The Nature of Explanation in Linguistic Theory

CSLI Lecture Notes
Number 162

The Nature of Explanation in Linguistic Theory

edited by
John Moore
Maria Polinsky

CSLI
PUBLICATIONS
Center for the Study of
Language and Information
Stanford, California

Center for the Study of Language and Information
Leland Stanford Junior University
Printed in the United States
07 06 05 04 03   5 4 3 2 1

Library of Congress Cataloging-in-Publication Data

Moore, John C., 1955-
The nature of explanation in linguistic theory /
by John Moore and Maria Polinsky.
p. cm. (CSLI lectures notes ; no. 162)
Includes bibliographical references and index.

ISBN 1-57586-454-1 (pbk. : alk. paper)
ISBN 1-57586-453-3 (hardback : alk. paper)

1. Explanation (Linguistics)
I. Polinsky, Maria. II. Title. III. Series.
P128.E95M66 2003
415′.01–dc21 2003006599
CIP

∞ The acid-free paper used in this book meets the minimum requirements of the American National Standard for Information Sciences—Permanence of Paper for Printed Library Materials, ANSI Z39.48-1984.

CSLI was founded in 1983 by researchers from Stanford University, SRI International, and Xerox PARC to further the research and development of integrated theories of language, information, and computation. CSLI headquarters and CSLI Publications are located on the campus of Stanford University.

CSLI Publications reports new developments in the study of language, information, and computation. In addition to lecture notes, our publications include monographs, working papers, revised dissertations, and conference proceedings. Our aim is to make new results, ideas, and approaches available as quickly as possible. Please visit our web site at

http://cslipublications.stanford.edu/

for comments on this and other titles, as well as for changes and corrections by the author and publisher.

Contents

Contributors

HAGIT BORER: Department of Linguistics, University of Southern California, Los Angeles, CA 90089-1693, USA.
borer@usc.edu

WOJCIECH BORKOWSKI: Institute for Social Studies, University of Warsaw, Krakowskie Przedmieście 26/28, 00-927 Warszawa, Poland.
wborkowsk@poczta.onet.pl

GREG CARLSON: Department of Linguistics, University of Rochester, Rochester, NY 14627-0096, USA.
carlson@ling.rochester.edu

PETER W. CULICOVER: Department of Linguistics, Ohio State University, Columbus, OH 43210-1298, USA.
culicover.1@osu.edu

JOHN HAIMAN: Linguistics Program, Macalester College, St. Paul, MN 55105, USA.
haiman@macalester.edu

JOHN A. HAWKINS: Department of Linguistics, University of Southern California, Los Angeles, CA 90089-1693, USA.
hawkins@usc.edu

EDWARD L. KEENAN: Department of Linguistics, University of California, Los Angeles, Los Angeles, CA 90095-1543, USA.
ekeenan@ucla.edu

RONALD W. LANGACKER: Department of Linguistics, University of California, San Diego, La Jolla CA 92093-0108, USA.
rwl@ling.ucsd.edu

JOHN MOORE: Department of Linguistics, University of California, San Diego, La Jolla CA 92093-0108, USA.
moorej@ucsd.edu

ANDRZEJ NOWAK: Department of Psychology, Florida Atlantic University, Boca Raton, FL 33431-0991, USA.
nowak@fau.edu

MARIA POLINSKY: Department of Linguistics, University of California, San Diego, La Jolla CA 92093-0108, USA.
polinsky@ling.ucsd.edu

FREDERICK J. NEWMEYER: Department of Linguistics, University of Washington, Seattle, WA 98195-4340, USA.
fjn@u.washington.edu

ROBERT D. VAN VALIN, JR.: Department of Linguistics, State University of New York, Buffalo, NY 14260-1030, USA.
vanvalin@acsu.buffalo.edu

Acknowledgments

This book represents a subset of papers presented at the conference "The Nature of Explanation in Linguistic Theory" which took place at UCSD in December 1999. In addition we have included an invited submission by Robert Kluender. In 1998, we co-taught an introductory seminar for incoming graduate students; we were astonished by how frequently the issue of explanatory adequacy came up in that course—and humbled by what seemed to us to be lack of clear answers. That experience gave us the idea to organize a conference addressing explanatory aspects of linguistic theory, and we would like to acknowledge the generous support from the Humanities Research Institute at the University of California, Humanities Center at UCSD, and the Office of the Dean of Social Sciences at UCSD that made the conference possible. The planning of the conference would not have been possible without helpful advice from our colleagues in the Department of Linguistics. The conference would not have been a success without the constant help from graduate students in the department; we would like to express our particular gratitude to Dan Brassil, Todd O'Bryan, Gina Taranto, and Ezra van Everbroeck.

The conference included talks and panel discussions by invited participants to whom we owe its ultimate success: Judith Aissen, Mark Baker, Hagit Borer, Greg Carlson, Sandra Chung, Peter Culicover, David Dowty, Charles Fillmore, Jane Grimshaw, John Haiman, Jack Hawkins, Edward Keenan, Angelica Kratzer, Yuki Kuroda, George Lakoff, Ronald Langacker, Howard Lasnik, Beth Levin, Fredrick Newmeyer, David Perlmutter, Ellen Prince, Ivan Sag, Robert Van Valin. It has been a pleasure working with them and we were very glad to extend that work to the papers included in this volume.

We thank the many anonymous referees who reviewed the papers in this volume, as well as Eric Potsdam and our colleagues in the department for their comments on our introductory chapter. We are also grateful to Russell Rhodes, Anne Sumnicht, and Antje Thiessen, for editorial assistance. Finally, we thank Dikran Karagueuzian and Christine Sosa for their support in bringing this volume to publication.

John Moore and Maria Polinsky

1

Explanations in Linguistics

JOHN MOORE AND MARIA POLINSKY

1 The Nature of Explanation

At least since the time of the Neogrammarians, elegance of analysis has been a point of pride among linguistic researchers. Since Chomsky's (1962) pioneering work on the goals of linguistic theory, this emphasis on elegance has gone under the rubric of EXPLANATION. While one wants an analysis to cover the empirical phenomena under study, it is generally assumed that descriptive adequacy is not enough. Rather, an analysis, if it is to be taken seriously must achieve EXPLANATORY ADEQUACY. However, what precisely renders an account explanatorily adequate? What are the empirical and theoretical trade-offs that come into play when pursuing this goal? These are the basic questions that we set out to answer when we organized the Conference on Explanation in Linguistic Theory that met at UCSD in December 1999. This volume presents a subset of the papers presented at that conference, plus an invited piece by Robert Kluender.

In this introduction we attempt to provide a background on the basic structure of an explanatory account and probe some of the oppositions that make explanation elusive. We view explanation as consisting of several steps: establishing the boundaries of a phenomenon, adequately describing this phenomenon, linking it to independently motivated generalizations, and making testable predictions about additional phenomena. Thus described, explanation is essentially an enterprise in scientific method, where theoretical accounts of empirical facts consist of falsifiable hypotheses formulated with the fewest possible number of auxiliary assumptions.

By way of an example, consider a classic problem from an introductory syntax class. The well-known example in (1) is ambiguous:

The Nature of Explanation in Linguistic Theory.
John Moore and Maria Polinsky (eds.).

(1) The ranger saw the moose with binoculars.

(1) admits two readings: one where the ranger looked through binoculars to see the moose and the other, less likely, where the moose was in possession of the binoculars. This example is used to show the importance of constituent structure, or strong generative capacity. That is, it is not enough to develop a grammar that puts the words in the right order – the words need to be grouped into constituents. The standard account of the ambiguity of (2) rests on two assertions:

(2) i. A PRINCIPLE OF MODIFICATION, which states that modifiers modify elements that stand in a structurally close relation (e.g. sisterhood), and
ii. An ambiguous constituent structure, whereby the PP *with binoculars* is respectively an NP and VP subconstituent.

If both (2i-ii) were stipulated, the account of the ambiguity in (2) would not transcend the facts in any interesting way. However, both (2i) and (2ii) can be established on independent grounds, yielding a truly explanatory account of the ambiguity. The effect of (2i) is observed, for example, in cases where adjectives modify head nouns by virtue of structural proximity. (2ii) is independently motivated by a number of constituency tests: the ability to be topicalized, clefted, etc. If *with binoculars* forms part of an NP constituent, then the whole NP should behave as a constituent:

(3) a. The moose with binoculars, the ranger saw.
b. What the ranger saw was the moose with binoculars.

Similarly, when *with binoculars* is part of a VP constituent, independent of the object NP, the NP should behave as a constituent independent of the PP:

(4) a. The moose, the ranger saw with binoculars.
b. What the ranger saw with binoculars was the moose.

Not only does (2) explain the ambiguity of (1) through independently motivated factors, it makes further predictions. Because the manipulations in (3) and (4) neutralize the structural ambiguity, we predict that these sentences will not show the semantic ambiguity found in (1). This prediction is borne out: the examples in (3) are only consistent with a situation where the moose possesses the binoculars, while those in (4) require that the ranger use the binoculars to see the moose.

This simple example, familiar to every first-year syntax student, has all the elements of an explanatory account: The range of relevant data and their description are clear: systematic ambiguities, such as the one in (1) require an account. This ambiguity is linked to independently established phenomena such as adjective modification and constituency tests. Finally, the account sketched above makes testable predictions regarding situations where the ambiguity will not obtain.

2 Oppositions

Notwithstanding the success of the account sketched above, several questions emerge; these questions can be stated in terms of oppositions – the resolution of these oppositions forms the basis for a number of competing approaches to theoretical linguistics.

One such opposition concerns the UNIVERSAL versus LANGUAGE-PARTICULAR aspect of the account. Are principles such as (2i-ii) parochial facts about English or are they universal facts about human language? If not universal, could they emerge through the interaction of various universal and, perhaps, language-particular principles?

Another opposition concerns the ontology of language principles such as (2i-ii). As stated, they appear to be autonomous facts about language. However, could they be emergent properties of other cognitive and/or functional systems? In other words, should linguists seek explanations via principles that are INTERNAL to language, or should EXTERNAL explanations be sought?

The final opposition compares SYNCHRONIC vs. DIACHRONIC explanations. This relates to both the language-particular/universal and internal/external oppositions. Language-particular phenomena may be the result of historical residue; phenomena that elude language-external accounts may be the result of grammaticalization.

In the following sections we consider aspects and trade-offs inherent in these three oppositions and their implications for the nature of explanation. As we show, explanation lends itself to a number of interpretations, simply because researchers may focus on different aspects and different implementations of scientific enterprise.

2.1 Language-Particular vs. Language Universal

The tension between universal and language-particular explanation has been a significant undercurrent in the history of linguistics. Faced with the seemingly limitless diversity in the world's languages, linguists have responded on a continuum between two extreme positions. At one end is the claim that linguistic diversity is only superficial. Under this position, all languages are manifestations of a single Universal Grammar and diversity stems from differing lexical items and small parametric differences in the grammars.[1] These parametric differences have been located in different components of the grammar and, most recently, have been claimed to reduce to the strength of a limited set of uninterpretable features. The other end of the spectrum is often characterized by Joos' (1957: 96) famous quote: 'languages could differ from each other without limit and in unpredictable ways.' From a modern perspective this way of thinking was necessary in its time to sever linguistic science from generally Eurocentric conceptions of language structure. However, need to counteract such socio-political prejudices cannot be sufficient reason to ignore underlying similarities that clearly exist amidst the diversity; hence, some middle ground must be found to explain the ways that language can vary and the ways they can be the same – finding this middle ground is, in essence, a fundamental goal of theoretical linguistics.

The universalist strategy has dominated the Principles and Parameters movement of the last twenty years. Although seeds of universal constraints, coupled with language-specific parameters were present in Transformational Grammar, at least since Chomsky's (1964) A-over-A Principle and Ross' (1967) account of island phenomena, a rather fundamental conceptual shift crystallized in Government and Binding Theory (Chomsky 1981). While explanation in linguistic theory once centered on the quest for an appropri-

---

[1] Sometimes Universal Grammar is equated with the INITIAL STATE of a language-acquisition device, which, through the acquisition of lexical items and the setting of parameters, yields a speaker's I-LANGUAGE (Chomsky 1986, among others). Given this (rather abstract) view of language-acquisition, a view of explanation emerges which evaluates linguistics theories on the basis of their ability to shed light on the language acquisition process (cf. Hornstein and Lightfoot 1981). Often this has been cast under the rubric of LEARNABILITY; given two competing accounts, the one which reduces 'the child's' learning space is viewed as more explanatory. Considerable research has addressed such learnability issues (Wexler and Culicover 1980, Lightfoot 1982, Wexler and Manzini 1987, among others), but it has been controversial (Bates and Elman 1996, Elman, et. al. 1996, Tomasello 1992, among others). Several consequences of using learnability as an explanatory metric have come under criticism: in order to determine the relative learnability of competing accounts, it is necessary to have a clearly delimited empirical domain; some view this as an artificial limitation on the empirical basis of linguistic research. At times, learnability considerations lead researchers to rather abstract representations; e.g., a binary branching structure is more learnable than an n-ary one (Kayne 1984, Larson 1988). However, strict binary branching complicates other components of the grammar, and eventually may undermine the strong generative capacity of the grammar. Finally, a common complaint has to do with the trade-off between Universal Grammar and parameters. It is possible to circumvent learnability issues by increasing the specificity of the initial state. That is, if a particular condition is unlearnable, it could be claimed to be part of the speaker's hard-wired language capacity. It is clear that the abuse of this practice has the danger of rendering learnability concerns entirely moot.

ately restrictive formalism – one that simultaneously limited the class of possible languages in a significant way, yet was able to express the full range of linguistic generalizations – the Principles and Parameters approach limited the class of possible languages through specific universal principles. Using a computational metaphor, this shift is similar to moving from an appropriately restrictive general-purpose computational model (e.g., locating natural language on the Chomsky Hierarchy) to finding an appropriately restrictive firmware chip. This new mode of explanation resulted in a wide range of putative universal principles: movement was strictly local (unless freed from locality through the interaction with other principles) (Subjacency, Antecedent Government, Principle A); anaphoric elements required antecedents in the appropriate local and structural configuration (Binding Theory); silent elements including traces of movement required proper identification and, some of them, a close association with a head (formal licensing, the ECP); and constituent structure conformed to a specific, endocentric scheme (X′-Theory). One strength of this approach was the manner in which it allowed linguistic generalizations to be directly encoded into the theoretical framework. A consequent liability was the development of a rather unconstrained research program where potentially parochial language phenomena might be reified as linguistic universals without regard for the consequences for other similar, but different accounts of similar, but different data sets.

Another challenge for the Principles and Parameters approach comes from its treatment of linguistic variation. Given the strong universalist character of the theory, variation should be superficial, and ideally, reducible to a finite (and small) set of universal parameters. A good deal of optimism was generated by the proposal that cross-linguistic variation in island phenomena might reduce to the choice of bounding nodes (Rizzi 1982) and that richness of agreement might determine the availability of *pro*-drop (Jaeggli and Safir 1989) (and that *pro*-drop itself correlated to seemingly unrelated extraction phenomena, Perlmutter 1971, Rizzi 1982). However, the facts ended up being less clear than originally thought, and the range of variation never fell neatly into the confines of a few parameter settings. The inability to constrain parametric variation led either to the abandonment of the overall program or to a seemingly endless proliferation of new parameters.

The late Principles and Parameters period of the 1990s and the Minimalist Program addressed some of these issues by overhauling the conceptual basis of the framework. For example by proposing a single, simple computational component, and limiting linguistic levels to lexicon, PF and LF, the Minimalist Program eliminated the unfettered proliferation of linguistic principles and the ad-hoc use of parameters. Ideally, language variation would reside in the lexicon, broadly construed to include abstract features. Since the Minimalist Program is relatively new, it remains to be seen how many of the empirical results achieved within the P&P Theory can be captured in a principled manner, given this rather narrow conception of parametric variation.

Another common criticism of the Minimalist Program has to do with the abstract nature of syntactic representations adopted in the framework. For example, while the assumption of binary right branching structures fits well with languages like English, it is less well suited for many other languages. Thus one wonders whether the structuralists' complaints about Eurocentric assumptions about language structure apply to the Minimalist Program as well.

While this discussion has highlighted problems with the universalist position, one should not lose sight of the fact that this research strategy has yielded considerable insight into language structure. By taking a strong position and pushing it to its consequences, the approach has uncovered hosts of new empirical discoveries. This pay-off is often cited as a major strength and accomplishment of the last few decades of generative research. This is very much to the theory's credit, even if it falls short of achieving explanation.

An alternative to the strongly universalist position seeks to explain linguistic data though the interaction of language-specific facts, coupled with universal principles. Under this approach, explanation is driven equally by the need to account for similarities and principled differences across languages. Such an approach has always been inherent in functional-typological view of linguistics and in Relational Grammar, which explicitly stated the division of labor between language universal and language specific principles. It is also implicit in Construction Grammar work and lexicalist theories such as HPSG and LFG. These frameworks provide a rather unconstrained formalism for stating language-particular generalizations; these generalizations potentially interact with each other, as well as with universal principles, to explain attested phenomena. Clearly this approach allows for a rather direct account of linguistic variation and, therefore, avoids many of the problems discussed above. The converse liability is, of course, that language-particular stipulations are essentially unconstrained, and the theories that employ them run the risk of becoming descriptive rather than explanatory.

In order to find the right breaking point between language-particular and universal generalizations, the descriptive component requires a database of relevant languages that is constructed in such a way as to guard against genetic, areal, and structural bias (Dryer 1989, 1992). Under this approach, the risk of Eurocentrism mentioned above with respect to the generative enterprise is mitigated. However, as one examines apparent similarities and differences across languages, the likelihood of uncovering solid generalizations is diminished, as each particular language is not well studied. While it is striking how many meaningful generalizations Joseph Greenberg established on the basis of a small, little studied sample (Greenberg 1963), it is no less telling how few new generalizations followed his pioneering work using the same method of surface sampling.

It is thus hard to predict where the right balance may be, but it seems that a promising approach may consist in studying a single language or a group of related languages closely, with the emphasis on the tension between language universal and language particular phenomena. Many promising results have been obtained within research based on such methodology, regardless of the framework employed, e.g., comparative studies of Germanic syntax (Vikner 1995, Haider et. al. 1995, and others), study of opacity in generative phonology and Optimality Theory (Kiparsky 1971, McCarthy 1999, among others), and hierarchies and alignment (Bresnan and Kanerva 1989, Levin and Rappaport-Hovav 1995, Ackerman and Moore 2001). In what follows, we will take the liberty of introducing detailed illustrations from our own research.

A largely framework neutral example of language-specific explanation is found in Perlmutter and Moore's (2002) account of Russian impersonal constructions. Descriptively, Russian impersonal constructions are limited to finite clauses:

(5) Na Gavajax ne morozit.
in Hawaii NEG freeze-3SG
'It doesn't freeze in Hawaii.'

Unlike English, Russian disallows impersonal constructions from infinitival contexts (note that the English counterpart, represented in the gloss, is grammatical).

(6) * Čtoby morozit' na Gavajax, ...
in order freeze-INF in Hawaii
'In order for it to freeze in Hawaii, ...'

Perlmutter and Moore attribute these data gaps to the interaction of two Russian-specific generalizations:

(7) i. Russian subjects of infinitives are dative.
ii. Silent pronominals, including silent expletives are nominative.

Both (7i-ii) are independently motivated in Russian; overt infinitival subjects of infinitival constructions are dative and Russian *pro*-drop is limited to nominative subjects. These two generalizations, which are clearly parochial to Russian, conspire to exclude silent expletives from infinitival contexts, yielding the gap illustrated in (6).[2]

This account achieves explanation in that it explains why the gaps occur by appealing to independently motivated generalizations. The fact that the generalizations are Russian-specific makes this explanation language-specific. Of course, the explanation also relies on certain universal principles, such as the proposal that all clauses have subjects - even impersonals where the subject is silent.[3] Thus, this account bases its explanation on a combination of universal and language-specific generalizations.

This type of explanation raises several questions. Are the Russian-specific generalizations in (7) really parochial facts about Russian, or are they part of a system of parameters? It is not clear that this question can be answered at this stage. Certainly case-marking rules that treat subjects of non-finite clauses differently from finite subjects are widespread, at least among Indo-European languages (cf. Andrews 1971). It is also true that English allows expletive subjects to be either nominative or accusative, but not genitive:

(8) a. There are flies in the soup.
    b. For there to be flies in the soup would be unfortunate.
    c. * There's being flies in the soup bothered everyone.

These facts show that (7ii) has an English counterpart that is similar (in that it explains gaps in the distribution of impersonals), but different (in that it yields a different class of gaps). The next step in this type of investigation would be to explore the typological possibilities in non-finite case marking and the case possibilities of expletive elements to see if the above account of Russian makes correct predictions for a wider range of languages.

The second illustration we would like to bring up has to do with the range of variation in CONTROL. Few phenomena have attracted as much attention from linguists as Control. Starting with Rosenbaum (1967), Postal (1970), and Bresnan (1972), the relevant constructions have been at the fore of syntactic and semantic analysis. Over thirty years of research into the

---

2 Perlmutter and Moore (2002) show instances of raising cases where infinitival subjects are not dative; in these cases, impersonal constructions are correctly predicted to be possible.

3 Several researchers have questioned this putative universal (Babby 1989, McCloskey 2001).

syntax and semantics of these constructions have produced several interesting theories of Raising and Control and have led to important discoveries in the nature and typology of empty categories. Most of the approaches built heavily on the facts of English and a small number of other well-studied languages.

The core property of the relevant English construction is a FORWARD CONTROL RELATION: an obligatory interpretational dependency between an overt argument NP and a lower unpronounced argument in the complement clause, represented atheoretically as a gap in (9b).

(9) a. Sandy tried to remain calm.
    b. $Sandy_i$ tried [$\_\_\__i$ to remain calm]

Virtually every currently existing syntactic theory has been constructed around the assumption that Backward Control, where the silent argument is structurally higher than the overt NP, is *not* possible:

(10) $\_\_\__i$ tried [$Sandy_i$ to remain calm]

For example, in the Principles and Parameters framework, Backward Control is specifically ruled out by the following set of assumptions:

(11) *PRO Control assumptions*
   a. every argument receives exactly one θ-role (Theta Criterion)
   b. PRO bears Null Case
   c. PRO must be bound for a referential interpretation

An initial problem with (10) is that PRO is not in a Null Case position.[4] The subject of tensed root clauses is uniformly a Case position cross-linguistically. Consequently, PRO should not appear there.

The structural requirements on referential PRO are also violated under Backward Control. The embedded overt controller cannot c-command the matrix NP. Since PRO is not bound, (11c) forces an arbitrary interpretation and nothing else. The final difficulty with the PRO analysis is that the structural configuration in (10) violates Condition C of the Binding Theory, which requires that referential expressions be free (Chomsky 1981). These

---

4 The assumption that PRO can only bear Null Case has recently come under scrutiny. In other languages, e.g. Icelandic (Andrews 1982; Thrainsson 1984), Russian (Babby 1998, Moore and Perlmutter 2000), Greek (Terzi 1997, Roussou 2001), PRO alternates with Case-marked NPs.

arguments indicate that the Principles and Parameters architecture quite generally rules out Backward Control. Thus according to the theory, Backward Control should not exist in natural language.

However, Backward Control is an empirical reality. To our knowledge, it was first identified in Kuroda's (1965/1979) dissertation and subsequently in Kuroda (1978) and Harada (1973), under the term Counter-Equi—a deletion rule that worked opposite to that of Equi. Counter-Equi was proposed to account for several classes of constructions in Japanese, for example, *tokoro*-clauses:

(12) Taroo-wa/?ga ~~ziroo-o~~ [ziroo-ga komatte iru]
Taro-TOP/NOM Ziro-ACC Ziro-NOM at a loss be.INF
tokoro-o tatsuke-ta.
occasion-ACC help-PAST
'Taro helped Jiro when Jiro was at a loss.' (Harada 1973: 115)

Polinsky (2000) and Polinsky and Potsdam (2002) established empirical evidence for Backward Subject Control in the Nakh-Dagestanian language Tsez, where a number of language-particular phenomena robustly attest to the validity of this construction. Tsez has a contrast between the two uses of the verbs *–oqa* 'begin' similar to the one found with the English *begin* (Perlmutter 1972), except that in Tsez the alternation is between the Raising construction in (13a) and the Backward Control construction in (13b); a Forward Control construction with - *oqa* 'begin' is not available, (3c).[5]

(13) a. Uži$_i$ [t$_i$ burti kura] Ø-oqsi.
boy.ABS ball.ABS throw.INF I-began
'The boy began to throw a ball.' (Raising)

b. PRO$_i$ [užā$_i$ burti kura] Ø-oqsi.
boy.ERG ball.ABS throw.INF I-began
'The boy began to throw a ball.' (Backward Control)

c. * Užā$_i$ [PRO$_i$ burti kura] r-oqsi.
boy.ERG ball.ABS throw.INF IV-began
('The boy began to throw a ball.' Forward Control)

Assuming that Backward Control is an empirically attested option, a question arises as to where in natural languages this pattern can be attested. This is where language specific grammatical properties become crucial. The analysis in Polinsky and Potsdam (2002) presents at least two preconditions

5 Following Hornstein (1999), Polinsky and Potsdam (2002) show that Backward Control is a theoretically tenable option in the Minimalist Program.

for the occurrence of Backward Control: (i) Case marking of subjects in Control complements; (ii) a particular subset of surface word orders which would not make Forward Control and Backward Control dramatically different. With respect to (i), such languages exist, and at least some of them are candidates for Backward Control: Malagasy (Polinsky and Potsdam 2001); Jacaltec (Craig 1974); Tsaxur (Kibrik 1999). With respect to (ii), Backward Subject Control is compatible with word orders SOV and VOS/VSO, in which Forward and Backward Control have the same surface realization:

(14)	Forward Control	Backward Control	Surface Order
a.	S [~~S~~OV]V	~~S~~ [SOV] V	SOVV
b.	V [VO ~~S~~] S	V [VOS] ~~S~~	VVOS

Again, the languages with attested or hypothetical Backward Control seem to fit the SOV or VOS type.

What lessons can we learn from the phenomena of Russian and Tsez briefly described here? If one extrapolates from the language-particular explanation of Russian impersonals or Tsez Control, one can imagine an approach whereby any of a number of language-particular idiosyncrasies interact to yield a host of language phenomena. This has the danger of bringing us back to Joos' assertion about the unfettered range of language variation. However, if language-particular generalizations can be built into general theory then Joos' variation can be embraced as part of such theory. The difficulty, of course, is to find the right breaking point between universal and language-particular explanation. At this stage of our understanding of grammar, our achievements in explaining linguistic structures and predicting their status lag behind more empirical work, which itself calls for major rethinking. This suggests that the time has come when empirical and theoretical research should zero in on similar questions.

2.2 Internal vs. External Explanation

The contrast between internal and external explanation is discussed in detail in work by Newmeyer (Newmeyer 1998: Ch. 3; this volume).[6] This section provides a brief overview of this opposition.

Internal explanation is one that exists within the context of a given theory of language, and is based on the principles of that theory. Under this type explanation, linguistic phenomena are accounted for by principles (i)

---

[6] Newmeyer also cites Hyman's (1984) paper where the opposition between formal and functional explanations is analyzed as the contrast between internal and external explanation; a similar dichotomy is presented and analyzed by Hall (1992: Ch. 1).

built into the theory (hence the term 'theory-internal') or (ii) inherent in the level of linguistic representation to which the phenomena belong. The more narrow conception (ii) has received most attention in the literature and is responsible for the often-criticized approach that assumes the AUTONOMY OF SYNTAX, grammatical phenomena are accounted for by syntax-internal principles. Nevertheless, the more general conception of internal explanation (i) is consistent with various theories of language and is not inherently linked to the Principles and Parameters framework.

Internal explanation is often linked to the explanation sought within the Principles and Parameters framework. Often this approach is criticized as emphasizing a deductive approach, putatively at the expense of descriptive adequacy. Other formal frameworks are often so keen on dissociating themselves from this approach that they insist on a different style of explanation. For example, Webelhuth et. al. (1999: 3) write that 'HPSG's methodology insists upon accepting linguistic analyses as explanatory only when they can be shown to be compatible with a broad and representative database of facts from a given language... What sets HPSG (and other ... frameworks with similar methodologies) apart from P&P is that its methodological underpinnings require a considerably more careful and complete demonstration of analytical success before one is entitled to the claim of having provided an explanatory analysis.' In other words, a successful internal explanation has to be based on a descriptively accurate account. This requirement is shared by any serious theory committed to the scientific method. Regardless of whether a particular account in any given framework falls short of this goal, it is probably unfair to characterize the framework as having a general disinterest in descriptive adequacy.

The essence of external explanation is in relating linguistic and extralinguistic phenomena as manifestations of the same principles. Thus, external explanation is one where a given linguistic phenomenon is linked to a phenomenon or principle that either (i) is not particular to language or (ii) is outside the level of linguistic representation where the phenomenon belongs. The broad and narrow conceptions of external explanation run in parallel to the two conceptions of internal explanation.

Linguists have explored two main domains that may provide us with external principles motivating linguistic phenomena. General cognitive ability is the first of those domains. Under this approach, language is viewed as part of human cognitive ability.

If language is similar to other cognitive systems (vision, attention), then linguists need to identify principles that are shared by language and the other systems. Significant advances towards identifying such cognitive principles have been made by Cognitive Grammar (Langacker 1991; this volume). Within Cognitive Grammar, many general principles motivating language structure are taken to be by-products of the structure of human cognition and attention. For example, an important property of language is construal defined as the observer's interpretation with regard to a particular scene. Construal includes the distinction between figure and ground, which goes back to Gestalt psychology, and the notions of perspective and focus, also recognized in cognitive psychology. However, in order for this approach to achieve a truly *external* mode of explanation, there needs to be independent corroboration of the relevant principles as belonging to language-external components. That is, experimental cognitive psychology and psycholinguistics must build upon the descriptive apparatus of Cognitive Grammar and test its hypotheses in such a way that would show their external explanatory power. Otherwise, being part of theory, and lacking independent corroboration through experimental methodologies, these notions run the risk of qualifying as internal, not external, factors.

The second source of external explanation is in the function of language as a communication device. Such external explanations have long been associated with functional approaches to language; they establish a causal relationship between the form of language and the need to express a proposition/concept efficiently and coherently (hence the well-known conversational implicatures), to facilitate the identification of referents (hence pragmatic and information structural principles), and to rule out as much ambiguity (again, Gricean principles, iconicity).

The cross-linguistic distribution of overt reflexive pronouns across grammatical persons, discussed by Comrie (1993), offers a good example of such causal principles at work. There are languages that have no overt reflexive pronouns, distinct from non-reflexives; Old English was one such language (Keenan, this volume). There are languages such as modern English that have distinct reflexives across all grammatical persons, and there are languages such as Romance where the reflexive/non-reflexive distinction is overtly expressed only for third person. There seem to be no languages where this distinction is overtly expressed for first or second person only. Is this gap in the distribution accidental? Comrie (1993) provides a functional external explanation by noting that the reflexive/non-reflexive contrast does not distinguish between different possible referents in the first and second persons (e.g., 'I hurt me' versus 'I hurt myself'), whereas it does make a difference in the third person ('She hurt her' versus 'She hurt herself'). Only in the third person does the overt non-reflexive/reflexive distinction allow for a more efficient tracking of referents.

Many complaints about functional explanations arise from cases where an external explanation is taken to replace an internal one or where a description of the function is taken to constitute both the description of a phenomenon and the motivation for that phenomenon. However, it is important to notice that Comrie's account of the cross-linguistic distribution of reflexive distinctions does not have any direct bearing on the binding principles and should not be taken as their replacement.

Another example of complementarity between functional motivations and internal explanations comes from passive constructions. A common, but not a necessary, function of the passive is to topicalize the referent of the subject. However, one cannot define passive as the theme-topicalizing construction, nor can one account for the structure of passive by the need to topicalize a referent other than agent. Hence, while the function of passives may be largely characterizable in terms of external factors, its form seems to require a language-internal account. This underscores that internal and external explanations are ultimately complementary — there is no intrinsic conflict between them. Given a high likelihood of multiple motivations underlying linguistic phenomena, both sets of explanations can benefit from integration. New advances in the experimental testing of linguistic hypotheses, be they in computational linguistics, study of language and brain, or acquisition, may eventually put an end to the contrast between internal and external explanation.

2.3 Historical Explanation

Ideally, grammar is a mental representation in the mind of a speaker (or a community of speakers). However, it is clear that grammars constantly change and are reshaped by new generations of learners as well as adults who innovate, evaluating and adopting or rejecting new usages in the community of speakers. This means that synchronic grammars reflect diachronic processes, ranging from abrupt change to the preservation of certain structures. Understanding what precedes and causes the development of a certain linguistic form, structure, or rule constitutes the first step towards an efficient explanation of language. It is therefore not accidental that linguists have long been concerned with mechanisms of language change and have widely used diachronic mechanisms to test existing theories of grammar (R. Lakoff 1968; Lightfooot 1999; Campbell 1999; Harris and Campbell 1995: Ch. 2, to name just a few).

In this section, we will discuss two major approaches to explaining synchronic facts through language change: diachronic accounts proper and performance-based accounts that motivate grammar by processing preferences. These apparently different approaches share a commitment to explaining the shape of grammar by relating that grammar to a prior stage where the grammar was different and to paying particular attention to multiple analyses available to a speaker.

2.3.1 Diachronic Accounts

Diachronic accounts, pioneered by early comparative linguists and refined by Neo-grammarians, relate synchronic grammar G_i to a prior grammar G_{i-1}, and explain the emergence of G_i by the operation of several recurring principles or mechanisms. Reanalysis is probably the most powerful mechanism appealed to in historical explanations. Reanalysis amounts to the change of the structure of a linguistic expression or linguistic subsystem, without modification in their overt expression (Langacker 1977; Harris & Campbell 1995; Campbell 1999). For example, in the Mantharta languages of Western Australia, the verb *kumpa-* 'be located at, sit' participates in the following biclausal structure, illustrated by an example from Jiwarli:

(15) kumpa-ja ngunha$_i$-rru
be located-PAST that.NOM-now
[__$_i$ jirriljipa-rnu walangu-wu thurupu-la]
frighten-IMPERF.SAME SUBJECT bird-DAT trough-LOC
'He frightened the birds away from the trough.'
(Austin 1998: 27, ex. (24))

In this example, as in quite a few others, the verb *kumpa* is semantically bleached, leading to its reinterpretation as an auxiliary with the ongoing reanalysis of the whole structure a monoclausal:

(16) kumpa-ja ngunha-rru jirriljipa-rnu
AUX-PAST that.NOM-now frighten-NON.FINITE
walangu-wu thurupu-la
bird-DAT trough-LOC
'He frightened the birds away from the trough.' (see also Austin 1998: 29)

Aside from the change in constituency in this structure, the reanalysis of (15) to (16) has deeper potential implications for alignment in Jiwarli. Jiwarli has a three-way distinction between the case of the single argument of an intransitive (nominative), the case of the transitive subject (ergative), and the case of the transitive object (accusative). In the biclausal structure, the object of the embedded imperfective must be marked by the dative case; the subject of *kumpa-* is in the nominative, because it is its single argument. In the reanalyzed monoclausal structure, the case of the subject should be ergative, the case of the object, accusative. However, as the (15)-to-(16) reanalysis preserves the earlier surface marking, the whole case system of Jiwarli may shift from the three-way contrastive type to a more common accusative type (subjects are in the nominative, objects, in the accusative/dative), thus from (17a) to (17b):

(17) a. 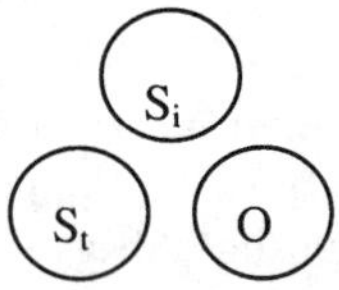

b. 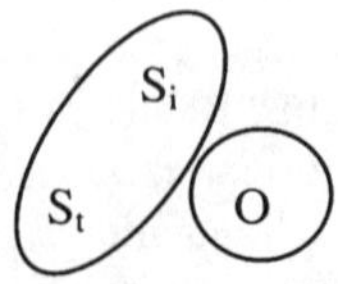

The syntagmatic reanalysis of a biclausal structure into a monoclausal is thus capable of triggering a paradigmatic reanalysis of the entire surface case system of Jiwarli (cf. Austin 1998: 29-30 about the potential for case reanalysis and parallels in other Australian languages).

By modifying the underlying representations, reanalysis brings about change in rules or constraints of a language. It is therefore a mechanism of language change potentially compatible with a number of linguistic theories. Reanalysis is thought to be the product of internal pressures (opacity, structural ambiguity) and/or of external influences. With respect to internal pressures, opacity or ambiguity is a common but not necessary prerequisite for reanalysis. As Harris and Campbell (1995:70-72) argue, reanalysis crucially depends on the availability of multiple interpretations of the same surface form. However, it is unclear whether multiple structures have to exist prior to reanalysis, in the reanalysis, or post-reanalysis. Examples of reanalysis brought up in linguistic literature seem to allow for all the three possibilities (Langacker 1977; Keller 1990; Campbell 1999).

Extension or analogical change is a major diachronic mechanism that prevents language from becoming completely chaotic by bringing new forms or new analyses in line with the existing structure.[7] A constant back and forth between extension and reanalysis prevents language from losing its complexity and also from becoming overly complex, to the extent of non-learnability.[8] While reanalysis changes the underlying representation of a linguistic expression, extension operates on the surface form of an expres-

[7] Harris and Campbell 1995: Ch. 5 present some good arguments for not using the notion of analogy. They find it too vague and show that it cuts across the more precisely defined mechanisms of diachronic change. We follow them in using the term extension instead.

[8] Complexity is a loaded issue in linguistic explanation, particularly in diachronic-based explanations. A simplistic view of language change may embed the idea that language becomes simpler over time. This is certainly a caricature view of grammaticalization, which is based on the idea that free lexical items lose part of their meaning and turn into functional words and then into bound morphemes (Kurylowicz 1948/1965; Givon 1971; 1977; Hopper and Traugott 1993, and many others). As Campbell (2001) argues, basic tenets of grammaticalization are compatible with the diachronic analysis that relies on reanalysis and extension.

sion, and this reliance on the surface manifestation explains why analogy plays such an important role in extension.

An interesting example of extension in grammar is in the rise of non-evidential marker in Estonian discussed by Harris and Campbell (1995: 98-100), who call this category INDIRECT or REPORTED SPEECH.[9] The category of evidentiality reflects the degree of certainty which the speaker assigns to his/her statement (Palmer 2001; De Lancey 1997, 2001). The main distinction in the grammatical expression is between evidential (directly witnessed) and non-evidential (everything else). Evidentiality can be marked on any constituent in the clause, but is typically marked on the VP.

In Estonian, evidentiality is marked on the verb by a zero marker (evidential) and the suffixes *–vat* (present non-evidential) and *–nud* (past non-evidential). The emergence of these overt suffixes starts with the reanalysis which transformed these endings, originally associated with the present and past participles, into the non-evidentiality markers used in embedded predication only. As the suffixes lost their participial flavor, they also lost the necessary association with embedded predication, and were extended over to all verbs, regardless of whether these verbs occur in the matrix or embedded clause. This is an example of a rather abstract case of extension, where the relevant feature is the lexical category of the word occurring with *–vat* and *–nud*. The end result of extension is the elimination of a contrast between two classes of verb forms; i.e., between those that take the suffixes and those that do not. The resulting system is more general.

This analysis of the rise of evidentiality in Estonian leads to two further questions. First, does the Estonian example shed any light on the nature of evidentiality distinctions in general? Second, how did the extension of the marker take place: as an abrupt change or as a gradual spread (diffusion). If as diffusion, is there a principled way to define the class of statements or predicates which formed the point of departure?

The answer to the first question is a weak 'maybe'. It is indeed true that, among other sources, evidential markers derive from tense morphemes across a number of languages (Comrie 1976: 110; Anderson 1986; Willett 1988; de Haan 1999, and many others). It is also true that in some other languages, the development of the category is due to the intrusion of non-finite forms into the finite verbal paradigm—such is the case, for example, in Turkic, Nakh-Dagestanian, Tibetan (Anderson 1986; Comrie and Polinsky 2002; Malchukov 2000, Garrett 2001, among others). Finally, the make-up of the category of evidentiality in Estonian also conforms to the widespread opposition of directly observed and inferred events. So, on the

---

[9] In the Estonian linguistic tradition, the category is referred to as INDIRECT.

positive side, diachronic extension in Estonian shows how the form has arisen and finds support from other languages whose grammars include evidentiality. However, there is nothing in the diachronic account that explains why this is the case or constrains the number of values within evidentiality. The extension account does not provide us with an obvious reason why the relationship between embedded clauses and matrix clauses should exist. In a sense, appealing to extension in this case explains the material shape of the form and the particular mechanism by which the form arose but defies a more principled, predictive, explanation. Knowing that extension of embedded participial forms to finite forms across all clauses took place in this particular case does not allow us to predict which non-finite clauses and under what conditions would undergo the similar kind of restructuring.

The second question raised by our discussion of extension has to do with the contrast between abrupt (rapid) and gradual (piecemeal) change. This contrast has been discussed in the phonological literature, particularly in attempts to depart from the overly deterministic Neogrammarian tradition (Wang 1969; Labov 1981). One wonders what the distinction between different types of change has to do with the nature of explanation in linguistics. The answer has to do with the fundamental difference in views on the mental representation of language in the mind of a speaker. Thus, the rapid/gradual change contrast hinges on architectural assumptions concerning acquisition and the overall structure of language. For a theory that relies on invariant principles of Universal Grammar, abrupt change is tantamount to the setting of parameters, which cannot be gradual — a parameter is either on or off. Under such a view, gradual change is also possible, as long as it does not affect the immediate setting of parameters (Lightfoot 1991, 1997, and 1999). In other words, gradual change belongs with E-language, while abrupt change belongs with I-language. But how does one decide on what is parametric and what belongs to E-language? The answer has never been clear.

For a theory that does not recognize UG or remains agnostic about it, gradual and abrupt change represents different manifestations of variation within a community of speakers.[10] Gradual change is much more common, especially outside phonology, and if one chooses to maintain the contrast, it is the existence of abrupt change that requires more of an explanation.

How does diffusion proceed? Factors that facilitate lexical diffusion include polysemy of lexical items, distributional criteria (Ard 1975), close

---

[10] Some researchers actually challenge the need to maintain the contrast between abrupt and gradual change (cf. Kroch and Taylor 1997; Kroch et. al. 2000, who argue for co-existing grammars, and Harris and Campbell 1995: 48, who emphasize the continuum from abrupt to gradual change).

formal or semantic similarity, which may trigger analogy (Wang 1977), and frequency of lexical or grammatical items (Bybee and Hopper 2001). Many approaches have resorted to frequency as the explanatory tool capable of accounting for language change. Interestingly, the appeal to frequency is found both in functional linguistics (e.g., Bybee 1985; 1988; 1995, among others) and in Principles and Parameters (e.g., Lighfoot 1991 and 1997). Several papers in this volume (Carlson; Hawkins; Culicover, Nowak, and Borkowski) appeal to frequency as an explanation. Frequency certainly plays a crucial role in shaping language (as shown for example in Bybee and Hopper 2001, and many others). However, it seems that often frequency itself may respond to a variety of factors (Newmeyer 1998) and it may play a less definitive role than one would assume. A typical example of the role played by frequency has to do with the correlation between frequency of use and phonetic reduction (Zipf 1935; Heine 1993: 109-111; 1997; Bybee 1995; Bybee and Hopper 2001): the more frequent a lexical item or a morpheme, the shorter it is. But do frequent lexical items continue to shrink in size? Judging by the behavior of most frequent lexical items in English, such as *come, see, think, do, very*, they are short but stable (Campbell 2001: 123).[11]

To summarize, many important discoveries have been made in trying to relate the current shape of language grammars to a prior grammar. It is still unclear, however, what the limits of such a historical explanation are and how to determine them (where should a historical explanation apply). It is very tempting to draw upon the successes of etymology and comparative linguistics, but since Hermann Paul, linguists have expressed immense frustration in the inability of the comparative method to capture language areas where the inventory of elements is small. In this enterprise, however, it has become rather clear that global explanations and predictions are quite unlikely. Linguists have been much more successful with smaller scale tasks, for example, explaining the emergence of modals (Bybee et. al. 1994) or certain functional words and categories (van Gelderen 1993). Success at the level of individual cases, however, cannot translate into the power of predicting language change on a large scale (Lightfoot 1999; Campbell 2001). Another lesson learnt from such explanations is that they cannot constrain the data in such a way that would predict an unambiguous outcome. Two lines of research seem possible and promising at this stage of our knowl-

---

[11] Even if very frequent items did shrink in size, that would presumably lead to another problem—redundancy in the lexicon. It is one of the basic tenets of grammaticalization that light items tend to become bound affixes, rather than free words; if so, they would bring in an additional cost to lexical memory by increasing complexity (see Hall 1992: 175-179 for a discussion).

edge: first, the understanding of how smaller scale, local changes can affect language subsystems (recall the reanalysis of evidentiality discussed above), and second, a better understanding of such fundamental mechanisms as frequency or extension. As our understanding of such mechanisms progresses, historical explanation has a chance of moving away from a post-hoc, causal approach to a more predictive, teleological theory.

2.3.2 Performance-Based Accounts

Performance-based accounts derive the existing linguistic structures from the needs of speakers and hearers; these needs define the shape of grammar and, since they are unlikely to vary from language to language, account for recurrent properties of languages. Just as reanalysis and extension serve as competing mechanisms in the diachronic approach, the often-competing needs of a speaker (production) and the needs of a hearer (perception) prevent languages from becoming too complex or too simple. A strong advantage of the performance-based approach to explaining linguistic structure is that it relies on an empirical field, well versed in making testable predictions, so more rigorous or at least more falsifiable hypotheses are readily available

One of the influential approaches to performance-based theory of grammar belongs to John A. Hawkins who outlined it in his 1994 book and a series of papers including the one in this volume. Hawkins' main idea is that natural language grammars are the way they are because they are shaped by performance factors. To account for the mapping of performance into grammar, Hawkins proposes EFFICIENCY PRINCIPLES. One of these principles, the MINIMIZE DOMAIN PRINCIPLE, formalizes the intuition that processing of shorter speech segments is easier than that of longer ones. It predicts that 'connected sequences of linguistic forms and their conventionally associated syntactic and semantic properties' over which the relationships between elements are computed should be as short as possible. Informally, this means that local domains are to be preferred over non-local domains, and minimal distance between related elements is to be preferred over longer distance. The preference for local domains and minimal distance is not new and is inherent in a number of theoretical frameworks—for example, Relativized Minimality (Rizzi 1990) or the presence of local domains in agreement or binding. However, the novelty of Hawkins' approach is that all these principles are derived from the need of a human parser to hold less information in working memory.

The other efficiency principle, MAXIMIZE ON-LINE PROCESSING, is also driven by memory limitations. This principle dictates that the online integration of a linguistic form should occur as soon as possible, in order to spare the parser the need to look back (as it happens in the repair of garden paths) and the need to look ahead by holding unassigned items in working memory. This principle predicts that structures such as (18a) would be preferable to (18b), because in the former the anaphor does not have to be held in the working memory until the parser reaches the antecedent:

(18) a. Stories about John_i amuse him_i
b. Stories about himself_i amuse John_i

According to Hawkins, the two major principles of parsing affect grammars and predict the shape of language-internal and cross-linguistic phenomena. These principles are often realized in a constraint-based system, which allows Hawkins to predict significant language variation and the co-occurrence of multiple analyses and expressive options available to a speaker.

The general spirit of this approach is extremely promising, and if this approach is developed in a comprehensive, globally constrained theory, it will be able to account for a wide range of language facts and bring together several sub-disciplines within linguistics. However, if the hypothesis that language is the way it is because of processing factors assumes explanatory power, it has to answer a number of general questions.

The first question has to do with the global versus local parsimony of the proposed principles: where within the language system do they apply? Implicit in Hawkins' discussion is the assumption that the proposed efficiency principles apply primarily at the level of phrase structure. Further research is needed to determine whether the proposed principles are global in nature or whether they are domain specific and work best in syntax.

The next question has to do with the nature of competing motivations: do these principles compete with other factors? Outside linguistics, many studies of non-deterministic, chaotic systems have long recognized the possibility of multiple determinations. For example, the complexity of linguistic material interacts with other sets of factors in addition to processing: information structure, the structure of the competence model, including the architecture of the lexicon. For example, with respect to the interplay between processing principles and information-structure principles,, four analytical options all seem possible: (i) the shape of grammars, constituent order in particular, is determined by the proposed efficiency principles, and information structure is derivative; (ii) the shape of grammars is determined by information-structural constraints and the efficiency principles are derivative; (iii) both sets of factors play a role, and their ordering is language-specific, phenomenon-specific, or domain-specific; (iv) both sets of factors play a role and can be ranked in a constraint-based system. The results of Arnold et al. (2000), which show that both complexity and information structure influence the form of linguistic expressions, suggest that (i) and (ii) are unlikely. Perhaps further psycholinguistic experiments may shed light on the interaction of these factors.

Hawkins' efficiency principles are also based on the assumption that processing takes precedence over production. This is based on the default assumption, going back to Clark (Clark 1973; Haviland and Clark 1974), that speakers do things to benefit their listeners. However, there is some independent evidence that production needs may take precedence over processing constraints (Ferreira 1996 and Ferreira and Dell 2000). For example, speakers do not hesitate to use garden paths if that makes production easier (Ferreira and Dell 2000), and are particularly unconcerned about the listener when they have a chance to access the lexically salient information sooner. While the overall thesis that grammars are shaped by processing remains unchanged, its realization may vary dramatically depending on whose needs, speaker's or listener's, are put first.

And finally, what is the ontological status of the efficiency principles? Let us return to the starting point of the whole enterprise: natural language grammars are the way they are because they are shaped by performance factors. Given evidence for the operation of the efficiency principles, one is tempted to conclude that they provide an adequate functional basis to grammar. The question that needs to be addressed is whether or not something is left for the grammar to do, and if yes, what are the limits of grammar. If there is a need for grammar, what is its status vis-à-vis the efficiency principles? Two main possibilities arise: either the efficiency principles constitute the diachronic motivation for certain grammatical phenomena or both efficiency principles and purely structural principles are psychologically real and are in competition with each other.

3 Conclusion

The interest in explanation in linguistics is a matter of fashion and often depends on the framework that dominates linguistic research. A cursory look at linguistic publications that explicitly mention explanation confirms that the interest in explanation comes and goes. It seems that periods marked by the interest in explanatory aspects of linguistic research alternate with stages that are marked by greater interest in methodology and descriptive approaches, a contrast that we can be described as the tension between RULES and TOOLS. In the structuralist tradition, which dominated the first half of the twentieth century, tools played the utmost role. The emphasis was on methodological precision, not on theory. This made the enterprise more descriptive than explanatory. With their strong emphasis on the structure, structuralists seldom bothered to ask why language forms and rules were the way they were. The task of uncovering linguistically important generalizations, a necessary step towards explanation, was often taken as the sufficient component of linguistic science.

The advent of generative grammar, with its insistence on explanatory adequacy pushed the issue of explanation to the fore (Chomsky 1962; Putnam 1967). This surge of interest led to important advances in what Newmeyer calls theory-internal explanation (Newmeyer 1998, and this volume). However, it also led to a strong subsequent disillusionment in the rather narrow and circular approach to explanation — the emphasis on competence, and the elimination of a range of explanations (e.g. historical, external, etc., cf. Julià 1983). In addition, the way of discovering the explanandum was becoming less and less satisfactory — not only did linguists not look outside language, but they were also to rely on introspection, which often led to questionable, conflicting, or too restricted data.

In reaction to the Chomskian approach, functional explanation was further developed, with a strong emphasis on performance-based data and variation. A particularly strong trend in this approach to explanation was apparent in the study of cross-linguistic variation and language universals, where the main explanatory mechanisms were to be sought outside language, in other cognitive systems, or in the community of speakers (Butterworth et al. 1984; Cutler et al. 1985; Hawkins 1988, among others). The immediate response to this approach was to criticize its lack of clarity with respect to the level at which the explanandum applied and the mechanisms that drove explanation. Partly in response, partly by way of natural development of ideas, generative grammar focused on Universal Grammar and introduced the concept of parametric variation as an explanatory device (cf. Hornstein and Lightfoot 1981; Lightfoot 1991). In the meantime, the pendulum in the functional literature swung towards diachronic explanations couched in terms of grammaticalization (Hopper and Traugott 1993; Keller 1990, and many others).

Despite heated debates on what is the explanans and what is the explanandum, what most of these approaches to explanation shared was the rejection of the discovery procedure promoted in structuralism, and heavy reliance on introspection and rather non-scientifically collected data. A paradigm shift that started in the 1990s led to a serious reconsideration of these approaches. Linguistics was becoming a more empirical field, and with it came the emphasis on psychological explanations. Tools, not rules, again became the focus of linguistic research. Language has increasingly been seen as part of MIND but MIND has no longer remained the philosophical black box of the generative revolution of the 1960s; rather, it has become a physical embodiment that can be measured, tested, modeled, and monitored.

It seems that the new generation of tools, which came to supplement the familiar introspection techniques, has begun to yield new explanatory mechanisms (Berg 1998; Kluender, this volume; Culicover et. al., this volume).

4 Summary of Papers in Volume

Papers in this volume offer different takes on the three main oppositions discussed above. The tension between external and internal explanations is addressed in the papers by Newmeyer, who develops the analysis of the opposition offered in his 1998 book, by Langacker, whose approach allows one to merge the external and internal dimension of explanation, and by Kluender, who addresses the potential limits of both internal and external explanation and discusses new tools at the disposal of modern linguistics. Carlson's paper, which also bears on this opposition of internal and external explanation, analyzes the reasons for 'linguistic isolationism'; Carlson argues that linguists sometimes get carried away by the technicalities of their own theories to such an extent that the desired explanation becomes inaccessible. The papers by Kuroda and Borer touch upon the choice between internal and external explanation; Kuroda discusses the philosophy underlying the quest for internal explanations in generative grammar, while Borer presents an interesting evaluation metric that can be used in the formulation and testing of theoretically informed hypotheses. The papers by Keenan and by Haiman both bear upon the diachronic aspects of explanation and underscore the need for historical explanations to rely upon a theoretically informed analysis of the earlier stage of language. Culicover, Nowak and Borkowski address the historical aspect of linguistic explanation and offer new tools that can be used to derive such explanations. Hawkins presents a good overview of his performance-based explanation for language phenomena, which develops the ideas outlined in his 1994 book.

References

Ackerman, F. and J. Moore. 2001. *Proto-Properties and Grammatical Encoding: A Correspondence Theory of Argument Selection.* Stanford: CSLI Publications.

Anderson, L. B. 1986. Evidentials, Paths of Change, and Mental Maps: Typologically Regular Asymmetries. *Evidentiality: The Linguistic Coding of Epistemology*, eds. W. Chafe and J. Nichols, 273-312. Norwood: Ablex.

Andrews, A. D. 1971. Case Agreement of Predicate Modifiers in Ancient Greek. *Linguistic Inquiry* 2: 127-151.

Andrews, A. D. 1982. Long Distance Agreement in Modern Icelandic. *The Nature of Syntactic Representation*, eds. P. Jacobson and G. K. Pullum, 1-33. Dordrecht: Reidel.

Ard, W. J. 1975. Raisings and Word Order in Diachronic Syntax. Doctoral dissertation, University of California, Los Angeles.

Arnold, J. et. al. 2000. Heaviness vs. Newness: The Effects of Structural Complexity and Discourse. *Language* 76: 28-55.

Austin, P. 1998. Crow Is Sitting Chasing Them: Grammaticalization and the Verb 'to Sit' in the Mantharta Language, Western Australia. *Case,Typology, and Grammar,* eds. A. Siewerska and J. J. Song, 19-36. Amsterdam: John Benjamins.

Babby, L. 1989. Subjectlessness, External Subcategorization, and the Projection Principle. *Zbornik Matice srpske za filologiju i lingvistiku* 32: 7-40.

Bates, E. and J. Elman. 1996. Learning Rediscovered. *Science* 274: 1849-1850.

Berg, T. 1998. *Linguistic Structure and Change*. Oxford: Clarendon Press.

Bresnan, J. 1972. Theory of Complementation in English Syntax. Doctoral dissertation, MIT.

Bresnan, J. and J. M. Kanerva. 1989. Locative Inversion in Chicheŵa: A Case Study in Factorization in Grammar. *Linguistic Inquiry* 20: 1-50.

Butterworth, B., B. Comrie, and Ö. Dahl. eds. 1984. *Explanation of Language Universals*. Berlin: Mouton.

Bybee, Joan. 1985. *Morphology: A Study of the Relation between Meaning and Form*. Amsterdam: John Benjamins.

Bybee, J. 1988. The Diachronic Dimension in Explanation. *Explaining Language Universals*, ed. J. A. Hawkins, 350-379. Oxford: Blackwell.

Bybee, J. 1995. Regular Morphology and the Lexicon. *Language and Cognitive Processes* 10: 425-455.

Bybee, J. and P. Hopper, eds. 2001. *Frequency and the Emergence of Linguistic Structure*. Amsterdam: John Benjamins.

Bybee, J., R. Perkins, and W. Pagliuca. 1994. *The Evolution of Grammar: Tense, Aspect, and Modality in the Languages of the World*. Chicago: University of Chicago Press.

Campbell, L. 1999. *Historical Linguistics: An Introduction*. Cambridge, MA: MIT Press.

Campbell, L. 2001. What's Wrong with Grammaticalization? *Language Sciences* 23: 113-161.

Chomsky, N. 1962. Explanatory Models in Linguistics. *Logic, Methodology, and Philosophy of Science,* eds. E. Nagel, P. Suppes, and A. Tarski, 528-550. Stanford: Stanford University Press.

Chomsky, N. 1964. The Logical Basis of Linguistic Theory. Proceedings of the Ninth International Congress of Linguists, Cambridge, MA, Aug. 27-31, 1962, ed. H. G. Lunt, 914-978. The Hague: Mouton.

Chomsky, N. 1981. *Lectures on Government and Binding*. Dordrecht: Foris.

Chomsky, N. 1986. *Knowledge of Language: Its Nature, Origin, and Use*. New York: Praeger.

Clark, H. 1973. Space, Time, Semantics, and the Child. *Cognitive Development and the Acquisition of Language*, ed. T. E. Moore, 27-63. New York: Academic Press.

Comrie, B. 1976. *Aspect*. Cambridge: Cambridge University Press.

Comrie, B. 1993. Language Universals and Linguistic Typology: Data-Bases and Explanations. *Sprachtypologie und Universalieforschungen* 46: 3-14.

Comrie, B. and M. Polinsky. 2002. Evidentiality in Tsez. *L'énonciation médiatisée*, ed. Z. Guentcheva, 2. Louvain/Paris: Peeters.

Craig, C. G. 1974. A Wrong-Cyclical Rule in Jacaltec? Papers from the Tenth Regional Meeting of the Chicago Linguistic Society, eds. M. W. La Galy, R. A. Fox, and A. Bruck, 103-116.

Cutler, A., J. A. Hawkins, and G. Gilligan. 1985. The Suffixing Preference: A Processing Explanation. *Linguistics* 23: 723-758.

de Haan, F. 1999. Evidentiality and Epistemic Modality: Setting Boundaries. *Southwest Journal of Linguistics* 18: 83-101.

de Lancey, S. 1997. Mirativity: The Grammatical Marking of Unexpected Information. *Linguistic Typology* 1: 33-52.

de Lancey, S. 2001. The Mirative and Evidentiality. *Journal of Pragmatics* 33: 371-384.

Dryer, M. S. 1989. Large Linguistic Areas and Language Sampling. *Studies in Language* 13: 257-292.

Dryer, M. S. 1992. The Greenbergian Word Order Correlations. *Language* 68: 81-138.

Elman, J. et. al. 1996. *Rethinking Innateness: A Connectionist Perspective on Development*. Cambridge, MA: MIT Press.

Ferreira, V. 1996. Is it Better to Give than to Donate? Syntactic Flexibility in Language Production. *Journal of Memory and Language* 35: 724-755.

Ferreira, V. and G. Dell. 2000. The Effect of Ambiguity and Lexical Availability on Syntactic and Lexical Production. *Cognitive Psychology* 40: 296-340.

Garrett, E. J. 2001. Evidentiality and Assertion in Tibetan. Doctoral dissertation, University of California, Los Angeles.

Givon, T. 1971. Historical Syntax and Synchronic Morphology: An Archaeologist's Field Trip. Chicago Linguistic Society. Papers from the Seventh Regional Meeting, 394-415. Chicago: Chicago Linguistic Society.

Givon, T. 1977. The Drift from VSO to SVO in Biblical Hebrew: The Pragmatics of Tense-Aspect. *Mechanisms of Syntactic Change*, ed. C. N. Li, 181-254. Austin: University of Texas Press.

Greenberg, J. 1963. The Languages of Africa. Bloomington: Indiana University. Research Center for the Language Sciences.

Haider, H., S. Olsen, and S. Vikner, eds. 1995. *Studies in Comparative Germanic Syntax.* Dordrecht: Kluwer.

Hall, C. J. 1992. *Morphology and Mind: A Unified Approach to Explanation in Linguistics*. London: Routledge.

Harada, S.-I. 1973. Counter Equi-NP-Deletion. *University of Tokyo Research Institute of Logopedics and Phoniatrics Annual Bulletin* 7: 113-47.

Harris, A. and L. Campbell. 1995. *Historical Syntax in Cross-Linguistic Perspective.* Cambridge: Cambridge University Press.

Haviland, S. and H. Clark. 1974. What's New? Acquiring New Information as a Process in Comprehension. *Journal of Verbal Learning and Verbal Behavior* 13: 512-521.

Hawkins, J. A., ed. 1988. *Explaining Language Universals.* Oxford: Basil Blackwell.

Hawkins, J. A. 1994. *A Performance Theory of Order and Constituents*. Cambridge: Cambridge University Press.

Heine, B. 1993. *Auxiliaries: Cognitive Forces and Grammaticalization*. Oxford: Oxford University Press.

Heine, B. 1997. *Possession: Cognitive Sources, Forces, and Grammaticalization.* Oxford: Oxford University Press.

Hopper, P. and E. Traugott. 1993. *Grammaticalization*. Cambridge: Cambridge University Press.

Hornstein, N. 1999. Movement and Control. *Linguistic Inquiry* 30: 69-96.

Hornstein, N. and D. Lightfoot, eds. 1981. *Explanation in Linguistics*. London: Longman.

Hyman, L. M. 1984. *Form and Substance in Language Universals*, eds. Butterworth et. al., 67–85.

Jaeggli, O. and K. J. Safir. 1989. The Null Subject Parameter and Parametric Theory. *The Null Subject Parameter*, eds. O. Jaeggli and K. J. Safir, 1-44. Dordrecht: Kluwer.

Johanson, L. and B. Utas, eds. 2000. *Evidentials: Turkic, Iranian and Neighbouring Languages*. Berlin: Mouton de Gruyter.

Joos, M. ed. 1957. *Readings in Linguistics*. Washington D. C.: American Council of Learned Societies.

Julià, P. 1983. *Explanatory Models in Linguistics*. Princeton: Princeton University Press.

Kayne, R. 1984. *Connectedness and Binary Branching*. Dordrecht: Foris.

Keller, R. 1990. *Sprachwandel. Von der unsichtbaren Hand in der Sprache*. Tübingen: Francke.

Kiparsky, P. 1971. Historical Linguistics. *A Survey of Linguistic Science,* ed. W. O. Dingwall, 576-642. College Park: University of Maryland Linguistics Program.

Kibrik, A. E. ed. 1999. *Elementy caxurskogo jazyka v tipologičeskom osveščenii.* Moscow: MGU.

Kroch, A., A. Taylor and D. Ringe. 2000. The Middle English Verb-Second Constraint: A Case Study in Language Contact and Language Change. *Textual Parameters in Older Languages*, eds. S. Herring, P. van Reenen, and L. Schosler, 353-391. Amsterdam: John Benjamins.

Kroch, A. and A. Taylor. 1997. Verb Movement in Old and Middle English: Dialect Variation and Language Contact. *Parameters of Morphosyntactic Change*, eds. A. van Kemenade, and N. Vincent, 297-325. Cambridge: Cambridge University Press.

Kuroda, S-Y. 1965 (1979). Generative Grammatical Studies in the Japanese Language. Doctoral dissertation, MIT.

Kuroda, S.-Y. 1978. Case-Marking, Canonical Sentence Patterns, and Counter-Equi in Japanese. *Problems in Japanese Syntax and Semantics*, ed. J. Hinds, 30-51. Tokyo: Kaitakusha.

Kuryłowicz, J. 1965 (1948). The Evolution of Grammatical Categories. *Diogenes* 51: 55-71.

Labov, W. 1981. Resolving the Neogrammarian Controversy. *Language* 57: 267-308.

Lakoff, R. 1968. *Abstract Syntax and Latin Complementation.* Cambridge, MA: MIT Press.

Langacker, R. W. 1977. Syntactic Reanalysis. *Mechanisms of Syntactic Change*, ed. C. N. Li, 59-139. Austin: University of Texas Press.

Langacker, R. W. 1991. *Foundations of Cognitive Grammar,* vol. 2. *Descriptive Application.* Stanford: Stanford University Press.

Langacker, R. W. 1995. Raising and Transparency. *Language* 71: 1-62.

Larson, R. K. 1988. On the Double Object Construction. *Linguistic Inquiry* 22: 103-199.

Levin, B. and M. Rappaport-Hovav. 1995. *Unaccusativity at the Syntax Lexical-Semantics Interface*. Cambridge, MA: MIT Press.

Lightfoot, D. 1982. *The Language Lottery: Towards a Biology of Grammars.* Cambridge, MA: MIT Press.

Lightfoot, D. 1991. *How to Set Parameters: Arguments from Language Change.* Cambridge, MA: MIT Press.

Lightfoot, D. 1997. Catastrophic Change and Learning Theory. *Lingua* 100: 171-192.

Lightfoot, D. 1999. *The Development of Language: Acquisition, Change, and Evolution.* Malden, MA: Blackwell.

Malchukov, Andrej. 2000. Perfect, Evidentiality and Related Categories in Tungusic Languages, in Johanson and Utas, 441-470.

McCarthy, John. 1999. Sympathy and Phonological Opacity. *Phonology* 16: 331-99.

Moore, J. and D. M. Perlmutter. 2000. What Does it Take to Be a Dative Subject? *Natural Language and Linguistic Theory* 18: 373-416.

Newmeyer, F. 1998. *Language form and Language Function*. Cambridge, MA: MIT Press.

Palmer, F. R. 2001. *Mood and Modality*. 2nd ed. Cambridge: Cambridge University Press.

Perlmutter, D. M. 1971. *Deep and Surface Constraints in Syntax*. New York: Holt, Rinehart and Winston.

Perlmutter, D. M. 1972. The Two Verbs *Begin*. *Readings in English Transformational Grammar*, eds. R. A. Jacobs and P. S. Rosenbaum, 107-119. Waltham: Ginn and Company.

Perlmutter, D. M. and J. Moore. 2002. Language-Internal Explanation: The Distribution of Russian Impersonals. *Language* 78: 619-650.

Polinsky, M. 2000. Variation in Complementation Constructions: Long-distance Agreement in Tsez. *Complementation*, ed. K. Horie, 59-89. Amsterdam: John Benjamins.

Polinsky, M. and E. Potsdam. 2001. Long-Distance Agreement and Topic in Tsez. *Natural Language and Linguistic Theory* 19: 583-646.

Polinsky, M. and E. Potsdam. 2002. Backward Control. *Linguistic Inquiry* 33: 245-282.

Postal, P. M. 1970. *On Raising*. Cambridge: MIT Press.

Putnam, H. 1967. The 'Innateness Hypothesis' and Explanatory Models in Linguistics. *Synthese* 17: 12-22.

Rizzi, L. 1982. *Issues in Italian Syntax*. Dordrecht: Foris.

Rizzi, L. 1990. *Relativized Minimality*. Cambridge, Mass.: MIT Press.

Rosenbaum, P. S. 1967. *The Grammar of English Predicate Complement Constructions*. Cambridge: MIT Press.

Ross, J. R. 1967. Constraints on Variables in Syntax. Doctoral dissertation, MIT.

Roussou, A. 2001. Control and Raising in and out of Subjunctive Complements. *Comparative Syntax of Balkan Languages, XX*, eds. M. L. Rivero and A. Ralli, 74-104. Oxford: Oxford University Press.

Terzi, A. 1997. PRO and Null Case in Finite Clauses. *The Linguistic Review* 14: 335-360.

Tomasello, M. 1992. *First Verbs: A Case Study of Early Grammatical Development*. Cambridge: Cambridge University Press.

van Gelderen, E. 1993. *The Rise of Functional Categories*. Amsterdam: John Benjamins.

Vikner, S. 1995. *Verb Movement and Expletive Subjects in the Germanic Languages*. New York : Oxford University Press.

Wang, W. 1969. Competing Changes as a Cause of Residue. *Language* 45: 9-25.

Wang, W. ed. 1977. *The Lexicon in Phonological Change*. The Hague: Mouton.

Webelhuth, G., J.-P. Koening and A. Kathol, eds. 1999. *Lexical and Constructional Aspects of Linguistic Explanation*. Stanford: CSLI Publications.

Wexler, K. and P. W. Culicover. 1980. *Formal Principles of Language Acquisition*. Cambridge, MA: MIT Press.

Wexler, K. and M. R. Manzini. 1987. Parameters and Learnability in Binding Theory. *Parameter Setting*, eds. T. Roeper, and E. Williams, 41-89. Dordrecht: Reidel.

Willett, T. L. 1988. A Cross-Linguistic Survey of the Grammaticization of Evidentiality. *Studies in Language* 12: 51-97.

Zipf, G. 1935. *The Psychobiology of Language*. New York: Houghton Mifflin.

2

Exo-Skeletal vs. Endo-Skeletal Explanations: Syntactic Projections and the Lexicon

HAGIT BORER

1 Introduction

Within generative traditions, the dominant approach to the projection of argument structure crucially links it to information in the lexical entry of argument selecting heads (verbs, adjectives, possibly nouns). Various executions of this leading idea may vary. Thus within many approaches, the argument structure associated with a particular lexical head is derived from the lexical semantics of that head (Jackendoff, 1990; Levin and Rappaport-Hovav, 1995; Carrier and Randall, 1992, among many others); within other approaches, the argument structure of a verb is a formal object, subject to formal manipulations, which do not represent direct mapping from lexical semantics (Williams, 1981; di Sciullo and Williams, 1987; Grimshaw, 1990; Reinhart, 1996, 2000). These approaches also differ on how argument-structure changing functions operate and where: in the lexicon, on lexical entries, as in Williams, (1981); di Sciullo and Williams (1987); Levin and Rappaport-Hovav (1995); Grimshaw (1990); Reinhart (2000) or alternatively, there are no argument structure changing functions as such, and what appears to be argument structure changing operations are the result of syntactic manipulations such as incorporation, as in the UTAH tradition, largely influential since Baker (1985, 1988). These approaches also differ on the nature of the relevant semantic roles (AGENT, THEME, GOAL, etc., or alternatively, SUBJECT OF CHANGE, SUBJECT OF RESULT, PATH, etc.). It is nevertheless fair to say that they all do have in common the assumption that the original, crucial locus for argument structure specification is a lexical entry

The Nature of Explanation in Linguistic Theory.
John Moore and Maria Polinsky (eds.).

of an assignor, and that at least some level of structure, whether syntactic or lexical, projects directly from that entry.[1]

In (1), I give a somewhat schematized representation of this class of approaches:

(1) (Semantics of Lexical item →) Predicate-Argument structure
→ structure (syntactic or lexical)

Consider, however, another approach, according to which much, if not the entire burden of argument structure is shouldered by the syntax. To consider a simple illustration, suppose it is not the case that AGENTS project externally (universally), but rather, that nominal expressions which project externally must be interpreted as AGENTS. Put differently, the syntactic structure gives rise to a template, or a series of templates, which, in turn, determine the interpretation of arguments. Within such approaches lexical items do not determine structure, but rather, function as its modifiers. Traditionally, this is a position that is associated with Construction Grammar (Fillmore and Kay, 1997; Goldberg 1995). More recently it has come to be associated with a number of models (often referred to as neo-constructionist models) which share to a varying degree a view of the grammar in which at least some argument structure interpretation is divorced from the lexical entry and rather, is determined by the structure. (see van Hout, 1992, 1996; Borer, 1994, 1998; Kratzer, 1994, 1996; Marantz, 1996, 1997; Harley, 1995; among others). Focusing here on the universal execution of this research agenda, the picture put forth within such models could be schematized as in (2):

(2) Syntactic structure → event structure → interpretation of arguments

Reaching beyond the representation of argument structure, the lexicon-driven approach and the syntax-driven approach are but the tip of a much deeper theoretical iceberg. Assumptions concerning the division of labor between the lexicon and various computational systems have always played a crucial role within linguistic theories. At one extreme of the continuum from lexicon to computation, we find a view of the human linguistic capacity fundamentally anchored in our demonstrable ability to acquire an intricate lexicon, based, at least in part, on a complex conceptual system.

[1] Nor is this assumption unique to the Extended Standard Theory, or GB and its direct descendent. It also characterizes Lexical Functional Grammar (LFG) and Head-Driven Phrase Structure Grammar (HPSG).

Within such a view, formal properties are deterministically projected from a listed item with fully articulated lexico-semantics, syntactic and morphological properties. Such properties include not just argument structure, but also syntactic category, syntactic projection environment, and morphological information. I will refer to such approaches as ENDO-SKELETAL, focusing, as they do, on the listed item as the skeleton around which the structure is built. At the other extreme, we find a view anchored in our equally demonstrable rule-governed behavior. Such approaches assume a linguistic ability which is fundamentally computational, with as small as possible repository of idiosyncratic information appended to it, by means of a lexicon, beyond the clearly arbitrary pairing of sound and meaning. While most grammatical models occupy some intermediate place on this continuum, it is, I believe, fair to say that these two extreme positions characterize what counts as a linguistic explanation within most models. Here, I will take a strong computational position.

It is in the nature of things that an endo-skeletal approach, with its ability to associate idiosyncratic as well as unpredictable syntactic properties with atomic listed lexical items, is both less restricted and more redundant, but also, potentially, more capable, at least prima facie, of describing the wealth of phenomena attested in natural language. Nonetheless, even though it turns out that some pairing of (some) listed items with syntactic properties is inevitable, the cause of explanatory adequacy could be greatly served by a systematic investigation of the extent to which the structure does determine the syntactic environment of inserted listed items, rather than the other way around. To this end, I will be pursuing here at least some of the consequences and the predictions of a strong computational position, illustrating specifically both modes of execution as well as a number of empirical advantages of such an approach.

More specifically, I will suggest that syntactic properties typically associated with listed items, notably argument structure and category type, are, in fact, properties of structures and not properties of the listed items themselves. While listed items may still convey an idea (e.g., *potato* is distinct from *pumpkin*), I will attempt to reduce as many as possible of the formal properties traditionally attributed to lexical listing to formal computational systems, be they syntax or morphology. I will call this view EXO-SKELETAL, given its focus on the way in which the structure, rather than the listed item, determines not only grammatical properties, but also the ultimate fine-grained meaning of lexical items themselves (an effect at times called COERCION).[2] If successful, then, an EXO-SKELETAL research program is

[2] With special thanks to Henry Davis for having suggested the term EXO-SKELETAL for this specific research agenda.

looking at a highly impoverished substantive lexicon which is a true interface with the conceptual system, and which contains little beyond the sound-meaning pair.

2 The Exo-Skeletal Approach

Consider the following execution of an exo-skeletal research program. Within such an approach there is a reservoir of sound-meaning pairs, where by 'meaning' we refer to the appropriate notion of a concept, and where by 'sound' we mean an appropriately abstract phonological representation.[3] Following tradition, I will refer to that reservoir as the ENCYCLOPEDIA, and to items within it as ENCYCLOPEDIC ITEMS (EIs). Crucially, an EI is not associated with any formal grammatical information concerning category, argument structure, or word-formation. It is a category-less, argument-less concept, although its meaning might give rise to certain expectations for a felicitous context.[4] It is EIs that are initially selected to form part of what I will call the conceptual array. In the absence of a category determination, however, they are inserted as an unordered set into an unmarked lexical phrasal domain (L-DOMAIN, L-D), as in (3):

(3) $[_{\text{L-D}}$ *sink, boat, dog*]

Alongside the encyclopedia and distinct from it the grammar does have a functional lexicon, including, in essence, grammatical formatives in the form of features (e.g., [+pl], [+pst]) as well as independent grammatical formatives (e.g., <*the,*[+def]>. Simplifying somewhat (but see Borer, 2001, for a fuller discussion), we may say that some grammatical formative α merges with L-D, in turn projecting some functional structure. Particular functional structures, in turn, will categorize whatever L-D they dominate. Consider, as an illustration, α to be equivalent to some value for Tense, e.g. <pst>, in a

---

3 We are making no claims here on the organization of conceptual systems, assuming this important issue to be within the domain of psychological and/or philosophical studies, but clearly extra-linguistic. We only claim that the conceptual system, however internally organized and constrained, is the appropriate input to the sound-meaning pairing.

4 It is within the domain of 'felicitous context' that we locate the selectional restrictions of Chomsky's (1965) Aspects model, assuming them to be fundamentally conceptual and not grammatical. We note that selectional restrictions can be, and are regularly over-ridden by the grammatical environment (i.e., coerced), but that the opposite is never true. Thus a noun with a denotation of 'stuff' (e.g., sand) will receive a count interpretation in the context of a plural marking or plural agreement (e.g., many sands), but a plural-marked noun will never receive a mass interpretation, no matter how salient the context (compare too little carpet for the money with *too little carpets for the money).

language in which the verb is inflected for tense. The merge of <pst>$_T$ and L-D would give rise to the structure in (4):

(4) [$_T$ <pst>$_T$ [$_{L\text{-}D}$ *sink, boat, dog*]]

Assuming free copy and merger (and abstracting away from the covert nature of verb movement in English), any of the items in L-D may now merge a copy in T, but under standard assumptions, only one may do so. Whichever element moves will become the head of L-D, as it must be a head, having merged a copy in a head position. In turn, L-D will become a VP in the context [$_T$ [$_{L\text{-}D}$]], making its head in T, as well as its copy effectively, a V. There only remains to be hoped that some post-derivational phonological storage area will be capable of dispensing, for the resulting V+<pst> structure, a well-formed phonological representation, for if it does not, the derivation would not converge and ungrammaticality would result.[5]

As it turns out, in English, there will be a phonologically felicitous representation for all the heads in (4), should they choose to merge a copy in T:

(5) a. [$_T$ [$_V$ *sink*]-<pst>$_T$ [$_{VP}$ [$_V$ ~~*sink*~~], *boat, dog*]] (*sank*)
b. [$_T$ [$_V$ *dog*]-<pst>$_T$ [$_{VP}$ *sink, boat,* [$_V$ ~~*dog*~~]] (*dogged*)
c. [$_T$ [$_V$ *boat*]-<pst>$_T$ [$_{VP}$ *sink,* [$_V$ ~~*boat*~~], *dog*]] (*boated*)

However, consider <fut> in English. A derivation in which an array item from L-D merges a copy in T would not converge due to the absence of an appropriate phonological representation for V+<fut>. On the other hand a well-formed derivation with a future interpretation could still result just in case the correct phonological formative <*will*> merges with T. Here as well, L-D will become VP in the context of TP. As for its head, if no relevant categorizing morphology can distinguish the items in L-D, any of them could, in principle, be the head. The structure will not, however, remain hopelessly ambiguous, quite simply because the non-head constituents will be themselves embedded under functional structure, categorizing them, so to speak, presumably as DPs or PPs. Should that not turn out to be the case the structure would become uninterpretable. The two modes of projecting functional structure, the one associated with English past tense, the other with English future, are, I believe, the two major strategies universally available. As is obvious, they do not characterize an inter-grammatical situation, but rather, an intra-grammatical one.

---

[5] The affinity with Anderson (1992) should be self evident here.

Schematically, then, our grammar looks as in (6):

(6) ENCYCLOPEDIA → $[_{\text{L-D}}$ conceptual array]

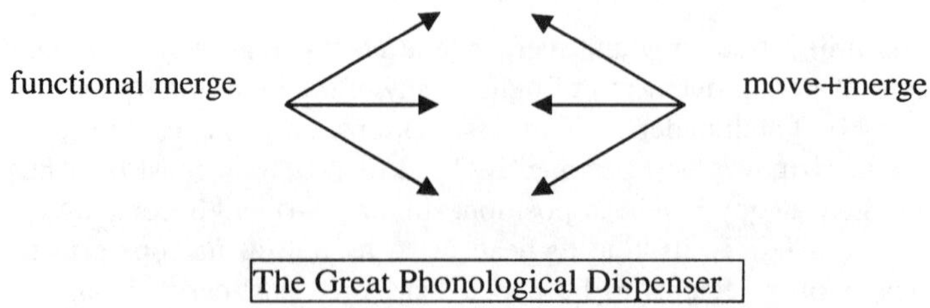

Categorizing, then, can be achieved by the phrase structure of functional projections, with straightforward examples given in (7):[6]

(7) $[_{\text{D}}$ <...>$_{\text{D}}$ $[_{\text{L-D}}$*dog*, *form*]] L-D → NP
$[_{\text{T}}$ <...>$_{\text{T}}$ $[_{\text{L-D}}$*dog*, *form*]] L-D → VP
$[_{\#}$ <...>$_{\#}$ $[_{\text{L-D}}$*dog*, *form*]] L-D → NP

In turn, categorizing can also be accomplished by a morphological structure (distinguished here from inflectional/functional features). Thus category-labeled morphemes such as *–ation, -ize, -al, -full,* etc. are members of the functional lexicon associated with a syntactic lexical category, and therefore can interact with the conceptual array. In turn, they not only carry a category themselves, but also categorize their morphological complements, should they happen not to have a category already:

[6] In English, and perhaps universally, there are no productive conversions with adjectives, productive adjectivizing typically requiring overt morphology. It would appear that for reasons that may or may not be English-specific, adjectives never originate as 'pure' category-less EIs.

(8) Categorizing by Morphological Structure:

a. *-ation,* N, [[$_{V}$] __$_{N}$]

b. N → V [$_{N}$-*ation*]; V: [$_{L}$*form*] ↓ [$_{V}$*form*]

N → V [$_{N}$–*ation*]; V: [$_{V}$*formalize*]

c. *-al*, A, [[$_{N}$] __ $_{A}$]

d. A → N [$_{A}$-*al*]; N: [$_{L}$*form*] ↓ [$_{V}$*form*]

A → N [$_{N}$–*al*]; N: [$_{N}$*formation*]

The morphological structures in (8) may operate on items of the conceptual array, in L-D, giving rise to (9), or alternatively, categorizing morphemes such as *–ation* or *–al* may merge independently in the syntax as N or A respectively, in turn heading an N^{max} and A^{max}. In this latter case, head movement would take place, and the structures in (8) would be applied to the output of head movement, as in (10):

(9) a. [$_{L\text{-}D}$ *dog*, *boat*, *form*]

b. [$_{L\text{-}D}$ *dog*, *boat*, [$_{V}$ [[[[$_{L}$*form*] *al* $_{A}$] $_{A}$] *-ize* $_{V}$]]

(10) a.

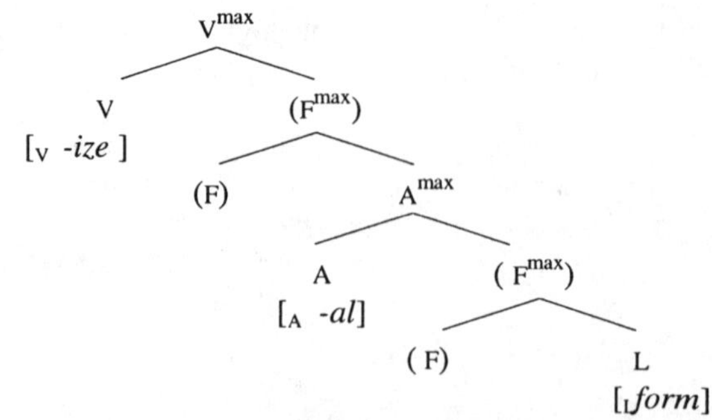

b. [$_V$ *form-al-ize* [$_{FP}$ [$_{AP}$ [$_A$ ~~*form*~~ ~~*al*~~ [$_{FP}$ [$_{L\text{-}D}$ ~~*form*~~]]]]]]

c.

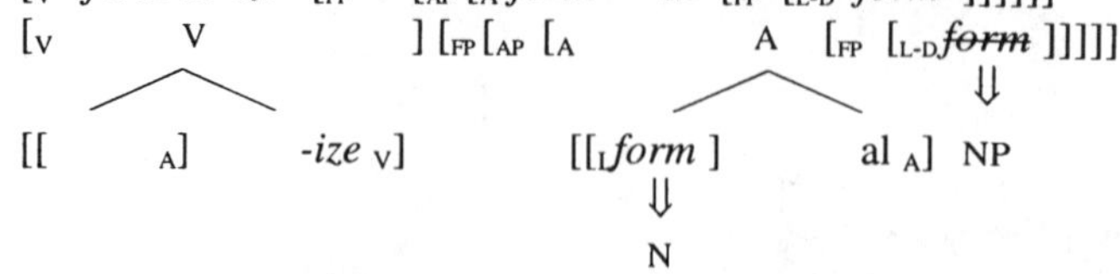

In, (10), note, [$_L$ *form*] becomes a noun through its morphological environment, in turn making its copy a noun, and the L-D dominating it, an NP.

As EI do not in and of themselves have arguments, by assumption, I will assume that argument structure, an event complex, emerges through functional syntactic structure, which has the effect of VERBALIZING an L-D, in the intended sense, in some event complexes, and possibly ADJECTIVIZING some other L-Ds, in other event complexes (e.g. stative ones, but see fn., 6). Specifically, and following a somewhat simplified version of Borer (1994, 1998, 2001), by virtue of being in the specifier of ASP$_Q$, *sink* in the structure in (11) is assigned a DP structure, thus allowing the merger of functional DP internal material (in this case, *three*). In turn, *three sinks* in [Spec,ASP$_Q$] is assigned a SUBJECT-OF-QUANTITY interpretation, in essence, equivalent to an interpretation associated with undergoing a structured change. *Boat,* in turn is assigned DP structure in [Spec, TP] thus licensing the merger of DP internal functional material (i.e. *the*). It then moves from [Spec, TP] to [Spec,EP], where it is assigned the role of an ORIGINATOR (of a non-stative event). Finally, and more crucially from the perspective of our focus here, all the functional nodes in (11) are verbalizers, turning L-D into a VP and categorizing *dog* as a verb (for concreteness, we assume overt short movement of the verb in English to a functional position above ASP_Q. See Johnson, 1991, Runner 1995, for discussion):[7]

(11)

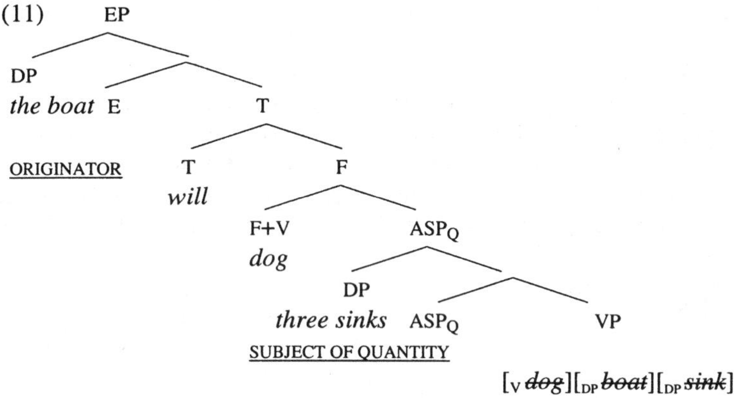

The output of (11) is in (12a). Likewise, the conceptual array in (5), together with the grammatical formatives *will, the, three*, could, in principle, give rise to all the sentences in (12) and more. Some are, of course, more compatible with world knowledge, or with selectional restrictions, than others. This we believe, however, to be outside the domain of the computational grammatical system, and strictly within the conceptual domain. Syntactically, note, they are all unambiguous, in assigning to the first DP the role of ORIGINATOR and to the second DP the role of SUBJECT OF QUANTITY entirely independently of plausibility:

---

[7] The terminology used in Borer (1994, 1998) is ASP_E, rather than ASP_Q as responsible for the assignment of OBJECTIVE roles in telic contexts, and ASP_P rather than EP, as responsible for the assignment of the ORIGINATOR role. See Borer (2001) for some discussion on the rationale for the modifications. The notion UNDERGOING STRUCTURED CHANGE is clearly reminiscent of notions such as INCREMENTAL or GRADUAL THEME, proposed in Dowty (1991) and Krifka (1992). In Borer (2001), however, I argue that SUBJECT-OF-QUANTITY need not be a theme, and that the change under consideration need not be incremental, as such.

We note that the focus here is not on the actual interpretation of arguments or the relevant functional structure, but on the fact that some such structure must exist if argument interpretation is to be assigned to DPs away from lexical listing.

(12) a. The boat will dog three sinks.
b. The dog will sink three boats.
c. The boat will sink three dogs.
d. Three sinks will boat the dog.
etc.

A striking illustration of the malleability of EI is available from the following paradigm, from Clark and Clark (1979). Note that *siren*, to begin with, is turned verbal by the syntactic contexts in (13), in which, in turn, it clearly functions as a modifier of an action, largely interpreted through the syntactic structure, rather than the determinant of the argument structure combinations available:

(13) a. The factory horns sirened throughout the raid.
b. The factory horns sirened midday and everyone broke for lunch.
c. The police car sirened the Porsche to a stop.
d. The police car sirened up to the accident site.
e. The police car sirened the daylight out of me.

It is worthwhile noting that if argument structure is determined by the structure and not by the projection of information in lexical entries, it may be the case that relationship between structure and argumental interpretation are fixed, but nevertheless, different for the same stem in different contexts. Thus, for instance, if the subject in the context of *destructible* is interpreted as a SUBJECT-OF-STATE, but an object in the context of *destroy* is interpreted as a SUBJECT-OF-QUANTITY, there is no particular reason to assume that they are projected in the same structural position. If, however, as endocentric, UTAH-driven approaches would have it, *destroy* assigns an internal (THEME) argument in all its realizations, we would be committed to claiming that in both *destroy* and *destructible* (and, of course, *destruction*), a THEME argument is projected in an identical position. For the paradigm in (13) this would mean that all occurrences of *siren* would have to be syntactically derived from a common source, a rather difficult fit. If, however, *siren* has no independent properties, and the argument structure in which it is embedded is syntactically, rather than lexically, driven, no such problems emerge. From this perspective, then, an exo-skeletal approach is more descriptively adequate here as well as theoretically simpler, without any need for compromising restrictiveness.

3 Some Questions and Some Goals

Any model which attempts to redefine the way in which category and argument structure come to exist must show not only that it is prima facie plausible and that it has some explanatory potential, but also that it makes at least some predictions which are fundamentally distinct (and, hopefully, correct) from those made by the model which it attempts to replace. In what follows I will attempt to show that some such predictions do exist, both within the syntactic and the morphological domain. I will further attempt to refine the notion of LISTED ITEM, as it is used in this work, elaborating, specifically, on the interaction between the morpho-phonological properties of words and structures. The specific subject matter on which I will focus concerns properties of nominals in general and derived nominals in particular.

Consider some of the obvious questions that do arise in the context of the treatment of categorizing and argument structure sketched above. First, note that the derivation of e.g., [$_{N}$ *dog*] and [$_{V}$ *dog*], as described in (7), gives rise immediately to the question in (14):

(14) Is it necessary, or desirable, to postulate, for English, a Ø-affixation rule mapping N→V or V→N (or alternatively, a rule of conversion mapping one to the other)? Alternatively, all such Ø-alternations are syntactically, rather than morphologically, determined, by inserting a category-neutral EI into a syntactically or morphologically deterministic structure. Even more importantly, does the assumption that *dog* is a category-neutral EI inserted into distinct syntactic environments have empirical consequences which are distinguishable from those which emerge if some categorical instance of *dog* (say the verb) is derived from the other?

Second, consider the issue of argument structure within derived nominals, and more specifically, the pair in (15):

(15) a. The enemy destroyed the city.
b. The enemy's destruction of the city

As of Chomsky (1970), it is standardly assumed that the relations which hold between the noun *destruction* and *the city* in (15b) parallel, and indeed have the same lexical source, as those which hold between *destroy* and *the city* in (15a). The fact that in the case of (15a) it is a verb which is thus related to the object, but in (15b) it is a noun is theoretically insignificant in this context. Consider, however, the pair in (15) from the perspective of an account which attributes the interpretation of arguments to functional structure, which has, in turn, verbalizing (or adjectivizing) properties. If such an approach is on the right track, it means not only that the role of *the city* cannot be assigned by either *destroy* or *destruction*, but also, that if, indeed, *the city* is assigned a role in (15b) on a par with the role assigned to *the city* in (15a) (e.g., in [Spec,ASP_Q], as SUBJECT-OF-QUANTITY), there must be a verbal constituent within (15b). Even more strongly, a strong semantic claim emerges from the specific syntactic execution here, according to which nouns, as such, may never have (event) argument structure, and every instantiation of (event) argument structure, by virtue of its categorizing properties, must include either a VP or an AP projection. Our next task, then, is to answer the question in (16):

(16) Can it be shown that there is, indeed, a verbal constituent in (15b), together with the relevant functional structure (as in e.g. (11)) responsible for the assignment of argument structure? Can it be shown that nouns, as such, never have (event) argument structure, and that (event) argument structure always requires the projection of either a verbal or an adjectival constituent, in the relevant functional configuration?

In the following sections I will address these issues. In sections 4-5 I review Grimshaw's (1990) analysis of derived nominals, assuming her descriptive conclusions to serve as the starting point for any adequate future research on derived nominals. Nevertheless, her specific analysis, crucially embedded within a lexical approach to role assignment, is reviewed and rejected. The conclusions I reach are summarized in (17):

(17) a. So-called complex event nominals (in the sense of Grimshaw, 1990), are derived from the presence of a nominal structure above an argument structure event complex, including either a VP or an AP alongside functional structure, e.g. as in (i):

i. [$_N$ –ation/*-ing* [$_{EP/ASPQ}$ [$_{L-D}$ ... L ...]]]

In (i), ASP_Q as well as EP are verbalizers, and hence L-D is a VP. In turn, L(= V for (i)) merges with *–ation/-ing* and is (or is not) assigned morpho-phonological structure. More specifically, the event interpretation of complex event nominals cannot be a property of nouns or of nominalizing affixes as such, contra Grimshaw (1990).

b. So-called result nominals are derived from the presence of a nominal structure directly above the EI, projected within the conceptual array.

Having elaborated on the properties of nouns which are derived from verbs with overt affixation, I turn to the status of so-called ∅-affixation or conversion, and to the question posed in (14). I address this question specifically in the context of so-called ∅-derived nominals such as *a walk, a talk, a drive, a break*, etc. An examination of their properties, undertaken in section 6, leads to the conclusions in (18):

(18) a. Ø-marked N⇔V alternations are not derivational, but represent category neutral EIs inserted in different syntactic environments. There is a Ø categorically-marked affix in English (universally?).[8]

b. The absence of '∅-derived' complex event nominals follows directly from the exo-skeletal model, combined with the absence of ∅-categorial affixation in English, in fact, provides strong evidence for the particular exo-skeletal model proposed here.

Within a neo-constructionist or exo-skeletal approach, with its impoverished listed representations that are devoid of category and argument structure information, yet another important question arises, concerning the degree to which encyclopedic entries are phonologically abstract. To consider a concrete example, suppose we look at the pair *eat-feed* in English, semantically displaying a rather similar relation to that associated with *sink.TRANSITIVE-sink.INTRANSITIVE*. Could we assume that there is one EI, say EAT with appropriate semantic value but no phonological (or syntactic) properties, and which, depending upon the existence or lack of a causative syntactic structure, would result in the picture in (19a-b):

(19) a. $[_V$ EAT] → */eat/*

b. $[_V$ CAUSE $[_V$ EAT]] → */feed/*

The conclusion to be reached here, as based on the discussion of derived nominals, will be that the representation in (19) must be rejected. Rather,

---

8 The scope of the possible universal here should be made clear. I am not suggesting that grammatical distinctions are never available without overt phonological marking. The claimed potential universal here, if indeed, shown to exist, would involve exclusively the absence of overt marking in the presence of categorial change.

we will conclude that EIs must be associated with (at least some abstract) phonological matrix. While some phonological manipulation is possible, some degree of phonological faithfulness must be preserved. What is possible, I will argue, are stem allomorphs conditioned by different syntactic or morpho-phonological contexts, hence [$destroy_V$] ⇔ [$destruct\text{-}_N$]; [$prógress_N$] ⇔ [$progréss_V$], and also [$grow_V$] ⇔ [$growth_N$],[$high_A$] ⇔ $height_N$] (but more on that below). Concretely, this means that */feed/* and */eat/* cannot be derived from the same EI.[9] In turn, the existence of phonological representation for EI will turn out to place well-defined morpho-phonological restrictions on what are and what are not syntactically possible derivations.[10]

This paper concludes with a brief comparison between the specific neo-constructionist execution proposed in this paper and other neo-constructionist executions, arguing, specifically, that a verbalizing (or adjectivizing) function is associated with all (event) argument structure, contra Marantz (1997) and Alexiadou (1999), and that the functional structure responsible for interpreting 'external' arguments may occur inside derived nominals.

4 Referential Nominals vs. Argument-Structure Nominals

4.1 Grimshaw's Diagnostics

Grimshaw (1990) diagnoses two types of nominals which I will refer to as *AS*-nominals (Grimshaw's complex event nominals) and *R*-nominals (Grimshaw's result nominals) respectively, and which are illustrated in (20)-(21). They have the properties in (22)-(23) respectively:

[9] In turn, to the extent that pairs such as *feed-eat* may be morphologically related, and hence derived from the same EI in some languages, this means that the encyclopedia cannot be considered the conceptual system proper, but rather, a true interface in which the presence of entry is determined by the conceptual system together with arbitrary, language specific vocabulary choices.

[10] The issue of the level of phonological abstractness of lexical items does not arise for strict lexicalist approaches, in which *feed* and *eat* are distinct lexical entries, but it does arise for approaches such as UTAH, in which *sink.TRANS* is derived from *sink.INTRANS*. As such, the conclusion that we will reach here is not just applicable to neo-constructionist models, but to any model which denies the independent listing of, e.g., *sink.TRANS* and *sink.INTRANS*.

(20) *AS*-Nominals

a. The instructor's (intentional) examination of the student
b. The frequent collection of mushrooms (by students)
c. The monitoring of wild flowers to document their disappearance
d. The destruction of Rome in a day

(21) *R*-Nominals

a. The instructor's examination/exam
b. John's collections
c. These frequent destructions took their toll

(22) *AS*-Nominals (Argument Structure Nominals)

a. θ-assignors, Obligatory arguments
b. Event reading.
c. Agent-oriented modifiers
d. subjects are arguments
e. *by* phrases are arguments; in Hebrew, selects *al-yedey*
f. Implicit argument control
g. Aspectual modifiers.
h. *frequent, constant* etc. possible without plural
i. Mass nouns

(23) *R*-Nominals (Referential Nominals)

a. Non-θ-assignors, No obligatory arguments
b. No event reading
c. No agent-oriented modifiers
d. Subjects are possessives
e. *by* phrases are non-arguments; in Hebrew selects *šel* (of) *me'et*
f. No implicit argument control
g. No aspectual modifiers
h. *frequent, constant* etc. possible only with plural nouns
i. Count nouns

The most powerful support for the classification in (22)-(23) comes from the impossibility of mixing and matching properties. Thus in the presence of an argumental *by*-phrase, a modifier such as *constant* cannot take a plural noun, nor is the omission of an object possible in (24a). Likewise, without arguments for *destruction*, the modification *in a day* gives rise to ungrammaticality.

(24) a. *The constant examination(s) by the students
b. *Mary's frequent collection
c. *The collection to document the disappearance of mushrooms
d. *The destruction in a day

To account for the differences between these two types of nominals, Grimshaw (1990) proposes that *AS*-nominals, her complex event nominals, have an event argument (*Ev*), and that the argument taking properties associated with the resulting nominal derive from the presence of such an event argument. On the other hand, *R*-nominals have a referential (*R)* external argument, responsible for the result interpretation associated with them. Fully endorsing the existence of two types of derived nominals, as argued by Grimshaw, there are, nevertheless, some problems with the idea that a noun may directly assign an event argument, or be associated with event structure, some pointed out in Grimshaw's own work. First, as Grimshaw notes (op. cit.), many nominals which denote an event behave like *R*-Nominals, and not like *AS*-Nominals. Among these are nouns such as *event, metamorphosis, journey, trip,* etc. as illustrated by (25):

(25) a. *The constant race to the mountains
b. *The event in three hours
c. *John's deliberate trip to the mountains
d. *A race from the station by Mary
e. *The metamorphosis of the town in order to win a medal

That nouns such as *event*, *metamorphosis*, *journey*, and *trip* are, indeed, event denoting, and that this event denotation appears to have at least some linguistic consequences is indicated by the grammaticality of (26), vs. the impossibility of (27) under a similar event interpretation (coercion notwithstanding):

(26) a. The three different races from the stadium lasted a long time.
b. The metamorphosis of Paris will last into the next century.

(27) *The table lasted a long time. (under an event reading, coercion notwithstanding)

Similarly, the contrasts in (28a,b), assuming, following Reichenbach (1948), that *happen, take place* and *occur* can only be predicates of events:

(28) a. The trip/metamorphosis/event/journey occurred last night.
b. *The table occurred last night. (coercion notwithstanding)

Thus it is clear that an event denotation, to the extent that it plays a role, cannot in and of itself induce the diagnostics in (22), and some means are necessary to distinguish between the event nominals in (20) and the event nominals in (25). To this end, Grimshaw introduces a distinction between Complex Event Nominals (=*AS*-Nominals) and Simple Event Nominals, as in (25). The distinction, primarily, is based on argument structure. While Complex Event Nominals, Grimshaw suggests, assign a role to an event argument (*Ev*), Simple Event Nominals pattern with *R*-Nominals in not assigning such a role, and instead, in assigning a role to a referential index, *R*. Because in Grimshaw's model derived nominals have a lexical entry which is independent of their derivational history, and because an entry for, e.g., *transformation*, is in essence ambiguous between an *AS*-Nominal and an *R*-Nominal, the fact that some nouns denoting events (e.g., *metamorphosis*) do not take arguments and do not assign an *Ev* role, while others (e.g., *transformation*) do, becomes a matter of arbitrary lexical listing.

And yet the classification is anything but arbitrary. Only nouns which are derived from verbs (or, as we shall see, from adjectives) by means of overt affixation can be *AS*-Nominals, while nouns which do not have a verbal or an adjectival source never are.[11] Viewed from that perspective, one is certainly tempted to view argument structure as well as event interpretation as deriving from the source verb or adjective, rather than the noun itself. But if this is indeed the case, then it would follow that nouns, as such, are never the source of event interpretation or argument structure. At the very best, they could be viewed as vehicles for passing on the roles and properties of stems embedded within them.

The problems for identifying what, exactly, is the relevant notion of event so as to apply it successfully to the diagnostic in (22)-(23) are further compounded by the fact that many *R*-Nominals derived from verbs denote an event and behave just like Simple Event Nominals, as (29)-(30) illustrate (see Zucchi, 1989):

(29) a. The destruction lasted for hours.
  b. The examination lasted for hours.

(30) a. The destruction occurred at dawn.
  b. The exam(ination) took place at 5pm.

What, then, is the lexical entry of *destruction*, such that it has two entries, both denoting event, but one which assigns an *Ev* role and the other an *R* role? We seem to be faced now with a difficulty which emerges directly

[11] Attributing it to A. Zucchi (p.c.), Grimshaw notes this fact, but does not pursue its consequences.

from the assumption that an event interpretation is the basic property of the derived nouns themselves, from which the presence of argument structure derives.

And finally, we note that while *AS*-Nominals do need to have an event interpretation in the episodic sense, they need not be eventive and may be stative. Such is the case for nominals derived from adjectives, clearly in evidence whenever the adjective in question can occur with complements, directly carried over to the nominal derived from it, as (31)-(32) illustrate:

(31) a. The court's awareness of the problem
b. Pat's consciousness of my presence
c. Jill's fondness of classical music
d. Robin's readiness to leave
e. Marcia's closeness to her parents
f. The party's satisfaction with the counting results

(32) a. The court is aware of the problem.
b. Pat is conscious of my presence.
c. Jill is fond of classical music.
d. Robin is ready to leave.
e. Marcia is close to her parents.
f. The party is satisfied with the counting results.

The existence of de-adjectival *AS*-nominals poses some difficulties for the Grimshaw model. First, we note that of the diagnostics in (22) only those in (33) are clearly applicable to de-adjectival nominals:

(33) a. θ-assignors, obligatory arguments
d. subjects are arguments
h. *constant* etc. possible without plural
(No agent-oriented modifiers; no implicit argument control, no aspectual modifiers)

In turn, the derived nominals in (31) do not behave like *R*-nominals either. Their subject is an argument, rather than a possessor, *constant* need not occur with a plural, etc. This state of affairs raises an important issue concerning the generality of Grimshaw's account. If *Ev* is assigned by the derived nominals in (31), the absence of event modification, event control, etc. becomes mysterious. If, on the other hand, *Ev* is not assigned by the derived nominals in (31), the presence of an argument structure identical to that of the source adjectives alongside the non-*R*-nominal properties of (31) must be argued to have a source distinct from the assignment of *Ev*. But if argument structure and non-*R*-properties can be assigned in (31) without an *Ev* argument, then the putative link between *Ev* and argument structure can no longer be generally maintained, and whatever mechanism is developed to account for the properties of (31) would need to be explicitly excluded in the domain of nominals derived from verbs.

One could suggest that some derived nominals assign *Ev*-STATIVE while others are assigned *Ev*-EVENTIVE. In Grimshaw's system, however, such assignment would have to be stated entirely independently of the derivational history of the relevant nouns, making the fact that stative interpretation is associated with nouns derived from adjectives, but not with nouns derived from verbs (and vice verse) a pure coincidence. In turn, of course, it could be suggested that the derived nominal inherits the nature of the *Ev* argument from the source verb or adjective, making a noun derived from an (eventive) verb *eventive,* and a noun derived from an adjective *stative.* That, of course, would be a fully workable solution, but here, again the conclusion must be that the source of any event interpretation as well as argument structure cannot be the derived nominal itself, but must be related in some fashion to the verb/adjective from which it is derived.

Suppose, then, that we assume that the arguments as well as the type of event involved are related in some crucial sense to the event complex dominated by the *AS*-nominal, an event complex which is headed by the very L-stem which incorporates into the nominalizer. What would be the ramifications of such an approach? Note that it has immediate ramifications for the level of phonological abstractness of EIs, or, for that matter, lexical items. To the extent that *AS*-nominals are precisely those which are morphologically derived from phonologically attested verbs or adjectives, and reflect directly a morpho-phonological relationship with them, we must assume that at least in this case, we are dealing with phonologically concrete objects, and not just with an abstract set of semantic or conceptual features. To see that this is so, consider the following hypothetical derivation:

(34) a. EI: [TRANSFORM] → [$_{V}$TRANSFORM] → */transform/*
b. [$_{V}$ TRANSFORM]+NOM→[$_{N}$TRANSFORMATION]→*/transformation/*
c. [$_{N}$ TRANSFORMATION]→ */metamorphosis/*; */shift/*; */turn/* (etc.)

Suppose, specifically, that an EI with the semantic and conceptual properties of [TRANSFORM] is inserted into an appropriate verbalizing structure, giving rise to [$_{V}$TRANSFORM]. Still maintaining its conceptual and semantic nature, now also associated with the syntactic category V, but still devoid of any phonological specification, [$_{V}$TRANSFORM] may now give rise to [$_{N}$TRANSFORMATION], associated with conceptual and semantic structure, as well as a category, but no phonological or morpho-phonological information. However, whatever semantic and conceptual properties are associated with the noun [$_N$TRANSFORMATION] are also associated with [$_N$ SHIFT], [$_N$ METAMORPHOSIS] or [$_N$ TURN], making the phonology of any of these nouns a proper phonological form for [$_N$TRANSFORMATION] in some post-derivational component. In turn, however, the derivation in (34c) must be blocked. If it is allowed, we would predict, contrary to fact, that *metamorphosis/shift/turn* may have argument structure associated with the event complex headed by [$_V$TRANSFORM]. While any ad hoc blocking of (34c) is, of course, possible, the near total absence of any such correlations, that is, the absence of phonological realizations for *AS*-nominals which do not record an actual morpho-phonological history of having been derived from a verb or an adjective, cannot be explained unless we assume that representations such as (34) must be rejected and replaced, at the very minimum, with the representations in (35), where π is a reference to an indexed phonological representation of some abstraction, and where EIs are sets referring both to some semantic/conceptual features and to some such phonological index:[12]

(35) a. EI: (TRANSFORM, π) → ([$_V$ TRANSFORM], π) → */transform/*
b. ([$_V$TRANSFORM], π)+NOM → ([$_N$TRANSFORMATION], π) → */transformation/*
c. ([$_N$ TRANSFORMATION], π) → **/metamorphosis/*, */shift/*, */turn/*)

The contrasts in (36)-(37) illustrate a similar effect in Hebrew. *Transformacia* is a borrowed word, meaning 'transformation'. *Šinui* is a (native Hebrew) nominal, derived from the verb *šina*, 'change, transform'. While the latter can occur both as an *AS*-nominal and as an *R*-nominal, the former, without any morpho-phonological derivational history in the language, can occur only as an *R*-nominal:

[12] A reviewer objects that *metamorphosis, shift, turn* and *transformation* might, in actuality, be sufficiently semantically distinct so as to make their interchanging in (35) impossible. We note that while one may subscribe to the view that true synonyms do not exist, and every encyclopedic entry, or lexical entry is maximally unique, at least the Hebrew example below shows that what is at stake here is very clearly the derivational history, and not the cluster of relevant meanings.

(36) a. Ha-šinui šel merkaz ha-'ir
the-transformation/change of center the-city
'al yedey ha-'iriya
on hands the-city hall
'The transformation of the center of the city by city hall'

b. Ha-šinui haya madhim.
the-change/transformation was amazing
'The transformation was amazing.'

(37) a. *Ha-transformacia šel merkaz ha-'ir
the-transformation of center the-city
'al yedey ha-'iriya
by hands the-city hall

b. Ha-transformacia hayta madhima.
the-transformation was amazing

The assumption that event structure in *AS*-nominals is associated with the verbal or the adjectival stem in turn has other consequences. As verbs and adjectives, themselves EIs, cannot have arguments as such, it follows that we must assume, within *AS*-nominals, a fully projected event complex, complete with whatever functional structure is responsible for the projection of argument structure. At a minimum then, *breaking* or *destruction* when occurring as *AS*-nominals, must embed a structure that includes not only *break* or *destroy*, but also a full VP and a full functional structure associated with whatever arguments *break* or *destroy* would otherwise be associated with. If we assume that e.g., (38) is the structure associated with *break* (transitive) or *destroy*, then we must assume that the structure in (39) is associated with the *AS*-nominals *breaking* or *destruction*:

(38) a. Kim broke/destroyed the vase.

b. $[_{EP}$ *Kim* $[_{TP}$ $[_{ASPQ}$ *the vase* $[_{L\text{-}D}$ *break/destroy*]]]] (L-D → VP)

(39) a. Kim's breaking/destruction of the vase

b. $[_{NP}$ *-tion*$_{NOM}$/*-ing*$_{NOM}$ $[_{EP}$ *Kim* $[_{ASPQ}$ *the vase* $[_{LD}$ *break/destroy*]]]]
(L-D → VP)

In accordance with an already established practice, L-D in (38)-(39) would become a VP, verbalized by ASP_Q, and *break* or *destroy,* its head, will become a verb. Argument structure and event interpretation will emerge exactly as they do for active propositions with *break* or *destroy* having an identical structure (TP aside). In turn, we may assume, for concreteness sake, that the verb, be it *break* or *destroy*, merges copies through the successive functional heads in (39) to *-ing*$_{\text{NOM}}$ or *-ation*$_{\text{NOM}}$, where *breaking* or *destruction* emerge, following the association of the appropriate morphological structure with the output of the head-to-head movement.

The evidence for the fact that the argument structure for derived nominals comes from the presence of some structure external to the nominal itself is surprisingly simple and straightforward. Consider, specifically, *R*-nominals, as in (40):

(40) a. The destruction was devastating.
b. The examination is over.
c. The formation is complete.

R-nominals, by definition, do not have an *Ev* interpretation, and do not have an event argument structure. Yet, morphologically, they are clearly very much the same creatures as *AS*-nominals, and must be assumed to be derived, morphologically, in an identical fashion. If we take the relevant morphological structure deriving both *AS*-nominals and *R*-nominals to be as in (8a-b), we can assume that morphological structure to be associated with the output of head-to-head movement in (39), but to be associated directly with some EI, within the conceptual array, in the case of *R*-nominals, as illustrated, for *formalize*, by (9b). Effectively, this means that a category neutral EI such as *form*, residing in the L-domain of (41a) as part of the conceptual array, may be associated, in the L-D, with an inserted nominal (and verbalizing) affix *–ation*, a member of the functional lexicon, to give rise to the structure in (41b). Of course, following the insertion of the relevant morphological structure *formation* is an N. If it is to become the head of L-D, it will force the existence of an NP, and would only allow the projection of nominalizing functional structure, e.g., DP, NumP, etc., but not the projection of verbalizing functional structure, such as TP or ASP$_{\text{Q}}$:

(41) a. [$_{\text{L-D}}$ *form*] b. [$_{\text{L-D}}$ N [*form* *-ation*]]
c. ([$_{\text{DP}}$) ([$_{\text{NumP}}$) [$_{\text{NP}}$ *formation*]
d. *[$_{\text{TP}}$ [$_{\text{ASPQ}}$ [$_{\text{NP}}$ *formation*]

That *formation*, as an *R*-nominal, does not have any argument structure in the representation in (41) emerges directly from the derivation. There is no argument structure here, quite simply because the nominalization was, so to speak, too low, and any attempt to add argument structure to it would involve the projection of structure that is incompatible with the existence of an N-head. Nothing else needs to be said. Much, however, must be said -and has been said - by any theory which assumes that either verbs or nouns assign argument roles, be they eventive or otherwise. Such theories must assume either that nouns are special in that their argument assignment properties are optional, unlike verbs in general, or the verbs from which they are directly derived (in essence Chomsky, 1970 and much subsequent literature) or alternatively, as Grimshaw assumes, that nouns are ambiguous, and that they are not related, argument-wise, to their source verbs. None of these complications, with their empirical and conceptual inadequacies, emerge if we assume that neither the noun *formation*, nor the verb *form* embedded within it have any arguments to assign.

Supposing this to be on the right track, there is a VP (or an AP) inside all *AS*-Nominals, alongside full functional event structure similar to that otherwise attested in propositions. On the other hand, *R*-nominals are simple nominal structures, with a nominalizing morphological structure as well as whatever compatible functional structure may co-exist with it.

That there is, indeed, a VP inside derived nominals has been, in turn, argued for extensively in a broad range of languages, including French (Valois, 1991), Hebrew (Hazout, 1990, 1995; Borer, 1993), Chinese (Fu, 1994), Russian (Schoorlemmer,1995) among many others, as well as most recently for English (Fu, Roeper and Borer, 2001), and I will assume the fundamental correctness of these approaches. Suppose we turn, however, to another question concerning the relations between particular nominalizing affixes and the resulting properties of *AS*-nominals. Grimshaw (1990) claims that *–ation* nominals are always ambiguous between an *Ev* and an *R* reading, that *–ing* nominals are always *Ev* nominals, and that Ø-derived nominals are always *R*-nominals, thus crucially linking the ±*Ev* property with nominalizers, rather than the stems from which they are derived. As I have now argued that event structure is never associated with nominals, but specifically with the event complex which is headed by the incorporated L-stem, these generalizations, if indeed correct, must be explained.

5 Do N-Affixes Determine Event Structure?

It has been claimed by Grimshaw (ibid.) and others that different nominalizing affixes have different effects on the output derived nominals, and that specifically, the picture in (42) holds, such that Ø-nominalizers only give rise to *R*-nominals, *-ing* nominalizers only give rise to *AS*-nominals, and –*ation* is ambiguous. That Ø-nominalizers, with few exceptions, do, indeed, give rise to *R*-nominals is very clear from the data in (43):[13]

---

[13] Alas, like all generalizations concerning WF, this one, too, has counterexamples. Thus, while at least some speakers reject (i)-(iii), others find them acceptable:

(42) Grimshaw: ∅(***R***); -ation({***R,Ev***}); -ing(***Ev***)

(43) a. *The/John's drive of this car
  b. *The/Mary's walk of this dog
  c. *The/Kim's break of the vase
  d. *The airforce's murder of innocent civilians

It is less than obvious, however, that Grimshaw is correct in suggesting that *–ing* nominals are always *Ev* nominals, *AS*-nominals in our terms. Certainly, the *–ing* nominals in (44) are not RESULT nominals, but as we have already seen, *R*-nominals need not be result nominals, and may be, instead, event nominals, or as the case appears to be at least for some of the nominals in (44), nominals denoting state.

(44) a. *a good living, a strong craving, a strong beating, a reading, (leftist) leaning, (good) standing, (one) sitting*, etc.
  b. 'Women are reared not to feel competent or gratified by *the questing, the competing, the outbidding* that collecting … demands.' (S. Sontag, *Volcano Lover*, p. 138)
  c. (this kind of) *fighting, fraternizing, parenting, writing*, etc.

In turn, if, indeed, both *–ing* and *–ation* allow freely *AS*-nominals and *R*-nominals, showing that at least for these two affixes the choice of N-affix is not the determinant of event structure, an important question concerns the absence of an *AS*-Nominal reading for Ø-nominalization, especially since at least prima facie, the relationship with the source verb is the most transparent, at least in (43a-c), and most so-called Ø-derived nominals do, indeed, have a salient event denotation:

(45) a. The walk lasted for five hours.
  b. The jump occurred before dawn.
  c. The (responsive) read took place in the law review office.

I suggested that the structure for *AS*-nominals with either *–ing* or *–ation* is in essence as in (39b). It would appear, then, that for some reason, the structure in (46) is not available, although the structure in (47), that of *R*-nominal with Ø, is available:

---

i. My constant change of mentors from 1992-1997
ii. The frequent release of the prisoners by the governor
iii. The frequent use of sharp tools by underage children

(46) $[_{NP}$Ø$_{NOM}$ $[_{EP}$ *Kim* $[_{ASPQ}$ *the vase* $[_{L\text{-}D}$ *break*]]]] (L-D → VP)
(47) $[_N$ $[_V$ *break*] Ø]

Viewed differently, however, the absence of *AS*-nominals with Ø-morphology is fully explained if we assume that what appears as a Ø-morpheme is in actuality a category neutral stem, unmarked for being either a noun or a verb. In effect, we suggest English does not have a Ø-morpheme which mediates conversion from verbs to nouns or from nouns to verbs. Rather, English has category neutral EIs, inserted into particular structures which render them verbs or nouns, syntactically. Consider, specifically, how such an account would work for the absence of *AS*-nominals with neutral stems, taking *break* as an example. For *R*-nominals, the derivation is straightforward. Rather than assume a Ø-affix, as in (47), consider instead a derivation in which a category neutral EI is inserted in L-D, and L-D becomes an NP as it is embedded under nominal functional structure (e.g., DP):

(48) a. $[_{L\text{-}D}$ *break*]
b. $[_D$ *the* $[_{L\text{-}D}$ *break*] L-D → NP, $[_L$ *break*] → $[_N$ *break*]

The derivation of a verbal *break,* within a propositional context, is likewise straightforward. As soon as ASP_Q (or TP) project, L-D will be verbalized, and one of its constituents will be targeted as a possible head, in turn verbalized as well:

(49) a. $[_{L\text{-}D}$ *break, Kim, vase*]
b. $[_{ASPQ}$ *the vase* $[_{L\text{-}D}$ *break, Kim,* $[_{DP}$ ~~*vase*~~]]
L-D → VP, $[_L$ *break*] → $[_V$ *break*]

Consider, however, *AS*-nominals. We suggested that a full VP event complex is projected within *AS*-nominals. This means that for a nominal such as *the breaking of the vase,* the merger of an ASP_Q with L-D is essential, to give a landing site for *the vase.* Likewise, a *subject-of-quantity* argument associated with *break* must project in the specifier of ASP_Q. Thus in attempting to derive (43d), we must start by projecting the structure in (50):

(50) $[_{EP}$ *Kim* $[_{ASPQ}$ *the vase* $[_{VP}$ $[_V$ *break*], $[_{DP}$ ~~*Kim*~~], $[_{DP}$ ~~*vase*~~]]

As in the case of (49b), ASP_Q will verbalize L-D as well as its head, *break.* If, e.g., *–ing* merges above EP in (50), an *AS*-nominal does emerge. However, if indeed English does not have Ø-nominalizers, and all Ø-alternations between verbs and nouns are instances of category-neutral stems, the representation in (50) cannot become nominalized without an overt nominalizer, and an *AS*-nominal derivation for [$_N$ *break*] is expected to never occur. As in the case of the missing arguments for *R*-nominals, here as well it is hard to see how a theory which attributes role assignment to lexical entries can likewise capture these facts.

6 More on the Absence of Ø Noun-Verb Alternations

We have, now, an interesting prediction. If, indeed, English does not have Ø-categorizing morphology, and all stems that appear to alternate between categorial types are, in actuality, category neutral stems categorized by the syntactic structure, we predict that the great freedom attested in English which allows any noun to be inserted in a verbal frame and any verb to be inserted in a nominal frame should be only attested with respect to category neutral stems, which is to say, stems that are not associated with any category morphology.

That this is indeed the case can be immediately illustrated by the ungrammaticality of (51b-c):

(51) a. *form, floor, table, chair, run, kiss, break, closet, wardrobe, telephone, brother, dog, cat,* etc.
b. **a formalize, *a fatten, *an enclose, *a bemoan,* etc.
c. **to formation, *to brotherhood, *to government*

The generalization here cannot be based on morphological complexity. Note that the forms in (52) are morphologically complex:

(52) *rerun, rebound, transport, import, export, subcontract*

Further, note that primary compounds do display a Ø N⇔V alternation:

(53) a. *to grandstand, to blackboard, to chicken-wire, to wall-paper,* etc.
b. *a white-out, a take-off, a sell-out, a buy-up, a take-over,* etc.

Rather, it seems that Ø N⇔V alternations are possible providing the morphological head is a category neutral EI. As prefixes in English do not change category, and neither do particles, as in (53b), the head remains a category neutral stem. Likewise, in primary compounds, the head, the right member, may be category neutral (but not so in synthetic compounds, note). Some illustrations of primary compounds that cannot enter Ø N⇔V alternations precisely because the right stem, the head, is not category neutral, are in (54):

(54) **to company executive*, **to compound director*, **to school teacher*, **to university professor*, etc.

The derivation for primary compounds as verbs such, as *wallpaper* is given in (55). We may assume, specifically, that both *wall* and *paper* are members of the conceptual array, being compounded by a morphological rule. In turn, the morphological rule assigns a morphological head status to the right stem, and either an N or an A category to the left stem. In turn, the entire compound, if headed by a category neutral EI, is categorized by the functional structure, as in (55b):[14]

(55) a. $[_{L}$ *wall...* $]$ $[_{L}$ *paper* $]$
b. $[_{L}$ $[_{A/N}$ *wall* $]$ $[_{L}$ *paper* $]$ $]$ (by the compounding rule)
i. $[_{D}$ $[_{L}$ $[_{A/N}$ *wall* $]$ $[_{L}$ *paper* $]$ $]$ L → N
ii. $[_{Asp}$ $[_{L}$ $[_{A/N}$ *wall* $]$ $[_{L}$ *paper* $]$ $]$ L → V

Note that the structure in (55a-b) would be the identical one to that assigned to exocentric compounds, in essence putting forth the claim that all primary compounds in English with an underived right member are syntactically exocentric.

While, of course, some counterexamples do exist, we note that of approximately 1300 denominal verbs studied by Clark and Clark (1979) and excluding instrumentals, there is a total of six counterexamples to the claim that nouns with categorial morphology do not participate in Ø-N⇔ V alternations: *to launderette, to laundress, to blockade, to allowance, to tourist,* and *to lover* (other than *blockade,* all rejected by native speakers). In the instrumental class, 12 out of 117 forms listed as possible verbs are derived, including *to elevator, to accelerator, to stopper, to trailer, to glider*, and others, very clearly re-analyzed and re-entered as independent EI.[15,16]

---

[14] But see footnote 6 on the possibility that adjectives are never categorized by the structure, leaving N as the only possibility for the left member in (55).

[15] Kiparsky (1982) argues that the Ø-affix converting verbs to nouns is unproductive and belongs to Level I morphology, while the Ø-affix converting nouns to verbs is fully productive and belongs to Level II morphology. The examples in (53b) as well as those in (54) are a straightforward counter-example to the level ordering assumed by Kiparsky, as is the ungrammaticality of *to transformation* and *to professor.* We also note that contra Kiparsky, V→ N alternations are extremely common and spontaneously produced on a regular basis, including cases which one would assume should be prohibited by blocking, such as *give it a think.* See Borer, forthcoming, for a fuller review.

7 On the Growth-Potential of Theories Based on GROWTH

The account for the properties of *R*-nominals as well as for the absence of an *AS*-nominal reading for '∅-derived' nominals relied heavily on two assumptions. The first concerned the claim that EI, as such, do not have any formal syntactic or morphological properties. To varying degrees, this claim is the defining feature of constructionist as well as neo-constructionist approaches, including the present one. The second assumption involved the claim that the functional structure which is associated with the assignment of all direct (event) arguments is a verbalizer (or alternatively possibly an adjectivizer), and most specifically, that it cannot be associated with an N-head. This, we note, is not a necessary assumption within a neo-constructionist approach, and in actuality, it does differentiate the account presented here from those put forth by Picallo (1991), Ouhalla (1991), and most recently Marantz (1997) and Alexiadou (1999) (and see also Harley and Noyer, 1998a,b). In all these accounts, which are neo-constructionist to varying degrees, it is assumed that in *AS*-nominals the L-D is headed by an N. To consider specifically Alexiadou (1999), who shares with the analysis presented here both a neo-constructionist approach to category determination, as well as the assumption that *AS*-nominals involve an articulated event structure separating the head from the DP, she nevertheless assumes that the relevant structure fundamentally does not have a verbalizing function, and that for, e.g. *destruction of the city*, the structure (somewhat schematically) is as in (56a), where neither ASP (grammatical aspect) nor ***v***, in essence an event licensing node (but not an external role assignor), are verbalizers, and hence L may be realized in situ as an N, and LP as NP, if dominated by a DP. In turn, non-event nominals involve the projection of a DP structure without the event node ***v*** (and without grammatical aspect) schematically as in (56b):[17]

---

[16] We note as an open issue here the mixed behavior of forms such as those in (i), where we have the appearance of a the nominal suffix *–tion*, but where there is no source morphological L-stem (or in turn, a source so drifted in meaning so as to give rise to the plausible assumption that the form has been entered separately in the encyclopedia from its erstwhile morpho-phonological source, as in the case of *proposition*). While some of these forms easily lend themselves to 'verbalizations', others seem more resistant, for reasons that do not seem obvious:

i. a. *to portion, to position, to condition, to proposition, to audition, to ration, to question, to motion*
   b. **to nation, *to ambition, *to potion, *to notion*

[17] Note that Alexiadou (1999), following Marantz (1997) also continues to subscribe to the view that internal arguments (but not external ones) are assigned by the root (our EI), and not

(56) a. $[_{DP}\ [_{ASP}\ [_{v}\ [_{LP}$ √*destroy the city*(*theme*)]]]] L→N
b. $[_{DP}$.......... $[_{LP}$ √*destroy*]]] L→N

Structures such as those in (56) fail, I believe, in two crucial ways. First, they entirely fail to predict the fact that only nominals that are morphologically derived from verbs (or from adjectives) may give rise to *AS*-nominals. There is nothing in the structure in (56a) which allows it to be sensitive to any morpho-phonological considerations. √*destroy* is nominalized in the context of DP, on a par with the nominalization of $[_{N}$*dog*] or $[_{N}$ *table*] or $[_{N}$ *transformation*], or, for that matter, on a par with the nominalization of √*destroy* in the *R*-nominal in (56b). Secondly, the representations in (56) entirely fail to predict the fact that Ø-alternations cannot occur as *AS*-nominals.

Ironically, (56a-b), at first sight so different from the lexicalist approach put forth by Grimshaw (1990), fail precisely where Grimshaw (1990) fails. Upon a closer look, this is not surprising, as they represent it is a syntactic execution of her very idea, endowing some nominals, but not others, with event structure. Both Grimshaw's (1990) analysis and Alexiadou's (1999) structures thus differ from the analysis presented here, whereby event structure is never associated with N, as such, but is always a property of an event structure embedded under a nominal head and associated with a distinct lexical head.

The analysis put forth by Alexiadou (1999) shares one more property with Grimshaw's account in disallowing, in principle, the projection of an external argument within *AS*-nominals. For Alexiadou (1999), following Marantz (1997), this follows from the fact that while neither *v*P nor EP in (56a) are verbalizers, a *v* which assigns an external argument is a verbalizer. Thus when such a node projects, a root embedded under it would become a V, rather than an N, and a derived nominal, quite simply, would not emerge. In the analysis proposed here, and regardless of whether or not *v* is, indeed, the relevant functional structure for the licensing of an external argument, nominalization crucially occurs above the event complex, which is always a verbalizer, and is possible because it gives rise to a verbal event complex embedded within a nominal structure. Thus there is little reason to assume that in principle external arguments are not possible within *AS*-nominals, contra Marantz (1997) and Alexiadou (1999).

Empirically, much of the support for the absence of external arguments within *AS*-nominals comes from Chomsky's (1970) account for the well-

---

through the structure, thereby requiring a special mechanism to allow its omission in *R*-nominals, involving, specifically, the presence vs. absence of structural case.

known ungrammaticality of (58a) with a transitive interpretation, as well as the ungrammaticality of (58b-c):

(57) a. The farmer grew the tomatoes.
b. The tomatoes grew.
(58) a. The growth of tomatoes (intransitive reading only)
b. *The farmer's growth of tomatoes
c. *The growth of tomatoes by the farmer

Chomsky (1970), and following him, Marantz (1997), suggest that the ungrammaticality of (58a) with a transitive reading as well as the ungrammaticality of (58b-c) derive from the fact that transitive *grow* is, in actuality, a complex form consisting of CAUSE+*grow*. If one assumes that CAUSE is an abstract entry which assigns an external *causer* role, say ***v***, and that ***v*** is a verbalizer, it follows, for Marantz (1997), that ***v*** cannot occur within *AS*-nominals, as its projection would lead immediately to the verbalization of the root embedded underneath it, blocking a nominal. Hence, the only possible derivation for *grow* would be one which does not involve ***v***, i.e., an intransitive derivation.

Marantz notes, nevertheless, that (59b) is grammatical, as is (59a) with a transitive derivation:

(59) a. The destruction of the city
b. The enemy's destruction of the city

To accommodate this, he assumes, along lines assumed by Grimshaw (1990) for similar structures, that *the enemy's* in (59b) is a possessor, and that the possessor may have a free interpretation in cases such as (59), including an interpretation that happens to coincide with that of AGENT. That such an interpretation is barred for (58) follows, in turn, from the lexical semantics of the root *grow* which requires an EXTERNAL CAUSER, not a possible interpretation for the possessor.[18]

There are a number of problems with the analysis, however, not the least of which being the grammaticality of (60) (and see also (61) as well)

---

[18] We note that by appealing to the lexical semantics of *grow* to exclude (58) Marantz effectively resurrects a lexical semantics for roots which determines not only the internal argument of an emerging form, but also its external argument, if only by means of excluding some roots, and thus effectively some syntactic structures, in the context of some types of external arguments.

already noted by Chomsky (1970) as problematic for the CAUSE analysis which he himself proposes:

(60) a. Mary's growing of the tomatoes
b. The growing of the tomatoes (ambiguous)

(61) a. The navy's sinking of the ship
b. Bill's melting of the wax
c. Kim's breaking of the vase

Nor is the grammaticality of (60)-(61) an artifact of some putative difference between *–ing* nominals and others (see Marantz, 1999). Harely and Noyer (1998a), investigating precisely this issue, cite the following examples in which an external argument interpreted as an EXTERNAL CAUSER does appear licensed within *AS*-nominals with *–ation* nominalizers, in contrast with (58):

(62) a. Kim's accumulation of dust
b. The accumulation of dust (ambiguous)
c. Robin's separation of Kim and Pat
d. The separation of Kim and Pat (ambiguous)
e. The government's unification of the city
f. The unification of the city (ambiguous)

And finally, a restriction against an external argument within *AS*-nominals as deriving from the impossibility of the projection of *v* has the hallmark of a linguistic universal. However in Hebrew where the forms for transitive *grow* and intransitive *grow* are morpho-phonologically related, but distinct, and each has a separate derived nominal, both are attested without any resulting ungrammaticality:

(63) a. Gidul ha-'agvaniyot ('al yedey ha-'ikarim)
growth.TRANS the-tomatoes (by hands the-farmers)
'The growing (trans) of tomatoes (by the farmers)'
b. Gdilat ha-'agvaniyot
growth.INTRANS the-tomatoes
'The growing (intrans) of tomatoes'

We therefore conclude that *growth* is rather isolated in exhibiting the behavior in (58), and that what is called for is an explanation for the exceptionality of *growth,* rather than an account which generalizes from its properties, thereby making wrong predictions for a broad range of derived nominals. What, then, could possibly be the reason for the ungrammaticality of (58)?

Following the lead of Pesetsky (1995), but with a very distinct execution, we would like to propose that the ungrammaticality of (58) has a morpho-phonological, language specific source, and not a syntactic one. We note that Pesetsky's claim, whereby *growth* is ungrammatical because it involves a Ø-affix attached to *grow.INTRANS* together with the assumption that Ø-affixation blocks all further affixation, could not possibly be adopted, or it would rule out, incorrectly, the transitive *AS*-nominals associated with *accumulation, separation* and *unification,* in a parallel fashion (Pesetsky does assume that *–ing* is special).[19]

Rather, I would like to propose that *grow* and *growth* do not represent a derivational relationship, but rather, they are stem allomorphs, much like what we find in *destroy/destruct(ion), prógress/progréss, louse/lice, break/broke* etc. We do not have here an actual derivational process, but rather, the selection of a particular allomorph from a paradigmatic set in particular morpho-phonological or morpho-syntactic environments. Thus *destruct* is a verb allomorph which is inserted in bound contexts, just like *broke* is the stem allomorph that is inserted both in past tense contexts and in bound contexts to give rise to *broken.* On the other hand *eat* is the stem allomorph that is inserted in present tense contexts and in bound contexts, to give rise to *eaten.* In neither case is the form *eat* present or *broke* past, or we would have to claim that *–en* is sometimes attached to past tense forms, and sometimes to present tense forms.

In turn, if *growth* is a stem allomorph inserted in nominal contexts, rather than an actually derived form, then whatever rationale applies to other category-neutral forms must apply to it – it may not be embedded within *AS*-nominals, quite simply because in order for an event complex, an inherent verbalizer, to become nominal, an overt nominalizer is required, but *–th* by definition is not such a nominalizer. Thus *growth,* in actuality, is an *R*-nominal, and *the growth of the tomatoes* has the same properties and the same structure as *yesterday's/the return of the Jedi (*in a day)* or *the design of the furniture.*

To support this claim, consider the distribution of nominals with *-th* in English which actually have a corresponding noun or adjective:

---

[19] The second half of Pesetsky's claim, according to which *annoyance* and similar nominals derived from psyche-predicates cannot be transitive, due to the presence of a Ø-causative affix which blocks *-ance* affixation, could not be adopted because unlike the behavior of *growth,* which is clearly language specific and morpho-phonologically conditioned, the behavior of *annoyance* is not language specific, and is not conditioned by the morpho-phonology. Thus in Hebrew, transitive nominalizations equivalent to *annoyance* are ungrammatical as well, although as in the case of *growth,* no Ø-affix could be assumed, and the transitive form and the intransitive forms are morpho-phonologically distinct.

(64) a. (*birth*), *breath*, *death*, *growth*, *stealth*, *health* (appears to be an exhaustive list)
b. *width*, *length*, *strength*, *warmth*, *truth*, *breadth*, *dearth* (appears to be an exhaustive list)

The list here is very limited indeed, nor is *–th* in any sense productive in the language. Consider, more strikingly, however, the following forms (with thanks to S. Anderson, p.c.):

(65) ***lengthen***, ***strengthen*** (and note also ***height***, ***heighten***, R. Kayne, p.c.)

As is well known, *-en* attaches to adjectives to give rise to verbs:

(66) *redden*, *blacken*, *thicken*, *fatten*, *shorten*, etc.

As is further well known, *-en* is morpho-phonologically constrained, and may not attach to adjectives which have a final sonorant, and hence (67):

(67) a. *-en* attaches to adjectives (*[+sonorant]#en)
b. **greenen*, **thinen*, **bluen*, **yellowen*, **brownen*, etc.

Consider, in view of this, (65). Both *long* and *strong* could not be affixed with *–en*, as both end in a sonorant, and such an affixation would give rise to **longen* or **strongen*. Instead, we find *lengthen* and *strengthen*, and also *heighten*, because the adjective *high* is similarly constrained, and here, too, *height* is a stem allomorph. If, now, we assume that *-th* forms are stem allomorphs, inserted, in the case of *lengthen* and *strengthen* in a morpho-phonologically conditioned environment, rather than derived forms, not only do we account for (65), but we also resolve the mystery surrounding the impossibility of (58), without needing to assume that the event complex within *AS*-nominals is different in crucial ways from that attested in propositions.[20]

---

[20] Marantz (1997) cites one more case which appears to pattern with *grow*, i.e., that of *rise/raise*, pointing, specifically, to the ungrammaticality of cases such as those in (ia), when contrasted with the grammaticality of (ibid.):

i. a.*Jane's raise of the crane
b. The rise of the sun

Note, however, that (ii) is morphologically well-formed, although it is both morphologically and semantically related to the transitive *raise*, and not to the intransitive *rise*:

8 By Way of Summary

By way of summarizing this paper, we consider briefly a number of interesting questions which arise here, in principle, and which are clearly worth pursuing. Note, first, that categories such as V, N, as associated with terminals, may emerge from this picture as not being universal, in the sense that there may be languages which do not distinguish between nouns and verbs on the TERMINAL level (i.e., any lexical item may be either a noun or a verb). On the other hand, the distinction between NP and VP is a universal one, and follows from the assumption that the inventory of functional structures is both limited and universal, giving rise to tense, argument structure, DP structure, etc. A stem which is neither a verb nor a noun may exist, but in the context of a VP (so verbalized by functional structure, e.g. TenseP) or in the context of an NP (so nominalized by functional structure, e.g. DetP), they will be formally equivalent to either N or V, by virtue of heading a categorically coherent constituent.

We further note that if the system outlined here concerning the licensing of the past and the future values in English is correct, and if, indeed, we are correct in assuming that functional structure is largely licensed through either the insertion of independent functional morphemes, or through head movement, then these are not inter-grammatical variations, but rather, intra-grammatical variations. This, in turn, raises the distinct possibility that there are no grammar-specific parametric settings, and instead, language variation represents a mix and match of universally available strategies, not always consistently used in any given language, but determined by the arbitrary phonological properties of the inventory of grammatical formatives.

Recalling now our discussion of the *feed/eat* problem we note that the encyclopedia obviously is not a pure conceptual component but an interface level. At the very least, it has phonological representations which may tease apart some related concepts and list them separately, as arbitrarily determined by a specific language's vocabulary. This, in turn, gives rise to typical interface questions. How does the encyclopedia relate to the conceptual system proper, and how many more language specific properties, in addition to phonological index, could it support? At least in the case of idioms, it

---

ii. I was given a raise this month.

The problem here, then, is that the *raise* does not appear to have an *AS*-nominal derivation, rather on a par, it would appear, with ∅-derived nominals in general, of which *raise* is certainly one. As such, it patterns exactly with our claim about the nature of *growth*, likewise, we suggested a ∅-derived nominal, subject to an allomorphy rule.

might appear that some syntactic information might be in order, resulting precisely in the rigidity typically associated with idioms.

And finally, we note, contra many current accounts, that morpho-phonological representation cannot be divorced from the grammar. Any attempt to disenfranchise it, so to speak, is empirically and explanatorily costly, precisely to those very computational systems which its elimination is an attempt to simplify.

References

Alexiadou, A. 1999. *On the Syntax of Nominalization and Possession: Remarks on Patterns of Ergativity.* Habilitation, University of Potsdam.

Anderson, S. 1992. *Amorphous Morphology.* Cambridge, UK: Cambridge University Press.

Baker, M. 1985, 1988. *Incorporation.* Chicago: University of Chicago Press.

Borer, H. 1991/1993. Derived Nominals. Unpublished manuscript, University of Massachusetts, Amherst.

Borer, H., 1994. The Projection of Arguments. *University of Massachusetts Occasional Papers in Linguistics* 17, eds. E. Benedicto and J. Runner. University of Massachusetts, Amherst.

Borer, H. 1998. Passive without θ-Grid. *Morphological and Its Relations to Phonology and Syntax*, eds. S. Lapointe, D. Brentari, and P. Farrell. CSLI, Stanford University.

Borer, H. 2001. The Exo-Skeletal Trilogy, Books I, II. Unpublished manuscript, University of Southern California.

Borer, H. forthcoming. The Exo-Skeletal Trilogy, Book III. Unpublished manuscript, University of Southern California.

Carrier, J. and J. Randall, 1992. The Argument Structure and Syntactic Structure of Resultatives. *Linguistic Inquiry* 23: 173-234.

Chomsky, N. 1965. *Aspects of the Theory of Syntax.* Cambridge, MA: MIT Press.

Chomsky, N. 1970. Remarks on Nominalization. *Readings in English Transformational Grammar,* eds. R. Jacobs and P. Rosenbaum, 184-221. Waltham, MA: Blaisdell.

Clark, E. and H. Clark. 1979. When Nouns Surface as Verbs. *Language* 55: 767-811.

di Sciullo, A.-M. and E. Williams. 1987. *On the Definition of Word.* Cambridge, Mass: MIT Press.

Dowty, D. R. 1991. Thematic Proto-Roles and Argument Selection. *Language* 67: 547-619.

Fillmore, C. and P. Kay. 1997. The Formal Architecture of Construction Grammar. Unpublished manuscript, University of California, Berkeley.

Fu, J.-Q. 1994. On Deriving Chinese Derived Nominals. Doctoral dissertation, University of Massachusetts, Amherst.

Fu, J., T. Roeper and H. Borer. 2001. The VP within Process Nominals. *Natural Language and Linguistic Theory* 19: 549-582.

Goldberg, A. 1995. *Constructions: A Construction Grammar Approach to Argument Structure*. Chicago: University of Chicago Press.

Grimshaw, J. 1990. *Argument Structure*. Cambridge, MA: MIT Press.

Harley, H., 1995. Subject, Events and Licensing. Doctoral dissertation, MIT.

Harley, H. and R. Noyer. 1998a. Formal vs. Encyclopedic Properties of Vocabulary: Evidence from Nominalizations. Unpublished manuscript, University of Pennsylvania.

Harley, H. and R. Noyer. 1998b. Mixed Nominalizations, Object Shift and Short Verb Movement in English. *Proceedings of North East Linguistic Society* 28, GLSA, University of Massachusetts, Amherst.

Hazout, I. 1991. Verbal Nouns: Theta Theoretic Studies in Hebrew and Arabic. Doctoral dissertation, University of Massachusetts, Amherst.

Hazout, I. 1995. Action Nominalization and the Lexicalist Hypothesis. *Natural Language and Linguistic Theory* 13: 355-404.

Jackendoff, R. 1990. *Semantic Structure.*, Cambridge, MA: MIT Press.

Johnson, K. 1991. Object Positions. *Natural Language and Linguistic Theory* 9: 577-636.

Kiparsky, P. 1982. Lexical Phonology and Morphology. Unpublished manuscript, MIT.

Kratzer, A. 1994. *The Event Argument.* Unpublished manuscript, University of Massachusetts, Amherst.

Kratzer, A. 1996. Severing the External Argument from the Verb. *Phrase Structure and the Lexicon*, eds. J. Orrick and L. Zaring. Dordrecht: Kluwer.

Krifka, M. 1992. Thematic Relations as Links between Nominal Reference and Temporal Constitution. *Lexical Matters*, eds. I. A. Sag and A. Szablocsi, 29-53. Stanford: CSLI Publications.

Levin, B. and M. Rappaport-Hovav, 1995. *Unaccusativity*. Cambridge, MA: MIT Press.

Marantz, A. 1996. Cat as a Phrasal Category. Unpublished manuscript, MIT.

Marantz, A. 1997. No Escape from Syntax. *University of Pennsylvania Working Papers in Linguistics* 4.2., eds. A. Dimitriadis et. al., 201-225.

Marantz, A. 1999. *Lecture Notes*. MIT, Cambridge.

Ouhalla, J. 1991. *Functional Categories and Parametric Variations*. London: Routledge.

Pesetsky, D. 1995. *Zero Syntax*. Cambridge, MA: MIT Press.

Picallo, C. 1991. Nominals and Nominalization in Catalan. *Probus* 3: 279-316.

Reichenbach, H. 1947. *Elements of Symbolic Logic*. New York: McMillan.

Reinhart, T. 1996. *Syntactic Effects on Lexical Operations: Reflexives and Unaccusatives.* UiL OTS Working Papers. Utrecht University, Utrecht.

Reinhart, T. 2000. *The Theta System: Syntactic Realization of Verbal Concepts.* UiL OTS Working Papers. Utrecht University, Utrecht.

Runner, J. 1995. Noun Phrase Licensing and Interpretation. Doctoral dissertation, University of Massachusetts, Amherst.

Schoorlemmer, M. 1995. Participial Passive and Aspect in Russian. Doctoral dissertation, Utrecht University.

Valois, D. 1991. The Internal Structure of DP. Doctoral dissertation, University of California, Los Angeles.

van Hout, A. 1992. Linking and Projection Based on Event Structure. Unpublished manuscript, Tilburg: Tilburg University.

van Hout, A. 1996. *Event Semantics of Verb Frame Alternations*, TILDIL Dissertation Series, 1996-1.

Williams, E. 1981. Argument Structure and morphology. *The Linguistic Review* 1, 81-114.

Zucchi, A. 1989. *The Language of Propositions and Events: Issues in the Syntax and Semantics of Nominalization.* Doctoral dissertation, University of Massachusetts, Amherst.

3

On the Notion 'Showing Something'[1]

GREG CARLSON

'show \'sho\ *vb* ... 1: to cause or permit to be seen'
--Webster's Seventh New Collegiate Dictionary

1 An Informal Introduction

In the final month of the last year of the last century (and the last millennium), certain predictable tasks came up, such as constructing 'greatest X of the century' lists. For example, the March 29th issue of *Time* magazine listed 'the century's greatest minds' ('scientists and thinkers' it said), and I noted that no linguists appeared on their list for their accomplishments. It's not that the area of language itself was neglected. Wittgenstein and Piaget appeared, but names like Sapir, Bloomfield, de Saussure, to name just a few, were absent (though Chomsky rated a small blurb and dated picture embedded within the Piaget article). And, it certainly had been an exciting century for linguistics. So, whatever it is we had done has, apparently, not sprung as brightly on the popular imagination as the work of Freud, Einstein, Fermi, Keynes, and the others.

It is clear that linguists work on something that matters to *Time*'s general readership. Granted, it takes the form of 'Increase your vocabulary', 'Learn Spanish in 30 days', worrying about Jimmie's stuttering, a fascination with dialect differences, fervent feelings about the English Only issue, and so forth. To suggest that the subject matter of linguistics is something that is

[1] I wish to thank Mike Tanenhaus, Steven Lapointe, David Perlmutter, Yuki Kuroda, and Jeff Pelletier for scattered and various conversations which influenced this paper. Comments from a variety of people, especially Ivan Sag, Ellen Prince, George Lakoff, and Robert Kluender, at the Explanation Conference itself helped sharpen and further my thinking. Finally, I wish to thank Tom Wasow for his helpful and insightful comments. None are to be held responsible for any of this.

The Nature of Explanation in Linguistic Theory.
John Moore and Maria Polinsky (eds.).

not important to people in general, and that's the source of the omission, is simply incorrect.

But perhaps instead we should ask ourselves what linguists have accomplished this past century that would merit the attention of *Time* magazine. Suppose, I'm sure contrafactually, that you were asked to edit a special issue of this magazine entitled 'Linguists of the 20th Century: Scientists and Thinkers'? Who would you put into this special issue? Who would be on the cover? And why? The point of this exercise is not to engage in some personality parade; it is instead to reflect on what we, as individuals, regard as the best of accomplishments that has gone under the rubric of LINGUISTICS, and what factors we employ to assess them.

Two criteria come most prominently to my mind: durability and impact. To illustrate what is intended by 'durability', consider what you would propose as the top ten accomplishments of linguistics of the nineteenth century? So, for instance, once the Egyptian hieroglyphs were deciphered, they stayed deciphered; or once Indo-European was 'discovered', it has likewise remained that way. What in the 20th century has this character?

As for impact, we might first think of influence within the field, that is, who has significantly shaped the way we think about our work the most? So, for instance, Leonard Bloomfield might be regarded by many as more influential than many of his contemporaries and, of course, Chomsky's dominant influence in the field in the latter decades should be obvious to all. In a somewhat different category, we might consider the standardization of a set of phonetic symbols--the IPA--this century as an accomplishment of this sort. Here's one thing we all use. But, perhaps even more important, is impact beyond linguistics, how an accomplishment or an idea has influenced other academic areas, and/or our society as a whole. How has it permitted us to do things we couldn't do before, or conceive of things in a way previously not possible? So, the influence of Structuralism in the earlier part of this century on sociology and cultural anthropology would be a possible example of this. Others might be the completion of the OED or the demonstration that signed communication systems used by people who are deaf or hard of hearing have the earmarks of normal human languages (and are thus not simply elaborated gestural systems). These have made a very real difference to many people. I'll just leave it to you to assess whether linguists have any noteworthy 20th century accomplishments.

The perspective I'm trying to take here is what we look like from the outside, and what it can tell us about who or what we are, on the inside. Here, I must gauge our broader image from piecemeal evidence. In any event, I am going to take it that our broader image—among other academics as well as with the general public—is largely produced by the most visible and articulate proponents of linguistic theorizing, which in the past decades has clearly been Chomsky and those who approach the puzzle of language in likeminded ways. Many linguists do not like this state of affairs, which is fair enough, and many more have misgivings about some of the particulars of prevailing rhetoric, myself included. But to give some circumference to this characterization of 'like-mindedness', I would count myself among this group, showing it to be a rather loose characterization I intend.

In conversation with someone outside (or even inside) academics, I and others often have had a hard time explaining what we do for a living. This is not experienced by all linguists, but I take it (though you well may not) as characterizing something central about the field in terms of our external presentation. As evidence, witness all the web pages of linguistics departments and note how many have 'What is linguistics?' as one of the topics addressed. Now go compare those to the home pages of history or physics departments. There is something going on here. The question I wish to pose is why this might be so. The less immediate question I wish to pose is, if linguists were good at explaining themselves to outsiders, might one or two have shown up in *Time* magazine's listings?

2 Some Quick Issues

2.1 Is Linguistics an Intellectually Incoherent Field?

No. The foundations of an intellectually coherent field are decently enough in place, despite the variety one finds. Linguistics has its own specific domain of data which is unshared by other enterprises: namely, human language and languages. There are distinguishing constructs and theoretical/descriptive vocabulary: notions like SUBJECT, CASE-MARKING, WORD, PREPOSITION, OBSTRUENT and so forth are, collectively, unshared by other enterprises either as a basic element of theoretical vocabulary, or as a phenomenon to be accounted for in other terms. Finally, the subject of this conference, linguists working on linguistic theory have their own methodologies and values, rightly or wrongly, for what constitutes a decent account of phenomena. Thus, it's not that the field itself is particularly less coherent than others. So what is it?

2.2 A Terminological Issue?

To many people, the term 'linguist' is synonymous with 'polyglot', as examination of popular literature will easily show. Using the term 'linguist(ics)' in general public forums, or even in the presence of other academics, does not call forth a rich set of concepts and associations from which people divine that they have a grasp of what this means. It seems more confusing than illuminating. To think a name change would solve any problems, though, is putting the cart before the horse.

2.3 Neglected Public Relations?

The field has (and always has had) relatively few practitioners, so there is in comparison to other fields a dearth of populizers, effective textbooks, or a critical mass of people with enough charm and charisma to grab the attention of the press. It might also be that linguists lack a popular iconographic image to project, no Margaret Mead sitting in a Samoan hut, Einstein writing abstruse but powerful formulas on a blackboard, or Freud and his cigar psychoanalyzing someone lying on a couch.[2] Is the difficulty one of not having a good PR firm? If so, it is hardly a current problem. If one lists some classically famous linguists and does a public survey on name recognition, the conclusion would be that linguistics lacks 'stars'. When the philosophers claim Socrates and Kant, linguists get to claim Dionysius Thrax and Bopp in return; when the physicists get Newton, Kepler, and Einstein, linguistics gets Panini, Priscian and, you know, what's-his-name, the guy that wrote the Port-Royale Grammar.

2.4 The Specter of Prescriptivism

The earliest experience with linguistics for most people is in the form of a prescriptive (and, proscriptive) approach to language. Even people who have since become linguists found this boring, simply another seemingly pointless set of classroom rules to be followed. Linguists thus become the Emily Posts of language, set your silverware this way, put your napkin here, do not split infinitives. It hardly seems to have anything to do with daily life. It also aligns linguists with an authoritarian view of the world, a view one would be very, very hard-pressed to achieve were one to examine actual working linguists.

2.5 Do People Really Want Their Languages Analyzed?

Unlike having dreams, desires, wishes and fears, the moment a person begins to speak, their thoughts and feelings are made public. Analysis brings a feeling of self-consciousness to this speaking process (particularly if one uses 'bad grammar' or speaks a socially identifiable dialect). This doesn't seem to bother working linguists very much, and if it did they wouldn't be linguists. But a good analogy that linguists might be able to connect better to is the study of gesture. If one has had the experience of the significance

---

[2] The closest I have been able to come as an iconographic image for linguists is the top-hatted Henry Higgins in 'My Fair Lady' (a character, I'm told, modeled after Henry Sweet).

of one's gesture being pointed out publicly, often a discomfort arises which others easily feel about language.

3 Some Longer Issues

3.1 Abstractness

Many linguists do not have such difficulties in communicating what they do. If one studies second language acquisition, for instance, as a specialty within the field, the responses to 'What do you do?' are fairly accessible and understandable. Something like 'I try to understand the way people learn a new language, so that we can teach them more effectively' leaves few questions in anyone's mind. Or, if one focuses on sentence processing by employing experimental methodologies, or computational routines for text retrieval, or constructing dictionaries and any manner of things, people readily have as good an understanding of what one does for a living as they do of any physicist or anthropologist. The same goes for language specialists--people who identify themselves as an expert in Greek, Southeast Asian languages, or Tibetan, have an entirely understandable if slightly arcane place in people's minds. The details and issues may be lost on all but the specialists, but a fundamental understanding of what the enterprise is *about* will not be. There is some phenomenon, out there, in time and space, that is the object of our knowledge, whether it is the process of learning a second language, a series of Runic inscriptions, producing and understanding utterances, or engineering a machine to understand what you're asking about over the telephone.

However, use the bare term 'linguist' or 'linguistics' without such further elucidation, and most understanding vaporizes. The reason why these terms seem so obscure to most people is the result of incomplete communication, I believe, not simply that obscure terms are being tossed around. What, after all, is the phenomenon in time and space that is the object of study?

The obvious answer would seem to be 'language'. But this is found unsatisfactory on at least two counts. Consider, for instance, what comedian Jerry Seinfeld means when he says, in an interview, that his (former) television show *Seinfeld* was 'about language'. Those who have watched the show would realize that he means USAGE, the various things people can do (in this case, socially) with language. Linguistics textbooks present a different view, that 'language' is not usage, but something else.[3]

---

[3] Just one example is Radford (1997: 2-3). The distinction, in this instance, is put in terms of competence and performance.

Linguistic work employing the methodologies distinctive of the field does not attempt to account for many aspects of linguistic behavior, such as average length of sentences in Faulkner or in Elvis Presley songs, or why the word 'party' might be used on some days more than others. Theorizing about language focuses on universals (in the philosophical sense of the term), and not particulars. Traditional notions like WORD, AFFIX, MEANING, and so forth, are abstracted from many particular token utterances, signs, or inscriptions, which are the particulars. Saying something so mundane as, 'In French, *chien* means 'dog'', or 'Old English had case-marking on nouns,' makes no reference to particular utterances in time and space. This focus on universals about language--what are traditionally called grammars--dissociates the contents of linguistic theorizing from the world of phenomena, and makes linguistics look a bit more like mathematics or philosophy than cognitive science. But linguistics is clearly an empirical area: unlike mathematics, proofs are not available to show most points; and unlike philosophy, there is a delimited domain of empirical data that primarily defines the area. As David Perlmutter and S.-Y. Kuroda have pointed out independently, the data of linguistic theorizing is (abstract) grammars, and its point is to theorize about how grammars could, and could not, be constructed. But (abstract) grammars are not phenomena in time and space to be understood, like historical events or observed planetary motion.

The other problem with concreteness is that one cannot just study 'language', as language appears in the world only in the form of particular languages, and it is almost universally assumed outside linguistics these do not have much in common. So 'language' remains this vague heterogeneous concept to most individuals. But many linguists consider it misleading to claim they work *on* particular languages (even if they work *with* them), as many see their work as aimed at trying to uncover and understand the basic design of language simpliciter. However, this can leave linguists, rhetorically, with little to say. Consider by way of analogy your reaction to the following:

You: What department are you in?
X: Biology
You: Oh, what do you study?
X: The principles of life.
You: Oh, how interesting. Now, what do you *really* study?
X: How life works.
You: (change of topic)

The focus on universals and 'language', rather than particulars and particular languages, can put linguists, on a public view, in the same position as the following professor:[4]

> 'I once heard of a course in esthetics given at a large Middle Western university in which an entire semester was devoted to Art and Beauty and the principles underlying them, and during which the professor, even when asked by students, persistently declined to name specific paintings, symphonies, sculptures, or objects of beauty to which his principles might apply. "We are interested," he would say, "in principles, not in particulars."'

No linguist I know of even remotely teaches or works this way, in practice. All work on some aspect of empirical data--some actual language or languages or language behavior. But something akin to this is a public impression which, if the universals are focused on a little too keenly, is all too easy to communicate.[5]

3.2 An Issue within Academics

One major development in the past twenty years or so is the slow departure of linguistics from cognitive science--or rather vice versa.[6] One thing that is clear is that this widening gulf is due in some significant measure to the increasing discrepancy between the types of explanations linguists routinely offer, vs. the types of explanations offered by colleagues in the other cognitive sciences.[7] From the standpoint of many psychologists and computer scientists, at least, it appears that most linguists have stuck to modes of explanation that may once have been acceptable in these adjacent fields, but are no longer. Such constructs as RULES, LOGIC, GRAMMATICALITY, and many others that many linguists make use of, have come under attack and have been increasingly discarded in other areas.[8] Linguists appear, in the eyes of some others, to be what's left on the beach after the tide went out, being unable to swim fast enough, and it is not always clear to others why linguists have not 'kept up'.

---

[4] Related in Hayakawa (1978: 164-165).

[5] Cf the discussion of linguistics by Dresher (1995: 9).

[6] See Ray Jackendoff (1988) for a discussion which, even more than a dozen years later, this article echoes.

[7] Discussions of this can be found in Miller (1990: 317-322) and in Osherson and Wasow (1976).

[8] See, for just one example, Seidenberg and McDonald (1999).

This view finds much favor among some of the closest colleagues, including a growing number within linguistics proper. The grounding assumption appears to be that linguistics is (in fact) a part of cognitive science, and if we take that seriously then it follows that we need to be serious about squaring the way linguists produce knowledge with the way knowledge is produced in other areas of cognitive science.[9] But more often, the critique becomes one of pure theory. The criticism is, to put it simply, that linguists' distinctive methodologies and modes of explanation stop short, somehow. That's the view, and it's not confined to the late 1990s or critiques from cognitive science. Here's what it looked like to one professor offering advice to a student about how to get through the language history examinations, some fifty years ago:[10]

> 'When you hit a word in a text you cannot identify, simply correlate it with some modern word it sounds like and then invent a bridge between them. Most of the examiners will be suspicious, but may consider, so imprecise is linguistic science, your little word history an interesting possibility.'

Or, consider a commonly-encountered type of example from your Linguistics 101 class, where students have been asked to give a morphological analysis of, say, the word *ridiculous*. While the *-ous* part is pretty cut and dried, what about the *ridicul-* part? And, if it's decomposable, is it *-ic -ul*, or *i-cul*, or what? Does appeal to Latin settle the issue? Is the existence of the word *risible* or *deride* a relevancy? Wherein lies the fact of the matter? And if there is no fact of the matter, what are linguists up to?

This criticism has enough content to sting some, despite the demonstrated productivity of applying linguistic methodologies in finding out new facts about language and languages. The issue is *not* whether linguistics has produced a significant bank of knowledge about language during, say, this century (just compare what is known now to what was known a hundred years ago!); rather, the issue seems to be whether the facts are as characterized by some form of current linguistic theory. It is a fact (to my knowledge discovered in the latter half of this century), for instance, that many languages have an unaccusative/unergative distinction in the domain of intransitive verbs. But is it a 'fact' that unaccusative subjects, in contrast to uner-

---

[9] Even simple quantification of judgment data would be a step in this direction. See, for instance, McCawley (1997).

[10] From Delbanco (1999).

gative subjects, are derived by movement from an underlying object position?

It is certainly an interesting and productive idea—but a fact? No. And, what's more, it is not clear what type of evidence would elevate this particular theoretical construct to fact-hood. Someone might become convinced enough to regard this idea of movement as something one is (intellectually) committed to and to incorporate it as a central and unshakable assumption of one's own work, and many have. But this is very different from someone *showing* that there is, in fact, movement.[11]

From the standpoint of linguists who work on such things, the issue turns on whether there is significant and systematic *insight* into a language or languages that is to be gained. But the amount of insight to be gained simply cannot be judged if one lacks requisite knowledge of how the theory works as a whole, what the existing alternatives are (and how they seem to miss the point), and some prior knowledge of significant patterns of data. Even among people with this kind of background, of course, not everyone ends up in agreement. While empirical coverage is expected, it is actually not, in practice, fully expected, for lingering counterexamples are almost always tolerated. This whole process can be mystifying to colleagues in the other cognitive sciences, who are used to the touchstone of increased empirical coverage as largely determining the success and value of a particular approach or analysis.[12]

3.3 The Descriptive Base

What is to be considered 'data' is itself not a theory-free concept, of course. Data need to be delimited, organized and interpreted in a satisfactory and largely agreed-upon way before anyone can proceed with anything empirical, in any domain. In Chomskyan linguistics, the competence/performance distinction is (partly) a rule-of-thumb proposal for delimiting what counts as data, as is a notion of GRAMMATICALITY. Both may be subject to question, but such notions as PAST TENSE, MASS TERM, WORD, PRONOUN, CLAUSE, AFFIX, etc., while not entirely theory-free, form a broad and shared basis for

---

[11] By 'movement' I intend any technical means of implementing this metaphor, such as copy-and-delete, 2 to 1 advancement, etc. I do not mean that one must literally detect spatial movement, though of course if this could be done somehow it would count.

[12] In lectures Chomsky has made the point that insight, and not prediction, is the key in linguistics (or any science). The following analogy is used: one can predict the next day's weather in Boston to a fair degree by reading the weather report of the current day in the Cleveland newspapers. Or, one can generate models of atmospheric dynamics. Even if the former turned out to be a better method of prediction, it still clearly lacks the ingredient of insight the alternative, even if less effective predictively, can offer.

common discourse about language structure.[13] Let us call this the 'descriptive base'. The descriptive base, like theoretical constructs, is open to question and revision; it can and does change, though more slowly. But it is not arbitrarily chosen. It reflects an interpretation of the data which is sufficiently justified by common standards to warrant presumption; it is a way of organizing data into reasonably justifiable classes of phenomena; it is that level which can be successfully shown to be so if pressed.

Hopefully, all linguists can show that there are words, or mass terms, or affixes, or vowels, to a level that would be acceptable to anyone respecting normal standards of evidence. This does not prevent people, of course, from turning right around and noting that the notion WORD (for instance) has problematic aspects to it, even to the point where, when you get right down to it, maybe there aren't WORDS after all. But this is theory-talk, not talk of phenomena. In claiming there are no WORDS one would not be claiming that such things as one utters or finds in the dictionary are a delusion; they remain. Try telling a roommate that *cat* isn't *really* a word and they'll be completely lost. In one sense there are, in fact, words. In another sense, there might not *really* be WORDS after all. This is the difference between a descriptive base and the theory.

This is a distinction which linguists may not always keep in mind. Why it hasn't been *shown* that there are movement transformations is, quite simply, this: an insufficient preponderance of linguists subscribe to this idea because evidence has not been produced up to the levels of normal standards of evidence (this is not to say other reasons don't come into play as well). Not everyone's convinced.

There is a somewhat artificial alternative to avoid the skeptics. To be much more persuasive, what one can do is to narrow the group addressed so that it has the effect of elevating a given theoretical construct to the level of fact-hood, by addressing only those who are 'on board'. The flip side of this coin is to simply ignore the work of those who are not in agreement. This limitation of the audience raises the richness of the descriptive base for that group (as everyone addressed basically agrees) and allows for increasingly abstract and deeper discussion and, presumably, for greater progress to be made.

Let's not argue the question of increased progress one way or another; let's instead consider the cost of this strategy. While one can, to a large extent, limit one's audience or who one listens to, what are considered 'normal standards of evidence' remains almost exactly the same no matter what one does. And as one's descriptive base becomes increasingly de-

---

[13] This constitutes what R.M.W. Dixon calls 'basic linguistic theory'.

pendent upon theoretical argument and conclusion, the implicit claim that this base encodes what can be satisfactorily shown--that is, what everyone pretty much agrees on-- becomes correspondingly less and less connected to the grounding of common standards of evidence in society at large, and also less and less connected to the standards of evidence invoked across academics in general. Note that this issue does not have to do with simple specialization per se; rather, it has to do with communicating to others what the results of all this work shows. If such statements as, 'Transderivational constraints exist' or 'Binding is expressible as three conditions', or 'The sound structure of language is a series of ranked universal constraints', are regarded as what has been shown, we're going to get the hearing we deserve. What, in terms of common experience, do such statements (whether correct or not) have to do with? Losing sight of this question results in others not being able to catch sight of what linguists, as a community, regard as answers, as what is known about language.

At the same time, there is no doubt as to both the necessity and worth of developing advanced, and highly abstract, forms of linguistic theory. This is what propels a huge amount of research that has advanced knowledge of language so much in this past century. It has proven massively productive. To present the theories themselves as what has been shown, however, communicates little to those outside.

3.4 Linguists as Scientists

It is common enough to speak as if linguistics is a science.[14] It is something worthwhile to think about and examine, as it implies a certain rigor that linguists can aspire to. But, as a public presentation, this characterization has its drawbacks. For one, natural science is fundamentally about events and their causes and effects. Despite the commonalities of theory construction and empirical orientation unless someone can articulate what the events are (and some linguists in their work certainly can), and how linguists are trying to understand causal relations, there's an uphill battle. Note, for instance, that a notion of PREDICTION in linguistic theorizing is only about future events in the derivative sense of order of observation, not actual order of occurrence (it's likely that in many papers some PREDICTIONS of an analysis were observed before the analysis itself was arrived at). Science also normally results, at least often enough, in some palpably engineered products that allow us to do things we couldn't do before. The point is not that linguists are unscientific (though my personal opinion is we're far more like

[14] For one recent discussion surrounding this topic, see Lappin, Levine, and Johnson (2000), and the series of Topic-comment responses in *Natural Language and Linguistic Theory* 18: 4.

philosophers than chemists). Rather, in asserting a scientific approach to others there is the risk of confusion because linguists don't wear white lab coats, often don't use expensive equipment and laboratories full of blinking lights and dials, the academic departments don't reside in science schools or divisions, and the scientists themselves don't appear to claim linguists in many important respects.[15] So, this discussion, as one publicly presented, does not immediately meet with very much that is already familiar in the minds of the outside world, including other academics.

3.5 Ontology of the Object of Study

The object of study for all linguists is (some aspect of) language. Most, however, have underlying motivations for studying language that are derived from other or broader intellectual or social concerns. It is important to articulate these concerns; in so doing, however, it is likewise important to distinguish them from what is the object of study. Let's take an obvious example first, and here I am more or less reiterating published comments by Geoff Pullum.[16] From one very common point of view, what linguistics is about is a particular endowment that human beings have by virtue of membership in a particular species, and that endowment is transmitted genetically. Thus, it is tempting to say that linguists are *really* doing genetics. Let us set aside the question of the correctness of this view--it is certainly not implausible. But people do read the job ads, and one thing all have failed to notice is medical schools or genetics departments advertising for linguists. If someone asks a linguist what they do for a living and hear 'genetics' in response, it counts, publicly, as wildly inaccurate.[17]

A slightly less pointed view that many find fascinating is this: that language is a creature of the mind. That is, linguists are *really* doing ('theoretical') psychology (Chomsky 1975:37). Again, this might be exactly right--and it is entirely plausible. But, as noted above, people read the job ads, and how many psychology departments are hiring linguists these days who do not share the experimental methodologies, and consequent modes of explanation, of others in such departments?

The basic claim examined is an ontological claim. That language is psychological (biological, genetic, chemical, on down the reductionist ramp). There exist competing ontological views--language as a social/cultural phe-

---

[15] In some ways they do. Inclusion of linguists in the National Academy of Science, and within the structure of the National Science Foundation are indicators. But linguistics articles, particularly theoretical articles, are absent from those regularly appearing in Science.

[16] For instance, Pullum (1995).

[17] People may not know what linguists do, but, to quote Will Rogers, 'It's not what you know, it's what you know just ain't so.' And people know linguists don't do this.

nomenon is one perfectly respectable alternative, or that language is an abstract mathematically-specifiable system. There is also the (to my mind, strong) possibility that 'language' is of mixed ontology (Pullum and Scholz 1997). Regardless, my own view is that ontological claims are the very, very toughest ones of all to put through, and hardly anyone can do it successfully. Now, one can believe that in fact this or that is what linguists are up to (say, studying the mind), and it may even be true, but when this agenda takes the form of a public representation of the character of an entire field, there's confusion sown, since not all linguists would agree that 'the mind' is what is being studied. It does seem, in contrast, that all would agree linguists study (some aspect of) human language, by studying particular languages and language behaviors, (linguists do not study digestive systems of reptiles, architecture, or comets, for instance), and all would agree (I assume) that it is studied from a variety of perspectives, some complementary, and some genuinely in conflict. There seems little more specific than this one can say that accurately characterizes the field as a whole.

Should linguistics be a branch of psychology, or of mathematics, of anthropology, of sociology, of biology, of philosophy?[18] Perhaps one or more of these answers is correct, perhaps not. More likely there is no 'correct' answer, but rather express judgments about the best ways to study language and languages--What is going to lead to more secure knowledge? What is going to attract more and better-qualified practitioners? What is going to lead to more productive research? These are questions that linguists differ on greatly. It may well, in the future, turn out that the methodologies which have buoyed the development of linguistic theory this century will have proven exhausted, and must be replaced by others. Perhaps some as-yet unenvisioned breakthrough will enable even more rapid development along the same lines, or in very different directions.

At this point, it might be an interesting thought experiment to transport oneself to the language world of December, 1899, and try and envision, given only what was known then, the next hundred years.

References

Chomsky, N. 1975. *Reflections on Language*. New York: Pantheon Books.

Delbanco, A. 1999. The Rise and Fall of Literature. *New York Review of Books* 46: 32-8.

Dresher, E. 1995. On the Tail of the Tiger. *Glot International* 3: 1-9.

[18] It is a fact of course that disciplines going by such names can be fluid, disjoint, with vague or even chaotic boundaries. Presumably, the publicly-presented labels will eventually catch up to these developments.

Hayakawa, S. I. 1978. *Language in Thought and Action.* San Francisco: Harcourt, Brace, Jovanovich, Inc.

Jackendoff, R. 1988. Why Are They Saying these Things about Us? *Natural Language and Linguistic Theory* 6:435-442.

Lappin, S., R. Levine, and D. Johnson. 2000. The Structure of Unscientific Revolutions, *Natural Language and Linguistic Theory* 18: 665-71.

McCawley, J. 1997. Acceptability Judgments in the Teaching and Doing of Syntax. *Chicago Linguistic Society* 32: 119-32.

Miller, G. 1990. Linguists, Psychologists, and the Cognitive Sciences. *Language* 66: 317-22.

Osherson, D. and T. Wasow. 1976. Task-Specificity and Species-Specificity in the Study of Language: A Methodological Note. *Cognition* 4: 203-14.

Pullum, G. 1995. Topic...Comment: No Trips to Stockholm. *Natural Language and Linguistic Theory* 3: 265-70.

Pullum, G. K. and B. C. Scholz. 1997. Theoretical Linguistics and the Ontology of Linguistic Structure. *Suomen kielitieteelisen yhdistyksen vuosikirja*, 25-47. Turku,Finland: Suomen kielitieteelinen yhdistys.

Radford, A. 1997. *Syntactic Theory and the Structure of English.* Cambridge: Cambridge University Press.

Seidenberg, M. and M. McDonald. 1999. A Probabilistic Constraints Approach to Language Acquisition and Processing. *Cognitive Science* 23: 569-88.

4

Linguistic Theory, Explanation and the Dynamics of Language[1]

PETER W. CULICOVER, ANDRZEJ NOWAK, AND WOJCIECH BORKOWSKI

1 Introduction

A central concern of linguistic theory is the nature of linguistic explanation, as exemplified by this conference. The goal is to gain as deep an understanding as possible of why human languages have certain properties and lack others. At the same time, we wish to understand better the limits of linguistic explanation. For example, are all apparent syntactic phenomena explained in terms of properties of the syntactic component of a grammar, or are some explicable in terms of the mappings between syntax and semantics, between syntax and phonology, between syntax and pragmatics, in terms of processing complexity, in more abstract computational terms, or otherwise?[2] It seems to be that in seeking to identify the status of one type of explanation, especially in the case of syntax where many different factors are simultaneously realized in a single string of words and morphemes, it is

[1] For stimulating discussion and helpful comments regarding this work we are indebted to Sarah Thomason, Michael Broe, Brian Joseph, audiences at the University of Illinois, Michigan State University, the University of Rochester, Keio University and the University of Stuttgart, and an anonymous reviewer. Naturally we are responsible for any errors. This work is part of a more extended collaborative project on the dynamics of language between the Center for Cognitive Science at The Ohio State University and the Center for Complex Systems at the University of Warsaw. Some of the material in this paper appears in a more elaborated form in a longer piece (Culicover, Nowak, and Borkowski 1999) and in Culicover and Nowak (2003). We gratefully acknowledge the James F. Mcdonnell Foundation for their support of this research.

[2] For some recent investigations of such questions, see the papers in Culicover and McNally (1998).

The Nature of Explanation in Linguistic Theory.
John Moore and Maria Polinsky (eds.).

essential to keep in mind the possibility that certain phenomena may properly fall under other mechanisms.

As our basic point of departure here, we adopt the sometimes (strangely) controversial proposition that human languages are *learned*, contrasting it with the view that knowledge of language is basically wired into the human mind/brain in some almost completely specified form and is rapidly refined through parameter setting in the course of language acquisition. Moreover, we take seriously the idea that language exists in a social context.

It is often proposed that the properties that languages may or must have are not accidental, but are in effect projections of the Language Faculty. This is certainly true to some extent, but we wish to argue here that there are, in principle, at least, other ways in which languages can get to be the way they are that does not directly reflect the Language Faculty. These other ways have to do with the dynamics of language, in particular language change, language learning, and language processing. We will focus here just on the first, although we believe that a good case can be made for the others as well. Moreover, we will suggest that at least in the case of language change, some explanations may be located entirely outside of the Language Faculty.[3]

2 Gaps

2.1 Gaps and the Language Faculty

The close study of the grammars of natural languages that has been pursued over the past forty-odd years has revealed that many if not most of the logically possible languages do not exist. We call these missing languages gaps. Linguistic theories have sought to account for some of the gaps by appealing to the structure of the Language Faculty. On such an approach, particular logically possible properties and correlations of properties are unattested because they are not allowed by the Language Faculty. They are biologically impossible, and their non-existence is explained in much the same way as are the non-existence of flying pigs or talking dogs. So the precise characteristics of the gaps may reveal something important about the Language Faculty.

This is in fact the standard approach that one takes when asymmetries are observed in some typological database. One of the earliest cases is Bresnan's (1970) account of the fact that if a language has *wh*-movement it

[3] There is a prominent line of research in historical linguistics that takes this view. See Thomason and Kaufman (1988).

is always to the left. The gap in this case consists of languages that have *wh*-movement to the right. Bresnan proposed that there is a node COMP that is universally a left sister of S, and that *wh*-movement is movement to this position. In recent years, many typological asymmetries have been tied to structural asymmetries such as these; see Kayne (1994) for development of the idea that there is in fact a universal asymmetry in branching structure, where all branching is binary and to the right, and all movement is to the left.

There are also gaps of a more specific nature. To take just one example, Zwart (1994) shows that not all of the possible orderings of three or four verbs in verbal clusters in West Germanic are possible. Let 1, 2, 3 and 4 represent the verbs in a syntactic structure, where 1 is the highest verb in the structure, 2 the second highest, and so on. An ordering such as 1-2 represents the surface order of the verbs in a main clause. While many orders are possible, Zwart shows that what apparently never occurs is *2-1-3. We will focus more closely on this example in section 2.4 in our discussion of the explanation of how such gaps might come about.

We stress that we have no quarrel with the methodology of seeking explanations for gaps in terms of linguistic structure, and in fact to reject this methodology would be irrational. We wish to suggest, however, that gaps may in principle reveal not just the structure of the Language Faculty, but also the structure of *social networks* of human beings in which linguistic knowledge is communicated. In fact, we will show that the way in which knowledge is communicated in such social networks makes it virtually inevitable that some combinations of properties will not appear. The combinations that do and do not appear are not necessarily predictable in terms of the linguistic content of the properties in question, although linguistic considerations may be relevant.

2.2 A Computational Simulation

In previous work, Nettle (1999) has shown through a computational simulation that the spatial distribution and particularly spatial clustering of languages can be attributed to interactions among speakers in the social network, assuming the Dynamic Theory of Social Impact (Nowak et. al. 1990; Latané 1996; Levenshtein et. al. 1992). We have replicated his results, and extended the approach to the clustering and correlation of linguistic features.

In our computational simulation, the social network is represented by a square matrix of k rows and k columns. Each of $k \times k$ locations can be occupied by an individual agent, so if all the locations are occupied there are $N = k \times k$ individuals. Each individual agent A is characterized in addition to its location in the matrix by the values of three linguistic features, and additionally by a strength parameter. The strength parameter describes how influential each individual is in inducing change in other individuals.

Each linguistic feature can have one of a discrete set of values. In the simplest case the value is a binary variable with values of 0 and 1. The linguistic features are assumed to be independent of one another. That is, there is no relationship between the values of different features.

The simulation proceeds according to the so-called Monte Carlo dynamic. An individual agent *A* is randomly selected from the matrix. For the chosen individual a specified number (*p*) of interaction partners are drawn randomly from a distance not greater than *d* cells from the agent, where *p* and *d* are chosen for the particular simulation. If the limiting distance *d* is equal to one, then only cells adjacent to the cell occupied by the agent can be selected as the interaction partners. The selection of interaction partners is independent for each agent so it is possible that a specific partner can be selected more than once.

For each of the linguistic features (independently of the two other features) the following procedure is repeated: for each value of the feature the social pressure to adopt this feature is computed by adding the strength of all the interaction partners (that were drawn in this round of simulation). If an agent has the value 1 for some feature, for example, and if enough of its neighbors have 0, then in the course of interaction with its neighbors, the 1 will be changed to 0 for this agent. Precisely how sensitive each agent is to external influence, which neighbors are potential interlocutors, and so on, are parameters of the simulation that can be adjusted.

Another parameter of the simulation model is whether or not there is self-influence. If self-influence is chosen, the agent is treated as one of the interaction partners and the strength of the agent is added to the value of influences of the appropriate value of the feature.

It is also possible to introduce noise into the simulation. If the value of noise is greater than 0 then the noise is added to the sum of the pressures from the interaction partners.[4]

In sampling the values of its interaction partners, an agent adopts the feature value that received the highest score. If two or more values have the same score then the value is chosen randomly from among them. After the values of all the three features have been updated for a given agent (the interaction partners are the same for all the three features of an agent), a new agent is randomly drawn. A simulation step corresponds to choosing N

---

[4] The noise is calculated as a random number drawn from a flat distribution (0..1) multiplied by the maximum strength of the individuals (to normalize it to the strength of individuals in the simulation) and multiplied by 4.5.

agents, so every individual is updated approximately once in a simulation step. Since the random drawings are independent of each other, some individuals may not be chosen in a given step and some possible interaction partners are not drawn at all in the course of the simulation.

We give a very simple illustration of a single iteration to show roughly how the simulation works.[5] For simplicity we have a 3x3 matrix consisting of nine agents. We assume that the features are binary valued, so that there are eight possibilities. A random distribution of feature values has a chance of realizing all possible combinations at least once; we generated such random distributions until this distribution occurred. The initial state is shown in Figure 1.

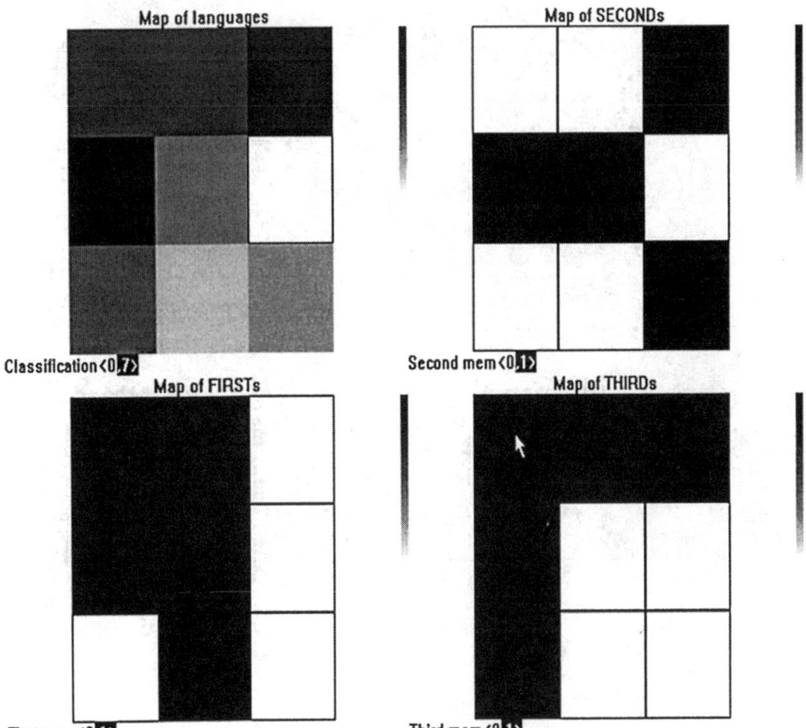

Figure 1. Simple Initial State

[5] The probabilistic nature of the simulation means that it is impossible to replicate precisely the course of change given the same starting configuration, so the example that we give is only illustrative.

The upper left image is a composite that represents the three feature values of each of the agents, using the gray scale. The individual feature values are shown in the 'Map of FIRSTs', 'Map of SECONDs' and 'Map of THIRDs'; they are either black (which we refer to as '+') or white (or '-'). The strengths are assigned randomly, and are shown in Figure 2.

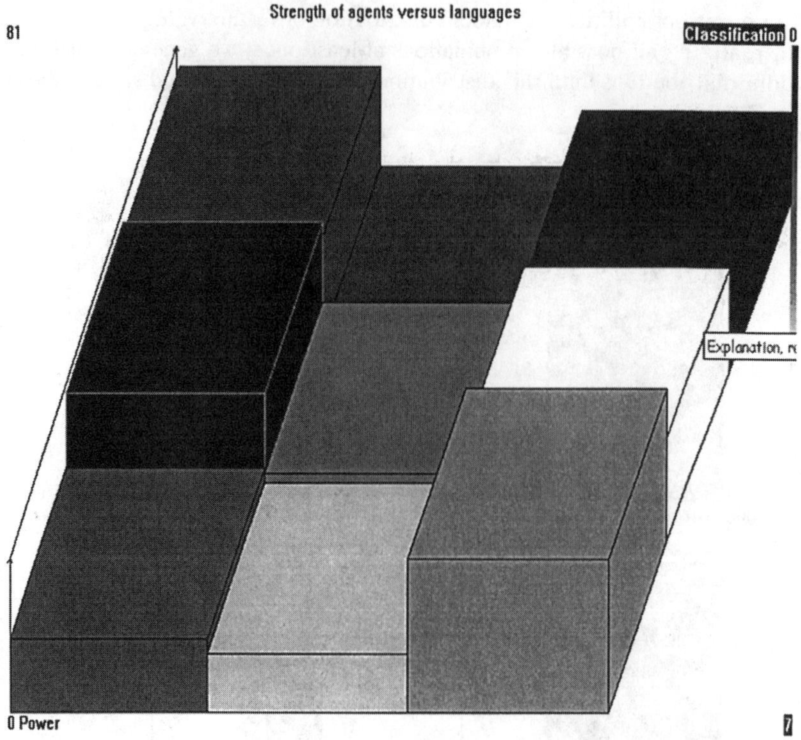

Figure 2. Strengths of Agents

On a single iteration, each agent interacts with those in its neighborhood and independently changes its values for each feature if the external influence is sufficiently strong. The result of doing so for one iteration in this example is shown in Figure 3.

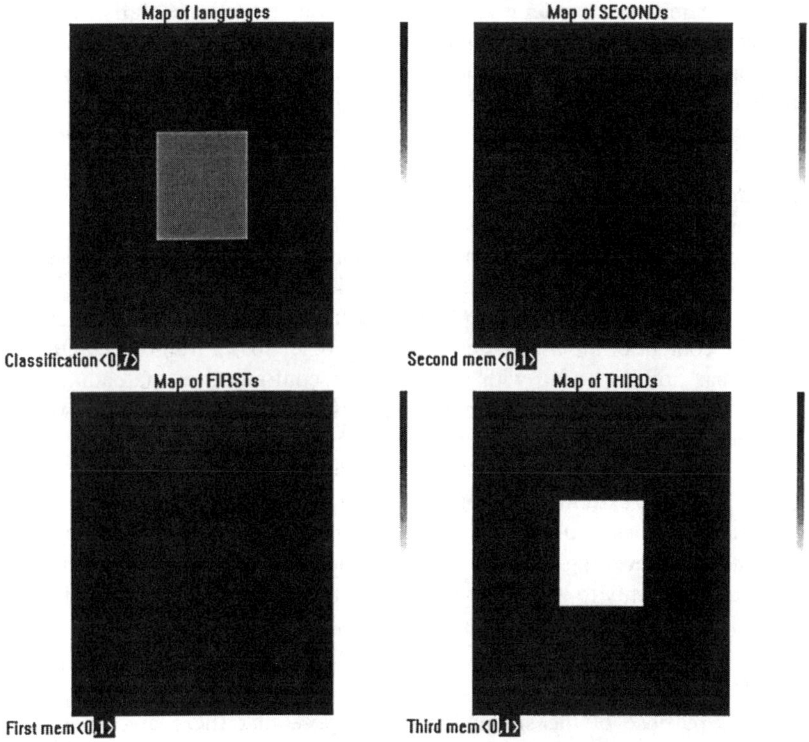

Figure 3. Result of Single Iteration

We can track the behavior of each agent for each feature by examining the result of a single iteration. For example, the agent in the middle row and middle column has the values +,+,- for the three features at the start. Looking just at the first feature, we see that four of its neighbors have the value + and four have the value -. The agent itself has the value + for this feature, and this is included in the calculation. So there are five +'s and four –'s, and the agent remains unchanged for this feature as we might expect. In the case of the other two features, however, the values of the neighbors outnumber that of the agent, and it should change its values, but doesn't. Recall that the agent does not interact with each neighbor once on this iteration, but with some neighbors that share its values more than once. Moreover, some agents are not chosen on every iteration. In the short run this means that an agent may resist change for a while, but in the long run the agent will eventually sample enough of its neighbors to change its values.

This simulation model is applicable to a wide range of socially transmitted attributions. In our computational simulation of language change, we interpret the simulation as modeling the distribution across the network of logically independent linguistic properties over time. The network consists of interactions and social relationships between individuals. There are linguistic communications across this network that pass between individuals. A language learner acquires knowledge of language by interacting with (a subportion of) this network, and by acquiring the linguistic features of the individuals with which it interacts, with some suitable weighting based on proximity, frequency of contact, social mobility, and so on.

Crucially, the Social Impact Theory that underlies this model presumes that the content of the linguistic features (or other social transmitted attributions) has nothing to do with the particular configuration of features displayed by a given agent or group of agents at any point in time. Agents change their feature values strictly as a function of the feature values of the agents that they interact with, and the strengths of the agents. While this presumption is extremely simplistic, and may well be controversial when the feature values in question correspond to social attitudes, it is fully consistent with prevailing views on how knowledge of language is transmitted from a community to its children. In brief, the children acquire the prevailing linguistic features of the community in which they live.

2.3 How Gaps Arise

For the purpose of the simulation we suppose that there are three two-valued features, which define eight distinct languages. Gaps occur when certain feature combinations are not attested. Our simulation shows that gaps may arise over the course of time, as the values of pairs of the features become strongly correlated. To take a very simple example as an illustration, suppose that there are two two-valued features that define four languages, as in (1):

(1) [+F1,+F2] [-F1,+F2] [+F1,-F2] [-F1,-F2]

If the geographical distribution of [–F2] becomes sufficiently restricted, it may fail to overlap with [+F1]. When this happens, one of the languages, namely [+F1,-F2], ceases to exist. Such a situation may occur simply as a consequence of the social structure, and in itself tells us nothing interesting about the relationship between [+F1] and [-F2].

Figure 4 shows the random distribution of feature values for three linguistic features in a population of 900 (=30x30). The upper left hand image shows the distinct languages as intensities on the gray scale. The other images show the distribution of + (black) and - (white) values for the three features FIRSTs, SECONDs and THIRDs.

Figure 4. Initial Random Distribution of Feature Values

The initial population of each of the eight languages is shown in the histogram in Figure 5. As can be seen, the languages are distributed more or less evenly over the entire population, as would be expected from a randomized assignment of feature values.

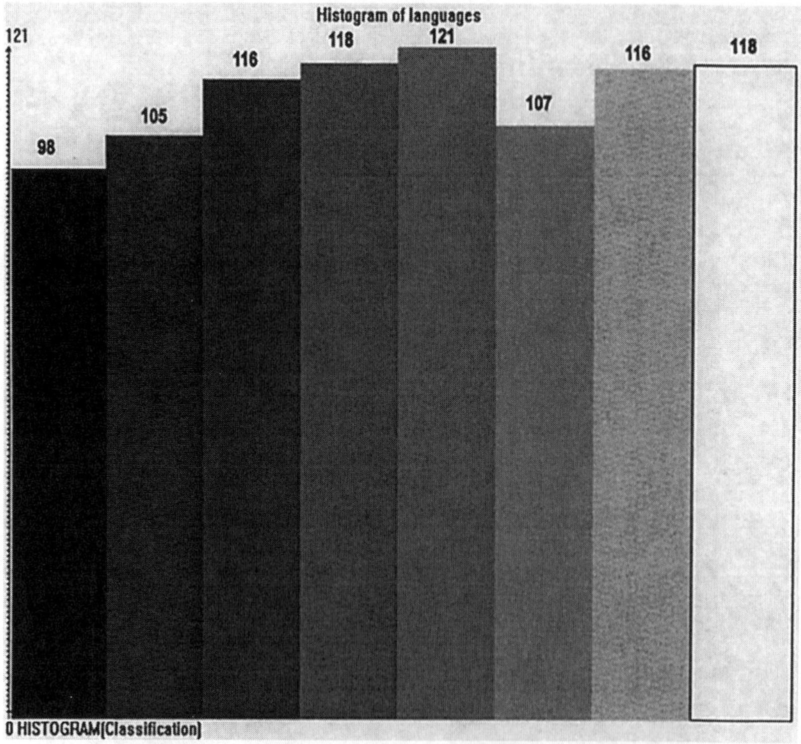

Figure 5. Initial Population of the Eight Languages

The picture at step 69 is shown in Figure 6.

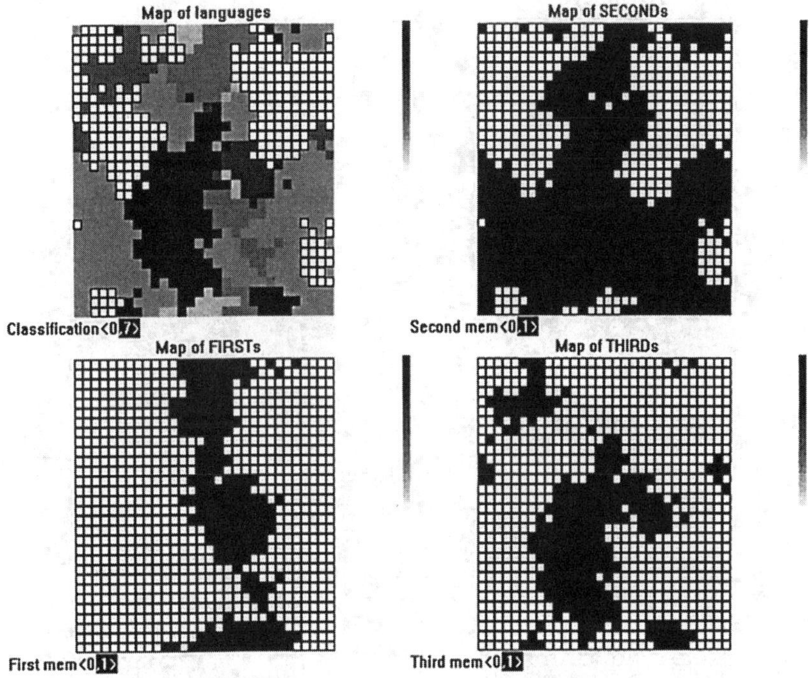

Figure 6. Distribution of Languages and Features at 69th Step

We have omitted additional intermediate steps in displaying the simulation for reasons of space. After 150 steps the distribution of languages and features is as in Figure 7.

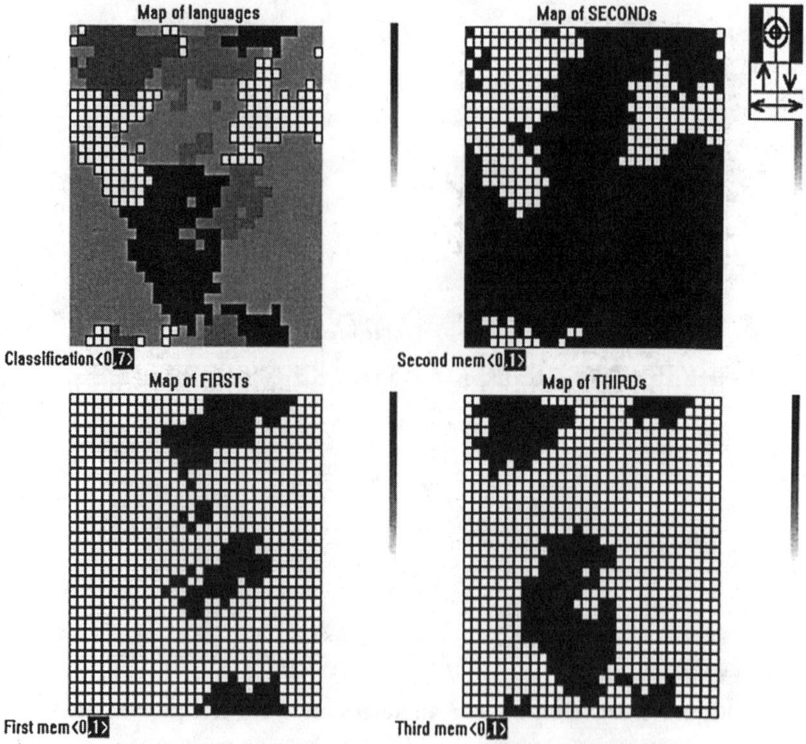

Figure 7. Distribution of Languages and Features at Step 150

It is clear from the images that there is significant clustering of feature values, and of feature value combinations, i.e. languages. The histogram in Figure 8 shows the population levels of the eight possible languages. Note that the third language (from the left) and the seventh language have entirely disappeared.

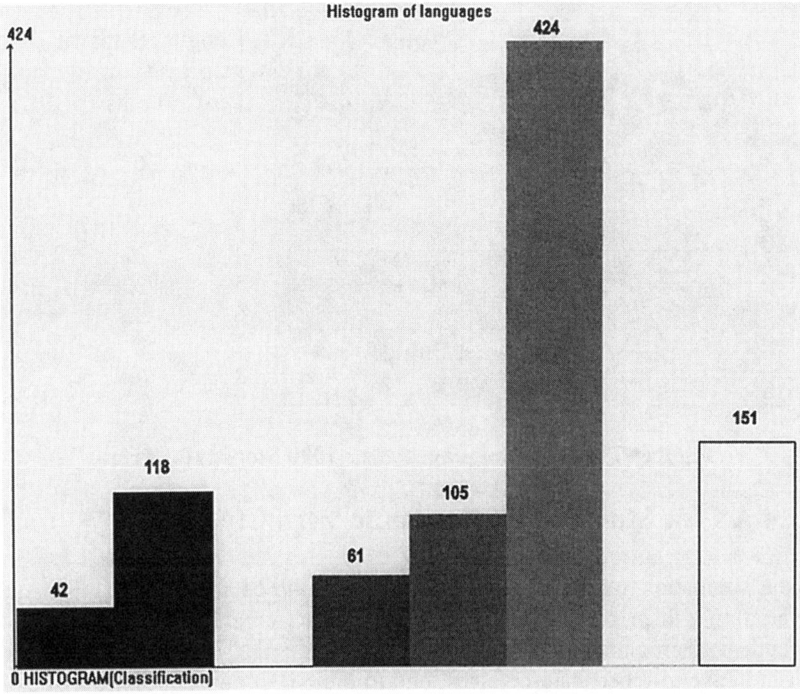

Figure 8. Population of Languages after 150 Steps

The loss of languages illustrated in this particular instance of the simulation is not unique. It is a consequence of the particular assumptions made in the simulation about how individuals interact in the network. Running the same simulation under the same parameters *p* and *d* yields a different pattern of features and languages each time; in most cases at least one language is lost. As an illustration, we repeated this simulation 100 times. The following chart shows the number of times a given number of languages remained after 1000 simulation steps. The results are also summarized in terms of number of languages lost.

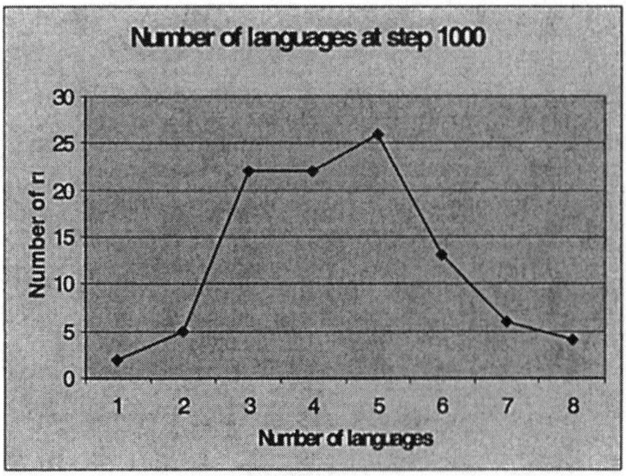

Languages lost at step 1000

Lost	Trials
0	4
1	6
2	13
3	26
4	22
5	22
6	5
7	2
8	0

Figure 9. Loss of Languages after 1000 Steps, 100 Trials

2.4 A Case Study: West Germanic Verb Clusters

The simulation suggests that the actual possibilities realized in linguistic variation will in general display a subset of the logical possibilities, independent of grammatical considerations. Feature values that are in a minority relative to other feature values tend to die out in non-equilibrium situations. The question of why it is that a particular feature value is in a minority is an independent question, and one of great importance. It may certainly have a linguistic as well as a sociological basis. Nettle (1999) shows that built-in biases against certain linguistic properties will produce clustering when coupled with the differential effects of social status and the dynamics of the social network model. Nettle characterizes properties with inherent bias as follows (1999: 112): they are hard to acquire, which causes languages to change away from them. In the context of current linguistic theorizing, this idea is a powerful one. It suggests that non-existing linguistic properties are in principle a consequence both of the social structure, and also of learnability, in some sense related to complexity of computation.[6] In effect, this is markedness, which takes us back to some essential insights of Chomsky's *Aspects*.

The linguistically interesting question is what constitutes computational complexity in the domain of grammar and language acquisition. We hypothesize that where there is grammatical structure, the logical possibilities

[6] See also Hawkins (1994) and Briscoe (2000).

in which the structure is more transparent, in the sense of correspondence with conceptual structure (CS), will be more highly favored, other things being equal.[7] Those possibilities that are minimally transparent will be rare if they exist at all, simply for this reason.

With this in mind we return to a consideration of the order of verbs in Continental West Germanic verb clusters, as described by Zwart (1994). The possibilities are summarized in Table 1.

1-2	Standard Dutch; dialects
2-1	Standard Dutch; dialects
1-2-3	Standard Dutch; High German
1-3-2	Standard Dutch; High German
*2-1-3	
2-3-1	West Flemish[8]
3-1-2	Dutch
3-2-1	Frisian; High German
4-3-2-1	Dutch
4-1-2-3	Dutch
1-4-2-3	Dutch
Others	

Table 1. West Germanic Verb Clusters

The set of possibilities clearly cannot be subsumed under a single ordering parameter that applies to sisters in a phrase marker. Zwart's solution is to assume that there is basically a single underlying ordering in a binary branching structure, 1-[2-[3-..., and that there are various leftward movements to designated positions.[9] These movements are constrained by grammatical factors, so that not all imaginable orderings occur. The major gap is that of *2-1-3.

Let us consider an alternative perspective, which is that the correct representation of the knowledge of the possible clusters can be expressed in terms of linear properties of the sequence of verbs. It is certainly true that even in theory of parameter setting, the learner must extract generalizations about the possible sequences prior to setting the parameters. Let us suppose that the relevant features are simply the relative orderings of pairs of verbs in the sequence. In a three-verb sequence, the features are 1>2, 2>3, and

[7] For discussion, see Culicover (1999) and Culicover and Nowak (2003).

[8] This order occurs only when V1 is an auxiliary verb (Zwart 1995). Zwart attributes the order to topicalization of the VP of which V2 is the head and V3 the head of the complement.

[9] Recall that 1 refers to the highest V in the structure, 2 to the next highest, and so on.

1>3 where one does not follow from the other two. These features will produce eight possible combinations, as shown in Table 2.

Language	**P1**	**P2**	**P3**	**Sequences**
D	1-2	2-3	(1-3)	1-2-3
G	2-1	2-3	1-3	*2-1-3
A	1-2	3-2	1-3	1-3-2
E	2-1	3-2	(1-3)	3-2-1
F	1-2	2-3	(3-1)	1-2-3
B	2-1	2-3	3-1	2-3-1
C	1-2	3-2	3-1	3-1-2
H	2-1	3-2	(3-1)	3-2-1

Table 2. Verb Clusters Generated by Simulation

All possible orders are produced by these three features, including the unattested *2-1-3. For languages A, F, E and H the value of P3 is irrelevant since 1-2 and 2-3 imply 1-3, and 3-2 and 2-1 imply 3-1. For the sake of the illustration we may take the feature P3 to be completely determined by the other two features when there is redundancy, recognizing that this is an unprincipled assumption.

Let us now consider the simulation. Suppose that there are in fact these three features, and that the unattested *2-1-3 is possible and actually exists at some point in a dialect of the language, but is relatively weakly attested; perhaps there is a functional bias against it. Figure 10 displays the development of a typical language group after 775 steps.

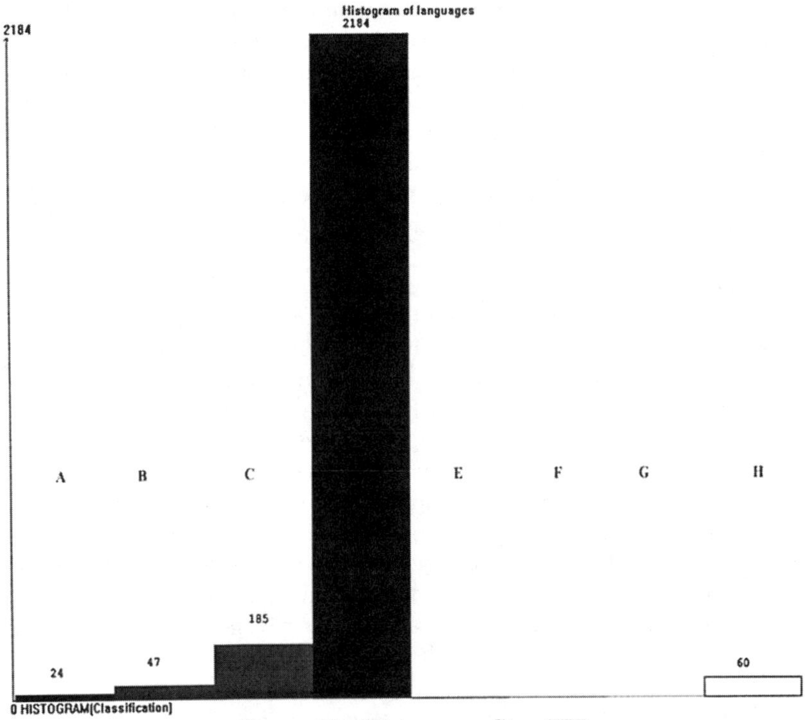

Figure 10. Histogram, Step 775

We can see that at this point there is one majority language (Language D), and there are three other more or less alive languages (B, C and H), three non-existent languages (E, F and G), and one that is very weak (A). Let the languages in the histogram be as defined above in Table 2. On this view, the non-existent *2-1-3 is not ruled out in principle, it simply does not exist as a consequence of the behavior of the network.

It is apparent that there is no linguistic content in this simulation, and we have chosen to name the languages in such a way that the simulation would illustrate the point. We do not claim to have explained the West Germanic data, and in fact Zwart's account could well be the correct one from a theoretical perspective. The point is simply to show that the non-existence of a particular combination of properties, in this case *2-1-3, is not *necessarily* linguistically interesting. Even if there are linguistic factors at play, it would be a mistake to conclude that the nonexistence of a particular combination of properties signifies that this combination is impossible for some deep principled reason. It may simply be, as suggested earlier, that this combination of features is possible but highly dispreferred, and hence dies out under pressure from more favored alternatives.

So we must consider the question, is there any way to predict which of the languages will in fact go extinct? In this simulation model there is no way to do these, because the three features and their values are equipotent. But, suppose that we add the further condition that a language property that is computationally more complex than its competitors in the set will be dispreferred. In the case of word order in West Germanic verb clusters, we may reasonably hypothesize that the processing of a head and its complement is facilitated by adjacency and consistent canonical order.[10] In the case of the order *2-1-3, the head of 2-3 is 2. The head 2 is not adjacent to 3, which may constitute a processing burden, perhaps a special instance of LOCALITY, or MINIMUM DISTANCE or MINIMUM LINK or RELATIVIZED MINIMALITY, all of which plausibly have a computational basis. Since the head 1 intervenes between 2 and 3 and is to the right of its (split up) complement, there is an additional burden with respect to the identification of 1 as the head of *2-3. Our suggestion is that while this particular state of affairs is not grammatically impossible, it is highly marked for computational reasons, and will be dispreferred by the language learner. It remains, of course, to provide an explicit characterization of relative computational complexity, a challenge that would take us far beyond the bounds of the present study.

3 Correlations

The appearance of gaps in the set of languages is an extreme case of a more general property of the simulation model, which is that feature values correlate. In other words, the model evolves over time so that there is a tendency for one feature value to appear when another appears. However, the correlation is not usually 100%, so that the opposite pattern may also occur, although less frequently.

In a random initial state the level of correlation between features is zero. Since the value of a feature for an individual is determined by the interactions between that individual and its interaction partners, over time all of the feature values of an individual tend to become more highly correlated with those of its interaction partners. An illustration of the history of correlation in a particular simulation is given in Figure 11.

[10] We leave open the question of whether or not there is a universal canonical order.

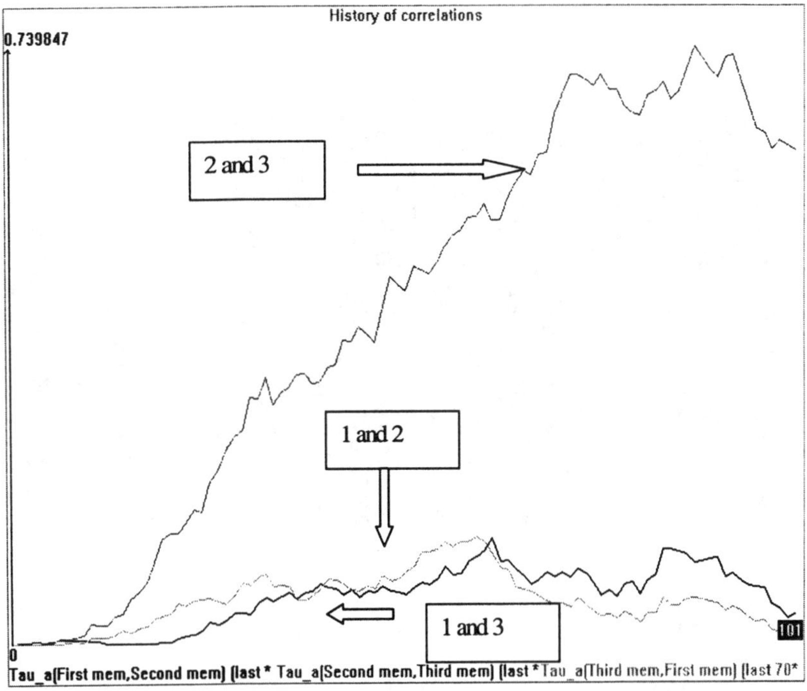

Figure 11. History of Correlations over 100 Steps

As can be seen, features F2 and F3 correlate increasingly closely over the course of the simulation, while features F1-F3 and F1-F2 do not.

It is instructive to observe the kind of pattern that is associated with such correlation. In Figure 12 we see the space for F2 and F3 after 100 steps.

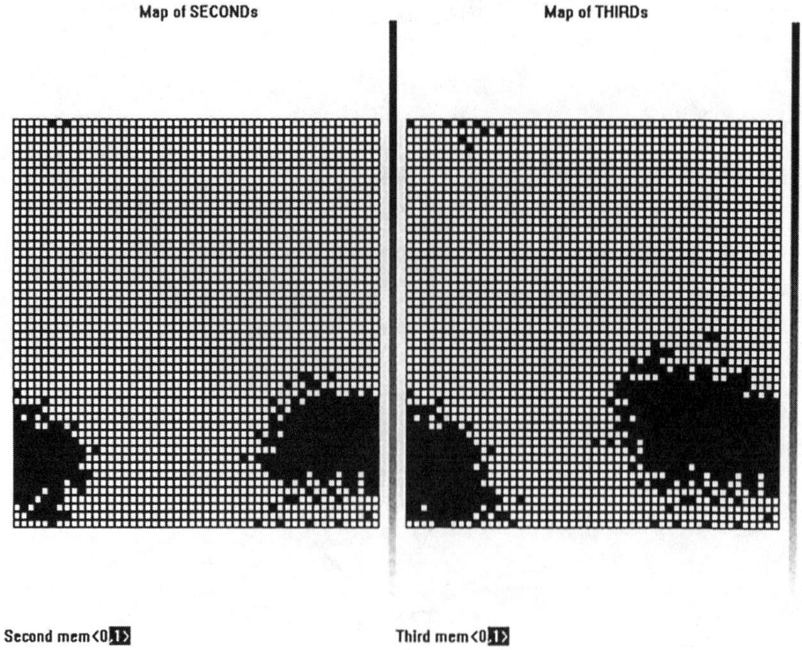

Figure 12. Features 2 and 3 after 100 Steps

The visual evidence reveals the tendency for F2 and F3 to have the correlated values, even though there are exceptions. The statistical correlation data confirms this observation. Such tendencies may have a linguistic interpretation along the lines of some Greenbergian universals (Greenberg 1963). Consider one chosen more or less at random, for example, Universal 4: With overwhelmingly greater than chance frequency, languages with normal SOV order are postpositional.[11] Let F2 be [+/-postpositional], and let F3 be [+/-OV]. Figure 12 can be understood as an illustration of the situation in which most SOV languages are postpositional, although some are not; we illustrate in Figure 13.

[11] Similar universals are:

UNIVERSAL 9: With well more than chance frequency, when question particles or affixes are specified in position by reference to the sentence as a whole, if initial, such elements are found in prepositional languages and, if final, in postpositional.

UNIVERSAL 17: With overwhelmingly more than chance frequency, languages with dominant VSO order have the adjective after the noun.

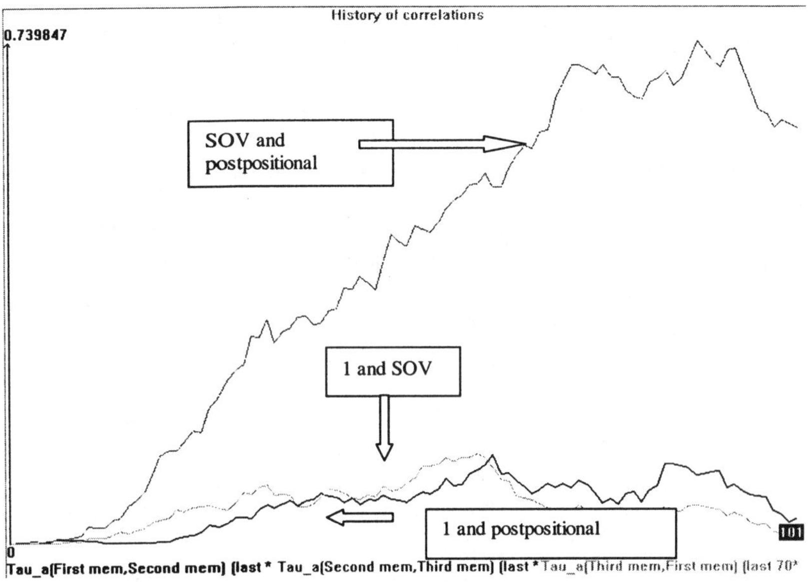

Figure 13. Hypothetical Correlation between SOV and Pre/Post-Position

While it is almost certainly true that there are other sorts of explanations for some implicational universals of this type, the possibility cannot be ruled out that at least some are due simply to the correlation of features through the interaction of the network.

4 Future Perspectives

We have argued that it is possible in principle to attribute to the social network such phenomena as gaps in the set of languages, and the tendency for certain properties to co-occur in languages. It is almost certainly the case that the intrinsic content of the features also plays an explanatory role as well in each of these categories of phenomena. The point is simply that there are at least two potential sources of explanation. This observation at first glance appears to complicate the task of the theorist, who is no longer able to posit without further investigation that the distributional patterns of linguistic phenomena reveal something interesting about the language capacity. But it does sharpen up to some extent our notion of what it means for something to count as an explanation of some linguistic phenomenon.

References

Abelson, R. P. 1979. Social Clusters and Opinion Clusters. *Perspectives on Social Network Research*, eds. P. W. Holland and S. Leinhardt. New York: Academic Press.

Bresnan, J. 1970. On Complementizers: Toward a Syntactic Theory of Complement Types. *Foundations of Language* 6: 297-321.

Briscoe, T. 2000. Grammatical Acquisition: Inductive Bias and Coevolution of Language and the Language Acquisition Device. *Language* 76: 245-296.

Chomsky, N. 1965. Aspects of the Theory of Syntax. Cambridge, MA: MIT Press.

Culicover, P. W. 1999. *Syntactic Nuts*. Oxford: Oxford University Press.

Culicover, P. W. and R. Jackendoff. 1999. The View from the Periphery: The English Comparative Correlative. *Linguistic Inquiry* 30: 543-71.

Culicover, P. W. and L. McNally. eds. 1998. *The Limits of Syntax*. San Diego: Academic Press.

Culicover, P. W. and A. Nowak. 2003. *Dynamical Syntax*. Oxford: Oxford University Press.

Culicover, P. W., Nowak, A., and Borkowski, W. 1999. Linguistic Features Cluster in a Social Network. Unpublished manuscript. The Ohio State University and the University of Warsaw.

Greenberg, J. 1963. *Universals of Language*. Cambridge, MA: MIT Press.

Kayne, R. S. 1994. *The Antisymmetry of Syntax*. Cambridge, MA: MIT Press.

Kayne, R.S. 1996. Microparametric Syntax: Some Introductory Remarks. *Microparametric Syntax and Dialect Variation*, eds. J.R. Black and V. Motapanyane, i-viii. Amsterdam: John Benjamins.

Latané, B. 1996. The Emergence of Clustering and Correlation Form Social Interactions. *Modelle sozialer Dynamiken: Ordnung, Chaos und Komplexität*, eds. R. Hegselmann and H.O. Peitgen, 287-310. Wien: Holder-Pichler-Tempsky.

Lewenshtein, M., A. Nowak, and B. Latané. 1992. Clustering Causes Correlation. Unpublished manuscript, University of Warsaw.

Nettle, D. 1999. Using Social Impact Theory to Simulate Language Change. *Lingua* 108: 95-117.

Nowak, A., J. Szamrej and B. Latané. 1990. From Private Attitude to Public Opinion: A Dynamic Theory of Social Impact. *Psychological Review* 97: 362-376.

Thomason, S. G. and T. Kaufman. 1988. *Language Contact, Creolization, and Genetic Linguistics*. Berkeley: University of California Press.

Zwart, C. J.-W. 1994. Verb Clusters in Continental West Germanic Dialects. Paper Presented at the 18th Annual Meeting of the Atlantic Provinces Linguistic Association, St. John, October 29, 1994.

Zwart, C. J.-W. 1995. A Note on Verb Clusters in the Stellingwerf Dialect. *Linguistics in the Netherlands 1995*, eds. M. den Dikken and K. Hengeveld, 215-226. Amsterdam & Philadelphia: John Benjamins.

5

Explaining Infixation

JOHN HAIMAN

1 Introduction

Ever since Bopp first proposed the idea in his Sanskrit grammar of 1816, we have recognized one source of bound grammatical morphemes: they are simply words that have been worn down by frequent use. Perhaps we do not always know exactly *which* words, but in principle, erosion offers a possible diachronic explanation for all prefixes and suffixes. Manifestly however, such an account is not available, even in principle, for the origins of infixes: morphemes that break up minimal morphemes. In this paper, I will try to justify a 'natural' explanation for the origins of infixation in Khmer (and, possibly, other Mon-Khmer languages).

I will call any explanation for a grammatical fact a NATURAL one (as opposed to FORMAL) when it crucially refers to something outside of the structural system wherein that fact occurs. Assuming the autonomy of grammar, all appeals to 'meaning' constitute (attempts at) natural explanations for grammatical facts. Assuming separation of levels or modularity within a grammar, appeals to syntax or phonology constitute attempts at natural explanations for morphological facts, and so on. Natural explanations may be synchronic or historical.

We turn now to the grammatical fact under review here, infixation. Why is it rare? What does its rarity explain? And why, in spite of everything, does it occasionally happen anyway?

The Nature of Explanation in Linguistic Theory.
John Moore and Maria Polinsky (eds.).

2 Synchronic Explanations for the Rarity of Infixation

There is a natural synchronic performance-based explanation for why infixation is rare: like center-embedding, infixation postpones parsing, and forces speakers and hearers to store something and then to retrieve it later on before it can be processed. It is therefore rare for the same reason that center embedding is (Miller and Chomsky 1963; for a survey of the recent literature, cf. Babyonyshev and Gibson 1999). Infixation is to the word what center embedding is to the phrase. More generally, center embedding increases simultaneous processing in working memory (Hawkins, this volume). It is important to bear in mind the contrast between centrally located LINKING MORPHEMES like the ones in *therm-o-meter* and *Geburt-s-tag*, which are easily tolerated, and cases of *TRUE* INFIXATION which tend not to be. Linking morphemes do not inhibit or postpone parsing. True infixation does. In a word like *ha-g-amu'* 'your namesake' in Hua (Haiman 1977), the root *hamu'* 'namesake' cannot be parsed or recognized until the whole word is uttered. The same is true of English words like *passer-s by.*

What this performance constraint explains is a remarkable fact. The well-known reversal of V and O constituents in verbal compounds like *life-saver*, etc. and adjectival compounds like *law-abiding*, *heartbreaking*, *heat-resistant*, etc. seems to contravene Bopp's principle of inertia, whereby morphology is nothing but congealed earlier syntax (cf. Meillet 1912, Givon 1971, Bybee et. al. 1990, Keenan, this volume, for restatements of this popular view). Less frequently, the reversal of V and Particle in adjectival compounds like *up-coming*, *out-going* is a parallel phenomenon. Inertia would call for structures like *pass-er by* consistently. The phenomenon is thus a textbook case of an apparent mismatch between syntax and morphology, and much of the literature in the generative framework has focused on whether the compound order is derived via a syntactic LEXICAL transformation (thus Roeper and Siegel 1978), or requires a distinct set of phrase structure rules in a separate morphological component of a grammar (thus Selkirk 1982). I am taking no sides on this issue, since my interest is primarily in the conditions under which this mismatch occurs.

Remarkably, where there is no agentive affix *-er*, or no adjectival affix *-ing*, *-ant*, the VO order of the sentential syntax is maintained: thus the nominal compounds *pickpocket*, *scarecrow*, *cutthroat*, *lickspittle*, *scofflaw*, *killjoy*, *spoilsport*, *daredevil*, *turncoat*, *post-It*,[1] and the adjectival compounds *kick-ass*, *breakneck* (VO); and nominal compounds like *hoe-down*,

---

[1] There are also compounds without an infix that reverse the syntactic order, such as *globe-trot* (cf. Selkirk 1982). Marchand (1969) has claimed that these are all back-formations from *globe-trotter* etc., however, and I will follow Selkirk in accepting this account.

hand-out or adjectival compounds like *drive-by* or *see-through* (V Particle). True infixation is, in general, only tolerated where it is repeated on the margin of the word: thus the still ludic *picker upper*, etc., which contrast with the perfectly acceptable internal affixation of words like *arm-s dealer*. The operative difference between forbidden infixation and tolerated internal affixation, as was correctly pointed out by Williams 1981, is that inflectional features associated with the non-final member of a compound must be interpretable within the affixing word itself (cited in Selkirk 1982).

German and Hungarian, which have agentive/ adjectival affixes like English, effect the same word order rearrangement: *Hand-trockn-er* 'hand drier' *kéz szárit-ó* 'hand drier'. French, Spanish, and Italian, which do not, form their VO compounds with syntactic VO order: *asciuga mani* 'dry hands' (Italian), *gratte-ciel* 'scrape skies' (French; cf. Bierbach 1983, Klingebiel 1989), *quebra ley* 'law break' [outlaw], *porta voz* 'carry voice' [spokesman] (Spanish). Where the agentive suffix *-er/-eur* appears in English or French, VO order is maintained, but only because of the particle *of* or *de*, which is here performing a word-separating function alone: *killer of sheep*, *cherch-eur d'asile* 'asylum seeker'/ 'seeker of asylum'.

This set of facts is usually explained by reference to something like a RIGHT-HEAD rule: affixes can only occur on heads, and heads are necessarily on the right. This purely formal (i.e. not NATURAL) explanation is descriptively adequate in English (cf. Williams 1981), and in other languages far more often than it deserves to be for two fortuitous reasons: many languages, like English, are right-headed, and most languages affix by suffixation, for most plausibly performance-related reasons that have been proposed by Hawkins (cf. Hawkins and Cutler 1988) and others. But when we consider the behavior of languages which are left-headed, and affix by prefixation, we see that the RIGHT HEAD explanation is not even descriptively adequate. Consider Khmer, a left-headed language where the agentive affix (like most affixes in Khmer) occurs as a prefix, on the left. VO word order is unexceptionably maintained in [affix + V + O] compounds like:

(1)	nɛək bɑɑ	dɑmraə	
	-er drive	elephant	'elephant driver'
(2)	nɛək koŋwiel	koo	
	-er tend	cow	'cowherd'
(3)	nɛək cok	baarej	
	-er smoke	cigarette	'cigarette smoker'
(4)	nɛək taeŋ	komnaap	
	-er compose	poem	'poet'

Affixation occurs neither on the left nor on the right a priori, but on the periphery of the construction, on the side opposite to the modifier.[2] The pattern which emerges from a display of tolerated and excluded structures:

(5) a. Affix + Head + Modifier
b. Modifier + Head + Affix
c. *Head + Affix + Modifier
d. *Modifier + Affix + Head

conclusively demonstrates the irrelevance of the HEAD HOSTING constraint. Avoidance of center-embedding of an affix is what prohibits monstrosities like

(6) a. *dri-er hand
b. *hand-er dry

and also accounts for all the other facts we have examined. VO is allowed where there is no potentially center-embedded affix at all as in the *turncoat* cases and their French, Italian, and Spanish congeners. VO is also allowed where the affix occurs as a prefix on V, as in Khmer; VO is transformed into OV in suffixing languages where the agent affix risks producing *V+Affix O compounds. Essentially the same arguments apply to compounds like *heat-resist-ant* and *up-com-ing*. They may extend as well to ludic doublings like *pick-er upp-er*. The etymologically motivated suffix is left in infixed position, but such infixation is allowed only if the buried affix is reiterated on the margin of the compound.

Nevertheless, infixation *does* sometimes occur: in some languages, systematically. Given the plausibility of both Bopp's conjecture, and of the center embedding constraint, and the fact that the active avoidance of center embedding at the word level is illustrated by words like *fire extinguisher* etc., our presumption is that all cases of systematic infixation are expensive enough that they must be explained in some way. And every explanation for the existence of infixation that I am aware of is historical.

3 Diachronic Explanations for the Existence of Infixation

Everything is the way it is because it got that way. So, to me, the most satisfying explanations for marginal or deviant phenomena such as infixation are evolutionary and historical accounts. In many (but not all) cases, evolution-

---

[2] The agent affix is homographic with the noun 'person', much like the *-man* in compounds like *gentleman, fireman*.

ary accounts identify external motivations for changes that occurred. We can access external motivations for the genesis of remarkable facts via performance constraints, comparative data from related languages, and typological comparison.

Infixation is not on a par with suffixation, or even with prefixation (the comparative rarity of which should also be accounted for by some theory cf. Hawkins and Cutler 1988, Bybee et. al. 1990) — it is really really rare, and every case should be accounted for. Not surprisingly, the diachronic explanations which have surfaced are different for different languages. Harris 1993 accounted for infixation in Udi, a Caucasian language, as entrapment of originally separate words under univerbation. (Her account is thus compatible with Bopp and Meillet.) Haiman 1977 accounted for object and possessive pronoun infixation in Hua, a Papuan language, as morpheme metathesis based on invisible paradigmatic restructuring given the empty 3sg. morpheme. (Something similar is attested in Turkish, although no infixation results.) Finally, in Haiman 1998, I proposed an account for the infixation of nominalizing and causative derivational affixes in Khmer: infixation assures the retention of a favorite inherited phonetic structure. This is an iambic bisyllabic word whose initial unstressed syllable is constantly being eroded by a number of processes which tend to eliminate the coda.[3] It was proposed there that the infixed syllable coda which restores bisyllabic words may have two possible sources:

(i) it may be infixed via metathesis of an inherited prefix; for example, the agentive infix -m-, found in a handful of nouns like *k-m-an* 'royal barber' (<*kan* 'hold (head)'), *c-m-uəɲ* 'tradesman' (< *cuəɲ* 'deal, trade, negotiate') also occurs as a prefix in a very few words like *m-cah* 'master, owner' (< *cah* 'mature, elder') and *m-hoop* 'food' (<*hoop* 'dine'), and is variously attested as a prefix or as a suffix in other Austroasiatic languages (cf. Pinnow 1963; Diffloth 1965). A similar origin is plausible for the instrument infix *-n-*, found in words like *s-n-ɔp* 'pump' (< *sɔp* 'to pump'), and whose cognates occur as a prefix in other Mon-Khmer languages (Schmidt 1906; Diffloth 1976);

[3] The productivity of these rules is illustrated not only in the native Khmer vocabulary (cf. Huffman 1970), but in the treatment of borrowings. *Mickey Mouse* for example is pronounced [kmaus]. My thanks to Jean Longmire for this observation.

(ii) it may result from excrescence (Jespersen 1921) or exaptation (Lass 1990) (the same process which is responsible for the morphologization of the originally meaningless syllables -*thon, -gate, -oholic*, in English), via the grammaticalization of what may have been once a register distinction.

The phonetic relation

(7) [C+**VC** + CVC] (Formal careful speech) ~
[C + _____ + CVC] (casual speech)

is reinterpreted as

(8) C + { derivational affix } + CVC ~ {C CVC }

on the basis of a NATURAL and very general iconic markedness principle that 'more form equals more content'. I now am disposed to be skeptical about metathesis as the best explanation for the majority of cases of *-Vm(n)-* infixation in Khmer, simply because there is not enough evidence within Mon-Khmer for this putative prefix.[4] I am much more enthusiastic about the second, which I now believe to be principally responsible for the genesis of this most productive infix, the nominalizing (and, less frequently, causativizing) infix *-Vm(n)-*. This is the explanation that I want to propose for between four and five hundred pairs of words (Long 1975) like the following:

[4] A single example in Khmer itself may be the doublet *(am)pii* 'about', which may be related to the preposition *pii* 'from'.

(9) Infix is Nominalizer

t-umn-ɛək	'connection'	< tɛək	'connect'
t-ɑm-laj	'price'	< tlaj	'valuable'
k-umn-ɯt	'thought'	< kɯt	'think'
k-ɑm-hoh	'mistake'	< khoh	'wrong'
k-ɑmn-aət	'birth'	< kaət	'be born'
c-ɑmn-eh	'knowledge'	< ceh	'know'
c-ɑm-laəj	'response'	< claəj	'respond'
k-um-liən	'hunger'	< kliən	'hungry'
d-ɑmn-aə	'voyage'	< daə	'travel'
c-ɑmn-ool	'entrance'	< cool	'enter'
c-ɑm-ŋaaj	'distance'	< cŋaaj	'far'
t-um-hom	'size'	< thom	'big'
k-ɑm-daw	'heat'	< kdaw	'hot'
c-um-hiən	'a pace'	< chiən	'(take a) step'
c-ɑmn-əj	'food'	< cəj	'eat'
k-ɑm-poh	'height'	< kpoh	'tall'
s-ɑmn-aəc	'(a) smile'	< saəc	'smile'
p-umn-ool	'recitation'	<pool	'utter'
b-ɑmn-ɑɑŋ	'goal'	<bɑɑŋ	'aim at'

Although infixation is often said to be a vestigial derivational fact, this particular nominalization procedure is so general that even in the current language it seems to be productive (cf. Lewitz 1968 for references to the prevailing view, and a native speaker-linguist's convincing rebuttal). Whatever its antiquity, it created new words from roots borrowed from Pali and Sanskrit. And, moreover, possibilities which are judged as plausible but nonexistent by one speaker, my teacher, Mr. Noeurng Ourn (and are not recorded in Cuen Naat's Dictionnaire Cambodgien) show up as neologisms in elementary school texts and doubtless other texts as well. Examples are:

(10)	s-am-rəp	'rustling'	< srəp	'rustle'
	c-ɑm -hɑk	'electric shock'	<chɑk	'shock'
	c-ɑm-hɛh	'arson, a fire'	<chɛh	'catch fire'
	k-um-həəɲ	'view, opinion'	<khəəɲ	'see'
	d-ɑm-nək	'transportation'	<dək	'transport, lead, carry'
	t-ɑm-hae	'caretaking'	<thae	'take care of'
	t-um-hiep	'comparison'	<thiep	'compare'

Less frequent, but still fairly common, are cases of another derivation, where the infix is causative:

(11) Infix is Causative

s-ɑm-ruəl	'facilitate'	< sruəl	'easy'
s-ɑm-'aat	'clean'	< s'aat	'clean'
t-um-lɛək	'drop'	< tlɛək	'fall'
k-ɑm-daw	'heat up'	< kdaw	'hot
l-um-hae	'relax'	< lhae	'empty,wide open'
c-ɑm-raən	'increase'	< craən	'lots'
s-ɑm-lap	'kill'	< slap	'die'
c-ɑm-lɑɑŋ	'help s.o. cross'	<clɑɑŋ	'cross (a river,etc.)'
t-um-loəp	'accustom'	<tloəp	'be used to'

The comparative evidence for an inherited nominalizing or causative prefix *-Vm(n)-* within Mon- Khmer is spotty — perhaps only because so little is known about most of the languages of the family. But the evidence for excrescence is considerable, both within and outside of Mon-Khmer.

Our best evidence for excrescence within Khmer itself is that there are a handful of pairs where the putative original semantic distinction (that is, virtually no semantic distinction at all) between the contrasting forms is ('still', ex hypothesi) maintained. Thus, the very earliest attested pair of such words was *c(aN)paar* 'garden', already attested in seventh century Khmer. Modern parallels are

(12)

s-(ɑm)-baəm	'grand, awesome, glorious'
c-(ɑm)- roh	'mixed'
c- (ɑmn)-ah	'mature'
c-(ɑm)-ŋaaj	'spend'
k-(om) -ruu	'teacher'[5]
c-(ɑm)-poh	'towards'
k-(ɑmn) aac	'fierce'
s-(ɑm)-ŋɑm	'hide, be or remain silent, lie quietly'
c-(ɑm)-bɑŋ	'main, principal, first'
t-(um)-roəm	'last, endure, be patient; until'
b-(ɑm)-roŋ	'ready, prepare'

There may be slight differences in meaning between these pairs of words, as exemplified in pairs like:

---

[5] Also: 'role model' (< *kruu* 'teacher' (< Skt. *Guru*))

(13) Wiə daə *d-am-raŋ* tək haəj coh tram nɑniəl phək.
it go direct water and descend wallow mud
'It (the water buffalo) goes directly to the water and wallows in the mud.'

(14) Nəj cam (nəj *traŋ)* kɯɯ ciə nəj
meaning central meaning direct : is meaning
krəh taam thoəmməciət.
basis follow nature
'The central meaning (the 'direct' meaning) is the basic meaning according to its nature.'

But this difference is very slight, and the perception of its very existence may be a consequence of the folk etymologizing that results from the universal (iconic) assumption that there is no true synonymy, and that *different form* must reflect some *different meaning*. In any event, there is nothing as concrete and categorical as a nominalizing or causative function in these examples.[6] Shorto (1962), Svantesson (1983) and Rischel (1995) report a similar meaninglessness for a number of infixes in the related Mon, Kammu, and Mlabri languages. For example, in Mon, *janok* 'size' is contrasted with *jamnok* 'chief', but each word seems to occur with both meanings. In Thai, which has borrowed several {C (VM)CVC} doublets from Khmer, the difference in meaning between the *bare* and the *infixed* form is one of 'relative formality' alone (Noss 1964).

A subset of these (*ex hypothesi*, more or less meaningless) syllable codas occur in causative doublets. There are two causative prefixes in Khmer: a somewhat productive prefix *bVN-*, found on several dozen verb stems, and a less frequent prefix *p-* found on only a handful. By my hypothesis, the latter is a reduction of the former via the totally productive process of erosion of the coda of the anacrusic syllable (and in fact, there is a low level rule which devoices initial stops before following consonants), and additional evidence for their identity is the existence of an *intermediate* (?) form pVN- on three or four verb stems. In any event, there are a small number of near synonyms which differ only in the nature of the causative prefix:

---

[6] Khmer is a language in which lexical roots are syntactically indeterminate: whether a root functions as a verb or a noun is largely determined by its morphological and syntactic trappings (Hopper and Thompson 1985; Borer, this volume). But remarkably, sometimes when a verb is marked as a derived nominalization, it will *still* function as a verb. This phenomenon of SYNTACTIC BACKSLIDING may bear witness to the originally meaningless nature of the infixation process. Cf. Haiman and Ourn, to appear.

(15) a.		b-aŋ-kap	'hide, conceal'	
	~	p - kap	'hide, conceal'	<kap 'be hidden'
b.		b-an-duəl	'knock down'	
	~	p-duəl	'fell, slay'	<duəl 'fall'
c.		b-aŋ-riən	'teach'	
	~	p-riən	'give moral instruction'	<riən 'study, learn'
d.		b-an-sam	'join'	
	~	p-sam	'join'	<sam 'yoke'

The synonymy is not perfect. For example, we may detect a minimal contrast between the final pair of words in (15) in the (tautological!) sentence from an elementary school primer but the differences in meaning are surely small and - most importantly - unsystematic.

(16) lbah	*psam*	kaət laəŋ	daoj saar	*bansam*	lbah.
sentence	compound	born up	along again	join	sentence

'A compound sentence arises from joining sentences.'

All of these near synonym pairs support the hypothesis that the infix may have begun its existence as an originally meaningless, phonetically labile part of a monolexemic sesquisyllabic root.

Our second best evidence for the excrescence hypothesis is that the iconic MORE CONTENT requirement is vague - and precisely this vagueness is matched by the variety of meanings that the excreted derivational affix may have: the two principal meanings of this infix, namely causative (as in *sam-lap* 'kill' , vs. *slap* 'die', etc.) and nominalizing (as in *s-am-lap* 'death' vs. *slap* 'die'), are fairly sharply defined: but they are by no means identical with each other, or even related to each other. In addition, the same or a very similar prefix occurs with other meanings, like the inchoative (as in *s-am-koəl* 'recognize (er-kennen)' vs. *s-koəl* 'know' (kennen)), factitive, and others which are quite idiosyncratic: for example *ksaan* 'Happy, tranquil' (<Skt. Ksanta 'patient') yields the derived verb *k-am-saan* 'enjoy oneself'; *braə* 'use' yields the derived noun *b-am-raə* 'servant, person used'.

Corresponding to vagueness of meaning is a similar vagary in the form of the infix. The nominalizing and causative infix is usually *-am(n)-* but the 'labile' syllable coda in the causative prefix *baN-* is actually *-aN-* (the final nasal assimilates in place of articulation to the following consonant, becoming *BVŋ-* before *k, g, h, r, w,* and the glottal stop, and *BVɲ-* before palatal consonants). Now, this *{-aN-}* is another form of the nominalizing infix as well:

(17)	s-ɑŋ-weeŋ	'a search'	<sweeŋ	'find out, discover'
	b-ɑŋ-'aem	'sweets, dessert'	< b'aem	'sweet'
	b-ɑŋ-'eek	'chair with a back'	<b'eek	'lean against'
	b-ɑn-dam	'testament'	<bdam	'entrust'
	p-ɑn-luɯɯ	'illumination'	<pluɯɯ	'illuminate'
	c-ɑŋ-han	'food'	<chan	'eat' (of a monk)
	c-ɑŋ-kəh	'chopstick'	<ckəh	'pick at'
	k-ɑŋ-wah	'insufficiency'	<kwah	'be insufficient'
	k-ɑŋ-wɔl	'agitation, spinning'	<kwɔl	'be agitated,spinning'
	t-uŋ-wəə	'making'	<twəə	'make, do' (an apparent neologism)
	k-ɑɲ-cɔp	'wrapping'	<kcɔp	'wrap'

as well as of the causative infix:

b-ɑŋ- 'əəl	'frighten away'	<b'əəl	'take flight, start'

There are also other forms, less frequently attested, for both the causative and the nominalizing infix, which are more idiosyncratic:

(18) a. *cap* 'grasp' provides both (regular) *camnap* and idiosyncratic *cambap* 'act of grasping; wrestling hold';
b. *rɔliej* 'melt (intr.)' provides the irregular *rumliej* 'melt (trans.)';[7]
c. *c-umŋ- ɯɯ* 'illness' < chɯɯɯ 'pain'

Finally, there are cases where both the form and the meaning of the infix are 'irregular'. The verb *kwiəl* 'to herd, guard a flock' yields the AGENT nominal *k-oŋ-wiəl* 'herder'. The noun *slək* 'leaf' yields the derived metaphorical nominal *s-an-lək* 'leaf, sheet of paper'.

This variation in the form of the labile infix accords well with the hypothesis that the reduced versions of two alternative forms are often the result of a common deletion processes which deletes syllable codas without reference to their exact structure. (It is easier to motivate deletion than insertion!)

Our best evidence for secretion from a comparative perspective is the fact that not all the of the languages of the Austroasiatic family exhibit in-

[7] This irregularity is only apparent: the surface form of the verb [rɔliəj] is probably a result of the insertion of an inorganic vowel between the first two consonants, the sequence [rl] being one of the few which are not tolerated word-initially in Khmer.

fixation. Vietnamese, for example, does not, and neither do the other languages of the Viet-Muong subfamily. Infixation is general among those Austroasiatic languages which still maintain the inherited iambic word as a favorite structure. Among them (though this list is very fragmentary) are Mundari (Osada 1992), Khmu (Svantesson 1983; Premsrirat 1987), Minor Mlabri (Rischel 1995), Jeh (Cohen 1966), Bahnar (Banker 1964), and Jah-Hut (Diffloth 1976).These are the only languages of Austroasiatic whose word stems exhibit what Matisoff 1973 has called a sesquisyllabic structure: a large part of the lexical stock of these languages is iambic, like the word *device*, or the phrase *good night.* And, as in these, the anacrusic presyllable undergoes considerable phonetic reduction (just as *good night* reduces to [gnajt]). In Khmer and other sesquisyllabic languages like Khmu (Premsrirat 1987), the anacrusic syllable, canonically [T(R)V(N)], optionally reduces to [T]; in others, like Sapuan (Jacq and Sidwell 1999), this reduction is a fait accompli (cf. Haiman 1998, and other references there). The fact that infixation is pretty much restricted to those languages which exhibit reduction of the anacrusic syllable of sesquisyllabic words strongly suggests that these two phenomena may be related as I am proposing.

Our best evidence for the plausibility of excrescence from a typological or cross-linguistic perspective is that exactly the same process of reinterpretation via secretion of an original register distinction has taken place demonstrably recently in another totally unrelated but very well-studied language. The excreted derivation affix is the infinitival suffixed syllable *-re* in Romanian. As recently as 1905 (Tiktin 1905) the formal contrast [X] ~ [X+*re*] could be construed as purely phonetic register alternations: there existed different (formal vs. casual) pronunciations of the infinitive. Already by this time, however, [X+*re*] could be interpreted as {Verb} + {derivational nominalizing affix} (ibid. 112), *and it is this use alone which is correct in contemporary Romanian.* Given our knowledge of the history of Romanian, we can say that only secretion (more strictly, exaptation, the reanalysis of an existing morpheme) has been at work. In Latin, the *-re* suffix marked nothing but the infinitive. But in modern Romanian, {X+*re*} words are not only semantically but also morphologically derived nouns. Deverbal nouns in *-re* are (like other nouns in final /e/) feminine in gender, take the singular definite article *-a*, form their plurals by changing the final /e/ to /i/, in which case they take the feminine plural definite article *-le*, and so forth:

(19) dure 'to hurt' : durere 'pain'
minca 'to eat' : mincare 'food'
aduna 'assemble' : adunare 'assembly'
uni 'unite' : unire 'union'
našte 'be born' : naštere 'birth'
întreba 'ask' : întrebare 'question'

(20) a. tace 'be silent' : tacere 'silence'
b. dupa o scurta tacere
'after a short silence'

(21) a. ave(a) 'have' :avere 'estate'
b. o avere mica
'a small estate'

(22) a. ieši 'exit' : iešire 'outburst'
b. iešir-i-le sale nervoase
outburst.PL.the.FEM.PL. her.FEM.PL. nervous.FEM.PL.
'her nervous outbursts'

(23) a. convorbi 'converse' : convorbire 'conversation'
b. convorbir-i-le telefonice
conversation.PL.the.FEM.PL. telephonic.FEM.PL.
'telephone conversations'

(24) a. fi 'be' :fire 'existence'
b. o fire independenta
a.FEM.SG. existence independent.FEM.SG.
'an independent existence'

(25) a. sta 'stand' : stare 'state'
b. stare de razboi
'state of war'

As in Khmer, there has been analogical extension. The *-re* derivational suffix occurs productively on verb stems which never had a final *-re*: from French, we have *epuiza-re* 'exhaustion' (<épuiser 'exhaust'), from Slavic , we encounter *iubi-re* 'love'(< Russian *l'ubi-t'* 'to love'); from Hungarian, *otarĭ-re* 'decision' (< Hungarian *határoz-ni* 'to decide').

Kurylowicz's IV law (1949) might seem to provide an alternative explanation for the reassignment of meanings in these cases of secretion. This is not the case. This law, it will be recalled, states that when analogy creates a novel form like *cows*, next to the inherited form (*kine*), then it is the novel form which will carry the former's basic meaning, while the archaic form, if it survives at all, will be relegated to some peripheral status. Here, in the cases we have been discussing, the novel (reduced) forms do carry on the older meaning of the inherited verbs, but these novel forms are created not by analogy but by the familiar erosion of sound change. The older inherited forms with which they *compete* and which they *relegate* to forms with which they *compete* and which they *relegate* to other meanings do not have the archaic or marginal connotations of traditional opaque survivors like *kine* and *brethren:* they have an entirely new meaning, which is (I believe) exclusively suggested by the iconic principle that more is more.

A final word. Infixation is deservedly a rare phenomenon. Even within Khmer, I am not certain that this mechanism is the only one which is responsible for the infixes that occur. In other languages, totally different mechanisms are undoubtedly at work: entrapment (Harris 1993), morpheme metathesis (Haiman 1977), and perhaps there are a plethora of others. The rarity and typological implausibility of infixation is perfectly compatible with the absence of a single well-defined general process whereby such an expensive and counterintuitive structure can arise.

References

Babyonyshev, M. and E. Gibson. 1999. The Complexity of Nested Structures in Japanese. *Language* 75(3): 423-450.

Banker, E. 1964. Bahnar Affixation. *Mon-Khmer Studies* 1: 99-118.

Bierbach, M. 1983. Les composés du type porte-feuille. *Travaux de linguistique et de littérature* 21: 137-55.

Bopp, F. 1816. *Über das Konjugations-System der Sanskritsprache.* Frankfurt: Andreäische Buchhandlung.

Borer, H. this volume. *Endo-Skeletal vs. Exo-Skeletal Explanations.*

Bybee, J. et. al. 1990. On the Asymmetries in the Affixation of Grammatical Material. *Studies in Typology and Diachrony* , eds. W. Croft et. al., 1-42. Amsterdam: Benjamins.

Chomsky, N. and G. Miller. 1963. Introduction to the Formal Analysis of Natural Languages. *Handbook of Mathematical Psychology* vol. 2, eds. R. Luce et. al., 269-321. New York: Wiley.

Cohen, P. 1966. Presyllables and Reduplication in Jeh. *Mon-Khmer Studies* 2: 31-40.

Deletant, D. 1983. *Colloquial Romanian.* New York: Routledge.

Diffloth, G. 1976. Jah-Hut, An Austroasiatic Language of Malaysia. *Southeast Asian Linguistic Studies*, ed. N. D. Liem, 73-118. Canberra: Research School of Pacific Studies, Australian National University.

Givon, T. 1971. Historical Syntax and Synchronic Morphology. *Chicago Linguistic Society* 7: 394-415.

Haiman 1977. Reinterpretation. *Language* 53: 312-28.

Haiman, J. 1985. *Natural Syntax.* Cambridge: Cambridge University Press.

Haiman, J. 1998. Possible Origins of Infixation in Khmer. *Studies in Language* 21: 597-617.

Haiman, J. and N. Ourn. (to appear). *Nouns and Verbs in Khmer.*

Harris, A. 1993. Explaining the Origins of Word-Internal Clitics. Paper Presented at the International Conference on Historical Linguistics, 1993.

Hawkins, J. and A. Cutler. 1988. Psychological Factors in Morphological Asymmetry. *Explaining Language Universals,* ed. J. Hawkins, 280-317. Oxford: Blackwell.

Hopper, P. 1997. When Grammar and Discourse Clash. *Essays on Language Function and Language Type*, eds. S. J. Bybee, J. Haiman and S. Thompson, 231-47. Amsterdam: Benjamins.

Hopper, P. and S. Thompson. 1985. The Iconicity of the Universal Categories 'Noun' and 'Verb'. *Iconicity in Syntax*, ed. J. Haiman, 151-86. Amsterdam: Benjamins.

Huffman, F. 1970. *Modern Spoken Cambodian.* New Haven: Yale University Press.

Jacq, P. and P. Sidwell. 1999. *Sapuan.* Munich: Lincom Europa.

Jakobson, R. 1936. Beitrag zur allgemeinen Kasuslehre. *Selected Writings,* vol. 2, 23-71. The Hague: Mouton.

Jespersen, O. 1921 [1964]. *Language: Its Nature, Development, and Origin.* New York: Norton.

Klingebiel, K. 1989. *Noun + Verb Compounding in Western Romance.* University of California Publications in Linguistics 113. Berkeley: University of California Press.

Kurylowicz, J. 1949. La nature des proces dits analogiques. *Acta Linguistica* 5: 121-38.

Lass, R. 1990. How to Do Things with Junk. *Journal of Linguistics* 26: 79-102.

Lewitz, S. 1968. Notes sur la dérivation par affixation en Khmer moderne. *Revue de l'école nationale des langues orientales* 5: 117-27.

Long, S. 1975. *Očerki po leksikologii kxmerskogo Jazyka.* Moscow: Nauka.

Marchand, H. 1969. *The Categories and Types of Present-Day English Word Formation.* 2nd ed. Munich: C.H. Beck'sche Verlagsbuchhandlung.

Matisoff. J. 1973. *A Grammar of Lahu.* Berkeley: University of California Press.

Meillet, A. 1912 [1958]. L'èvolution de formes grammaticales. Reprinted in *Linguistique historique et linguistique générale*, 130-49. Paris: Champion.

Osada, T. 1992. *A Reference Grammar of Mundari.* Tokyo: Tokyo University of Foreign Studies.

Pinnow, H.-J. 1963. The Position of the Munda Languages within the Austroasiatic Language Family. *Linguistic Comparison in Southeast Asia and the Pacific*, ed. H. Shorto, 140-5. London: School of Oriental and African Studies.

Premsrirat, S. 1987. A Khmu Grammar. *Khmu, a Minority Language of Thailand,* 1-144. Canberra: Research School of Pacific Studies, Australian National University.

Rischel, J. 1995. *Minor Mlabri.* Copenhagen: Museum Tusculanum Press.

Roeper, T. and M. Siegel. 1978. A Lexical Transformation for Verbal Compounds. *Linguistic Inquiry* 9: 199-260.

Schachter, P. 1973. Focus and Relativization. *Language.* 49: 19-46.

Schiffrin, D. 1983. *Discourse Markers.* Cambridge: Cambridge University Press.

Schmidt, P. 1906. *Die Mon-Khmer Völker: Ein Bindeglied zwischen Völkern Zentralasiens und Austronesiens.* Braunschweig: Friedrich Vieweg und Sohn.

Selkirk, E. 1982. *The Syntax of Words.* Cambridge: MIT Press.

Shorto, H. 1962. *A Dictionary of Spoken Mon.* Oxford: Oxford University Press.

Svantesson, J.-O. 1983. *Kammu Phonology and Morphology.* Lund: CWK Gleerup.

Tiktin, H. 1905. *Rumänisches Elementarbuch.* Heidelberg: Carl Winter.

Williams, E. 1981. On the Notions 'Lexically Related' and 'Head of a Word'. *Linguistic Inquiry* 12: 245-74.

6

Efficiency and Complexity in Grammars: Three General Principles[1]

JOHN A. HAWKINS

1 Introduction

An interesting general correlation appears to be emerging between variation data in performance, in languages that dispose of several structures of a given type, and the fixed conventions of grammars, in languages with fewer structures of the same type. The performance data come from corpus frequencies and processing experiments, the grammatical data from our expanding samples of languages and from the growing number of languages that have now been subjected to in-depth analysis.

The Keenan-Comrie Accessibility Hierarchy was an early example of such a correlation, whereby an implicational hierarchy in cross-linguistic relativization possibilities (SU>DO> IO/OBL>GEN) was argued to correlate with ease of relativization and with relativization preferences in a language (English) with many relativizable positions (Keenan and Comrie 1977, Keenan 1975, Keenan and Hawkins 1987). The preferred word orders in languages with choices have also been argued to be those that are productively grammaticalized in languages with fixed orders, and in almost exact proportion to their degree of preference, in Hawkins (1994, 1998a, 2001).

The goal of this paper is to define a hypothesis concerning the relationship between performance and grammars, and to propose three general prin-

[1] I would like to thank Jeff Elman for a very helpful and detailed review of the original version of this paper.

The Nature of Explanation in Linguistic Theory.
John Moore and Maria Polinsky (eds.).

ciples of efficiency and complexity that appear to underlie the preferences of performance and their correlations with grammars. The hypothesis will be referred to as the Performance-Grammar Correspondence Hypothesis (PGCH). The three principles are supported by data from several areas of syntax and morpho-syntax. If this hypothesized correspondence between performance and grammars is even partially correct, it needs to be seriously pursued in order to see how much of core syntax and of cross-linguistic syntactic variation can be derived from whatever explains the preferences of performance. If there is a common explanation for both, this will have far-reaching consequences for the ultimate explanatory basis of grammatical conventions.

The PGCH is defined in (1):

(1) PERFORMANCE-GRAMMAR CORRESPONDENCE HYPOTHESIS
Grammars have conventionalized syntactic structures in proportion to their degree of preference in performance, as evidenced by frequency of use and ease of processing.

From (1) we can derive a number of predictions, including those of (2):

(2) Predictions of the PGCH
   a. If a structure A is preferred over an A′ of the same structural type in performance, then A will be more productively grammaticalized, in proportion to its degree of preference; if A and A′ are more equally preferred, then both A and A′ will be productive in grammars.
   b. If there is a preference ranking A>B>C>D among structures of a common type in performance, then there will be a corresponding hierarchy of grammatical conventions (with cut-off points and declining frequencies of languages).
   c. If two preferences P and P′ are in (partial) opposition, then there will be grammatical variation, with both P and P′ being conventionalized, each in proportion to the degree of motivation for that preference in a given language type.

In order to test these predictions we need performance data from languages with a plurality of structures of a common type, e.g. different orderings of the same phrasal constituents, or relativizations on different positions of a clause using the same relative clause type (e.g. a Filler-Gap construction), and so on. We then need cross-linguistic grammatical data from languages with fewer structures of these types, i.e. with more conventionalized and fixed phrasal orderings, and with relativizations on fewer positions. If the degree of preference in performance matches the relative productivity of structures in the cross-linguistic grammatical conventions, then the PGCH will be supported. If not, it will not be.

More generally, we need to identify general principles of preference in performance and to search for corresponding principles in grammars. In this way we can rise above a discussion of individual structures and languages, with their possible idiosyncracies, and focus on general properties of preference that hold for a large number of structures in a large number of languages. This paper will attempt to do this by outlining three general principles.

2 Principle 1: MINIMIZE DOMAINS

One clear principle of efficiency and complexity involves the size of the syntactic domain within which a given grammatical relation can be processed. How great is the distance separating interrelated items and how much material needs to be processed simultaneously with the processing of the relation? Hawkins (1994, 1998a, 1999a, 2001) argues that there is a correlation between performance and grammar with regard to domain sizes. In those languages and structures in which domain sizes can vary in performance, we see a clear preference for the smallest possible domains. In those languages and structures in which domain sizes have been grammatically fixed, we see the same preference in the conventions.

(3) MINIMIZE DOMAINS
The human processor prefers to minimize the connected sequences of linguistic forms and their conventionally associated syntactic and semantic properties in which relations of combination and/or dependency are processed. The degree of this preference will be proportional to the number of relations whose domains can be minimized in competing sequences or structures, and to the extent of the minimization difference in each domain.

COMBINATION is defined here as: two categories A and B are in a relation of combination iff they occur within the same syntactic mother phrase or maximal projection. And DEPENDENCY is defined as: two categories A and B are in a relation of dependency iff the processing of B requires access to

A for the assignment of syntactic or semantic properties to B with respect to which B is zero-specified or ambiguously or polysemously specified.[2]

2.1 Domain Minimization in Phrasal Combination Domains

The immediate constituents (ICs) of a phrase can typically be recognized on the basis of less than all the words dominated by that phrase. Some orderings reduce the number of words needed to recognize all ICs compared with other orderings, making IC recognition faster. Compare (4a) and (4b):

(4) a. The gamekeeper $_{VP}$[looked $_{PP1}$[through his binoculars]
1 2 3 4 ...
$_{PP2}$[into the blue but slightly overcast sky]].
... 5

b. The gamekeeper $_{VP}$[looked $_{PP2}$[into the blue but slightly
1 2 3 4 5 6 ...
overcast sky] $_{PP1}$[through his binoculars]].
... 7 8 9

The three items, V, PP1, PP2 (where the higher subscript refers to a phrase with greater or equal length in words) can be recognized on the basis of five words in (4a), compared with nine in (4b), assuming that head categories such as P immediately project to mother nodes such as PP, enabling a parser to construct them in the assignment of on-line structural representations (cf. Hawkins 1993, Jackendoff 1977, Pollard and Sag 1994). In Hawkins (in prep) I argue that the greater efficiency of (4a) applies both in production and in comprehension and I define a Phrasal Combination Domain as follows:

(5) PHRASAL COMBINATION DOMAIN (PCD)
The PCD for a mother node M and its I(mmediate) C(onstituent)s consists of the smallest possible string of terminal elements (plus all M-dominated non-terminals over the terminals) on the basis of which the processor can construct M and its ICs.

To identify PCDs, proceed from the terminal node that constructs the first IC to the terminal node that constructs the last IC (at least one of which will

---

[2] Notice that the definition for DEPENDENCY given here is a processing one, in terms of the required access by the processor to one category while processing another. This is, I believe, the most descriptively adequate approach, see Hawkins (in prep.) for extensive discussion.

also construct M). The greater efficiency of (4a) can then be captured by dividing the number of ICs by the number of words in each PCD and by expressing the result as a percentage, following the procedure in Hawkins (1994: ch.3).[3] The higher the percentage, the more efficient the ordering is, since the same constituency information can be assigned on the basis of less terminal material:

(4a) VP PCD: IC-to-word ratio of 3/5 = 60%
(4b) VP PCD: IC-to-word ratio of 3/9 = 33%

My earlier principle of Early Immediate Constituents (EIC, cf. Hawkins 1990, 1994) is now subsumed under Minimize Domains and can be redefined as follows:

(6) EARLY IMMEDIATE CONSTITUENTS (EIC)
The human processor prefers linear orders that minimize PCDs (by maximizing their IC-to-word ratios), in proportion to the minimization difference between competing orders.

EIC's predictions remain as they were.

A possible explanation for the EIC preference is that small PCDs reduce simultaneous processing in working memory. If, in (4a), the same VP constituency information can be assigned on the basis of five words, whereas nine words are required in (4b), then the production and comprehension of phrase structure can be accomplished sooner, there will be fewer additional (phonological, morphological, syntactic and semantic) decisions that need to be made simultaneously with this one, and less demands on working memory (cf. Hawkins 1999b, 2001).

2.1.1 Performance Data Testing EIC

For a language like English, EIC defines a quantitative preference for shorter PPs before longer ones overall, and the degree of this preference is predicted to be directly proportional to the length difference between them. Structures like (4a) and (4b) were examined in which the two PPs were

[3] See Hawkins (1994: Ch.3) and also Wasow (2002) for discussion and testing of alternative ways of quantifying the EIC preference, in terms of IC-to-word ratios and IC-to-nonIC ratios using different non-IC nodes (e.g. phrasal nodes only or all non-terminal nodes). Wasow (ibid.) concludes that the different quantification procedures are statistically undistinguishable and that the simpler IC-to-word ratio fares as well as any.

freely permutable with truth-conditional equivalence (Hawkins 1999b).[4] Only 15% were ordered long before short, with 67% short before long and 18% of equal length (n=71). The short before long orders plus the equal length PPs (in which either ordering is as efficient as it can possibly be) collectively account for 85% of the data. Moreover, within the 15% of long before short PPs, almost two thirds involved only a one-word difference in length and there was a gradual reduction in long before short orderings the bigger the length difference, as predicted by (6). This is shown in (7), in which the top row gives the figures for short before long, PP^1 before PP2, and the second row long before short.

(7) n=323	$PP_2 > PP_1$ by 1 word	by 2-4 words	by 5-6	by 7+
[V PP1 PP2]	60% (58)	86% (108)	94% (31)	99% (68)
[V PP2 PP1]	40% (38)	14% (17)	6% (2)	1% (1)

Data from Japanese reveal an equally principled set of preferences, but for the mirror-image long before short pattern. This is predicted by EIC. Postposing a heavier phrase to the right in English shortens PCDs and increases IC-to-word ratios. Preposing heavy phrases in a head-final language has the same effect, since the relevant constructing categories (V for VP, P for PP, etc) are now on the right. In a structure like $[\{[\text{NP P}]_{PP1}, [\text{NP P}]_{PP2}\}\ \text{V}]_{VP}$, the PCD for VP will proceed from the first P(ostposition) encountered to the verb, and will be shorter if the shorter PP1 is adjacent to the verb than if the longer PP2 is adjacent. The preferred pattern overall should be long before short in Japanese, therefore, and the degree of this preference should increase with increasing relative weights. In this way the time course from construction of the first PP to the VP-final verb will be faster than if the long PP is adjacent to V.

Consider some illustrative data collected by Kaoru Horie and involving orderings of $[\{NP_o, PP_m\}\ V]$, where NP_o stands for a direct object containing an accusative case particle *o*, in combination with a postpositional phrase (PP_m, i.e. with right-peripheral projection from P to its mother PP, hence the *m* subscript on the right). I assume that o̲ is the projecting and constructing category for this case-marked NP, paralleling the final postposition in PP and the final V in VP, and that these heads have left-branching phrasal sisters that are processed bottom-up. I.e. the NP within PP_m is

---

4 The corpus that was used for sequences of PPs following intransitive verbs consisted of 500 pages of written English, comprising 200 pages of fiction, 225 pages of nonfiction, and 75 pages of a diary. Eight different texts were used, and the full references and page numbers are given in Appendix 1 of Hawkins (1999b).

processed before PP itself is constructed on the basis of P, the NP within NP_o before the case particle is processed projecting to a case-marked NP, and both are processed before the containing VP is constructed on the basis of V. The distance and time course from the first constructing category (P or *o*) to V is then shorter when the longer sister phrase precedes the shorter one. I.e. [PP_m NP_o V] is preferred when $PP_m > NP_o$, and [NP_o PP_m V] is preferred when $NP_o > PP_m$. An example of the relevant sentence type is given in (8):

(8) Tanaka ga {[sono hon o] [Hanako kara]} katta.
Tanaka SU that book OBJ Hanako from bought,
'Tanaka bought that book from Hanako.'

The data (cf. Hawkins 1994:152) reveal that each additional word of relative weight resulted in a higher proportion of long before short orders, as shown in (9), in which IC_2 refers to the longer phrase, whether NP_o or PP_m, and IC_1 to the shorter.[5]

(9) n=153	$IC_2 > IC_1$ by 1-2 words	by 3-4	by 5-8	by 9+
[IC_2 IC_1 V]	66% (59)	72% (21)	83% (20)	91% (10)
[IC_1 IC_2 V]	34% (30)	28% (8)	17% (4)	9% (1)

An additional 91 sequences had ICs of equal length (total n = 244). The preferred long before short sequences plus those with equal lengths (in which either order was as efficient as it could possibly be) amounted to 201/244 = 82%, the dispreferred short before long to 43/244 = 18%. A full 30 of these 43 involved a length difference of only 1-2 words and hence EIC defined its weakest possible dispreference in these cases. Further support for the long before short preference in Japanese is given in Yamashita and Chang (2001).

2.1.2 EIC in Grammars

Grammatical conventions across languages reveal the same EIC preference for minimal domains. Minimal PCDs are preferred in the vast majority of languages, and as PCD sizes increase, the relevant orders are conventionalized in progressively fewer languages and structures.

[5] The Japanese data in (9) are taken from three written texts referenced in Hawkins (1994).

The cross-category ordering correlations in Greenberg's (1963) universals, two of which are presented in (10) and (11), illustrate the minimal domain preference in VP and PP respectively:

(10) a. $_{VP}[V\ _{PP}[P\ NP]]$ = 161 (41.4%)
IC-to-word: 2/2 = 100%
b. $[[NP\ P]_{PP}\ V]_{VP}$ = 204 (52.4%)
IC-to-word: 2/2 = 100%
c. $_{VP}[V\ [NP\ P]_{PP}]$ = 18 (4.6%)
IC-to-word: 2/4 = 50%
d. $[_{PP}[P\ NP]\ V]_{VP}$ = 6 (1.5%)
IC-to-word: 2/4 = 50%

Assume: V = 1 word; P = 1; NP = 2
EIC-preferred (10a)+(10b) = 365/389 (94%)

(11) a. $_{PP}[P\ _{NP}[N\ PossP]]$ = 134 (39.9%)
b. $[[PossP\ N]_{NP}\ P]_{PP}$ = 177 (52.7%)
c. $_{PP}[P\ [PossP\ N]_{NP}]$ = 14 (4.2%)
d. $[_{NP}[N\ PossP]\ P]_{PP}$ = 11 (3.3%)

EIC-preferred (11a)+(11b) = 311/336 (93%)

The adjacency of V and P, and of P and N, guarantees the smallest possible domain for recognition and production of the two ICs in question (V and PP within VP, P and NP within PP): two words suffice, hence 100% IC-to-word ratios. In the non-adjacent domains of the (c) and (d) orders, the ratios are significantly lower and exemplifying languages are significantly fewer. The preferred (a) and (b) structures collectively account for 94% or 93% of all languages (see Dryer 1992 for the data of (10), Hawkins 1983 for (11)). These data support prediction (2a) above.

It is patterns like this that have motivated the head-initial (or VO) and head-final (OV) parameters in typological and generative research. The two language types are mirror images of one another, and EIC offers an explanation for this: both (a) and (b) are optimally efficient. They are equally good orderings for phrase structure recognition, and we expect both to be productive by prediction (2a) above.

When non-optimal domains are grammatically permitted they appear to be arranged in hierarchies whose internal organization reflects the complexity of the relevant domain, as predicted by (2b). For example, it has been well-known since Miller and Chomsky (1963), Bever (1970) and Kimball (1973) that center embeddings are hard structures to process. EIC predicts that the larger a center-embedded constituent is relative to its sisters, the greater will be its degree of dispreference. For example, the heavier an NP relative to a PP in $_{VP}$[V NP PP] and the longer the PCD for this containing VP, the more infrequent and the harder to process this structure is in English performance, as shown in Hawkins (1994), Stallings (1998) and Wasow (2002) using both frequency data and processing experiments. Correlating with this are hierarchies of tolerance for center embeddings of different degrees of complexity in cross-linguistic grammatical conventions, cf. Hawkins (1994).

For example, in the center-embedding environment between a preposition and the head noun within a sister NP, i.e. $_{PP}$[P $_{NP}$[__ N]], we find the following implicational pattern:

(12) If a language is prepositional, then if RelN then PosspN [Exceptionless]; if PosspN then AdjN [Strongly supported in Hawkins (1983)]; and if AdjN then DemN [Massively supported but e.g. Sango is exceptional, cf. Dryer (1993)].

and the following distribution of preposed to postposed noun modifiers in the prepositional languages of Hawkins' (1983) sample:

(13) Prep lgs:	RelN	1%	NRel	99%
	PosspN	12%	NPossp	88%
	AdjN	32%	NAdj	68%
	DemN	49%	NDem	51%

Relative clauses are on aggregate longer than possessive phrases, which are on aggregate longer than single-word adjectives. As center embedded categories of increasing aggregate length intervene between P and N, the distance between them increases and IC-to-word ratios decline. As they do so the, the numbers of attested languages decline, and the proportion of languages with postposed rather than preposed modifiers increases. Indeed the only center-embedded category that is productive at all is the single-word adjective (at 32%). Prenominal possessive phrases are found in only 12% of prepositional languages, and prenominal relatives in only 1%. Demonstrative determiners construct the same phrase (NP) as head nouns in the theory of Hawkins (1993, 1994) and both [P [DemN]] and [P [NDem]] are therefore equally efficent.

Grammatical structures are avoided across languages in proportion to EIC's dispreference, therefore, resulting in this center-embedding hierarchy.

2.2 Domain Minimization and Adjacency

More generally, principle 1 (MINIMIZE DOMAINS) can be used to explain adjacency effects in syntax. Categories that prefer adjacency are argued in Hawkins (2001, in preparation) to be those that contract more combinatorial and/or dependency relations with one another, and whose processing domains are minimal when adjacent. Hawkins (ibid.) proposes the following hypothesis:

(14) ADJACENCY HYPOTHESIS
Given a phrase {H, {X, Y}}, H = a head category and X and Y phrases that are potentially adjacent to H, then the more combinatorial and dependency relations whose processing domains can be minimized when X is adjacent to H, and the greater the minimization difference between adjacent X and adjacent Y in each domain, the more H and X will be adjacent.

Consider again the PP sequences in the English corpus data of (7). Hawkins (1999b) examined not only syntactic weight and the relative sizes of phrasal combination domains, but also various relations of semantic dependency holding between the (intransitive) verb and the PPs. Two entailment tests were conducted. The first, the Verb Entailment Test, asked: does V PP1 PP2 entail V alone, or does V have a meaning dependent on either PP1 or PP2? For example, 'the man waited for his son in the rain' entails 'the man waited'; but 'the man counted on his son in old age' does not entail 'the man counted'. The second, the Pro-Verb Entailment Test, asked: can V be replaced by some general Pro-verb, or does one of the PPs require that exact V for its interpretation. Thus, 'the girl played on the playground' entails 'the girl did something on the playground'; but 'the girl depended on her mother' does not entail 'the girl did something on her mother'. When there was a dependency between V and one of the PPs by these tests, then 73% (151/206) had the dependent PP (PP_d) adjacent to V, i.e. their processing domains were minimal. 82% (265/323) of the sequences in (7) had short PP before long PP, i.e. minimal PCDs. For PPs that were BOTH shorter AND semantically dependent, the adjacency to V was even higher, at 96% (102/106). The combined adjacency effect exerted by semantic dependency and EIC was statistically significantly higher than for each factor alone.

I conclude that the more syntactic and semantic processing operations whose domains can be minimized in a given order, the greater is the preference for that order since each combinatorial and dependency relation can then be processed faster and with fewer simultaneous demands on working memory.[6]

The full figures illustrating this interaction are given in (15), in which P_d is the PP semantically dependent on V by the Verb or Pro-Verb entailment tests and P_i is the semantically independent PP by these tests:[7]

(15)	$P_d > P_i$ by			$P_d = P_i$	$P_i > P_d$		
n=206	5+	2-4	1		1	2-4	5+
[V P_d P_i]	7% (2)	33% (6)	74% (17)	83% (24)	92% (23)	96% (49)	100% (30)
[V P_i P_d]	93% (28)	67% (13)	26% (6)	17% (5)	8% (2)	4% (2)	0% (0)

I would argue further that these entailment tests provide empirical evidence in favor of assigning COMPLEMENT rather than ADJUNCT status to the P_d. If the relevant V or P cannot be semantically interpreted independently of the other, this would appear to constitute a sufficient criterion for complementhood and for the listing of the P_d within the lexical co-occurrence frame for the V. These data therefore reveal a preference for complements before adjuncts in performance, and an almost exceptionless preference for short complements before adjuncts (and before longer complements in sequences of two complements).

Complements also prefer adjacency to their heads in the basic grammatical orders of numerous phrases in English and other languages and are generated in a position closer to the head than adjuncts in the grammars of

---

[6] There is an interesting processing difference between lexical-semantic dependencies like *the man counted on his son in old age* (in which the verb *counted* is dependent on *on his son* for the assignment of its appropriate meaning, but not on *in old age*) and the phrasal combination data and EIC effects. Minimizing the domains for processing the latter can be argued to benefit both the speaker and the hearer (Hawkins 1998a, in preparation), since the relevant (phrasal combination) domains are defined on the basis of the construction or projection potential of terminal elements, and these constructions/projections can define the same domain minimizations are being produced in an on-line fashion (within the Formulator of a production model such as Levelt 1989) or comprehended within a comprehension model. For the lexical-semantic dependencies, on the other hand, the speaker is at an advantage since he/she knows the intended sense of *count* in advance, and yet production data are still highly sensitive to the minimal domains on the basis of which the hearer can disambiguate!

[7] In corresponding tables cited in Hawkins (1999b, 2001) I included five additional sequences, making 211 in all, in which both the PPs involved an interdependency with V by the entailment tests, but one involved more dependencies than the other. I have excluded these five here, making a total of 206 sequences, in all of which one PP is completely independent of V by both entailment tests discussed in the main text, while the other PP is interdependent with V by at least one entailment test.

Jackendoff (1977) and Pollard and Sag (1987). Tomlin's (1986) Verb Object Bonding principle provides further cross-linguistic support for this by pointing to languages in which it is impossible or dispreferred for adjuncts to intervene between a verbal head and its subcategorized direct object complement. The Adjacency Hypothesis of (14) provides an explanation for this. There are more combinatorial and dependency relations linking complements to their heads whose processing domains can be minimized under adjacency, compared to the relations linking adjuncts and heads. Adjacency of complements is predicted in grammars, therefore, for the same reason that more interdependent and combinatorial processing results in tighter adjacency between V and PP_d in English performance.

Complements are listed in a lexical co-occurrence frame defined by, and activated by, a specific head (e.g. a verb). Adjuncts are not so listed and occur in a wide variety of phrases with which they are semantically compatible. Processing the lexical co-occurrence frame of a verb therefore favors a minimal surface domain in which the verb can be linked to its complements as rapidly as possible.

There are also more productive relations of semantic and syntactic interdependency between heads and complements than between heads and adjuncts, i.e. more cases in which the meaning or grammar of one of these categories requires access to the other for its assignment. E.g. a direct object receives a theta-role from the verb (typically a subtype of Dowty's (1991) Proto-Patient theta-role); adjuncts do not receive theta-roles. The direct object is also syntactically required by a transitive verb; adjuncts are not syntactically required sisters. A transitive verb in turn regularly undergoes what we might call FUNCTION CATEGORY RANGE REDUCTION (following Keenan 1979) by a direct object NP. Compare the different interpretations of *run* in *run the advertisement/run the water/run the race (in the afternoon)*. The verb is lexically dependent on the choice of direct object for its interpretation here, not on an adjunct phrase such as *in the afternoon*. Similarly an intransitive verb is frequently dependent on a PP complement for range reduction (e.g. *count on X*). Adjuncts may, however, be lexically dependent on a verb by Keenan's principle, as function categories (compare the different interpretations of *smoothly* in *sailing smoothly/landing smoothly/talking smoothly*), but the number of semantic and syntactic interdependencies linking them to their heads are fewer, since adjuncts do not receive theta-roles, are not grammatically required, and their heads are not lexically dependent on them.

To these considerations must be added EIC effects. Direct object complements are significantly shorter on aggregate than PP adjuncts or complements (Hawkins 1994), hence their relative adjacency to the verb is predicted for constituent recognition. In fact, given that adjuncts are less interdependent with their heads than complements, the current theory predicts that they will only be adjacent to their heads if they are shorter than accompanying complements, thereby minimizing PCDs.

I therefore see adjacency as motivated by domain minimizations in syntactic and semantic processing. In this way the surface domains in which phrase structure recognition, lexical-semantic dependencies, theta-role assignments and complement relations can be processed will each be smaller and more efficient and will involve less simultaneous processing and less demands on working memory as each relation is processed.

2.3 Domain Minimization in Filler-Gap Domains

When a dependency exists between a c-commanding category A and an asymmetrically c-commanded category B dominated by a sister to A, namely C, then categories A and C can regularly be adjacent, but the precise positioning of the dependent B will depend on its role within category C. Consider the relation that holds between the nominal head of a relative clause and the gap, subcategorizor or resumptive pronoun within the clause that is co-indexed with the head. I have argued in Hawkins (1999a) that numerous hierarchies can be set up on the basis of the increasing domain sizes for relative clause processing, measured in terms of the number of nodes and structural relations that need to be computed in order to match the relative clause head with the co-indexed gap, subcategorizor or resumptive pronoun. One of these is the original Keenan and Comrie (1977) Accessibility Hierarchy, which is formulated as (16) in Comrie (1989) (SU=subject, DO=direct object, IO=indirect object, OBL=oblique, GEN=genitive):

(16) SU > DO > IO/OBL > GEN

Examples of relative clauses formed on each of these positions are given in (17):

(17) a. the professor$_i$ [that O$_i$ wrote the letter] *SU*
b. the professor$_i$ [that the student knows O$_i$] *DO*
c. the professor$_i$ [that the student showed the book to O$_i$] *IO/OBL*
d. the professor$_i$ [that the student knows his$_i$ son] *GEN*

Some performance support for this hierarchy as a complexity ranking comes from a repetition experiment conducted by Keenan and Hawkins (1987) on English speakers, children and adults. The prediction was that repetition accuracy would correlate with postions on the hierarchy, subjects being easiest. The data, shown in (18), bear this out (GEN-SU stands for relativization on a genitive within a subject, GEN-DO for relativization on a genitive within a direct object as in (17d)):

(18) Repetition accuracies for relativization in English

	SU	DO	IO	OBL	GEN-SU	GEN-DO
Adults	64%	62.5%	57%	52%	31%	36%
Children	63%	51%	50%	35%	21%	18%

The relative ranking SU > DO has been corroborated by a number of further studies in the psycholinguistic literature. For example, Pickering and Shillcock (1992) found significant reaction time differences between the two positions in a self-paced reading experiment (cf. Hawkins 1999a for further references).

As the surface domains grow that must be processed in order to link the relative clause head with the position relativized on, the amount of simultaneous processing and the demands on working memory increase. If the position relativized on is a gap, then the very identification of this position is difficult and requires access to the gap's subcategorizor and/or its structural environment, and to the filler (i.e. the relative clause head) upon which the gap is dependent. All of these considerations are reflected in the definition of a Filler-Gap Domain given in Hawkins (1999a), which identifies the smallest amount of surface structure containing information sufficient for the unambiguous parsing of a filler-gap dependency.[8] Hawkins (1999a) formulates the following general prediction for cross-linguistic variation in relative clauses with Filler-Gap domains:

(19) RELATIVE CLAUSE GAP HIERARCHY

If a relative clause gap is grammatical in position P on a complexity hierarchy H, then gaps will be grammatical in all higher positions on H.

Applied to the Accessibility Hierarchy, this prediction turns out to be exceptionlessly supported. Keenan and Comrie's relative clauses with [-Case] strategies are those containing no nominal element to indicate which posi-

[8] A FILLER-GAP DOMAIN (FGD) is defined as follows in Hawkins (1999a): An FGD consists of the smallest set of terminal and non-terminal nodes dominated by the mother of a filler and on a connected path that must be accessed for gap identification and processing; for subcategorized gaps the path connects the filler to the gap's subcategorizor and includes, or is extended to include, the gap's dependent and disambiguating arguments (if any); for nonsubcategorized gaps the path connects the filler to the gap site; all constituency relations and coocurrence requirements holding between these nodes belong to the description of the FGD.

tion is being relativized on and are Filler-Gap structures, therefore. All the languages with [-Case] in their sample (40 in all) limit this gap strategy to all and only the following hierarchically arranged possibilities (sample languages only given here):

(20) [-CASE] GAP LANGUAGES in Keenan and Comrie's Data

SU only:	e.g. Arabic (Classical), Toba Batak, Malagasy, Minang-Kabau
SU & DO only:	e.g. Chinese (Pekingese), Fulani, Hebrew, Malay
SU & DO & IO/OBL only:	e.g. Basque, Korean, Tamil
SU & DO & IO/OBL & GEN:	Japanese

Hierarchy prediction (19) is a particular instance of prediction (2b) defined by the Performance-Grammar Correspondence Hypothesis of (1). Further complexity rankings of relevance to Filler-Gap relativizations discussed in Hawkins (1999a) are: gaps in CNPC (Complex NP Constraint) environments are more complex than those in non-CNPC environments (see Ross 1967); WH-island environments are more complex than non-WH-island environments; environments with semantically rich bridging verbs or complementizers are more complex than those with semantically weaker items; and others. The cut-off points between grammatical and ungrammatical Filler-Gap relatives across languages are structured by hierarchies of complexity that include these ranked positions.

3 Principle 2: MINIMIZE FORMS

The second principle of efficiency and complexity to be proposed here is (21):

(21) MINIMIZE FORMS

The human processor prefers to minimize the formal complexity of each linguistic form F (its phoneme, morpheme, word or phrasal units) and the number of forms with unique conventionalized property assignments, thereby expanding the compatibility of F with a larger set of properties {P}. These minimizations apply in proportion to the ease with which a given P1 can be assigned in processing to a formally reduced F with expanded property compatibilities.

The processing of linguistic forms requires effort. This effort is minimized, first, by reducing the set of formal units in a form or structure. It is minimized, secondly, by reducing the number of forms with unique property assignments. It is not efficient to have a distinct form F for every possible property P that one might wish to express. To do so would greatly increase the number of form-property pairs in a language and the length and complexity of each proposition. Choices have to be made over which properties get priority for unique assignment to forms, and the remaining properties are assigned to forms that are ambiguous, vague or zero-specified with respect to the property in question. It is up to the *context*, broadly construed, to permit assignment of the intended P1 to a form F that is compatible with a larger set of properties {P}. (21) asserts that there is a trade-off between form minimization as defined here and the ease with which such additional properties can be assigned to forms through processes that are variously described as processing enrichments, inferences, implicatures, and sentence-internal dependencies of various sorts (e.g. filler-gap dependencies).

Examples abound whose patterning suggests that a reduction in form processing is an advantage, as long as the relevant information can be recovered, from discourse, from real-world knowledge, or from some accessible linguistic structure. Consider the use of pronouns versus full NPs (*he/she* versus *the professor*), Zipfian (1949) effects (the shorter *TV* for *television)*, compounds (*paper plate* for *plate made of paper*; *paper factory* for *factory that makes paper*; *paper clip* for *clip for use on paper*; etc), coordinate deletions (*John cooked 0 and Fred ate the pizza*), and control structures involving understood subjects of verbs within non-finite subordinate clauses (versus corresponding finite clauses with overt subjects). Filler-gap dependencies in e.g. relative clauses are also plausibly motivated by (21). Gaps can be identified by reference to their subcategorizor and to the filler with which they are co-indexed, but the resulting structure is a difficult one for processing and this difficulty is plausibly motivated by the compensating advantage of more minimal form processing (compared with a structure in which the filler is explicitly copied within the relative).

(21) is further supported by the ECONOMY PRINCIPLE of Haiman (1983) and by the data that he summarizes from numerous languages. It is also reminiscent of Grice's (1975) second Quantity maxim for pragmatic inferencing ('Do not make your contribution more informative than is required'), and more specifically of Levinson's (2000) Minimization principle derived from it ('Say as little as necessary', that is, produce the minimal linguistic information sufficient to achieve your communicational ends, cf. Levinson ibid.).

3.1 Form Minimization Predictions

Minimizing forms and assigning properties through processing enrichments reduces overall processing effort in these cases. But one cannot minimize everything and assign all properties through enrichment. Otherwise human languages would be reduced to a few highly polysemous grunts, beyond the capacity of the processing mechanisms to enrich to the intended P1. There has to be a balance between conventionalized forms and their linguistic properties on the one hand, and on-line inference on the other, and the need for such a balance leads to the following predictions:

(22) FORM MINIMIZATION PREDICTIONS
- a. The formal complexity of each F is reduced in proportion to the frequency of that F and/or the processing ease of assigning a given P1 to a reduced F (e.g. to zero).
- b. The number of unique F:P1 pairings in a language is reduced by grammaticalizing or lexicalizing a given F:P1 in proportion to the frequency and preferred expressiveness of that P1 in performance.

In effect, form minimizations require compensating mechanisms. (22a) asserts that frequency and processing ease regulate reductions in form, while frequency and preferred expressiveness regulate the grammaticalization and lexicalization preferences of (22b).

The factors that facilitate form reductions and processing enrichment include high accessibility for the entities and events in the current discourse (whence the use of shorter pronouns and anaphoric VPs rather than full NPs and VPs, cf. Ariel 1990), and real-world knowledge (whence the structurally reduced compounds like *paper plate* in lieu of more explicit post-modifiers such as *made of paper* precisely when the semantics of the post-modifier can be readily inferred, cf. Sperber and Wilson 1995, Levinson 2000). High frequency is also important. Zipf (1949) proposed an inverse correlation between word size and frequency of use in English: short words are more frequent than longer ones in general; and as lexical meanings gain in frequency of usage their formal expression often becomes shorter (whence *TV* for *television*). In grammars, high-frequency closed-class grammatical categories are typically more minimal than their lower-frequency counterparts. Auxiliary verbs are often reduced and contracted in comparison with lexical verbs, each of which has a frequency that is significantly less than that of each auxiliary. Pronouns are generally shorter than full NPs containing lexical nouns, each of which will be less frequent than a grammaticalized pronoun. When definite and indefinite articles emerge historically from demonstratives and from the numeral *one* respectively, the greater frequency of the articles is matched by a reduction in phonological and/or morphological structure (*the* versus *that*, *a(n)* versus *one* in English, etc). And so on.

Why should frequency be so predictive? This follows, I believe, from the efficiency logic of MINIMIZE FORMS (21). By assigning reduced forms to high-frequency properties, and by reserving more complex forms for lower frequency properties, the overall number of formal units that the processor has to process, in a given sentence and in a lifetime of sentence usage, is less. By contrast, if reduced forms systematically conveyed low-frequency properties and more complex forms high-frequency properties, or if reduced forms were neutral to frequency with the result that some reduced forms expressed frequently used properties while others did not, then more processing of formal units would be required in performance overall. Frequency effects in form reduction therefore accomplish the same minimization in articulation and processing that property expansions and the exploitation of contextual clues do.

Frequency is also relevant to (22b). There are numerous semantic and syntactic properties that are frequently occurring in performance and that have priority in grammatical and lexical conventions across languages. The property of causation is invoked often in everyday language use and is regularly conventionalized in the morphology, syntax or lexicon (Comrie 1989, Shibatani 1976). Agenthood and patienthood are frequently expressed and are given systematic (albeit partially different) formal expression in ergative-absolutive, nominative-accusative and active languages (Primus 1999). The very frequent speech acts (asserting, commanding and questioning) are each given distinct formal expression across grammars, whereas less frequent speech acts such as baptizing or bequeathing are assigned separate lexical items, but not a uniquely distinctive construction in the syntax (Sadock and Zwicky 1985). Within the lexicon the property associated with *teacher* is frequently used in performance, that of *teacher who is late for class* much less so. The event of *X hitting Y* is frequently selected, that of *X hitting Y with X's left hand* less so. The more frequently selected properties are conventionalized in single lexemes or unique categories, phrases and constructions in all these examples. Less frequently used properties must then be expressed through word and phrase combinations and their meanings must be derived by a process of semantic composition.

It is this last point that holds the key to the explanatory question that is raised in connection with (22b): why are frequently used properties given priority when assigning unique properties to forms? The answer is plausibly the same as we gave for form reductions and Zipfian effects. Sensitivity to high frequency results in more minimal forms within a sentence and in a lifetime of sentence usage. If less frequently used properties were given priority for unique F:P1 assignments, or if these assignments were neutral to frequency with the result that some were high frequency and some were low frequency properties, then more word and phrase combinations would be needed overall whenever the enrichment to P1 was not contextually guaranteed. If *teacher* meant *teacher who is late for class*, then the meaning of *teacher* would have to be expressed by semantic composition through appropriate word and phrase combinations (e.g. by *someone who gives instruction at school level*) since the closest single word would be pre-empted by its low-frequency property assignment. If the relatively infrequent dual number were the base form for a grammatical number system, then the much more frequent singularity and plurality concepts would need to be expressed by longer and more complex combinations (two minus one, two and more, etc). The conventionalization of high-frequency properties in unique F:P1 pairings minimizes forms, therefore.

3.2 Greenberg's Feature Hierarchies

One of the best documented and cross-linguistically researched set of data that test, and support, (22a) and (22b) comes from the FEATURE HIERARCHIES or MARKEDNESS HIERARCHIES of Greenberg (1966) and Croft (1990). Examples are given in (23):

(23) Nominative > Accusative > Dative > Other (for case marking)
Singular > Plural > Dual > Trial/Paucal (for number)
Masculine/Feminine > Neuter (for gender)
Positive > Comparative > Superlative

Greenberg argued that these hierarchies define relative frequency rankings for the relevant properties in each domain. For example, the relative frequencies of number inflections on nouns in a corpus of Sanskrit are:

(24) Singular = 70.3%; Plural = 25.1%; Dual = 4.6%.

The other hierarchies have similar frequency correlates. In other words, these hierarchies are PERFORMANCE FREQUENCY RANKINGS defined on entities within common grammatical and/or semantic domains. These performance rankings are then reflected in cross-linguistic grammatical patterns that conventionalize morphosyntax and allomorphy in accordance with the predictions of (22).

One prediction that is made is (25):

(25) QUANTITATIVE FORMAL MARKING PREDICTION
For each hierarchy H the amount of formal marking (i.e. phonological and morphological complexity) will be greater or equal down each hierarchy position.

(25) follows from (22a). For example, in Manam the 3rd Singular suffix on nouns is zero, the 3rd Plural is *-di*, the 3rd Dual is *-di-a-ru* and the 3rd Paucal is *-di-a-to* (Lichtenberk 1983). The amount of formal marking increases from singular to plural, and from plural to dual, and is equal from dual to paucal, in accordance with the hierarchy in (23). Similarly English singular nouns are zero-marked whereas plurals are formally marked, generally with an *-s* allomorph.

(26) MORPHOLOGICAL INVENTORY PREDICTION
For each hierarchy H (A > B > C) if a language assigns at least one morpheme uniquely to C, then it assigns at least one uniquely to B; and if it assigns at least one uniquely to B, it does so to A.

(26) follows from (22b). A distinct Dual implies a distinct Plural and Singular in the grammar of Sanskrit, and a distinct Dative implies a distinct Accusative and Nominative in the case grammar of Latin and German (or a distinct Ergative and Absolutive in Basque, cf. Primus 1999). A unique number or case assignment low in the hierarchy implies unique and differentiated numbers and cases in all higher positions.

(27) DECLINING DISTINCTIONS PREDICTION
For each hierarchy H any combinatorial features that partition references to a given position on H will result in fewer or equal morphological distinctions down each lower position of H.

(27) also follows from (22b). For example, unique and gender-distinctive pronouns can exist for the singular and not for the plural in English (*he/she/it* versus *they*), whereas the converse uniqueness is not predicted.

I have argued in Hawkins (1998b, c) that we should view the performance frequencies of different hierarchy positions not just as correlations of these hierarchies, but as causes of the grammatical asymmetries in the conventionalization of morpho-syntactic distinctions, in accordance with (22).

These grammatical distinctions and their degrees of formal marking reflect usage: the more frequently a form can be used to identify some property in performance, the more it will be grammaticalized, and the more reduced its surface marking can be. Singular entities are referenced more frequently in performance than plurals and duals, nominatives more frequently than accusatives and datives, and these frequencies are then reflected in the conventionalized preferences of grammars, favoring more grammatical distinctions but less explicit marking in the higher positions compared to the lower ones. The ultimate causes of the frequencies, in turn, can be diverse and can reflect real-world frequencies of occurrence (pairs are less frequent than singular entities and undifferentiated plurals) and communicative biases (in favor of animates rather than inanimates, cf. gender systems). The frequencies of use for the different hierarchy positions can also reflect degrees of syntactic and semantic complexity predicted by other efficiency principles (which is plausibly what we see in the declining use of the lower case forms in increasingly complex clauses with more argument positions).

All of these data exemplify the testing of prediction (2b) of the PERFORMANCE GRAMMAR CORRESPONDENCE HYPOTHESIS in section 1.

3.3 Form Minimization and Adjacency

There is an interesting interaction between MINIMIZE FORMS (21) and MINIMIZE DOMAINS (3) that can be seen both in performance and in correlating grammatical data across languages. When one structure involves fewer overt forms than an alternative, then the syntactic or semantic properties that are conveyed by the missing forms must be recovered from their environments. As a result there are more relations of syntactic or semantic dependency between categories, whose processing assigns the properties in question, while fewer properties can be derived from these categories independently of their environments. There are also often longer domains for processing these properties when overt forms are absent. As a consequence, constructions with fewer forms define a stronger preference for minimal domains of processing compared with their explicitly marked counterparts, for the same basic reason that additional semantic dependencies result in tighter adjacency in the prepositional phrase data of section 2.2.

Consider the alternation in English between WH or THAT relativizers versus ZERO in restrictive relative clauses. ZERO relatives, e.g. *the Danes you taught*, involve a clause (*you taught*) that requires more dependent processing on the head. For example, processing the subcategorization frame and the precise semantics of this subordinate verb requires access to the subject *you* and to the second (direct object) argument. If that argument is represented by a WH pronoun (*the Danes whom you taught*) the appropriate properties can be assigned to *taught* on the basis of material within the relative clause itself (as happens also in pronoun-retaining languages like Hebrew, see below). But in the absence of WH, the processing of *taught* must access the head, *Danes*, and this introduces a dependency on the head whose processing prefers a minimal domain. Processing the co-indexation relation between the head and the relative also requires direct access to the subcategorizor *taught* (or to its gap position, depending on one's theory) since there is no intervening WH word to bear the index. As a result of these and additional processing dependencies that are defined explicitly in Hawkins (in preparation), tighter adjacency is predicted between ZERO relatives and their heads than between WH and THAT relatives and their heads. The following data are from Quirk (1957):

(28) a. Restrictive (non-subject) relatives adjacent to the head
WH = 28% (152) THAT = 32% (174) ZERO = 41% (222)
b. Restrictive (non-subject) relatives with intervening material
WH = 50% (31) THAT = 44% (27) ZERO = 7% (4)

Only 4/226 (2%) of the more dependent ZERO relatives are non-adjacent to the head.

Across languages grammatical rules have conventionalized such preferences of performance: zero-marked dependencies require adjacency to their heads, formally marked dependencies occur in non-adjacent and adjacent domains. Consider the following agreement universal for languages with case copying, from Moravcsik (1995):

(29) If agreement through case copying applies to NP constituents that are adjacent, it applies to those that are non-adjacent.

For example, case copying is quite systematic in the Australian language Kalkatungu (a word-marking language according to Blake 1987) and occurs when NP constituents are both adjacent and non-adjacent:

(30) a.	thuku-yu	yant-tu	yanyi	itya-mi
	dog-ERG	big-ERG	white-man	bite-FUT
b.	thuku-yu	yanyi	itya-mi	yaun-tu
	dog- ERG	white-man	bite- FUT	big- ERG

But in Warlpiri (a phrase-marking language) case copying is found only on non-adjacent NP constituents, cf. (31b), while adjacent sisters (cf. (31a)) have only one occurrence of case marking in conjunction with zero-marking:

(31) a. tyarntu wiri-ngki+tyu yarlki-rnu
dog big- ERG +me bite-PAST
b. tyarntu-ngku+tyu yarlku-rnu wiri-ngki
dog- ERG +me bite- PAST big- ERG

Similarly in highly inflected languages like Latin, separation of Adj and N is made possible by rich morphological agreement (see Vincent 1987), suggesting more generally that if a language permits separation of N and Adj, then Adj must agree with N.

The grammatical variation here reveals a conventionalization of exactly the preferences that are evident in English performance data such as (28). Under conditions of adjacency both formal marking and zero have been grammatically fixed, the former in Kalkatungu and Latin, the latter in Warlpiri, and these two options are both productive in performance, cf. (28a). But under conditions of non-adjacency only formal marking is productive in grammars, and only this option is productive in performance as well, cf. (28b).

3.4 Form Minimization in Filler-Gap Domains

Similarly the gap strategy in relativization prefers a processing domain that is smaller and simpler than that of relative clauses with explicit marking of the position relativized on. Explicit marking can be achieved by using a copy pronoun, as in Hebrew:

(32) ha-isha$_i$ [she-Yon natan la$_i$ et ha-sefer]
the woman that John gave to-her DO the book
'the woman that John gave the book to'

Copy pronouns make identification of the position relativized on as easy as it can possibly be. They also permit the processing of the verb's subcategorization and semantics to take place locally in the relative clause and without having to access the head noun, which the gap-containing structures must do, as in the English ZERO relative construction. This leads to the prediction that gaps will prefer more minimal domains for processing, while copy pronouns fill the more complex positions on hierarchies such as the Accessibility Hierarchy, in proportion to the degree of complexity involved. We therefore predict that if a copy pronoun is grammatical in position P on a complexity hierarchy H, then it will be grammatical in all lower positions that can be relativized at all (cf. Hawkins 1999a). 27 of Keenan and Comrie's (1977) languages have copy pronouns (as a subinstance of their

[+Case] relativization strategy), and this prediction holds exceptionlessly for these languages (sample languages only given here):

(33) Pronoun-retaining Languages in Keenan and Comrie's Data

GEN only:	e.g. Japanese, Javanese, Malay, Turkish
GEN & IO/OBL only:	e.g. Toba Batak, Hausa, Welsh
GEN & IO/OBL & DO only:	e.g. Chinese (Pekingese), Kera, Slovenian
GEN & IO/OBL & DO & SU:	Urhobo

The grammatical data from relative clauses reveal two opposite implicational patterns overall: gaps go from low to high on a complexity hierarchy (see (20)), copy pronouns from high to low. In Hawkins (ibid.) I quantified the distribution of gaps to copy pronouns in 24 languages (like Hebrew) that have both: the occurrence of gaps declined down the Accessibility Hierarchy of (16) by 100% to 65% to 25% to 4%, while that of pronouns increased (0% to 35% to 75% to 96%). The gapped relatives involve more dependencies between relative and head, therefore, and the attested Filler-Gap Domains are smaller than corresponding Filler-Copy Pronoun domains in languages like Hebrew, in accordance with Minimize Domains (3).

4 Principle 3: MAXIMIZE ON-LINE PROCESSING

The third principle I propose is (34):

(34) MAXIMIZE ON-LINE PROCESSING

The human parser prefers to maximize the set of properties that are assignable to each item X as X is parsed. The maximization difference between competing orders and structures will be a function of the number of properties that are misassigned or unassigned to X in a structure/sequence S, compared with the number in an alternative.

This principle asserts that it is preferable to be able to recognize syntactic and semantic properties productively throughout the processing of a sentence.[9] What is dispreferred is, first, any significant delay or LOOK AHEAD

---

[9] Notice that Maximize On-line Processing is formulated in terms of parsing and the hearer, since the speaker does not make structural missassignments on-line and can enrich unassignments based on knowledge of what is to be produced later. Nonetheless there is evidence for the speaker's accommodation to the hearer's needs here, in proportion to the degree of misas-

(Marcus 1980) in on-line property assignments, and second a misassignment of properties on-line. Misassignments result in so-called garden path effects whereby one analysis is chosen on-line and is then subsequently corrected in favor of a different analysis when more material has been processed. A famous example is *the horse raced past the barn fell* which is first assigned a main clause reading and then a reduced relative reading when the (matrix verb) *fell* is encountered (see MacDonald et. al. 1994). Such backtracking is difficult for the processor, but more importantly it is inefficient since initial property assignments are wasted and make no contribution to the ultimate syntactic and semantic representation of the sentence. Similarly any processing delay followed by a late surge of property assignments towards the end of a clause or sentence does not maximize on-line property assignments.

This principle is discussed and exemplified in detail in Hawkins (in press-ab). I believe that it is ultimately responsible for a large number of linear precedence asymmetries across languages which contrast with the kinds of symmetrical orderings associated with the head-initial and head-final typology illustrated in (10) and (11) above. These asymmetries involve a clear preference for just one ordering of categories across languages. Many involve cases in which there is an asymmetric dependency between some category D and another category I.

4.1 Fillers First

For example, gaps are dependent on their fillers in Filler-Gap structures for coreference and co-indexation and also for recognizing the position to be filled (in conjunction with access to the subcategorizor, if there is one), whereas fillers are not so dependent on their gaps. This results in a preference for fillers before gaps, or Fillers First (Hawkins 1999a, J.D. Fodor 1983). When the gap follows the filler, I ... D, then the filler (I) can be fully processed on-line, and the grammatical properties that are assigned by reference to I can be assigned to the gap on-line as well, resulting in an efficient distribution of property assignments throughout the sentence. But if the gap precedes, D ... I, its full properties can only be assigned retrospectively when the filler is encountered, resulting in a processing delay and in frequent garden path effects as matrix and subordinate clause arguments are redistributed to take account of the gap that is activated by late processing of the filler (cf. Antinucci et. al. 1979, Clancy et. al. 1986). I ... D maximizes on-line property assignments, therefore.

When the filler is a WH-word in a WH-question there is unambiguous cross-linguistic support for Fillers First: almost all languages that move a

---

signment and unassignment involved in various structures, and a quantified metric for testing Maximize Online Processing is proposed in Hawkins (2002a).

WH-word to clause peripheral position move it to the left, not to the right (Hawkins 1999a: in press-ab). In relative clauses there is also clear support, but Fillers First is now in partial conflict with the EIC preference for noun-final NPs in head-final languages. Head-initial languages have consistently right-branching relatives (e.g. [V [N S]]), which are motivated both by EIC and by Fillers First. But head-final languages have either left-branching relatives ([[S N] V]), which is good for EIC but which positions the gap before the filler, or right-branching relatives ([[N S] V]), which is good for Fillers First but which creates non-adjacency between heads and makes PCDs longer.

The variation here points to the existence of two preferences, whose predictions overlap in one language type but conflict in another. This illustrates prediction (2c) of the PERFORMANCE-GRAMMAR CORRESPONDENCE HYPOTHESIS in (1). Each of the structural variants is motivated. There is also suggestive evidence that each principle is exemplified across grammars in proportion to its own degree of motivation. The head-final languages that prefer left-branching relatives are the *rigid* ones like Japanese, in which there are more containing V-final and P-final phrases, etc, that prefer the head of NP to be final as well (by EIC). *Non-rigid* head-final languages have fewer containing phrases that are head-final and so define a weaker preference for noun-finality, allowing Fillers First to assert itself more, which results in more right-branching relatives (cf. Lehmann 1984 for numerous exemplifying languages).

4.2 Other Linear Precedence Asymmetries

A related structure involves topicalized XPs with gaps in a sister S. These generally precede S across languages (Gundel 1974, 1988; Primus 1993, 1999). The reverse ordering could be optimal both for EIC and for scope marking, but it is either ungrammatical or dispreferred and this provides further evidence for Fillers First. The asymmetry disappears when a co-indexed pronoun replaces the gap, resulting in left- or right-dislocation structures, suggesting that it is the gap that contributes substantially to the linear precedence asymmetry.

The dispreference for D ... I here is motivated by the dependence of D (the gap) on I (the filler) for gap identification and filling, as before. In addition the ABOUTNESS relation between the predication and the topic (Reinhart 1981), coupled with the regular referential independence or givenness of the topic, means that the semantic processing of the predication is often incomplete without prior access to the topic (cf. Keenan 1978, Gundel 1988), whereas the topic can be processed independently of the predication. For example, Tsao (1978) gives numerous examples from Mandarin

Chinese of the topic phrase providing information that is required for interpretation of the predication, making these predications *dependent* on the topic as this term is defined here. The topic can provide the understood possessor for a possessee within the predication, a class or set relative to which some entity in the predication is understood to be a member, a domain relative to which a superlative claim in the predication is interpreted, a restrictive adjunct for a noun in the predication, a locative or time adjunct for a verb, and so on. In all these cases the proper interpretation of the predication depends on the topic and these asymmetric dependencies motivate an asymmetric topic before predication ordering across languages, I ... D, thereby maximizing on-line processing efficiency (Hawkins 2002a).

Further ordering asymmetries that are plausibly motivated by (34) include the preference for wide scope before narrow scope operators and quantifiers, and also the preference for restrictive before appositive relatives exemplified in the English (35a):

(35) a. Students that major in mathematics, who must of course work hard, ... R + A

b. *Students, who must of course work hard, that major in mathematics, ... A + R

In the on-line processing of (35b) there would always be a semantic garden path. The appositive relative would first be predicated of all students, and would then be predicated only of that subset of which the restrictive relative was true, once the latter was encountered and processed. The ordering of (35a) avoids the regular garden path by placing together all the items that determine the reference set of which the appositive clause is predicated, and by positioning them before an appositive claim that would make an erroneous predication on-line if it preceded the restrictive clause. The positioning of the restrictive is also motivated by the Adjacency Hypothesis in (14), since the nominal head is semantically dependent on the restrictive but not on the appositive clause for the restriction in its reference. Principles (34) and (14) therefore reinforce one another in this case.

5 Conclusions

I conclude that there is a profound correspondence between performance data and grammars, see the Performance-Grammar Correspondence Hypothesis of (1) and (2). Structural types that are preferred in performance are also preferred in grammars (2a), preference rankings in performance are matched by hierarchies of grammatical conventions (2b), and partial competition between preferences results in grammatical variation (2c).

Three general principles of efficiency and complexity have been proposed: MINIMIZE DOMAINS (3); MINIMIZE FORMS (21); and Maximize ON-LINE PROCESSING (34). These principles, individually and in combination, can motivate a broad range of preference data in performance and in grammars. They are simple and intuitive principles that reflect an even more general Zipfian principle of least effort (cf. Zipf 1949), yet they can explain many subtle properties of syntax that have been largely viewed as innate and non-functional hitherto, in accordance with Chomsky (1965) and subsequent publications. Yet when precise functional principles are formulated, I would argue that they provide an alternative to this view, with wide-ranging empirical support, less stipulation, and more independently motivated explanation.

It remains to be seen how much of core syntax and of syntactic variation can be explained in these terms. This general approach views grammars and grammatical evolution as complex adaptive systems (Gell-Mann 1992), with efficiency and ease of processing driving the adaptation in response to prior changes. Innate syntactic knowledge is not the ultimate explanation, although the processing architecture that defines ease of use is most plausibly innate.

It will also be necessary to answer questions that are raised by this general approach. How exactly do the preferences of performance gradually become fixed conventions in language evolution, whereby only the preferred structure is generated and dispreferred options are eliminated altogether? Kirby (1999) gives a clear discussion of the issues here and provides an intriguing computer simulation of grammars evolving out of performance preferences. Haspelmath (1999) discusses the question from the perspective of Optimality Theory and argues that the constraints of this theory can be functionally motivated by performance preferences such as those proposed here which become grammaticalized through a process of diachronic adaptation. There are also psycholinguistic issues that are raised by these performance preferences. How exactly can the kinds of efficiencies described here be implemented in current production and comprehension models with the result that they could actually be predicted? And to what extent do the needs and benefits of the speaker overlap with those of the hearer, to what extent are they different, and to what extent does the speaker accommodate to the hearer?

These are big issues that arise independently of the central hypothesis of this paper, which is that there is a profound correspondence between the preferences of performance and those of grammars, whatever the precise causality of the performance data turns out to be. This hypothesis is at variance with the proposed autonomy of grammars from performance which has dominated generative thinking since Chomsky (1965). The evidence of this paper suggests that syntax is, to a significant extent at least, PERFORMANCE-DRIVEN and that we can achieve a richer and more explanatory theory of grammar if we combine generative insights with a theory of processing efficiency of the type outlined here.

References

Antinucci, F., A. Duranti, and L. Gebert. 1979. Relative Clause Structure, Relative Clause Perception, and the Change from SOV to SVO. *Cognition* 7: 145-176.

Bever, T.G. 1970. The Cognitive Basis for Linguistic Structures. *Cognition and the Development of Language*, ed. J.R. Hayes, 279-362. New York: Wiley.

Blake, B. 1987. *Australian Aboriginal Grammar*. London: Routledge.

Chomsky, N. 1965. *Aspects of the Theory of Syntax*. Cambridge, MA: MIT Press.

Clancy, P.M., H. Lee, and M. Zoh. 1986. Processing Strategies in the Acquisition of Relative Clauses: Universal Principles and Language-Specific Realizations. *Cognition* 14: 225-262.

Comrie, B. 1989. *Language Universals and Linguistic Typology*. 2nd ed. Basil Blackwell, Oxford.

Croft, W. 1990. *Typology and Universals*. Cambridge, Cambridge Univer-sity Press.

Dowty, D.R. 1991. Thematic Proto-Roles and Argument Selection. *Lan-guage* 67: 547-619.

Dryer, M.S. 1992. The Greenbergian Word Order Correlations. *Language* 68: 81-138.

Dryer, M.S. 1993. Modifying Hawkins' Prepositional Noun Modifier Hier-archy. Paper Presented at the Annual Meeting of the Linguistic Society of America, Los Angeles.

Fodor, Janet D. 1983. Phrase Structure Parsing and the Island Constraints. *Linguistics and Philosophy* 6: 163-223.

Gell-Mann, M. 1992. Complexity and Complex Adaptive Systems. *The Evolution of Human Languages*, eds. J.A. Hawkins and M. Gell-Mann, 3-18. Redwood City, CA: Addison-Wesley.

Greenberg, J.H. 1963. Some Universals of Grammar with Particular Refer-ence to the Order of Meaningful Elements. *Universals of Language* 2nd ed., ed. J.H. Greenberg, 73-113. Cambridge, MA: MIT Press.

Greenberg, J.H. 1966. *Language Universals, with Special Reference to Feature Hierarchies*. The Hague: Mouton.

Grice, H.P. 1975. Logic and Conversation. *Speech Acts. Syntax and Semantics* vol.3, eds. P. Cole and J. Morgan, 41-58. New York: Academic Press.

Gundel, J.K. 1974. The Role of Topic and Comment in Linguistic Theory. Doctoral dissertation, University of Texas, Austin.

Gundel, J.K. 1988. Universals of Topic-Comment Structure. *Studies in Syn-tactic Typology*, eds. M Hammond, E.A. Moravcsik, and J.R. Wirth, 209-239. Amsterdam: John Benjamins.

Haiman, J. 1983. Iconic and Economic Motivation. *Language* 59: 781-819.

Haspelmath, M. 1999. Optimality and Diachronic Adaptation. *Zeitschrift für Sprachwissenschaft* 18:180-205.

Hawkins, J.A. 1983. *Word Order Universals.* New York: Academic Press.

Hawkins, J.A. 1990. A Parsing Theory of Word Order Universals. *Linguis-tic Inquiry* 21: 223-261.

Hawkins, J.A. 1993. Heads, Parsing, and Word Order Universals. *Heads in Grammatical Theory,* eds. G.G. Corbett, N.M. Fraser, and S. McGlashan, 231-265. Cambridge: Cambridge University Press.

Hawkins, J.A. 1994. *A Performance Theory of Order and Constituency.* Cambridge: Cambridge University Press.

Hawkins, J.A. 1998a. Some Issues in a Performance Theory of Word Order. *Constituent Order in the Languages of Europe,* ed. A. Siewierska, 729-781. Berlin: de Gruyter.

Hawkins, J.A. 1998b. Morphological Hierarchies in the History of Ger-manic. *Interdisciplinary Journal for Germanic Linguistics and Semiotic Analysis* 3: 197-217.

Hawkins, J.A. 1998c. A Typological Approach to Germanic Morphology. *Historische Germanische und Deutsche Syntax*, ed. J.O. Askedal, 49-68. Frankfurt: Peter Lang Verlag.

Hawkins, J.A. 1999a. Processing Complexity and Filler-Gap Dependencies across Grammars. *Language* 75: 244-285.

Hawkins, J.A. 1999b. The Relative Order of Prepositional Phrases in Eng-lish: Going beyond Manner-Place-Time. *Language Variation and Change* 11: 231-266.

Hawkins, J.A. 2001. Why Are Categories Adjacent? *Journal of Linguistics* 37: 1-34.

Hawkins, J.A. 2002a. Symmetries and Asymmetries: Their Grammar, Typology and Parsing. *Theoretical Linguistics* 28: 95-150.

Hawkins, J.A. 2002b. Issues at the Performance-Grammar Interface: Some Comments on the Commentaries. *Theoretical Linguistics* 28: 211-226.

Hawkins, J.A. in prep. *Efficiency and Complexity in Grammars.* Oxford: Oxford University Press.

Jackendoff, R. 1977. *X-bar Syntax: A Study of Phrase Structure.* Cam-bridge, MA: MIT Press.

Keenan, E.L. 1975. Variation in Universal Grammar. *Analyzing Variation in English*, eds. R. Fasold and R. Shuy, 136-148. Washington DC: Georgetown University Press.

Keenan, E.L. 1978. The Syntax of Subject-Final Languages. *Syntactic Ty-pology: Studies in the Phenomenology of Language*, ed. W.P. Lehmann, 267-327. Austin: University of Texas Press.

Keenan, E.L. 1979. On Surface Form and Logical Form. *Studies in the Lin-guistic Sciences* 8: 163-203.

Keenan, E.L. and B. Comrie. 1977. Noun Phrase Accessibility and Univer-sal Grammar. *Linguistic Inquiry* 8: 63-99.

Keenan, E.L. and S. Hawkins. 1987. The Psychological Validity of the Accessibility Hierarchy. *Universal Grammar: Fifteen Essays*, ed. E.L. Keenan, 60-85. London: Routledge.

Kimball, J. 1973. Seven Principles of Surface Structure Parsing in Natural Language. *Cognition* 2: 15-47.

Kirby, S. 1999. *Function, Selection and Innateness: The Emergence of Language Universals*. Oxford: Oxford University Press.

Lehmann, C. 1984. *Der Relativsatz*. Tübingen: Gunter Narr Verlag.

Levelt, W.J.M. 1989. *Speaking: From Intention to Articulation*. Cambridge, MA: MIT Press.

Levinson, S.C. 2000. *Presumptive Meanings: The Theory of Generalized Conversational Implicature*. Cambridge, MA: MIT Press.

Lichtenberk, F. 1983. *A Grammar of Manam*. Honolulu: University of Ha-waii Press.

MacDonald, M.C., N.J. Pearlmutter, and M.S. Seidenberg. 1994. The Lexi-cal Nature of Syntactic Ambiguity Resolution. *Psychological Review* 101: 676-703.

Marcus, M.P. 1980. *A Theory of Syntactic Recognition for Natural Lan-guage*. Cambridge, MA: MIT Press.

Miller, G.A. and N. Chomsky. 1963. Finitary Models of Language Users. *Handbook of Mathematical Psychology* vol.2, eds. R.D. Luce, R.R. Bush and E. Galanter, 419-492. New York: Wiley.

Moravcsik, E.A. 1995. Summing up Suffixaufnahme. *Double Case: Agreement by Suffixaufnahme*, ed. F. Plank, 451-484. Oxford: Oxford University Press.

Pickering, M. and R. Shillcock. 1992. Processing Subject Extractions. *Is-land Constraints: Theory, Acquisition and Processing*, eds. H. Goodluck and M. Rochemont. Dordrecht: Kluwer.

Pollard, C. and I.A. Sag 1987. Information-Based Syntax and Semantics, Volume 1: Fundamentals. *Center for the Study of Language and Infomation Lecture Notes No.13*. Stanford: CSLI Publications.

Pollard, C. and I.A. Sag 1994. *Head-Driven Phrase Structure Grammar*. Chicago: University of Chicago Press.

Primus, B. 1993. Word Order and Information Structure: A Performance-Based Account of Topic Positions and Focus Positions. *Syntax: An International Handbook of Contemporary Research* vol. 1, eds. J. Jacobs et. al., 880-896. Berlin: de Gruyter.

Primus, B. 1999. *Cases and Thematic Roles: Ergative, Accusative, Active*. Tübingen: Max Niemeyer Verlag.

Quirk, R. 1957. Relative Clauses in Educated Spoken English. *English Studies* 38: 97-109.

Reinhart, T. 1981. Pragmatics and Linguistics: An Analysis of Sentence Topics. *Philosophica* 27: 53-94.

Ross, J.R. 1967. Constraints on Variables in Syntax. Doctoral dissertation, MIT.

Sadock, J.M. and A.M. Zwicky. 1985. Speech Act Distinctions in Syntax. *Language Typology and Syntactic Description* vol. 1, *Clause Structure*, ed. T. Shopen, 155-196. Cambridge: Cambridge University Press.

Shibatani, M. ed. 1976. *The Grammar of Causative Constructions*. New York: Academic Press.

Sperber, D. and D. Wilson. 1995. *Relevance: Communication and Cogn-tion*. 2nd ed. Oxford: Blackwell.

Stallings, L.M. 1998. Evaluating Heaviness: Relative Weight in the Spoken Production of Heavy-NP Shift. Doctoral dissertation, University of Southern California.

Tomlin, R.S. 1986. *Basic Word Order: Functional Principles*. London: Croom Helm.

Tsao, F-F. 1978. *A Functional Study of Topic in Chinese*. Taipei: Student Book Company.

Vincent, N.B. 1987. Latin. *The Romance Languages*, eds. M.B. Harris and N.B. Vincent, 26-78. Oxford: Oxford University Press.

Wasow, T. 2002. *Postverbal Behavior*. Stanford: CSLI Publications.

Yamashita, H. and F. Chang. 2001. 'Long before Short' Preference in the Production of a Head-Final Language. *Cognition* 81: B45-55.

Zipf, G. 1949. *Human Behavior and the Principle of Least Effort: An Introduction to Human Ecology*. New York: Hafner.

7

An Historical Explanation of Some Binding Theoretic Facts in English

EDWARD L. KEENAN

1 Introduction

Drawing on Keenan (1994, 1996, 2000) I provide an historical explanation of the facts in (1) in MSE (Modern Standard English). I use co-indexing for semantic binding, distinct indices for independent reference:

(1) a. Every worker$_i$ criticized himself$_{i,*j}$/him$_{*i,j}$.
b. John$_i$ lost *himself$_{i,j}$'s / his$_i$ own watch
c. John$_i$ thought that no one but himself$_i$ would get an A on the exam.
d. He$_i$ denied that either himself$_i$ or his wife was there.
e. He$_i$ tackled a problem that only himself$_i$ and the teacher could solve.
f. No one$_i$ likes to work with anyone$_j$ smarter than himself$_{i,j}$.

Using [pron+*self*] as a cover term for the *self*-forms in ME (Middle English: c1150 - 1300) and MSE (e.g. *himself, herself, themselves,* ...), (1a) instantiates the familiar fact that, when occurring as a DO (object of a verb) [pron+*self*] must be locally bound (= bound to a co-argument) and the bare pronouns (*him, her, them,* ...) must not be (but may be non-locally bound: *John$_i$ thinks that she criticized him$_{i,j}$*).

(1b) states that [pron+*self*] does not occur as a possessor in MSE; possessor binding is expressed by *his own* (*her own, their own*...).

The Nature of Explanation in Linguistic Theory.
John Moore and Maria Polinsky (eds.).

(1c) recalls (Keenan 1988, Safire 1992) that [pron+*self*] within ICEs (Inherently Contrastive Expressions) may be non-locally bound.

1.1 Dismissing a dismissal

Some might suggest that these facts are just special cases of universal facts given by Binding Theory (BT) and thus can not receive an historical explanation: they hold of all languages and so of all 'stages' of a given language, and hence are not subject to historical change. But in fact there is something to explain. Here first is the formulation of BT we use:

(2) A. Anaphors are locally bound
B. Pronominals are not locally bound but may be bound
C. R-expressions are free (= not bound)

The facts in (1a) follow if *himself* is an anaphor and so subject to (2A), and *him*, etc. are pronominals and so subject to (2B). But these are just claims about English words; they are not remotely universal. In fact *himself* need not be locally bound in ME and doesn't exist in OE (Old English c750–c1150). *him* is often locally bound in OE and ME.

Thus our historical explanation of (1a) is first an explanation of how [pron+*self*] comes to exist (c1200) and be interpreted as locally bound (c1500), and second, how the pronouns lose their local binding interpretation. Similarly, (1b), we account for why [pron+*self*] don't occur as possessors, and (1c), why [pron+*self*] may escape locality requirements in ICEs.

1.2 Historical explanations

Historical explanations of synchronic facts raise many conceptual issues for which I offer no general theory here. But I do present two examples to illustrate how they can be enlightening. The examples introduce specific changes and forces of change operative in the BT phenomena we study here and which, like language change in general, are subject to the Principle of Inertia:

INERTIA Things stay as they are unless acted upon by an outside force (including decay)

INERTIA applies to language change as a very special case. And in that case it derives, at least in part, from considerations of learnability and social utility. Imagine that English changed a century's worth per day: so Chaucer drafted the contract you signed a week ago; ten days ago you lectured in the language of the monk Ælfric, and a scant two weeks ago the news was broadcast in the alliterative verse of Beowulf. A 'language' that changes that rapidly is neither learnable nor functional in ordinary social contracts.

INERTIA tells us that in comparing a language over time 'No Change' is the default expectation. When there are changes we account for them by appeal to outside forces or decay (below). What we don't need to explain is absence of change. Curiously however it is precisely this absence which enables us to explain many properties of MSE. For example many of the properties of the newly created *him+self* in 1250 are inherited from the OE dative pronoun *him* and the adjectival contrastor *self* that *him+self* is derived from.

> *Example 1:* Imagine putting the speech of London under a metaphoric microscope during the ME period. We observe that in 1250 the 3rd pl pronouns in use are *hy* (nom), *hem* (dat/acc) and *here* (gen). But in 1450 we find *þai*, *þaim*, *þayr* (with much spelling variation in both periods). A change has taken place.

We might try to explain this change phonologically, guessing that word initial *h-* changed to /þ/. But this was not the case: *ham* 'home' did not become *þam*, *halten* 'halt, be lame' did not become *þalten*, etc. Only the pronouns changed in this way. Expanding our data base we see (as is well known) that the *th-* pronouns are Scandinavian, and that the Northeast of England came under extensive Scandinavian influence beginning with incursions in the 8th century, then settlements and the imposition of Danelaw through the mid-11th cent.

So now we understand that the change from *hem* to *them* was due to external, Scandinavian, influence. Our understanding has improved, though questions remain – How did it propagate? Why did it just affect 3rd plural? Why did the nominative forms spread first, then dative/accusative and genitive forms? As a second example, illustrating decay rather than external forces, consider:

> GEN: Single word modifiers of nouns occur prenominally in MSE

We say *a sleepy child* not **a child sleepy*; *every burning issue* (was discussed) not **every issue burning* (was discussed). Equally noun modifiers are prenominal: *a bone doctor, a silver spoon*, not **a doctor bone* or **a spoon silver*.

But many single word modifiers in *a-* are exceptions to Gen: We say *no man alive*, not **no alive man*; *a lion asleep*, not **an asleep lion*, *the pas-*

sengers aboard, not **the aboard passengers*. Here is our historical explanation: First, from Late OE through ME FUNCTION WORD PROCLISIS was taking place:

FUNCTION WORD PROCLISIS (FWP) A short closed class item ω forms a phonological word with a following word W. ω loses stress (if it had it) and may phonologically reduce.

(3) a. on+weg ⇒ away on+slep ⇒ asleep on+life ⇒ alive
b. bi+cause ⇒ because be+sidan⇒bi+siden⇒beside(s) beȝeondan ⇒ beȝeond((e)n) ⇒ beyond
c. eal(l)+ane ⇒ alone/lone all+theigh (< þeah) ⇒ although all+to+gædere ⇒ altogether

The main stresses on forms derived by FWP are those of W. When W has rightmost stress (e.g. is monosyllabic), so does the derived word. Recall that, ignoring some prefixes, Germanic roots are stress initial .

SPLIT Cliticized items generally do not cease to exist as independent words. We even say *all alone*. We did not lose *on* or *by* (< ME *bi/be*) in MSE. In some cases we still have both forms: *on fire*, *afire*; *on board*, *aboard*. The unreduced form occurs when separated from W by a possessive: ***beside** me vs.* ***by** my side*; *They sent him* ***away*** *vs* ***on his way***. When Fr. *avoir* 'to have' encliticized to infinitives forming a future tense: *parler**ai*** 'I will speak', *parler**as*** 'you(sg) will speak', ... it did not cease to function as a main verb. This, common, type of change is called SPLIT, in Heine and Reh (1984), 'Divergence' in Hopper (1991).

Corollary to FWP+INERTIA: Expressions created by FWP preserve, by INERTIA, the distribution and interpretation of the least constituents that contain them.

FACT: In ME, as in MSE, PP modifiers of Ns followed them. From Chaucer (1385):

lordshipe over youre persone,	folk in sorwe,
moththes in the shepes flees,	recours to the juge,
recchelesnesse in spekynge,	servauntz and thralles to synne,
another remedie agayns Leccherie,	humylitee in confession.

The Corollary *explains* Gen on the grounds that the postnominal modifiers (*alive*, …) position like PPs because they used to be PPs and (INERTIA) didn't change position after FWP cliticized *on* to *a*-.

FWP was also operative in creating the paradigmatically related *what(so)ever*, *how(so)ever* and later *who(so)ever* from non-constituents (C. Allen 1980). *so* (< *swa*) and *ever* originate inside relative clauses, *what*, *how* and *who* outside, as in (4a). But by the late 1300s we see (4b,c), with separation possible as late as 1607, (4d). Note that *hwat*, *swo*, and *aeure* are not adjacent in (4a) and do not by themselves constitute a syntactic unit, nor are they interpreted as a semantic unit.

(4) a. Luue ðine nexte al swa de seluen, hwat manne swo he aeure bie!
'Love thy neighbor as thyself, whatsoever man he be!'
V&V 1.67 (c1200)

b. And what as evere that ye seie, riht as ye wole so wol I.
'And whatsoever that you say, just as you will so will I.'
Gower (c1390)
(< Allen)

c. But what-som-ever woo they fele, they wole not pleyne.
'But whatsoever woe they feel, they will not complain.'
Chaucer (c1385)
(< Allen)

d. Hee would...patronize his caufe againft all opponants of what fort foeuer,
Horsman (1607)

Another instance of decay relevant to our concerns is the loss of word final unstressed vowels in ME: early ME bisyllabic *name*, derived from OE bisyllablic *nama*, becomes monosyllable *name* (= /nem/) in MSE. This change was among those that eliminated inflexional endings in the passage from OE to MSE.

Like INERTIA decay (entropy) is an unexplicated force of change. If I could really explain why houses need repairs or people die I would be off collecting my Nobel Prize. And like INERTIA decay is not specific to language change:

DECAY: Things wear out.

2 [Pron+*Self*] Become Words Around 1200

The dative pronouns procliticize to nominative *self* (FWP). Below we study the properties of these components and show how they determine the distribution and interpretation of [pron+*self*].

2.1 Personal pronouns and local binding

Personal pronouns in OE were used to express local binding (indicated by underlining). They could also be non-locally bound and deictically interpreted. OE lacked BT ANAPHORS – expressions, like *himself* in MSE, which must be locally bound when an argument of a V, A, N or P.

(5) a. syðþan he hine to guðe gegyred hæfde.
once he(nom) him(acc) for battle girded had *Beowulf* 1473
'once he girded himself for battle' (c750)

b. Wit unc wið hron-fixas werian þohton
we (1.nom.du) us (1.dat/acc.du) whale-tusks
werian þohton.
to protect thought *Beowulf* 540
'We thought to protect ourselves from whale-tusks.' (c750)

c. þa gegyrede heo hy mid hærenre tunecan ond ...
then dressed she(nom) her(acc) in a tunic of hair and
'then she dressed herself in a tunic of hair'... *Mart.*190 (c850 – 900)

d. þonne ðæt mon gadrige ðæt ðicke fenn on hine,
when that man gathers that thick mud on him(acc)
& hine mid ðy gehefegige,... *CP*.XLIV.329
and him(acc) therewith loads down c880
'when that man gathers that thick mud on himself and therewith loads himself down'

e. ...ðæt hie sylf hie ðeowen nemde
...that she(nom) self(nom) her(acc) handmaiden calls
'...(that was undoubtedly modesty) that she herself calls herself handmaiden' *BlHom* 5.I.13 (c971)

f. hu he him on þas world þingian ongan, ...
how he him in this world to insert began *BlHom*.105
'how he began to insert himself in this world' (c971)

g. ...hweðer he hine gefreclsian wolde
...whether he(nom) him(acc) set-free would *BlHom* III.29
'...whether he would set himself free' (c971)

h. Sibyrhtes broðor and swiðe mænig oþer ...
Sibyrht's brother and very many others...
cene hi weredon.
bravely them(acc) defended
'Sibyrht's brother and very many others bravely defended themselves.' *Maldon*.282 (c1000)

2.2 Non-Theta (Pleonastic) Pronouns

The locally bound pronouns in (5) are +*THETA*, meaning they satisfy a semantic role requirement of their governing verb. But from Late OE through ME we also find many non-theta (pleonastic) occurrences of pronouns. They do not satisfy either a semantic role requirement or a syntactic requirement of the verb. In OE they are usually dative, sometimes accusative, never genitive or nominative. They are always bound to the local subject, agreeing with it in person, number and gender and serve semantically to heighten the *involvement* of its referent: e.g. the subject acted intentionally or was involved in the action in some way other than the role it has in virtue of being the subject argument. At times they suggest a telic interpretation. They are almost obligatory with 'fear' and 'pray', (6b, d; but absent in 6h). They may take quantified NP antecedents, not just definite ones (6b, f). At times, (6i), passages are peppered with them. The *Saxon Chronicles* from 999 to 1067 has 58 locally bound dative pronouns: 57 are non-theta.

(6) a. ond hig lyfedon hym þa samod on clænnysse ond... *Mart*.214
'and they lived them then together in purity and ...' (c850-900)

b. ...on þæm magon nigon men standende him gebiddan, ...
'...on which may nine men stand and them pray...' *Mart*. 52 (c850–900)

c. he...ferde to þæm casere...ond hine aþenede
'he...went to the caesar...and him(acc) prostrating'
beforan þæm...cwæð *Mart*.86
'before him...said' (c875)

d. forðæm hi him ondrædað ða frecenesse ðe hi ne gesioð
'because they fear them the danger that they do not see'
CP.433 (c880)

e. ...& namon him wif of eallum ðam ðe hi gecuron
'...and (they) took *them* wives from all those that they chose'
...acceperunt *sibi* uxores ex omnibus quas elegerant
(Latin original)
ÆGen 6.2 (c1000)

f. Aledon hie ðær linwerigne, gestodon him æt his lices heafdum.
'Laid *they* there (his) limbs+weary, (and) stood *them* at his body's head.' *Dream* (c974)

g. forþam hi ondreddon þ he hi fordon wolde
because they feared that they them destroy would
'because they were afraid that they would destroy themselves' *Chron(E)* (1013)

h. ...ge swicon þa þære fyrding. & færde ælc mann him ham
...(they) abandoned then the expedition and went every man *him* home
'(they) abandoned then the expedition and everyone went home' *Chron(E)* (1016)

i. Ac he ne wandode na him metes to tylienne. ... & nam him on orfe & on mannum & .... gewende him þa east werd to his feder. & gewendon heom þa begen east weard ...
'But *he* not hesitated at all *him* provisions to provide... and took *him* in cattle and in men & ... and went *him* then eastward to his father, and went *them* then both eastward ...' *Chron*(E) (1052)

NB: *Pronoun changes* Already by 1000 1st and 2nd person accusative pronouns are replaced by their dative counterparts. This happens by 1250 in 3rd person (Southeastern dialects lag a little). So e.g. *hine* (3acc.masc.sg) gives way to *him.*

2.3 *Self* in OE

Self in OE functions to contrast (= identify from a set of alternatives) the referent of a definite NP (proper noun, personal pronoun, demonstrative+N), its ANTECEDENT, which it follows and agrees with as an adjective (usually strong) in case, number and gender. We use α as a variable ranging over case.

(7) [X_α+*self*$_\alpha$] is always contrastive and X_α, pronoun or full NP, is always +theta.

a. hwæt ***Crist self*** tæhte and his apostolas on þære niwan gecyðnisse
what Christ self (nom.sg.) and his apostles taught in the New Testament
'what Christ himself and his apostles taught in the NT' *ÆO&N* (c1000)

b. ***Þe hæðenan selfe*** hæfdon his wundor on þære mæstan are.
the pagans self(nom.pl) held his miracles in the greatest honor
'The heathens themselves held his miracles in the greatest honor.' *Mart* 12.150 (c850-900)

c. ond he geseah ***þone hælend sylfne*** standan on his godþrymme
'and he saw the Lord self(acc.m.sg) standing in his divine glory' *Mart*.8 (c850-900)

d. menn þa gearwiaþ clæne wununga on heor heortum ***Criste sylfum***
men who prepare a clean habitation in their hearts for Christ self (dat.m.sg.)
'men who prepare a clean home in their hearts for Christ himself' *BlHom*.73 (c971)

Self$_{\alpha}$ occurs immediately after its antecedent except *self*$_{\text{nom}}$, which occurs about 30% of the time (Farr 1905) in the predicate separated from its subject antecedent by small adverbs and object pronouns, which cliticize to the left edge of the VP (van Kemenade 1987):

(8) a. þa beoð swilce lareowas, swa swa ***Crist*** eft ***sylf*** cwæð:..
they are like those teachers of whom Christ also self (m.sg.) said:
'they are like those teachers of whom Christ also said himself…' *ÆO&N* (c1000)

b. Ðæt ***hi*** hit ***selfe*** dydon.
that they it(neut.acc.sg) self (nom.m.pl) did *CP*.LV.427
'That they did it themselves.' (c880)

c. swa ***he*** hyne ***sylf*** stafode, be hys sunu wifunge.
as he$_i$ had asked him$_j$(acc) self$_i$(m.sg.), concerning his son's wifing
'as he had asked him himself concerning his son's taking a wife' *ÆGen* 24.9 (c1000)

d. Se hælend him cwæð to. ***Ic*** beo ***sylf*** mid þe.
The Lord him said to I will be self (m.sg.) with thee
'The Lord said to him: I will myself be with thee' *ÆLS*.IV.16 (c1000)

e. ond ***he***$_i$ him$_j$ sæde ***sylf***$_i$ þæt his nama wære 'spiritus fornicationis',
and he$_i$ told him$_j$ self$_i$ that his$_i$ name was 'spiritus fornicationis'
'and he told him himself that his name was "spiritus fornicationis"' *Mart.*22 (c850-900)

NB nominative *sylf* in (9c) unambiguously contrasts the nominative subject not the accusative object *hyne*, otherwise it would have been *sylfne*, accusative. Had *sylf* contrasted *him* in (9e) it would have been dative *sylfum*.

(9) ***self***$_\alpha$ **has main stress and counts for alliteration** (Mitchell 1979, Ogura 1989)

Hi hyne þa ætbæron	to brimes faroðe,	
They him(acc) then bore	to the seas' edge	
<u>S</u>wæse ge<u>s</u>iþas,	swa he <u>s</u>elfa bæd	*Beowulf* 29-30
(His) beloved followers,	as he self bade	(c750)

(10) ***self***$_\alpha$ **occurs, as expected, in ICEs** (Inherently Contrastive Expressions): Coordinations (a,b,c), Gappings (d,e), Comparatives (f,g).

a. his gastlican gesihþe be þam Hælende sylfum & his ge laðunge &...
'his spiritual vision concerning the Lord self and his church & ...' *ÆO&N* (c1000)

b. He us æt urum assum bereafige & æt urum þingum & us sylfe þeowige.
'He may take our asses and our things and us selves as bonds.' *ÆGen* (1000)

c. þa underþeoddon hi hi selfe ond eall þæt mænnisce cynn to sare ond…
'then subjected they them selves and all mankind to pain and…' *Mart* (c850-900)

d. Selð Goðe his æhta, & hine selfne diobule.
'(He) gives to god his goods and him(acc) self(acc) to the devil.' *CP* (c880)

e. ac hie gearwiaþ deoflum eardunga, & him selfum ece wite
'but they prepare for devils a dwelling, & for them selves eternal punishment.' *BlHom* (c971)

f. þa afulode he sona, swa þæt nænig mon ne meahte aræf nan þone stenc ne furðor he sylfa;
'Then he soon became rotten, so that nobody could bear the stench any more than he self (nom.sg.weak)' *Mart* (c850-900)

g. ...suelce we maran earfe hæbben ðæt hie geðeon ðonne hie selfe, &..
'...as if we have more need that they prosper than they selves (nom.pl)' *CP* (c880)

Note that if a coordinate expression is +theta we count each conjunct as +theta.

(11) Given an occurrence of [X_α + *self*$_\alpha$]
a. if X_α is a full NP then it usually denotes an exalted personage
b. if X_α is a pronoun it denotes an exalted personage less than half the time; the contrast required by *self* is satisfied in linguistically local ways.

Farr (1905:19) already remarks that 'The noun modified [by *self*$_\alpha$, ELK] is, with few exceptions, an expression for the Deity (God, Crist, Drihten, etc.), a superhuman personage (heahengel, deofol, etc.), or a person of exalted rank (cyning, eorl, David, Petrus, etc.).' See König & Siemund (1998) for a more refined analysis. So when the antecedent of *self* is an exalted personnage it contrasts with whatever objects the personnage is exalted with respect to. Mere mortals in the case of God.

But when X_α is a pronoun it happens more than half the time in my data that the contrast required by *self*$_\alpha$ is established locally as in (10b-d) and (12a,b):

(12) a. 'Ne sohte ic na ***hine***, ac ***he sylf*** com to me. *ÆLS*.III.1.445
'Not sought I not him, but he self came to me.' (c1000)

b. forðæm ***nan mon*** ne bitt oðerne ðæt he ***hine*** rære, gif ***he self*** nat ðæt he afeallen bið;
'because no man$_i$ asks another$_j$ to lift him$_i$ if he$_i$ self knows not that he has fallen' *CP*.LVIII.441 (c880)

(13) **In [pron$_{\alpha}$+*self*$_{\alpha}$], pron$_{\alpha}$ may have a non-local antecedent.** It always does when α = nom, as in (12b) and (13a,b,c). This follows from (14).

a. ***Heora*** earmes wæron swylce ormæte beames. ***heora*** clawa scearpe. and *hi sylfa* un-mild-heorta.
'Their arms were like immense beams, their claws sharp, and themselves merciless.' *ÆLS* IV 288 (c 1000)

b. ***Abraham*** soðlice ymbsnað hys sunu Ismahel on þone ylcan dæg, swa swa God him bebead. & ***he sylf*** wearð ymbsniden þa he wæs nygan & hundnygantig geara.
'Abraham verily circumcised his son Ishmael on the same day as God him bade, and he self was circumcised when that he was nine and ninety years old.' *ÆGen*16.24 (c. 1000)

c. ***Abraham*** þa het Isaac beran þone wudu to þære stowe and ***he self*** bær his sweord and fyr
'Abraham then ordered Isaac to carry the wood to the place and he self bore his sword and fire.' *ÆGen* 22.6 (c 1000)

(14) ANAPHORA INVARIANT: At all stages of English subject pronouns cannot be locally bound (a fact which is unchanged by contrasting them with *self*$_{(\alpha)}$).

(15) **[pron$_{\alpha}$+*self*$_{\alpha}$] may also take non-local antecedents when $\alpha \neq$ nominative**:

a. ...æppelbære treow..., ***ðæs*** sæd sy ***on him syluum*** ofer eorðan ...
'the fruit tree ..., whose seed is in itself upon the earth ...' *ÆGen* 1.11 (c 1000)

b. Uþe ic swiþor þæt ðu ***hine selfne*** geseon moste...!
'How I wish that you could have seen him self (= Grendel) .' *Beowulf* 960 (c 750)

c. Hi þa hrædlice ...gewendan eft ongean ***þone cyning***...& ***hiene selfne*** gefengon
'They then quickly ...turned again toward that king$_i$ ...and himself$_i$ captured' *Alf. Orosius* <Mitchell 1985;1992

d. ***Him selfum*** ðincð þæt he nænne næbbe.
'(It) seems to him self that he has nothing.' *Alf. Boethius* 29.66.11 <Traugott 1992; 211

e. 'Selre is þæt man ***me selfne*** bærne þonne þa godcundan gewritu.'
'It is better that one burns myself rather than the holy scriptures.' *Mart.*158 (c850-900)

f. ..., for þam þa ***he*** deð swa swa ***hine selfne*** gewyrð,
'..., therefore he did just as it pleases himself, ...' *Æ Pref Gen* (c1000)

(16) Locally bound objects of verbs of bodily harm are regularly [$pron_\alpha$+$self_\alpha$]

(16) supports the contrast interpretation of $self_\alpha$, as in OE times one fought others endlessly to survive; suicide was not an expected option. In Ogura's (1995) study, of Vs that had at least 5 occurrences of locally bound objects, there were 10 which always took them with $self_\alpha$. They include *acwellan* 'to kill', *ahon* 'to hang', *fordon* 'to destroy', *forseon* 'to scorn, renounce', *(ge)haelan* 'to cure, castrate', *ofslean* 'to slay' *(ge)swencan* 'to afflict, oppress', and *þrea(ga)n* 'to threaten, torture'. My data present only one counterexample. (17) is representative.

(17) ac heo lyfde sceand-lice . swa swa swin on meoxe.
and mid healicum synnum hi sylfe fordyd
'but she lived shamefully, even as swine on a dunghill,
and by deadly sins her self(acc.f.sg.) destroyed' *ÆLS* III.528

(18) $Self_\alpha$ does not occur as a possessor.

By 1000 AD (Mitchell 1985) pronominal possessors are expressed by the personal pronouns in the genitive case: *his*, *hire*, *hira*, ... When emphatic or contrastive they are augmented with the adjective *agen* (< *agan* 'to own, possess'). Thus the MSE possessive is established by 1000ad. *agen*, like *self*, (19a), may modify referentially autonomous NPs. In (19b) *his agen* has a local antecedent. In (19c) it takes the DO as antecedent, and in (19d) it has a non-local antecedent.

(19) a. ...and seo sawl nis na of ***godes aȝenum*** gecynde
'...and the soul is not of God's own nature' *ÆLS*.1.16 (c1000)

b. & ***Laban*** aras on night ...& cyrde to ***hys aʒenum*** hame
'& Laban arose in the night and returned to his own home'
ÆGen.31.55 (c 1000)

c. & hie ***hine*** ongyredon ***his aʒenuym*** hrægle & ...
'and they stripped him of his own raiment and ...' *Hom3*III.324 (1025-50)

d. ond þa ***he*** ut eode, þa flugon hine ***his aʒene*** mæn...
'and when he came out, then his own men fled (from) him'
Mart 52 (c850-900)

Thus we explain half of (1b) by INERTIA: Contrastive possessors were established with *own* by 1000 and nothing has happened to change that.

3 The Creation of *Him+Self*: 1000-1250, by Function Word Proclisis

$$\text{(20) } [\text{prón}_{dat}] + [\text{sélf}_{nom}] \overset{\text{FWP}}{\Rightarrow} [\text{prŏn}_{dat}\text{+sélf}_{nom}] \Rightarrow [\text{prŏn + sélf}])$$

$$\alpha\text{-theta} \qquad \alpha\text{-theta} \qquad \alpha\text{-theta}$$

Thus by 1250 we have a paradigm [pron+*self*] of phonological words, derived from the dative pronouns and the nominative contrastor *self*. Once formed the internal pronoun ceases to be felt as dative, as the derived forms do not contrast with others that differ by the case of the pronoun. Similarly *self* in [pron+*self*] ceases to be felt as nominative, not contrasting with *self* in any other case. Case marking on adjectives is basically lost by 1200 (C. Allen 1995). So [pron+*self*] is *caseless*, like *John* or *the man*, meaning that it is not marked for case and thus is not constrained by case requirements predicates impose on their arguments. But [pron+*self*] do vary for person, number and gender, as the dative pronouns they are built from do. Also during this period bare $self_{\alpha}$, all cases α, dies out as an independent definite NP contrastor (Our last, isolated, attestation is in 1272).

We first support the correctness that OE evolved in the way (20) indicates. Then we consider the distribution and interpretation of the derived forms, which we sometimes represent by [*him+self*] for concreteness.

3.1 Enabling (20)

By Ælfric, c1000, we find non-theta dative pronouns followed by nominative *self* frequently enough to interpret them by function composition as a unit (even though they are not a syntactic constituent, Farr 1905:26), meaning 'identify the referent of the subject from among the alternatives and heighten its involvement'. Interpreting [*him+self*] as a unit just meant not having to identify the subject referent twice. [*him+self*] must have a meaning as soon as it is created. We don't first use words for a generation or two and then start assigning them meanings. We posit (Keenan 2000):

THE INTERPRETATIVE PRINCIPLE (IP)
The constituents of an expression φ are meaningful.

(21) a. ðæt he ... in mynster eode, þæt he him seolf ær getim brade
'that he ... entered a monastery that he_i self had earlier built for him_i'
Bede 208.14

b. Hu mæg se ðonne bion orsorg se ðe him self wat ðæt he gesyngað?
'How may the one be confident who himself knows that he sins?' *CP* 425 (c880)

c. & he ys geworden nu...þæra sceaðena ealdor, þe he him sylf gegaderode
'and he_i has now become....the leader of the robbers that he_i self has gathered (to) him_i' *ÆO&N* (c1000)

d. ...he is him sylf angin. na gesceapen. ne geworht.
'...he is himself the beginning, neither created nor made'
ÆLS 1.14 (c1000)

e. He næs na ofslagen, ac he him sylf gewat, ...
'He not+was not slayed, but he departed (= died) on his own.'
(Non-theta *him* is common with *witan* 'to depart' from the earliest OE) *ÆO&N* 661 (c1000)

In (22) it is hard to avoid treating *him self* as both a syntactic and a semantic unit.

(22) a. & he com him sylf æfter — *ÆGen* 3.18 (c1000)
'and he himself comes later'

b. On þam dæge sealde God him sylf hys wed Abrame, & Cwæð...
'On that day God himself gave his covenant to Abram, & said...' — *ÆGen* 15.18 (c1000)

c. God foresceawað, min sunu, him sylf ða offrung
'God himself foresees, my son, the offering' — *ÆGen* 22.8 (c1000)

These data show that *him* and *self* were in positions where procliticization was plausible given our other attested cases. And of course

(23) [pron+*self*] carries main stress on *self*, just where FWP predicts.

3.2. Alternate Hypothesis (AH)

AH: [pron+*self*] result from reanalyzing *self* as a N.

The main motivation for AH is to account for the 1st and 2nd sg forms *miself/þiself* by taking *mi* and *þi* as possessive adjectives, which combine independently with Ns and so with *self*. Also, mainly after 1300, we find occasional occurrences of *his self* and *myn owyn self* (Mustanoja 1960; van Gelderen 2000). Finally AH rightly predicts that *him+self* occurs as a subject since it is an NP and NPs occur as subjects. But AH fails to account for the *creation* of [pron+*self*].

First, it makes incorrect predictions: (1) If *self* is an N we should have, contrary to fact, attestations of Det+*self* in general: **each self*, **no self*, **most self/selves*. (2) And certainly we should have other possessive NPs with *self*, but **John's self*, **no man's self*, ... (3) And crucially, why are there no attestations of *min(e) self*, *þin(e) self* or *mire self* in this period? In 1200 these are by far the most widely used possessive forms, even in *Lay(A)* with the first productive attestations of *miself*. (In our 5,000+ lines of *Lay(A)*, there were 282 1st and 2nd sg possessors. Of these 83% were full forms, dominantly *mine* and *þine* but also *min/þin*, *mire/þire*, *minne/þinne*, and *mines/þines*. Only 17% were the reduced forms *mi/þi*. So H1 predicts that 83% of 1st /2nd sg [pron+*self*] should be built from full forms. But *none* are. Similarly the *Ormulum*, *Siriz* and *F&W* use both full and reduced forms of possessive adjectives, but [pron+*self*] never appears with full forms. (4) If *self* is a N we should expect to find possessive adjective + *self* in 1st and 2nd plural and in 3rd person, all numbers. But here we find only the dative pronouns until the late 1300s, as in (24); the datives continue into the 1400s, (24g), and possibly into the 1500s (24h,i). (5) Lastly, AH predicts the wrong date for the appearance of *itself.* It is attested in the late 1300s: ... *pouerte of temperal goodes in hitself is no vertu,...* (*Lollard Sermons* 1390–1400) but possessive *its* is only attested at the end of the 1500s.

(24) a. Ye kouthe noght rule *yow selve* — *Piers Pl* 399; (1372-79)
b. For I have saved *yowself* and your sonnes. — ibid. 11049
c. Wher ȝee demen not anentis *ȝou self,* — Wiclyffe, *James*.II.4 (c1390)
d. He scheweth us by ensamples *usselve* to wisse. — *Piers Pl* 4748
e. we schulden ... mekeli knowleche *vs self* as oon of hem,... — *Lollard* (1390s)
f. ...& stiriþ vs to many grete synnes & to forȝete *vs self* — Wycliffe X.192
g. We commende not *vs silf* eftsoon to ȝou... — *Donet* 1443-9
h. I do not greatly mistruste *meselfe* — *Utopia* 1551
i. if thou ...art bounde to procure it to others, why not chiefly to *theself* — *Utopia* 1551

Second, our proposal makes correct predictions that AH fails to make: it fails to predict that [pron+*self*] occur as non-NPs: *I'll do it myself, John himself did it.*

But most crucially, AH fails to predict the forms which actually occur when [pron+*self*] become words. Through 1250, *all* the ME texts in our corpus with any 1st or 2nd person forms use dative *me/þe* + *self.* Only a few also use *mi* and *þi* with *self.* During 1250 -1300 *miself* and *þiself* become dominant. But the dative pronouns remain for another hundred years in 1 and 2 pl. (24), and they remain in third person both numbers through MSE.

Clearly the first *-self* forms in ME are built from dative pronouns. We account for these forms and the absence of *mine/þine self* (*self* is not an N, so not modifiable by possessive adjectives), as well as the absence of [(*h*)*it self*] as *hit* was not dative; the neuter dative was *him. miself* and *þiself* derive from vowel reduction in unstressed syllables. Note that of the dative pronouns in OE, only 1sg and 2sg are light monosyllables. All others (*him, hire, us, eow*) are either bisyllabic or consonant final. The third person cases *himself, hemself* are among the phonological types (C)VC'CV with C' nasal which Fidelholtz (1975) shows do not undergo vowel reduction: *ambitious, anticipate.*

Once the vowels have reduced we can reinterpret *mi* and *þi* as possessive adjectives. Pattern Generalization from the singular cases accounts for the later change to *ourself* and *yourself.* This reanalysis also allows analyzing *self* in *myself* as an N, a possibility consciously played with by authors from EME on. 'To thine own self be true' saith the Bard. But equally this possibility has not been grammaticized in MSE.

3.3 Deriving the Distribution and Interpretation of [Pron+*Self*] in the 1200s

1. OE *him* has both + and – theta occurrences; so does ME [*him+self*] (INERTIA). More explicitly ME [*him+self*] accepts a theta role assignment from a predicative, but does not require one.
2. So on the one hand [*him+self*] behaves as *self* with a prefix: it inherits (INERTIA) completely the distribution and –theta interpretation of nominative *self* in OE, occurring in the VP or in apposition to subjects, contrasting the referent of the subject in both cases (INERTIA).
3. On the other hand [*him+self*] accepts theta role assignments and, since it is not marked for case and thus not case constrained in its distribution, it may occur wherever +theta NPs do: DO and OPrep positions, as well as Subject and Object of Comparison (see below for Possessor position). It retains (INERTIA) its contrastive meaning on all occurrences.

3.3.1 Adverbial Occurrences

[*him+self*] inherits immediately the adverbial occurrences of OE $self_{nom}$. (25a-f) are all from EME (Early ME: c1150-1300):

(25) a. ...he wass himm-sellf þær hidd *Orm* H. 1090
'...he was himself hidden there (c1200)

b. þat Crist sade himself us to forbisne, *V&V* 141
'what Christ said himself to us as an example' (c1200)

c. and heo werð hire solf waschen of hire fule sunnen
'and she became herself washed of her foul sins'
Lay(A) XVII.157 (c1205)

d. Arh ich was meself and ... *Wohunge* 277
'Fearful I was myself and ...' (c1220)

e. And alle his feren twelf / He schal kniȝten himself
'And all his twelve comrades he shall knight himself'
King Horn 489 (c1225)

f. Betere is i go miself and se: *Havelok* 2097 (c1270)
Hweþer he sitten nou and wesseylen [= drink healths]

3.3.2 Subject Apposition

[*him+self*] occurs in apposition to the subject in EME:

(26) a. bute þane mete þat hie hire self et — *OE Hom* 47
'except the meat that she herself did eat' — c1150-1200

b. ...þa þa he him solf com alse he hefde bihaten
'... when then he him self came as he had promised'
Lambeth 153 (c1150-1200)

c. & tu þe sellf narrt rihht nohht wurrþ — *Orm* H. 5020
'& thou thyself are not at all worthy' — (c1200)

d. ðeih ic me selu none ne habbe swa (swa) me behofde;
'though I myself have none as it behooved me' — *V&V* 53 (c1200)

e. þe orl himseolf ferde beforen al his genge,
and Arður himseolf arnde biuoren al his ferde.
'The earl in person led his whole company, — *Lay(A)* 10589
and Arthur himself ran before all his followers.' — (c1205)

f. godd him feolf feið þurh þe prophete: ... — *H. Meidenhad* 240
'God himself says through the prophet ...' — (c1200-1250)

g. mi swete lefmon poure þu þe self was — *Wohunge* 279
'my sweet beloved one, poor thou thyself was' — (c1220)

h. He him felf wurð ðanne circumcif — *Gen&Exod* 999
'He himself was then circumcised' — (c1250)

i. þerof shall i meself borw be. [= safe/rescued be]
Havelok 1667(c1270)

Fact Adnominal [pron+*self*] occurs only on subjects in my texts before 1300. Then it spreads to other theta positions.

3.3.3 Theta [*Him+Self*] Occurs in INHERENTLY CONTRASTIVE EXPRESSIONS (ICEs)

(27) Coordinations

a. he nemnede hire cun to more. and hire su[l]f to gerde and…
'he compared her kin to a root and herself to a rod and ...'
OEHom 34 (c1150-1200)

b. …hit bieð sume de...want hem seluen and iec sumen odre te michele hearme,
'there are some who...turn themselves & also some others to great harm, ...' — *V&V*65 (c1200)

c. Godd Allmahhtiȝ ȝife us...to cnawenn & to sen himm sellfenn & hiss kinde
'and God Almighty allows us...to know and to see himself and his nature' *Orm* H. 19476 (c1200)

d. Heo feol on hir bedde, / þer heo knif hudde,
To sle wiþ King loþe / and hurselue boþe
'She fell on her bed, / where she a knife hid / to slay with the hated King / and herself both' *King Horn* 1195 (c1225)

e. ...he fulden famen, ðor hem-felf & here orf framen
'...they should together there themselves and their cattle serve' *Gen & Ex* 1641 (c1250)

f. And helpes me and yuself baþe, *Havelok* 2592 (c1270)

(28) Objects of Comparison

a. Luuie we god ... and vre emcristene alse us suelf...
'Let us love God ... and our fellow Christians as ourselves ...' *Lambeth*.PM 77 (c1150-1200)

b. ȝef hit if godd [leof], þet if, him feolf fwa ilich, hit na wunder
'If it is dear to God, that is, so like himself, no wonder' *H.Meid*141 (c1200-1250)

c. hwen euchan luueð godd mare þen him seoluen ant þen alle þe odre;
'because each one loveth god more than himself and than all the others' *S. Warde* 263 (c1200)

d. & te birrþ ec, ... firrþrenn iwhillc oþerr mann / All all swa summ þe selfenn
'you ought also, ... to assist each other man/just as yourself' *Orm* H.5082 (c1200)

(29) Focus words

a. þat he had newe imaked to him sealf one
'that he had recently made for himself alone' *OE Misc. PofL* 512 < Farr

b. ...hie bieð ut-iworpen ðurh dieules lore, naht for hem se luen ane, ac for oðre ec awei to affleien
'...they are thrown out through the devil's lore, not for themselves alone, but also to put others to flight' *V&V* 65 (c1200)

c. þu...wakien i moni care, nawt ane for þe-felf...ah...for monie oðre
'Thou lie awake in many a care, not only for thyself but for many others' *H.Meid* 421 (c1200)

d. None lay by hemself a-lone, But eche on oþer, ...
H. Synne 2517 (1303)

Even without a focus word like *ane*, 'one' or *alone* 'all one', *by+self* is used in ME with the contrastive modern sense of 'without the presence or help of others' .

(30) a. ȝie ðe senegin be ȝew seluen, doð scame ȝew seluen
'Ye who sin by yourselves (= on your own), do shame yourselves' *V&V* 123 (c1200)

b. & sone summe he cuþe be/Himm ane bi himm self enn /He flæh till weste
'& as soon as he was able / him alone, by himself, / He flew to the desert' *Orm* H. (c1200)

(31) Exception Phrases

a. Nat þah na mon bute ham feolfen hwet ham fticheð ofte
'Not-knows though no man but themselves what often pains them' *H. Meidenhad* 97 (c1200)

b. Wel hie mihte ða [witen] þat hie scolde bien heiȝest ourer alle þing on heuene and on ierðe,...,wid-uten him seluen
'Well might she then know that she should be highest over all things in Heaven and on earth,...,except Himself' *V&V* 53 (c1200)

c. ...þat no mon of al þis word.ne þar me wiþ delen: but þi self al one
'...which no man in this whole world is to share with me but Thyself alone ...' *Talkyng* 58.8 (c1380)

d. Sche was vanyssht riht as hir liste, That no wyht bot hirself it wiste
'She sped off just as she wanted to, so that no one but herself knew it' Gower *CA* (c1390)

Explaining (1c)

The data in (27) – (31) show that [pron+*self*] occur in ICEs from their inception in Early ME. And we expect them to as [pron+*self*] inherits its contrastive meaning from that of $self_{nom}$ in OE. Further [pron+*self*] is not constrained to have a local antecedent in these environments. It is non-locally anteceded in (27a,c), (28b), and (31d). In (31c) it is used deictically (no antecedent). In (31b) it either has no antecedent or a non-local one. Thus the anaphora pattern we see in ICEs since the very inception of [pron+*self*] is the one we see today. We account for the facts in (1c) by INERTIA.

(32) +theta [pron+*self]* accept QUANTIFIED NP (QNP) antecedents

In OE [pron$_\alpha$+*self*$_\alpha$] accepted QNP antecedents only when α = nom, as per inspection of our earlier data. By INERTIA this pattern was extended, given that +theta dative pronouns could take QNP antecedents: (28c), (29d) and (33a,b).

(33) a. and leren <u>elch man</u> to helpen <u>him seluen</u> þe hwile he mai.
'and let each man learn to help himself while he may'
OE Hom 29.185 (c1150-1200)

b. <u>Sume odre</u> ...nimeð cloðes of religiun, and sone <u>hem se luen</u> healdeð for hali,
'Some others ... take the clothes of a religious order and at once themselves hold for holy' *V&V* 5 (c 1200)

Of course bare pronouns retain (INERTIA) the possibility of QNP antecedents:

(34) a. <u>Moni</u> halt <u>him</u> til an make, ... *H. Meidenhad* 35
'Many keep them to one mate,...' (c1200)

b. Ne mei <u>nan mon</u> habben al his wil. and blissien <u>him</u> mid þisse wordle
'No man may have all his will and rejoice himself with this world,' *Lambeth* 33 (c 1200)

Consider now the claim in 3.3.2 that [pron+*self*] occurs freely in +theta positions. Most of our examples above have been of DOs, though a few cases of OPreps have been given: (29c,d), (30a,b), (31b). Here are a few more:

(35) a. Fiftene Salmes seggeð…þe eareste fiue <u>for ouseolf</u> ant alle þet…
'Fifteen Psalms recite ... the first five for yourself and all that ...' *A.Riwle*.60 (c1200)

b. Wiþ him ȝe wolden pleie / <u>Betwex ȝou selue</u> tweie
'With him ye will play / between yourselves two'
KingHorn 35 (c 1225)

c. An he wurðe <u>in him-seluen</u> prud *Gen&Exod* 272
'And he became in himself proud' (c1250)

We have also noted a few cases of Objects of Comparison in (28) and arguments of Exception Phrases in (31). Further, contrary to Modern English (post 1700), [pron+*self*] leads a lively existence as a Subject.

(36) **[pron+self] as Subject in ME and Early Modern English**

a. þanne bie we turnd to him; and he to us alse him self seið
'Than shall we be turned to him and he to us as himself saith'
OE Hom 61 (1150-1200)

b. Swa haueð þe ðouel ... and onde to monne...þeh him solf þe betre nere.
'So hath the devil and hatred towards man, ...; though himself the better not+were' *Lamb* XVI.153 (c1150-1200)

c. ʒif he gifð bleðeliche to eten and to drinken, ..., and him self lið on sume heaued-senne, ...
'if he gives blithely to eat and to drink, ..., and himself lies in some cardinal sin, ...' *V&V* 37 (c1200)

d. Fulle seue ʒere/þat to Rymenild he ne sente, / Ne him self ne wente
'full seven years / that to Rymenild he didn't send, / nor himself didn't go' *K. Horn* (c1225)

e. ...hys bere he fonde,/Besyde hys shepe, slayn on a londe Asswyþe hym self gan to rede / who hadde do þat yche dede;
'... his bear he found, / Beside his sheep, slain on a "londe" Immediately himself began to consider / who had done that evil deed' *H.Synne* 4097 (1303)

f. Behold, himself has laid him down, / In length and breadth ...
(Roman soldier wondering how to get Christ on the cross; note the non-theta *him* anteceded by Subject *himself*)
York Play 75 (c 1425)

For some of these cases, (36c,d), one might claim that the apparent subject *him+self* results from dropping a *he* from *he him+self* in contexts comparable to Conjunction Reduction ones in MSE. But I think this not to be a viable analysis in the general case. First, scholars of diverse stripes (Hulk and van Kemenade 1995, Mustanoja 1960, Mossé 1979, Roberts 1993, van Gelderen 2000) agree that ME is not Pro-Drop (expletives aside). Secondly, subject pronoun retention in ME seems fully regular following a complementizer. Of the 65 relative clauses in Moessner (1989), Mossé (1979), Fischer (1992), and Mustanoja (1960) whose subjects would be pronouns in MSE, all were in fact pronouns. (37) illustrates the relative clause cases, (38) sentence complements. (Note the ECP violation in (37a) and the resumptive subject pronoun in (37d)).

(37) a. þa men þe hi wenden ðat ani god hefden *Chron*
'the men that they thought that had any money' (c1137)

b. al þat þu mist mid cliure smiten *Owl & Nightingale* (c1200)
'all that thou might with (your) claws smite' (Moessner p.162)

c. eurich man mit þet he haueð mai beggen heueriche
'every man with what he has may buy heavenly bliss'
Poema Morale (c1200) (Moessner p.162)

d. Wot ic ðor non ðat he ne biueð
'I know no one there who wouldn't tremble (...that he wouldn't tremble)' *Gen & Exod* 2280 (c1250)

e. Ich wende ... þat ich i-seie were soþ *The Fox and the Wolf*
'I think ...what I saw was true' (c1275)

f. bondes þat þu leidest on min hondes *Havelok*
'fetters which you laid on my hands' (c1285)

g. God hadde herd þat he besoght *H.Synne* 4044
'God had heard what he asked for' (< Mossé)

(38) a. hwat mai ic don ðat ic mihte hauen ðat eche lif? *V&V* 67
'What may I do that I might have that eternal life?' (c1200)

b. ðanne ðu ðus hauest ðine luue te gode, ðanne behoueð
ðat ðu bie wel warr ðat tu luuiȝe ðine nexte,
'When thou thus hast thy love in God (it) behooves thee
that thou be well aware that thou shouldst love
thy neighbour...' *V&V* 39 (c1200)

c. himm bidde icc þatt he't write rihht *Ormulum* D97
'him bid (order) I that he it write correctly' (c1200

d. beseche ich þe ... þet tu luvie me *Ancrene Wisse* 80
'I beseech thee ...that you love me' (c1225) (< Mossé)

e. he wolde þat he ded wor *Havelok* 504
'he wished that he were dead' (c1285)

And we get [*him+self*] as subject following the *that* and *wh*-complementizers.

(39) **post-complementizer occurrences of Subject [pron+*self]***

a. There preched a Pardonere as he a prest were, ...
And seide that hymself myghte assoilen hem alle
Piers. Prol. 68 (c1375)

b. And he shal venge yow after that hymself witnesseth,
Chaucer *Mel* 191 (C1390)

c. thei seiynge that hem silf weren wise, Wycliffe; *Rom*1.22. LV. (c1390) < Warner

d. ...whyuche thynge hym selfe can not denye,...
More: Conf 227 (1532)

e. Two glasses where herself herself beheld Sh: *Venus & Adonis* (c1600)

f. but he...protefted...that himselfe was cleere and innocent.
Horsman 37 (1607)

g. But there was a certain man, called Simon, which ... bewitched the people of Samaria, giving out that himself was som great one: *KJ Acts 8.9* (1611)

Further support are cases where *him+self* coordinates with full NP subjects:

(40) a. the forseide John Norhampton...& hym self most y-maked assembles and gadringes of companyes...
London English (1384)

b. So that himself and al his host were of defalte of drinke almost Destruid,... Gower CA (1393)

c. ...tak hede, /how that ȝour-silf and ȝoure brother blyve/ for the croune Lydgate 1915 (1421)

d. ye send me no letter from Caleys,
neder thy broder nor thyselve, *Cely* (1475)

e. his Imperial Majesty...desired that himself, and his Royal Consort ... might have the happiness ...of dining with me
Swift 283 (1726)

The Drop hypothesis would have to distinguish the many cases where we don't drop – (26a, b, c, d, g, h, i) from those where we do. By contrast our approach predicts both *him+self* and *he him+self* as Subject. We also have one piece of textual evidence that supports the existence of bare *him+self* as Subject.

Namely, there are two manuscripts of *Laȝamon's Brut*, Lay(A) and Lay(B), c1200–1250. Lay(A) shows many archaic features, such as the accusative pronoun *hine* and, crucially for us, *he self* as a contrastive pronominal subject . Lay(B) by contrast rarely uses *hine* and in the 5,000 lines I studied, always uses *him+self* (not *he him+self*) where Lay(A) uses *he self.* Here is one line (10180):

(41) a. and ȝif he cumeð riden sorȝe he scal ibiden; *Lay*(A)
he seolf and his ferde faeie scal iwuðen

b. and ȝef he comeþ ride; sorwe he sal a-bide; *Lay*(B)
him-seolf and his ferde; faeie sal worþe
'If he comes riding (there) he shall suffer misfortune;
he and his army shall be doomed.'

Repeated examples of this sort persuade me that the scribe of Lay(B) was using *him+self* as subject with the same meaning that *he self* in Lay(A) expressed.

POSSESSORS are a counterexample to our claim in 2.3.2. Possessor of N is a +theta position, but [pron+*self*] does not occur there in any stage of English: *John prefers *himself's bike / his own bike*. Explanation of this fact invokes a possibly new learnability principle. As we have seen, (18), *his+own* in OE was the contrastive possessor construction. But once the [pron+*self*] forms existed as caseless NPs why did we not also say *himself's bike*, just as we say *John's bike*?

The reason, I believe, is that the independent meaning of *him+self* would yield synonymy between *himself's* and *his own*. [pron+*self*] and [poss adj+*own*] would be isomorphic paradigms (*myself's/my own*, *yourself's/your own*, etc.) whose corresponding items are synonymous referentially dependent contrastive forms. This systemic synonymy is incompatible with the language learning dynamic called CONTRAST in E. Clark (1993) and GAINFUL LEARNING here:

GAINFUL LEARNING (GL): New words have new meanings

'Why buy something you already have?'.[1] Less metaphorically: to express desires, make requests, engage in social intercourse, etc. language learners are motivated to master the ambient language(s). Learning to say new things contributes to that goal, learning to say something you can already

---

[1] The effect of Clark's CONTRAST and our GL on learning behavior is the same, so we can accept her evidence in support of its correctness. We seem to differ with regard to the causal and logical link to Anti-synonymy. Clark (1993) sees Contrast 'Words contrast in meaning' as driving GL: 'For children to assume contrast offers considerable economy of effort in acquisition'. In contrast I see Clark's CONTRAST as deriving from the learning dynamic: what we're doing in learning a language is learning new expressions.

say does not. Thus I see the ANTI-SYNONYMY PRINCIPLE *Different words have different meanings* as a corollary of GL, deriving from how languages are learned. See Carstairs-McCarthy (1998) for helpful discussion of this principle.

Thus we explain the absence of [pron+*self*]'*s*: we inherit (INERTIA) a paradigm [poss+*own*] that works well, and we don't learn synonymous paradigms.

Two remarks on GAINFUL LEARNING:

1. GL is plausibly a special case of INERTIA: You have already learned X for meaning A so you won't start using Y unless acted on by an outside force – such as the Norman Conquest and later French influence, which threatened native *pig* with *pork*, *sheep* with *mutton*, *brotherly* with *fraternal*, etc. but where semantic or pragmatic differentiation usually led to avoidance of pure synonymy (though a few cases may have slipped through: *guarantee* vs. *warranty).*

2. GL plausibly entails a related learning dynamic, which I called in earlier versions of this paper the INITIAL EXPOSURE EFFECT:

   INITIAL EXPOSURE EFFECT (IEE)
   If two words compete for meaning X in context Y, learners favor the word they were exposed to first, which increases early exposure for new learners, ...

By *favor* here I mean 'use as the default': the later learned word being reserved for special circumstances. More clearly than GL the IEE is a positive feedback principle. If *w* and *w'* are equally frequent expressions for meaning X in context Y and, for whatever reason w becomes more frequent, this increases early exposure for new learners, which further increases *w*'s frequency (one's contemporaries being more important models than the +1 generation), which further increases early exposure, ... Possibly the IEE accounts for some of the language changes with S-shaped data curves (Kroch 1989, Bailey 1973). We conclude now with an explanation for (1a).

4 The Creation of Anaphora and Pronominals c1500

The ME period saw the creation of a paradigm of referentially dependent contrastive words [pron+*self*] formed by FWP from historically dative pronouns and nominative *self*. By SPLIT the pronouns remain in the language, continuing to express local binding except (though when contrast was intended [pron+*self*] were used). In fact the use of non-theta pronouns (always bound to the local subject recall) expanded until the 1400s. Here are some representative examples:

(42) *Think:*

a. Now beþenke þe weyl on þys — *H.Synne* 151 (1303)
b. Floripe bythought hir on a gyle [trick] — *Sultan* 1571 (c1400)

Repent:

c. wharto shuld y þan me repente — *H. Synne* 4497 (1303)
d. but [unless] thou repente the here anone — *Sultan* 2517 (c1400)

Possession:

e. He chofen hem wiwes of caym — *Gen & Exod* 543 (c1250)
'They chose them wives of Cain's seed'
f. He gate hym grete powere and myʒt — *H.Synne* 3807 (1303)

Fear:

g. Slep wel faste, and dred þe nouth: — *Havelok* 661 (1272)

Motion:

h. tatt he comm himm siþþenn ut … — *Ormulum* 1710 (c1200)
'that he came him later out …'
i. þe King him rod an huntinge. — *King Horn*.645 (c1225)
[rode a-hunting]
j. He wente him to þen inne — *Siriz* 2.19. (1272-83)
k. ʒho ras hire upp, & … — *Ormulum*.2655 (c1200)
[she rose up…]
l. Hauelok sette him dun anon — *Havelok* 927 (c1285)
m. Þan restyd he hym fro al erþly werkys — *H.Synne* 831 (1303)
n. And for he bare hym so meke and softe, — *H.Synne* 5835 (1303)

During the 1500s there is a sharp drop in local binding by pronouns and a corresponding rise in the use of [pron+*self*] for local binding. The percentages and the absolute figures, based on an extensive study of about 100 texts with some 6,400 examples (Keenan 2000) are given below.

Percentage of Locally Bound [Pron+*Self*] vs Bare Pronouns

100% 99

87

80% 81

60%

40%

20% 18 19 20 18

750-1154 1154-1303 1303-1405 1405-1495 1495-1605 1605-1700 1700-1777

Table 1: Number of Local Bindings: Bare Pronouns vs [$\text{Pron}_{(\alpha)}$+$\textit{Self}_{(\alpha)}$]

750-1154	1154-1303	1303-1405	1405-1495	1495-1605	1605-1700	1700-1777
pron-self	pron-self	pron-self	pron-self	pron-self	pron-self	pron-self
419-89	735-167	753-191	915-203	291-1232	138-930	3-335

So up until the 1500s about one in five local bindings was expressed by [pron+*self*] (pron_α+$\textit{self}_\alpha$ in the OE period). During the 1500s this figure shoots up to four out of five, and increases thereafter. Clearly a change has taken place.

4.1 Triggers for this Change

Triggers for this change are two. MINOR TRIGGER: There was some shift in the balance of local bindings by pronouns vs [pron+*self*] due to: (1) several verbs that commonly licensed non-theta pronouns die out or become rare: *gebiddan* 'pray', replaced by *preien* (< French *preier*), *greiþen* 'prepare', *schapien* 'make', *schriven* 'confess, prescribe penance', *bethink* and others. And (2) by INERTIA the verbs of bodily harm, with +theta objects, continue to use [pron+*self*] for local binding. In consequence the percentage of local bindings expressed by [pron+*self*] would have increased slightly, an effect that could be magnified by the IEE. But many verbs – *set*, *lay*, *remember*, *repent*, *went*, and many others – that often took pleonastic objects did not die out, they just ceased to be used with a pleonastic pronoun, always an option. Possibly also a minor reinforcing effect on the change once begun was the removal of referential ambiguities. Several verbs–*set*, *lay*, *shrive*– that often took non-theta objects also had transitive uses with theta objects: from Chaucer's *Knyghtes Tale* (c1385), cited from Keenan (1976):

(43) a. Upon a nyght in sleep as he$_i$ hym$_i$ leyde — line 1384
b. He leyde hym, bare the visage, on the beere — line 2877
(He = Theseus, hym = Arcite)

MAJOR TRIGGER: In the 1400s the +theta [pron+*self*] lose their obligatory contrast interpretation when DOs and OPreps. Compare (44a,b,c) in MSE:

(44) a. The king himself defended the children
b. The king defended the children himself
c. The king defended himself in the castle

The non-theta [pron+*self*] in (44a,b) are obligatorily contrastive. They refer to the king as opposed to others. But the +theta *himself* in (44c) is not necessarily contrastive. (44c) could felicitously be followed by *and so did everyone else*. I'm claiming that this interpretative difference arose in the 1400s and that it is a case of semantic DECAY, comparable to vowel reduction in unstressed syllables. Objective evidence that the contrastive interpretation of *him+self* weakened in this period is not easy to present, as even contrastive uses are often not obvious in a single sentence, the larger context being required to provide the contrast set.

One small fact however can be cited. Namely, in a few later texts in the 1400s, the *Donet* and Malory's *Morte Darthur*, we find a 'flickering' use of non-theta [pron+*self*]. Essentially this never happens in Early ME texts, *self*-forms being limited to theta positions. Nor does this practice ever become common, even in one author. Still observe in Malory:

(45) a. Than he remembird hymselff that he wolde [go] to the justis…
b. …ye muste remembir you what ye ar,..
c. I pray you remembir what I have don…

Most uses of *remember* in this text are as in (45c), with no object. When there is an object it is pleonastic bare pronoun (*remember* can not mean *remind* here). But we find this one example of [pron+self], (45a). Similarly in the *Donet* we find:

(46) a. In þe first of þese ij casis, a man schal bere him silf þus: …
a′. In þe ij caas of pacience bifore seid, a man schal bere him þus:

b. …and he muste remembre him silf vpon þe entent and purpose….
b′. and þat he schulde in þis wise remembre him þat crist, …

bare is used with a pleonastic object from the late 1200s through Shakespeare (c1600), so its use with a *self*-form is surprising.

So the contrastive interpretation of (non-subject) argument [pron+*self*] decayed. As usual we cannot explain why it happened just when it did, but we can say something about which occurrences of [pron+*self*] were affected.

Obviously Contrast Reduction did not apply to [pron+*self*] in ICEs: *The king defended everyone but himself / both himself and his children*, etc. since the ICE forces a contrastive interpretation. So only bare [pron+*self*], ones that constitute the entire argument, lose their contrastive interpretation. And non-theta [pron+*self*], as in (44a, b) cannot lose their contrast value, as then they would have no semantic role, in violation of the IP (INTERPRETATIVE PRINCIPLE). And if [pron+*self*] has a non-local antecedent then it is usually (though not necessarily) contrastive, since there are many loci where a non-local antecedent may lie, so there are many other possible local antecedents which then contrast with the actual one. Now by (14) subject [pron+*self*] must have a non-local antecedent, so these are not easily non-contrastive. This leaves bare objects (DOs and Objects of prepositions) with local antecedents as the only realistic candidates for loss of contrast. Thus

(47) Contrast reduction is limited to bare theta [pron+*self*] with local antecedents.

Now, what allows the reduction to happen at all? The crucial fact is that the [pron+*self*] that reduce are +theta. *himself* in (44c) satisfies the IP by virtue of satisfying an argument (semantic role) requirement of the verb: it identifies its Theme (as its Agent). So the propositional content of (44c) is comparable to that of *The king defended Bill*, but with this additional identification of arguments. Let us sum up these changes so far, as a remarkable pattern from the perspective of Binding Theory is beginning to emerge.

(48)a. In c1200 [pron+*self*] are selected for their contrastive value – that is what they contribute to the meaning of the Ss they occur in.

b. In c1450 [pron+*self*] lose their obligatorily contrastive interpretation when occurring as bare theta objects with local antecedents. So their semantic contribution to the Ss they occur in now consists in identifying an object argument with a local antecedent (virtually always the subject)

(49) **The Creation of Binding Theory**

a. If locally bound object [pron+*self*] lose their contrastive interpretation they become a synonymous paradigm with locally bound bare pronouns. But ANTI-SYNONYMY is preserved by limiting [pron+*self*] to local antecedents (their most common interpretation anyway) and forcing bare pronouns not to take local antecedents (always a common possibility), and

b. Non-theta uses of pronouns, never obligatory, die out since they must be locally bound.

Two comments on (49a):

1. In my data for the 1400s there are 204 instances of locally bound [pron+*self*] and 10 non-locally bound ones, of which only 4 are 3rd person (and so depend on identification with their antecedent for their reference), two of which are in ICEs. This is striking confirmation of the local binding interpretation of [pron+*self*]. The figures for OPreps are less striking, but still support a non-trivial correlation. We have 157 locally bound OPrep *self*-forms and 35 non-locally bound, of which 18 or 10% are 3rd person.

2. The threat of synonymy would be absent if the choice of locally bound *him* vs *him+self* was conditioned in some way. The natural suggestion is the choice of verb, and there is some conditioning: verbs of bodily harm choose [pron+*self*] for local binding. And some verbs of motion take either a pleonastic pronoun (locally bound) or no object at all, but never a [pron+*self*]. Still many verbs allow both, the meaning difference being one of contrast, and when that function weakens synonymy arises. Here are examples from two works for illustrative purposes. (50) is from *OE Homilies* (1150-1200), early

in ME, and (51) is from *H. Synne*, (1303), halfway through this period.

(50) a. Ne wreck þu þe mid wussinge. ne mid warienge XXIX
'Avenge thou not thyself by [evil] wishes nor with maledictions'

a′. ac…he þe … wolde him seluen wreke gif he mihte XIII
'but …he who…would avenge himself if he might'

b. …hit is time. þat we rise …and clensen us of ure fule synnes II

b′. Swo fasteð þe sinfulle man…to clensen him seluen of his fule sinnen X

c. ac turne we to ure drihten…and maken us wei to him XXII
'but let us turn to our Lord…and prepare our way to him'

c′. And þus man makede him sulfen fo þer he fren[d]shipe sholde VII
'And thus man made himself a foe where he should (have made) friendship.'

d. we … don us in to helle wite IX
'we … put ourselves into hell-torments'

d′. and him þat sore reu ... and dude him seluen mid hem þaron II
'and he had great sorrow…and put himself thereon with them'

(51) a. wyþ þe tokene he gan hym blesse line 3875
'with the token he began to bless himself'

a′. Hys ryʒt hand vp he lyfte/And blessede hym-self stedfastly
'His right hand up he lifted/And blessed himself steadfastly' line 3588

b. …þese wymmen…preysed hem to seynt Makayre line 2003

b′. þat none can preyse hym self by name line 3125

c. Alle þese coude hem neuer were/From treytur ne from bakbytere
'All these could them never save / from traitors nor from backbiters' line 4213

c′. ʒyf he ne myʒt with noun answere / Or ouþer manere hym seluen were line 3669
'if he might not with any answer/or other manner himself save'

d. And þou þat fedyst þe so rychely line 6753
'And thou that feedest thyself so richly'

d′. þe boldlyere þey myʒt hem self fede line 6621
'the more boldly they might themselves feed'

A comment on (49b): In fact the non-theta uses of the dative/accusative pronouns drop sharply by the end of the 1400s, supporting the synonymy avoidance analysis proposed here. In Keenan (1994, 1996) I took this loss as a mammals vs dinosaurs explanation. Now I see it as a consequence of the loss of contrast on [pron+*self*] plus ANTI-SYNONYMY. Still once the loss has triggered a shift in the balance of [pron+*self*] vs bare pronouns in the expression of local binding the IEE can reinforce that.

So, (49a) gives us Principle A of the Binding Theory in so far as it is true: it does not hold for [pron+*self*] in ICEs. (49b) added to (49a) gives us Principle B. This completes our historical explanation of the Binding Theoretic facts in (1).

Concluding Reflection: THE EIFFEL TOWER PRINCIPLE

The creation and interpretation of *him+self* in English is an instance of a type of change Gould & Vrba (1982) call *exaptation* in a biological context. An organ, say, may be selected for some function X but redundantly satisfy some other function Y to some extent. Later changes in selection pressure or the organ itself may make satisfying Y more important or satisfying X less important to the survival of the organism, so that the organ is now primarily selected for Y. Examples suggested in the literature are (1) the selection of jaws in bony fish, originally useful in forcing water over the gills increasing oxygen exchange, later useful for capturing and holding prey, or (2) the selection of feathers in birds as temperature controllers, later useful in flight.

In our case, pursuing the biological analogy, *him+self* was initially selected as a contrastor. Secondarily *him+self* often identified co-arguments, as adverbial self_{nom} always referred to the local subject in OE. Later routinization (Haiman 1997) weakened the contrast function of *him+self* in argument position and the pleonastic pronouns died out, leaving local binding as its primary function.

The biological examples have some appeal due to the long time periods over which the change is effected, plus the role they play in explaining how a complex organ can come to satisfy some function without having been selected for it initially. But, as Deacon (1997: 350) notes, exaptive changes are rampant and rapid in human technology. Melissa Epstein (p.c.) points out to me the case of Kleenex: invented as a means of removing facial make-up, it quickly became selected for its utility in nose blowing. Many examples can be found in Burke (1978), cited by Deacon, and in Panati 1987). My preferred example (perhaps because I noticed it myself) is the Eiffel Tower. It was constructed in the late 1890s for an international fair and was intended to be destroyed twenty years later. In the interim however radio became prominent and the tower was an ideal locus for a radio antenna. Thus the Eiffel Tower survives in part because of a role it came to play in radio transmission, a role that had nothing to do with its creation in the first place.

Open questions

I have focused here on attempting to document and explain several changes in the anaphora system of English over time. This work raises many questions, of which here are two broad ones: (1) What is the status of Binding Theory for OE and ME? And (2) How does the account of change here, given in terms of general, not language specific forces of change, relate to current parameter changing models (see Briscoe 2000)? Discussion of these questions would be another paper.

Let me just say in answer to (1) that classical Binding Theory for OE is vacuously true: there are no anaphors or pronominals (expressions which must / must not be locally bound) so Principles A and B are vacuously true. But Trichotomy–All NPs/DPs are eitheranaphors, pronominals or R-expressions–fails. *him* for example is not an anaphor since it need not be locally bound; it is not a pronominal since it need not be locally free; and it is not an R-expressions since it can be bound.

Regarding (2), the work presented here shares with parameter resetting models the focus on language learning as a locus of language change; it is analogous to reproduction in the biological case. And certainly forces like INERTIA and DECAY could trigger a parameter resetting. But application of this idea remains open.

References

Allen, C.L. 1980. *Topics in Diachronic English Syntax.* New York: Garland.

Allen, C.L. 1995. *Case Marking and Reanalysis.* Oxford: Clarendon Press.

Bailey, C-J. 1973. *Variation in Linguistic Theory.* Washington, D.C.: Center for Applied Linguistics.

Battye, A. and I. Roberts., eds. 1995. *Clause Structure and Language Change.* Oxford: Oxford University Press.

Briscoe, T. 2000. *Grammatical Acquisition: Inductive Bias and Coevolution of Language and the Language Acquisition Device.* Computer Laboratory, University of Cambridge. http://www.cl.cam.ac.uk/users/ejb.

Burke, J. 1978. *Connections.* London: Little, Brown and Company.

Carstairs-McCarthy, A. 1998. *Synonymy Avoidance, Phonology and the Origin of Syntax.* Oxford: Oxford University Press.

Clark, E. 1993. *The Lexicon in Acquisition*. Cambridge: Cambridge University Press.

Deacon, T. 1997. *The Symbolic Species*. New York: W.W. Norton and Company.

Farr, J. M. 1905. *Intensives and Reflexives in Anglo-Saxon and Early Middle English*. Baltimore: J.H. Furst.

Fidelholtz, J.L. 1975. Word Frequency and Vowel Reduction in English. *Chicago Linguistic Society* 11*: Parasession on Historical Linguistics*, 200–213.

Fischer,O. 1992. Syntax. *Cambridge History of the English Language,* vol. 2, ed. N. Blake, 207–398. Cambridge: Cambridge University Press.

van Gelderen, Elly. 2000. *A History of English Reflexive Pronouns.* Amsterdam: John Benjamins.

Gould, S.J. and E. Vrba. 1982. Exaptation: A Missing Term in Evolutionary Theory. *Paleobiology* 8: 4-15.

Haiman, J. 1997. Repetition and Identity. *Lingua* 100: 57–70.

Heine, B. and M. Reh. 1984. *Grammatical Categories in African Languages.* Hamburg: Helmut Buske.

Hogg, R.M., ed. 1992. *The Cambridge History of the English Language*, vol. 1, *The Beginnings to 1066*. Cambridge: Cambridge University Press.

Hopper, P.J. 1991. On some Principles of Grammaticization. *Approaches to Grammaticalization*, vol. 1, eds. E. Traugott & B. Heine, 17-35. Amsterdam: John Benjamins.

Hulk, A. and A. van Kemanade. 1995. Verb Second, Pro-drop, Functional Projections and Language Change. *Clause Structure and Language Change*, eds. A. Battye and I. Roberts, 227–256. Oxford: Oxford University Press.

Hurford, J.R., M. Studdert-Kennedy, and C. Knight. 1998. *Approaches to the Evolution of Language.* Cambridge: Cambridge University Press.

Keenan, E. L. 1976. Logical Expressive Power and Syntactic Variation in Natural Language. *Formal Semantics for Natural Language,* ed. E. L. Keenan. Cambridge: Cambridge University Press.

Keenan, E. L. 1988. Complex Anaphors and Bind Alpha. Papers from the 24th Annual Regional Meeting of the Chicago Linguistic Society, eds. L. MacLeod, G. Larson, and D. Brentani, 216-232.

Keenan, E. L. 1994, 1996. Creating Anaphors: An Historical Study of the English Reflexive Pronouns. Unpublished manuscript, University of California, Los Angeles.

Keenan, E. L. 2000. Creating Anaphors. Unpublished manuscript, University of California, Los Angeles.

van Kemenade, A. 1987. *Syntactic Case and Morphological Case in the History of English.* Dordrecht: Foris.

König, E. and P. Siemund. 1998. On the Development of Reflexive Pronouns in English: A Case Study in Grammaticalization. Unpublished manuscript, Institut fuer Englische Philologie, Freie Universitaet Berlin.

Kroch, A. 1989. Function and Grammar in the History of English Periphrastic *Do*. *Language Change and Variation*, eds. R.W. Fasold and D. Schiffrin, 133-172. Amsterdam: John Benjamins.

Mitchell, B. 1979. Old English *Self*: Four Syntactical Notes. *Neuphilologische Mitteilungen* 80: 39–45.

Mitchell, B. 1985. *Old English Syntax*. 2 vols. Oxford: Clarendon Press.

Moessner, L. 1989. *Early Middle English Syntax*. Tuebingen: Max Niemeyer Verlag.

Mossé, F. 1979. *Handbook of Middle English*. trans. James A. Walker. Maryland: The Johns Hopkins University Press.

Mustanoja, T.F. 1960. A Middle English Syntax: Part I. *Mémoires de la Société Néophilologique de Helsinki, XXIII*. Helsinki.

Ogura, M. 1989. *Verbs with the Reflexive Pronoun and Constructions with* ***Self*** *in Old and Early Middle English*. Cambridge: D.S. Brewer.

Roberts, I. 1993. *Verbs and Diachronic Syntax*. Dordrecht: Kluwer.

Panati, C. 1987. *Panati's Extraordinary Origins of Everyday Things*. New York: Harper & Row.

Safire, K. 1992. Implied Non-Coreference and the Pattern of Anaphora. *Linguistics and Philosophy* 15.1: 1-53.

Traugott, E.C. 1992. Syntax. *The Cambridge History of the English Language I: Old English*, ed. R.M. Hogg, 168-286. Cambridge: Cambridge University Press. Traugott, E.C. and B. Heine. eds. 1991. *Approaches to Grammaticalization*, 2 vols. Amsterdam: John Benjamins.

8

In Search of the Golden Slash: Prospecting for Biological Explanations of Language

ROBERT KLUENDER

1 Introduction

The question of the proper relationship between mental representations and underlying physical (i.e. brain) states, the so-called 'mind/body problem,' has been with us for some time now, at least since Plato. Most intellectually minded folk are at least superficially familiar with Descartes' dualist solution to the problem of how to get the mind to line up with the body: namely by allowing the former to more or less free-float vaguely in the vicinity of the latter, but critically anchored to it, so as not to float away entirely, via the pineal gland in the brain. And there things still sit quite comfortably and pleasantly for the vast majority of the world's population. Academic types, however, seemed unable to leave well enough alone and let this thorny problem and its felicitous solution be. In the last century, the behaviorists made valiant attempts to get rid of the whole mess altogether by adopting a don't-ask-don't-tell policy: if we simply don't talk about the mind, then perhaps we won't have to worry too much about what it's doing there hanging out about the body. As is again generally well known in academic circles, this attitude turned out to be as untenable in the philosophy of mind as it was in linguistics and the rest of psychology, and thus it was supplanted toward the latter half of the last century by two still competing theories of mind, commonly referred to as reductionism and functionalism.

The Nature of Explanation in Linguistic Theory.
John Moore and Maria Polinsky (eds.).

Reductionism is perhaps the easier of the two to define and comprehend: the mind is the body, or more specifically the brain, period; end of story. The discomfort associated with this view was expressed quite succinctly by Herder already in 1770 in his famous `Essay on the Origin of Language': 'Should physiology ever progress to a point where it can demonstrate psychology—which I greatly doubt—it would derive many a ray of light for this phenomenon, though it might also divide it in individual, excessively small, and obtuse filaments' (Herder 1966: 87-88). In more modern terms, synaptic connections and neurotransmitters and long-term potentiation might not be the most fortuitous level at which to define, say, locality.

There thus arose an alternative view that admits quite frankly that mental states may indeed be reducible to brain states, but that the latter are not the level at which we should be seeking our explanations. The inspiration for this view ultimately came no doubt from the simultaneous advent of artificial intelligence in the latter half of the 20th century, which held out the bold promise of autonomously thinking machines. The conclusion was that if a computer could walk like a human, talk like a human, and think like a human, then it must perforce have humanlike mental states—think HAL in Stanley Kubrick's *2001*. But no brain. Or at least not a carbon-based brain like yours and mine. This is the argument from MULTIPLE INSTANTIABILITY. In light of this conclusion, it became popular to define mental states in terms of their causal relations with other mental states, rather than in terms of their corresponding, underlying physical substrates. This is the view that came to be known as functionalism.

Modern linguistics has been a functionalist enterprise (in the above philosophical rather than the traditional linguistic sense) *par excellence*. Chomsky (1980) leaves no doubt about that in the following passage:

> In the natural sciences, when a theory is devised in some idealized domain, we ask whether the theory is true and try to answer the question in various ways. Of course, we expect that the theory is probably false, and even if on the road to truth, that it does no more than describe at some appropriate level of abstraction properties alleged to be true of whatever the real elements of the world may be when considered at this level of description; it has, in short, some of the properties of so-called 'functionalist' theories in psychology. (Chomsky 1980: 11)

The phrase LEVEL OF ABSTRACTION in the above passage is a recurring one in Chomsky's writings. It turns out that this is quite simply a basic theme of functionalism writ large, to wit.

> What it all comes down to is that there seems to be a level of abstraction at which the generalizations of psychology are most naturally pitched. This level of abstraction cuts across differences in the physical composition of the systems to which psychological generalizations apply. In the cognitive sciences, at least, the natural domain for psychological theorizing seems to be all systems that process information (J.A. Fodor 1981: 118).

Chomsky (1993) has more recently referred to this view as COMPUTATIONAL.

> A naturalistic approach will assume that like other complex systems, the human brain can be profitably viewed as an array of interacting subcomponents, which can be studied at various levels: atoms, cells, cell assemblies, neural networks, computational systems of the kind pioneered, at a primitive stage, by the Cartesians, and so on. We cannot know in advance which (if any) of these approaches will provide insight and understanding. In several domains, including language, the computational approaches currently have the strongest claim to scientific status, at least on naturalistic grounds (Chomsky, 1993: 42-43).

Note the commonality of the misgivings about reductionism indirectly expressed here with those expressed by Herder over 200 years prior.

If it is true then that our linguistic generalizations 'are most naturally pitched' (Fodor 1981) 'at a certain level of abstraction from mechanisms' (Chomsky 1986: 11), and if this is one of the main tenets of a functional/computational approach to language, then there immediately arises what may at first blush seem to be something of a paradox. And that is this: one of the main tenets of modularity (Fodor 1983) is that modules such as the language faculty, or subcomponents thereof such as syntax or phonology, are associated with fixed neural architecture. How does this work? Why fix an otherwise autonomous mental property to a piece of wetware? Well, for one thing, the modularist view of the mind draws much of its inspiration by way of analogy from anatomical and physiological modularity in the body itself. Just as physiological function is not distributed randomly across the internal anatomy of the body, in the interest of optimizing functioning through specialization, so, the argument goes, mental functions must be similarly localized in the brain in the interest of functional optimization. And in this sense, the physical instantiation of a system will place significant constraints on its optimal functional nature. For another thing, one must bear in mind that even on its own (i.e., independent of modularity), functionalism does not deny the obvious basis of human mental states in states of the human brain. As Fodor (1981) puts it,

> The functionalist would not be disturbed if brain events turn out to be the only things with the functional properties that define mental states. Indeed, most functionalists fully expect it will turn out that way. Since functionalism recognizes that mental particulars may be physical, it is compatible with the idea that mental causation is a species of physical causation. ...It is possible for the functionalist to assert both that mental properties are typically defined in terms of their relations and that interactions of mind and body are typically causal in however robust a notion of causality is required by psychological explanations. (J.A. Fodor 1981: 119)

So where does this leave us? Basically, with the status quo in theoretical linguistics. The trend has been for linguistic research to proceed on its own, to do as it does, so to speak, in seeking relevant explanations, with that trend firmly rooted in a functionalist view of mind. What this means in practical terms is that for the last 50 years or so, the causal relations between mental representations (in the form of linguistic utterances) and other mental representations (in the form of intuitions about the relative well-formedness of those utterances, and their interpretations) have been not only the driving force behind the methodology, but also the veritable substance of linguistic research. A real advantage of this particular tack has been that explanations can be pursued, and have been pursued, without much concern for what physically underlies the whole process. There is a vague assumption that eventually our explanations can probably be made to map on to what we know about the underlying substrate, somehow, somewhere—but this is not essential, let alone an impediment, to progress. It's simply not a concern in an enterprise with a functionalist agenda. Thus this prevailing attitude in linguistics might be—not unfairly, I think—construed as the functionalist version of the behaviorist don't-ask-don't-tell policy in converse form: if we simply don't talk about the brain, then perhaps we won't have to worry too much about what it's doing there hanging out underneath the mind, and in any case, that's for the neuroscientists to figure out.

At the same time, we find ourselves in the somewhat curious situation of witnessing a burst of neural imaging studies designed to do precisely that, i.e. verify in very specific detail Fodor's (1983) claim that input systems (= modules) are associated with fixed neural architecture, in this case subserving language. In particular, there has been a rather frenetic effort to pin the syntactic tail on the donkey/brain—preferably in a different place from the semantic tail—to varying degrees of success (see Section 4). Be that as it may, the result of all this is that at this juncture in the intellectual history of the field, in our explanations of linguistic phenomena, theoretically we do not concern ourselves overly much with what's going on in the brain, while simultaneously fretting quite a bit experimentally about just where inside the head the whole business is taking place. One might correctly point out that the respective subsets of researchers who worry about these two sides of the equation are not necessarily coextensive. Even in that case, however, one might wish to entertain the possibility of a Central Pacific/Union Pacific-type problem: will independent efforts to forge a link between mind and brain result in a fortuitous driving of the golden spike at Promontory, Utah, or end up missing each other by a mile (or more)?

It is the aim of this chapter to consider some of the consequences of this particular state of affairs. In section 2, we will consider the issue of reduction, which raises a whole series of questions about direction of explanation and burden of proof liability. Section 3 will entertain some methological considerations as to how we might best go about gathering data in the service of linguistic theory. Section 4 will summarize the current state of neural imaging studies and suggest some possible alternatives.

2 The Direction of Explanation

In addition to my initial perplexity at the recurring expression 'level of abstraction' in Chomsky's writings, I spent a good deal of my time in graduate school wondering out loud what the slash in the equally frequent expression 'mind/brain' referred to. I was thus recently amused to discover the same question posed by Eric Wanner in his comments on Chomsky's (1993) Language and Thought lecture: 'If the state of information on the mind/brain is so rosy, why don't we have an answer to this fundamental question: What does the '/' mean in Chomsky's succinct formulation, mind/brain?' (Chomsky 1993: 72). Chomsky's answer to this question is essentially, we don't know, and moreover, it doesn't matter (ibid. 1993: 79-87), about which more below. This is pretty much the standard functionalist response to this question.

It turns out that the expressions 'level of abstraction' and 'mind/brain' have far more to do with each other than a mere relationship of coincidental and collocational co-occurrence. In fact, the whole notion of 'mind/brain' seems to rest pretty squarely on the notion of 'level of abstraction', as is evident in the following passage from Aspects of the Theory of Syntax (Chomsky 1965: 193).

> To accept traditional mentalism, in this way, is not to accept Bloomfield's dichotomy of 'mentalism' versus 'mechanism'. Mentalistic linguistics is simply theoretical linguistics that uses performance as data (along with other data, for example, the data provided by introspection) for the determination of competence, the latter being taken as the primary object of its investigation. The mentalist, in this traditional sense, need make no assumptions about the possible physiological basis for the mental reality that he studies. In particular, he need not deny that there is such a basis. One would guess, rather, that it is the mentalistic studies that will ultimately be of greatest value for the investigation of neurophysiological mechanisms, since they alone are concerned with determining abstractly the properties that such mechanisms must exhibit and the functions they must perform (Chomsky 1965: 193, fn. 1).

The idea that emerges here is that the abstract characterization of properties at the functional level is to be determinative in specifying not only the direction of linguistic explanation, but also the agenda adopted by neuroscientific research when it ventures into cognitive domains. Moreover, the expectation usually accompanying this idea is that this abstract characterization of cognitive properties, will, or should, map straightforwardly onto what is known about the underlying substrate, the brain. If it does not, then the assumption is that the fault must lie not with linguistic explanation, but with neurophysiological explanation, and that in that case neuroscience would be well advised to go back to the drawing board. This view is expressed even more directly in some of Chomsky's later writings.

> From this point of view we can proceed to approach the study of the human mind much in the way that we study the physical structure of the body. In fact, we may think of the study of mental faculties as actually being a study of the body—specifically the brain—conducted at a certain level of abstraction (Chomsky 1980: 2).

The most extreme version of this position is the following.

> In fact, the belief that neurophysiology is even relevant to the functioning of the mind is just a hypothesis. Who knows if we're looking at the right aspects of the brain at all. Maybe there are other aspects of the brain that nobody has even dreamed of looking at yet. That's often happened in the history of science. When people say the mental is the neurophysiological at a higher level, they're being radically unscientific. We know a lot about the mental from a scientific point of view. We have explanatory theories that account for a lot of things. The belief that neurophysiology is impli-

> cated in these things *could* be true, but we have very little evidence for it. So, it's just a kind of hope; look around and you see neurons; maybe they're implicated (Chomsky 1993: 85).

One of the more comforting aspects of cognitive science (perhaps) is that we are not alone in our discipline-internal debates. The following passage, while not at all intended to address the particular linguistic manifestation of the problem that immediately confronts us, nonetheless applies to it transparently without much need for discipline-specific translation.

> As Pylyshyn (1980) sees it, the research labor can be divided along these lines: the cognitive scientists will figure out the functional/cognitive theory, and the neuroscientists can untangle the underlying physical devices that instantiate the cognitive 'program'. On an extreme version of this view, nothing much of the details of neuronal business need be known by the cognitive scientist—or the philosopher, either—since the way the functional organization is instantiated in the brain is a quite separate and independent matter from the way our cognitive economy is organized (P.S. Churchland 1986: 354-355).

It is this position that neuroscientists like Wanner on the other hand take exception to, predicated on the reductionist view shared by most neuroscientists that the brain simply *is* the mind. The extreme variant of this position is that it is hopeless to even discuss mental phenomena. As Wanner states, 'At their worst, my colleagues warn me to stick to molecules, because it is the only hard-nosed approach. They solve the problem by denying it, echoing the currently popular school of philosophy called Eliminative Materialism [i.e. reductionism—RK]. This school claims that mentalist explanations of psychology (folk psychology like my grandmother's) ultimately must reduce to neuroscience anyhow' (Chomsky 1993: 72). This might easily be construed as the reductionist spin on don't-ask-don't-tell: If we don't worry about the (epiphenomenal) mind, then we can focus our attention and our efforts more exclusively and more effectively on the brain, which is where it's at anyway.

So: How do we extricate ourselves from this impasse? There are multiple options. Two of the more extreme are summarized above. One, the functionalist extreme, is that linguists should pursue linguistic explanations based on introspective data, and if the results of this approach don't end up mapping onto anything known about the brain and how it operates, oh well - the neuroscientists must have gotten it all wrong in the first place. The other, the reductionist extreme, is that neuroscientists should study language representation and processing in the brain in benign disregard of the results of traditional (mentalistic) linguistic inquiry; to some extent, this is what one already sees a fair amount of in the neuroimaging literature. It seems obvious that neither alternative is going to get very far in solving the 'mind/brain' slash problem by staunchly refusing to acknowledge what's lurking on the other side of that slash. Are we thus left with nothing but the dualist solution we inherited from Plato via Descartes?

Mercifully, these are not the only alternatives. Descartes himself gave us the pineal gland as an escape hatch. And as it turns out, positions less extreme than those cited above have also been voiced in the public domain. Even Chomsky in less confrontational mode has acknowledged, to a certain extent, the degree of cooperation that is required between neuroscience and linguistic science in solving this particular aspect of the 'mind/brain' slash problem.

> We observed that it is a task for the brain sciences to explain the properties and principles discovered in the study of the mind. More accurately, the interdependency of the brain sciences and the study of mind is reciprocal. The theory of mind aims to determine the properties of the initial state S_0 each attainable state S_L of the language faculty, and the brain sciences seek to discover the mechanisms of the brain that are the physical realizations of these states. There is a common enterprise: to discover the correct characterization of the language faculty in its initial and attained states, to discover the truth about the language faculty. This enterprise is conducted at several levels: an abstract characterization in the theory of mind, and an inquiry into mechanisms in the brain sciences (Chomsky 1986: 38-39).

While it is true that this proposal is still cast firmly in functionalist terms, and that the role it envisions for the neurosciences is still largely one of implementation, nonetheless there seems to be at least some room for accommodation here. Moreover, in a lecture given in UC Irvine in 1993, Chomsky went so far as to suggest that relying on primary linguistic data alone may not be adequate for determining well-formedness in language, and thus for deciding between competing theories. Instead he advocated turning to other sources of evidence, including neurophysiological data, in linguistic theory construction. The issue of data sources will be taken up again at greater length in Section 4.

In the meantime, I would like to offer the following quote as a possible compromise solution, one that falls between the extremes of the don't-ask-don't-tell approaches to the mind/body problem. There is a slight risk involved here in citing a document conceived during the death throes of both behaviorism and American structuralism, but with a modicum of charity on the part of the reader, I believe the point can still be well taken without making too much of its historical provenance and context. Moreover, the advantage of going back in time to seek a compromise position is that with 20/20 hindsight, both reductionists and functionalists seem to be able to find much of substance to relate to, and to agree with, in it.

> The essential difference between the [analytical] process in the child and the procedure of the linguist is this: the linguist has to make his analysis overtly, in communicable form, in the shape of a set of statements which can be understood by any properly trained person, who in turn can predict utterances not yet observed with the same degree of accuracy as can the original analyst. The child's 'analysis' consists, on the other hand, of a mass of varying synaptic potentials in his central nervous system. The child in time comes to *behave* the language; the linguist must come to *state* it.
>
> ...The structure of a language may be regarded as the end-product of a game; in this sense structure is created by the person who plays the game. But every speaker of a language plays just such a game, the end-product being a state of affairs in his nervous system rather than a set of statements. The linguistic scientist must regard the structure of language as consisting precisely of this state of affairs. His purpose in analyzing a language is not to create structure, but to determine the structure actually created by the speakers of the language. For the scientist, then, 'linguistic structure' refers to something existing quite independently of the activities of the analyst: a language is what it is, it has the structure it has, whether studied and analyzed by a linguist or not (Hockett 1948: 280).

In particular, note that Hockett is perhaps unique in implying that neither side of the 'mind/brain' slash can be safely ignored, and that a double-pronged approach to the mind/body problem in the domain of language would be well advised. Not only are both aspects of the mind/brain equation equally important, but the role of the neural side of things is elevated from one of mere mechanical implementation to that of a causal factor in the determination of linguistic structure. At the same time, while strongly advocating that linguists should acknowledge the neural basis of linguistic structure (ironically enough, at a time when not much was known about it), by no means does Hockett advocate that they should abandon their analytical procedures at the (waxing slightly anachronistic here) functional level. He merely reminds us not to mistake the nature of our overtly stated linguistic explanations as that which must of necessity be implemented in the human nervous system.

To extend the analogy—perhaps to the breaking point—this seems to be more a position of please-ask, show-and-tell. In other words, if language researchers can merely manage to pay more attention to the infamous binding violation of *what each other are doing*, the field would be well served, and the progress might well turn out to be faster and better directed, with fewer false starts and dead ends.

Certainly it is unreasonable to expect all linguists to bone up on the brain and run positron emission tomography (PET) studies—though some have taken up even this challenge—or to expect all neuroscientists to head back to graduate school in linguistics. If this were the only option, prospects might indeed look bleaker than they actually do. But this is hardly required at this point in the history of the field, as evidenced by the prevalent trend for linguistics departments to announce and fill positions in psycho- or neurolinguistics routinely of late. In short, a new generation of scholars is currently being trained who at least have passing familiarity with, and in some cases are well versed in, both sides of the mind/brain slash as far as language is concerned. This can only augur well for the field, which stands to gain great benefits from such a joint endeavor. In the meantime, if the rest of us can just hold off making premature pronouncements in dichotomous fashion on the utility of adhering to either a functionalist (computational) or a reductionist (eliminative) approach, as if one had to choose between them, things can simply proceed as history generally does anyway, namely inexorably. That is, the conditions have already been set for a merger of these two strands of research, and so it remains to the rest of us to simply sit back (and sit tight) and wait for the results, which should speak for themselves.

This seems on the face of things like a perfectly doable game plan, and also points to a solution to the direction of explanation problem. It is true that relying exclusively on neuranatomical and neurophysiological study alone would not get us very far, reducing language to 'excessively small and obtuse filaments' of which not much practical sense could be made. However, relying exclusively on functionally derived explanations as a guide for to how to proceed neurally would seem to rob us of half the potential benefit in this enterprise as well. If, on the other hand, functionally (computationally) derived linguistic explanation can seek confirmation in experimental studies of language representation and processing in the brain, while remaining amenable to falsification, and accommodating of unexpected findings, that should seem like everyday, garden-variety science to everyone involved.

Having proposed a do-nothing path of least resistance out of the mind/brain slash impasse, then, let us now turn our attention to questions of data, actual or expected.

3 The Thorny Question of Data Collection

Recall Chomsky's (Chomsky 1965: 193) statement from *Aspects* cited at the beginning of the previous section that 'Mentalistic linguistics is simply theoretical linguistics that uses performance as data (along with other data, for example, the data provided by introspection) for the determination of competence....' This statement, in combination with Chomsky's (Chomsky 1993: 43) assertion that 'In several domains, including language, the computational approaches currently have the strongest claim to scientific status' might lead one who didn't know any better to believe that the findings of theoretical linguistics are based on a variety of measures using standard, agreed-upon methodology. This is pretty clearly not the case. The methodological discussion in *Aspects* (Chomsky 1965: 18-21) makes this apparent, and rings nearly as true today as it did almost 40 years ago.

At the risk of presuming to do an exegetical summary of Chomsky's writings, the discussion in Aspects points out the difficulty of obtaining information about the native speaker's linguistic competence, a mental state well hidden from observable view. As above, the suggestion is made that the only sources available are linguistic performance or introspective report by the native speaker, or by a linguist *who has learned the language*. However, Chomsky goes on to point out that at the time, there were very few experimental or data-processing procedures available for zeroing in on facts of native speaker intuition, and then proceeds to cast serious doubt on the utility and reliability of performance measures altogether. The conclusion is that the only reliable source of data is native speaker intuition via introspective report.

> It is important to bear in mind that when an operational procedure is proposed, it must be tested for adequacy (exactly as a theory of linguistic intuition—a grammar—must be tested for adequacy) by measuring it against the standard provided by the tacit knowledge that it attempts to specify and describe. Thus a proposed operational test for, say, segmentation into words, must meet the empirical condition of conforming, in a mass of crucial and clear cases, to the linguistic intuition of the native speaker concerning such elements. Otherwise, it is without value. The same, obviously, is true in the case of any proposed operational procedure or any proposed grammatical description. If operational procedures were available that met this test, we might be justified in relying on their results in unclear and difficult cases. This remains a hope for the future rather than a present reality, however. This is the objective situation of present-day linguistic work; allusions to presumably well-known 'procedures of elicitation' or 'objective methods'

> simply obscure the actual situation in which linguistic work must, for the present, proceed. Furthermore, there is no reason to expect that reliable operational criteria for the deeper and more important theoretical notions of linguistics (such as 'grammaticalness' and 'paraphrase') will ever be forthcoming (Chomsky 1965: 19).

Putting on my linguist's hat, this makes perfect sense: we all know that we have good intuitions about language or we wouldn't be linguists, and we certainly want our experimental results to coincide with and reflect those intuitions. But putting on my experimentalist's hat, it makes almost no sense: why would one want to assume that our introspection, or the theory being tested, is *a priori* true, and reject experimental results if they do not support it? Part of the problem here is that there seems to be a too easy conflation of theory and intuition in the above passage. It starts out by asserting that *both* grammatical theory and operational procedures need to answer to our linguistic intuitions, arrived at via introspection. But even at this point, surely one wouldn't want to say that linguistic theory can never be counterintuitive; don't some of the most interesting, even revolutionary and influential theories fly directly in the face of our introspective intuitions? Isn't that precisely what makes linguistics so fascinating, the unexpected explanatory result?

Moreover, the appeal to native speaker intuitions about word segmentation seems highly suspect, since the elusive definition of the word is perhaps the best kept secret of our disciplinary dirty laundry. Native speaker intuition about word segmentation is highly influenced by orthographic convention. Do we take this as the determinant norm? If so, why does it then take a linguist to tell us what a clitic is? Even at the most mundane level, we don't know the simplest answers regarding wordhood: is *living room* one word or two? What about *any more* or *all right*? I was drilled in elementary school that these phrases consisted of two words, not one, but in recent years the quality print media have adopted *anymore* and *alright* as the standard. So where are the native speaker intuitions here? All over the map. Why should either a theory of morphology or an operational procedure conform to what is in this case clearly a linguistic muddle?

The end of the above passage, however, seems to suddenly equate 'deeper and more important theoretical notions of linguistics (such as 'grammaticalness' and 'paraphrase')' with native speaker introspection. It's not clear that these are well-defined notions, either, however, as anyone who has ever taught introductory syntax can attest to. Introspective verbal report of global sentence evaluation is a very highly subjective performance measure, and, in view of the tremendous advances in technology and scientific methodology over the past century, curiously primitive. Elicitation does not occur under anything resembling experimental laboratory conditions; at most a few tokens of a given sentence type can be tested at any given time before native speakers begin to fatigue, and their judgments start becoming erratic; there are no established criteria for selecting subject populations (in dying languages, of course, one has to take what one can find in the way of linguistic competence); no attempt is made to determine the effects of individual variation in the data, or to control for factors known to correlate with verbal ability, such as age, gender, working memory capacity, socioeconomic class, level of education, handedness, or family history of handedness; subject pools generally number less than ten; and most crucially, the data gathered are seldom subjected to statistical analysis.

Beyond this, in practice this procedure also tends to involve the subjectivity of the investigator to a large degree. For one thing, in many cases linguists who are native speakers of the language under investigation have relied primarily on their own intuitions. Yet even when this is not the case, the ultimate decision as to the grammaticality of a particular sentence often ends up being a compromise between consultant and investigator. Subjects will often resist giving judgments on pragmatically odd or ambiguous sentences, and even when they have no trouble making such judgments, one still cannot be sure exactly what the elicited behavior reflects. A judgment of grammaticality is usually interpreted as a measure of purely grammatical competence, yet it is notoriously difficult to factor out the influence of lexical, semantic, pragmatic, discourse, processing, and prescriptive factors. Extensive probing can be required to determine what reasons subjects have for rejecting particular sentences. This tends to make the interpretation of the subject's response a judgment call on the part of the investigator. This is particularly the case when subjects give conflicting judgments on sentences which the investigator considers to be of the same syntactic type, or for that matter on the same sentence tokens they have been presented with on different occasions.

Furthermore, although subjects are traditionally presented with a forced choice, i.e. a decision as to whether or not one can say a given sentence, they typically respond in non-dichotomous fashion. The proliferation of diacritical markings used to index the grammatical status of subjects' responses (no marking, ?, ??, ?*, ??*, *, **, etc.) demonstrates this fact (see also Langacker 1987: 15). Yet aside from one or two isolated earlier proposals (e.g. Timberlake 1979, 1980), no attempts were made until recently to define or systematize the range of these symbols either within or across subjects, let alone across studies. While reliable operational procedures have surfaced in recent years that seem to give us a much better handle on what constitutes grammaticality without requiring any technology over and above pencil and paper, or computerized tests (Kluender and Kutas 1993b; Bard, Robertson, and Sorace 1996; Cowart 1997), these have not been widely adopted in linguistic practice. So it seems curious indeed that operational procedures are deemed the odd man out with respect to reliability. This may be simply another consequence of a functionalist approach to the study of the mind/brain in relation to language.

In short, the standards of rigor applied to theories of linguistic competence are frequently missing from the empirical methodology on which they are based. From the perspective of other empirical disciplines in either the natural or the social sciences, this constitutes a puzzling phenomenon. Ironically, where standards of experimental rigor are observed, namely within the subfield of psycholinguistics, the domain of investigation has traditionally been confined to territory left largely unoccupied by theoretical linguistics: How innate grammatical competence interacts with pressures of time and limitations of memory to yield on-line performance, and questions of modularity. Until recently, the role of pscholinguistics in questions of sentence processing has largely been one of implementing established theoretical models.

Later in the methodological discussion in *Aspects*, Chomsky raises the question 'whether the necessity for present-day linguistics to give such priority to introspective evidence and to the linguistic intuition of the native speaker excludes it from the domain of science' (Chomsky1965: 20). His answer is of course no, based on a crucial distinction that he draws between insight and objectivity; if the latter does not lead to the former, then it serves no useful purpose. The next paragraph is prophetic in this regard.

> In any event, at a given stage of investigation, one whose concern is for insight and understanding (rather than for objectivity as a goal in itself) must ask whether or to what extent a wider range and more exact description of phenomena is relevant to solving the problems that he faces. In linguistics, it seems to me that sharpening of the data by more objective tests is a matter of small importance for the problems at hand. One who disagrees with this estimate of the present situation in linguistics can justify his belief in the current importance of more objective operational tests by showing how they can lead to new and deeper understanding of linguistic structure. Perhaps the day will come when the kinds of data that we now can obtain in abundance will be insufficient to resolve deeper questions concerning the structure of language. However, many questions that can realistically and significantly be formulated today do not demand evidence of a kind that is unavailable or unattainable without significant improvements in objectivity of experimental technique (Chomsky 1965: 20-21).

To Chomsky's credit, as mentioned earlier, he himself came to question this premise in the early nineties, when he conceded that data derived from grammaticality judgments might no longer be able to distinguish between competing theories of grammar, and suggested that appeal be made in such cases to experimental, particularly neurophysiological techniques of investigation. And this is essentially where we sit nowadays, almost exactly ten years after this concession was first made in public. In that time, we have witnessed the development of a burgeoning field of neurophysiological research into language processes, in part thanks to the vision of the first president Bush, who saw fit before leaving office to proclaim the nineties *The Decade of the Brain*.

4 On the Proper Treatment of Neuroimaging

In a seminal article entitled *On the Proper Treatment of Connectionism*, first published in 1988, Paul Smolensky argued that connectionist architectures should be properly understood as a refinement of classical models of cognition, rather than as mere implementations of them. The heading of this section, shamelessly lifted from that work (which may in turn have been lifted from Montague's classic paper on quantification in English), points to a similar thesis: it will be suggested here that neuroimaging may not best serve linguistics by playing a purely implementational role, but that neural imaging data, along with other psycholinguistic measures, may help to refine our theories of grammar in the larger sense of the term.

Neuroimaging techniques can be divided roughly into two broad categories: those that provide temporal information on the time course of language processing in the brain, and those that provide spatial information on the localization in the brain of particular language functions. Temporal information is gathered from the electrochemical changes that occur when assemblies of neurons communicate with each other, and spatial information is derived from the metabolic processes occurring in the blood that support these electrochemical processes. Electrochemical changes taking place in groups of pyramidal cells aligned perpendicular to the scalp are registered by the electroencephalogram (EEG), while the same changes taking place in groups of pyramidal cells arranged orthogonally to the scalp are picked up by the magneto encephalogram (MEG); this distribution of sensitivity by recording technique is simply determined by the physical relationship of electrical and magnetic fields to each other. The EEG elicited in response to particular types of linguistic stimuli can be computer averaged to yield an aggregate response known as the event-related potential (ERP). While these techniques can be used in conjunction with other procedures to ascertain the location of electrochemical changes in the brain, their real advantage lies in their fine-grained temporal resolution, on the order of milliseconds. The metabolic processes supporting electrochemical changes in the brain are blood flow, which can be tracked by positron emission tomography (PET), and blood oxygenation, which can be picked up by functional magnetic resonance imaging (fMRI). Because changes in blood flow and blood oxygenation take place more slowly than the electrochemical changes they subserve, these techniques provide better spatial than temporal resolution.

As hinted at in the introduction, there is currently a great fascination with regard to the localization of language in the brain, particularly on the part of language researchers with functionalist (again, in the philosophical rather than the linguistic sense, i.e. as opposed to reductionist) leanings. This is because of the close association of the functionalist approach to the study of language, which has dominated our field in its modern incarnation for the last fifty years, with the theory of modularity (Fodor 1983), which predicts mental language modules to be supported by dedicated neural systems. Thus many if not most of the brain imaging studies that have been conducted to date have been devoted to issues of modularity. In all fairness, this can only be expected, insofar as a modularist view of language representation in the brain at least makes clear and simple (at times, I would contend perhaps overly simple; see below) predictions about what mental modules we should be looking for in the brain.

There have thus been numerous studies aimed at dissociating types of language processes, most notably syntactic and semantic ones. In terms of temporal processing, overall there does seem to be a bifurcation in the types of event-related potential (ERP) waveform components elicited by semantic as opposed to morphosyntactic violations, though certain unaccounted for anomalies remain. In these cases, the presumed semantic component appears in response to certain morphosyntactic violations (Coulson, King, and Kutas 1998), and the supposed morphosyntactic component shows up in response to certain semantic/pragmatic violations (Shao and Neville 1996). There have also been attempts to associate particular ERP components with particular stages of processing in a modularized, serial parser (Friederici 2002). In terms of spatial location, the dissociation of syntax and semantics has been less clear-cut in PET and fMRI studies. Most of these aim to tie relevant parts of Broca's area, in the inferior frontal gyrus of the frontal lobe, exclusively to syntactic processing. Often the dissociations between syntactic and semantic processing do not fall out neatly along these pre-specified lines. At best, syntactic conditions generally elicit greater or more highly (left-)lateralized activation in Broca's area compared to semantic conditions, but the same regions of Broca's area are nonetheless activated by both semantic conditions and syntactic conditions alike (Kang et. al. 1998; Dapretto and Bookheimer 1999; Ni et. al. 2000).

A related but separate line of research has been devoted to the processing of subject vs. object long-distance Ā-dependencies. This is perhaps a little closer to home with regard to theoretical linguists' concerns. In ERP studies, object dependencies seem to be reliably indexed by slow anterior negative brain potentials, sometimes, but not always, lateralized to the left side of the head. These have been interpreted as indexing processes of verbal working memory involved in maintaining long-distance parsing relationships (Kluender and Kutas 1993a; King and Kutas 1995). In PET and fMRI studies, object dependencies generally activate regions within Broca's area more strongly than subject dependencies (Stromswold et. al. 1996; Caplan, Alpert, and Waters 1998; Caplan, Alpert, and Waters 1999; Caplan et. al. 2000), though there have been anomalous cases as well. In an early study, both subject and object relative clauses activated Broca's and Wernicke's areas equally, with object relative clauses eliciting overall greater activation in both traditional language areas (Just et. al. 1996). In a more recent fMRI study by the same group reporting consistent activation of Broca's area by object relative clauses in a series of studies using PET, object relative clauses instead activated the left angular gyrus, in the border region between temporal and parietal and occipital cortices (Caplan et. al. 2002). Also, to the extent that the processing of long-distance object dependencies has been localized to inferior frontal regions (Broca's area), the exact interpretation of this phenomenon is under discussion (Cooke et. al. 2002).

So, are we simply left with yet another hopeless muddle when we expand our horizons to add new operational procedures to our well-worn bag of introspective tricks? I think not. That would be the council of despair assessment of the situation. Note that the objective is not to replace all that has been accomplished over the last fifty years. The position taken here, however, is that the aim should not be merely to substantiate all that has been accomplished on the basis of introspection over the last fifty years, either. The aim of the proper treatment of neuroimaging should rather be to both substantiate and refine our models of language when they seem out of line with the data available from powerful imaging techniques.

Let us begin at the most fundamental level: the model of language representation in the brain that most of us are familiar with, and that is taught in virtually all introduction to linguistics classes, has been with us for the last 150 years or so. It so happens that major portions of this model are being proven false: the relationship between lesion sites and aphasic symptoms is turning out to be far more complex and differentiated—and interesting—than traditional associationist accounts of the 19th century led us to believe.

It has been known for some time now that Broca's area is not the main or even the only cause of Broca's aphasia, because when only Broca's area proper is damaged, aphasic symptoms are transitory, and patients recover (Damasio 1992). Recent comparative MRI scans of living aphasic brains indicate that the loci of certain symptoms associated with Broca's aphasia reside nowhere near Broca's area itself (Dronkers 1996, 2000; Dronkers et. al. 2000). So this must surely be considered a significant advance, and one that significantly alters our conceptions of mind-to-brain mapping.

However, this has obvious consequences for imaging studies of normal brains as well: there is no longer any reason to expect that all of what we consider (i.e. introspect) to be syntactic processing should light up Broca's area, and Broca's area alone. What we have also known for a long time now is that brain systems are distributed (Ojemann 1991); cognitive, in this case linguistic functions just don't map nicely onto clearly defined, unique areas of cortex, they're spread out all over the cortical surface, and below it as well. This is not to say that specific areas of cortex, Broca's area in particular, are not involved in certain language processes. They clearly are. But they also seem to be involved in other functions. One of the more startling findings in recent years has been that Broca's area is activated not only by linguistic stimuli, but also by the observation and imitation of non-linguistic motor actions of both hand and mouth (Buccino et. al. 2001; Krams et. al. 1998). Given the technologies at hand, expecting to localize what we presume to be linguistic primitives to predetermined areas of cortex may not be the best way to go about things. We may in fact find out much more about how language is handled by the brain by not making too many assumptions about what should be where, or where what should be. Note that this is not an exhortation to give up all hope of localizing anything related to language function in the brain whatsoever. It is a mere reminder that it is probably not a good idea, based on what we have discovered so far, to rely overly much on our received preconceptions about where language functions ought to park in the brain.

This much as to localization. But localization has never been that near and dear to the hearts of theoretical linguists anyway. So what vested interest should the theoretical linguist expect to have in what's going on in the brain? Here are some suggested possibilities. For one thing, to the extent that it proves possible using neural imaging techniques to cleanly dissociate semantic from syntactic processing, or syntactic from lexical and phonological processing, this could be of tremendous value in helping to nail down exactly where proposed levels of linguistic analysis reside in the *cognitive* (not just the neural) architecture. For example, most linguists recognize that such a thing as information structure exists, but no one can agree on its exact nature: is it more of a semantic/pragmatic or a syntactic animal? Another possibility is that we may finally be able to decide where morphology is (Anderson 1982). These are just two cases where the results of imaging may be of very direct and practical use to theoretical linguists.

Another is in the analysis of dependencies alluded to above. Already we have found out by using experimental techniques a number of things that weren't so clear before. While locality is less of a linguistic concern for displaced grammatical objects than it is for displaced grammatical subjects, the human brain has quite a time dealing with long-distance object dependencies. From the mid-eighties to the present, one has been under the mistaken impression that scrambling in Japanese is a pervasive and ubiquitous phenomenon. It turns out that it is far from that: corpus studies show that it is extremely rare, with an occurrence rate of about 1% (Yamashita, in press). Neural imaging studies show that the simplest permutations of canonical SOV word order in Japanese to OSV order are as big a deal for the Japanese-speaking brain as a long-distance object dependency is for the English- or German-speaking brain (Ueno and Kluender, in press). Moreover, residual effects at sentence end in all these languages (Kluender and Kutas 1993a; Kluender and Münte 1998), i.e. after filler-gap dependencies have already been successfully resolved, suggest that it is the disruption of canonical word order itself rather than the notion of a syntactic chain that most disturbs the brain. With this knowledge in tow, it is then possible to look again at information structure, and begin to investigate the relationship between *wh*-focus constructions and contrastive (vs. informational) focus (Cowles, in preparation). It also raises the possibility of addressing the unresolved question of just how it is that *wh*-scope gets assigned in *wh*-in-situ languages (Ueno, in preparation), and/or languages with partial *wh*-movement.

These are just a random sampling of some of the linguistic issues that have been investigated, or are under investigation, in my own lab, but this hardly exhausts the possibilities. There are a number of linguistic issues that with some thought could well profit from careful experimental manipulation—and it seems obvious that there is no paucity of careful thought in theoretical linguistics. Likewise, experimental design, while more complicated than one usually assumes before one actually attempts it, is not rocket science, either – it merely requires the same kind of deliberate analysis that theoretical linguists do every day of their lives anyway. So, should one choose not to do experimental work oneself, which certainly seems a valid stance, finding someone to collaborate with on experimental work is becoming increasingly hard to avoid, as we continue to turn out increasing numbers of linguistics Ph.D.'s with experimental training under their belts. Just look down the hallway.

So, in sum, far from bleak, I think the prospects look quite rosy if not golden for linguistics as a field, and for the incorporation of additional data sources in its bag of tricks. In this chapter I have only addressed the utility of neural imaging data, but there are myriad other data sources to be exploited: lesion studies, attrition studies, acquisition studies, corpus studies, computational simulations, laboratory phonology, the list goes on and on. With careful planning, extensive and open collaboration, and a large measure of good luck and good will, we may yet be able to mine that elusive golden slash and use it to drive the last spike in the mind-brain (inter) continental railway.

References

Anderson, S.R. 1982. Where's Morphology? *Linguistic Inquiry* 13: 571-612.

Bard, E.G., D. Robertson, and A. Sorace. 1996. Magnitude Estimation of Linguistic Acceptability. *Language* 72: 32-68.

Buccino, G. et. al. 2001. Action Observation Activates Premotor and Parietal Areas in a Somatotopic Manner: An fMRI Study. *European Journal of Neuroscience* 13: 400-404.

Caplan, D., N. Alpert, and G. Waters. 1998. Effects of Syntactic Structure and Propositional Number on Patterns of Regional Cerebral Blood Flow. *Journal of Cognitive Neuroscience* 10: 541-552.

Caplan, D., N. Alpert, and G. Waters, 1999. PET Studies of Syntactic Processing with Auditory Sentence Presentation. *Neuroimage* 9: 43-51.

Caplan, D., N. Alpert, G. Waters, and A. Olivieri, 2000. Activation of Broca's Area by Syntactic Processing under Conditions of Concurrent Articulation. *Human Brain Mapping* 9: 65-71.

Caplan, D. et. al. 2002. Vascular Responses to Syntactic Processing: Event-Related fMRI Study of Relative Clauses. *Human Brain Mapping* 15: 26-38.

Chomsky, N. 1965. *Aspects of the Theory of Syntax*. Cambridge, MA: MIT Press.

Chomsky, N. 1980. Rules and Representations. *Behavioral and Brain Sciences* 3: 1-61.

Chomsky, N. 1986. *Knowledge of Language: Its Nature, Origin, and Use*. New York, NY: Praeger.

Chomsky, N. 1993. *Language and Thought*. Wakefield, RI: Moyer Bell.

Churchland, P. S. 1986. *Neurophilosophy*. Cambridge, MA: MIT Press.

Cooke, A. et. al. 2002. Neural Basis for Sentence Comprehension: Grammatical and Short-Term Memory Components. *Human Brain Mapping* 15: 80-94.

Coulson, S., J. W. King, and M. Kutas. 1998. Expect the Unexpected: Event-Related Brain Response to Morphosyntactic Violations. *Language and Cognitive Processes* 13: 21-58.

Cowart, W. 1997. *Experimental Syntax: Applying Objective Methods to Sentence Judgments.* Thousand Oaks, CA: Sage Publications, Inc.

Cowles, H. W. (in preparation). Processing Information Structure: A Multi-Methodological Approach to Language Comprehension and Production. Doctoral dissertation, University of California, San Diego.

Damasio, A.R. 1992. Aphasia. *New England Journal of Medicine* 326: 531-539.

Dapretto, M. and S. Y. Bookheimer. 1999. Form and Content: Dissociating Syntax and Semantics in Sentence Comprehension. *Neuron* 24: 427-432.

Dronkers, N.F. 1996. A New Brain Region for Coordinating Speech Articulation. *Nature* 384: 159-161.

Dronkers, N. F. 2000. The Gratuitous Relationship between Broca's Aphasia and Broca's Area. *Behavioral and Brain Sciences* 23:30-31, 64-71.

Dronkers, N. F. et. al. 2000. Broca's Historic Cases Revisited. *Brain and Language* 74: 553-555.

Fodor, J. A. 1981. The Mind-Body Problem. *Scientific American*, January 1981, 114-123.

Fodor, J. A. 1983. *The Modularity of Mind: An Essay on Faculty Psychology.* Cambridge, MA: MIT Press.

Friederici, A.D. 2002. Towards a Neural Basis of Auditory Sentence Processing. *Trends in Cognitive Sciences* 6: 78-84.

Herder, J. G. 1966. Essay on the Origin of Language. *On the Origin of Language*, eds. J. H. Moran and A. Gode, 87-166. Chicago, IL: Chicago University Press.

Hockett, C. F. 1948. A Note on 'Structure'. *International Journal of American Linguistics* 14: 269-271.

Just, M. A. et. al. 1996. Brain Activation Modulated by Sentence Comprehension. *Science* 274: 114-116.

Kang, A. M. et. al. 1998. An Event-Related fMRI Study of Implicit Phrase-Level Syntactic and Semantic Processing. *NeuroImage* 10: 555-561.

Kluender, R. and M. Kutas. 1993a. Bridging the Gap: Evidence from ERPs on the Processing of Unbounded Dependencies. *Journal of Cognitive Neuroscience* 5: 196-214.

Kluender, R. and M. Kutas. 1993b. Subjacency as a Processing Phenomenon. *Language and Cognitive Processes* 8: 573-633.

Kluender, R. and T. F. Münte. 1998. ERPs to Grammatical and Ungrammatical Wh-Questions in German. *Poster presented at the 11th annual CUNY Conference on* Human Sentence Processing, Newark, NJ.

Krams, M. et. al. 1998. The Preparation, Execution and Suppression of Copied Movements in the Human Brain. *Experimental Brain Research* 120: 386-398.

Langacker, R.W. 1987. *Foundations of Cognitive Grammar, vol. 1: Theoretical Prerequisites.* Stanford, CA: Stanford University Press.

Ni, . et. al. 2000. An Event-Related Neuroimaging Study Distinguishing Form and Content in Sentence Processing. *Journal of Cognitive Neuroscience* 12: 120-133.

Ojemann, G. 1991. Cortical Organization of Language. *Journal of Neuroscience* 11: 2281-2287.

Pylyshyn, Z. 1980. Computation and Cognition: Issues in the Foundation of Cogntive Science. *Behavioral and Brain Sciences* 3: 111-134.

Shao, J. and H. Neville. 1996. ERPs Elicited by Semantic Anomalies: Beyond the N400. Paper presented at the Cognitive Neuroscience Society, Third Annual Meeting, San Francisco, CA.

Smolensky, P. 1988. On the Proper Treatment of Connectionism. *The Behavioral and Brain Sciences* 11: 1-23.

Stromswold, K. et. al. 1996. Localization of Syntactic Comprehension by Positron Emission Tomography. *Brain and Language* 52: 452-473.

Timberlake, A. 1979. Reflexivization and the Cycle in Russian. *Linguistic Inquiry* 10: 109-141.

Timberlake, A. 1980. Reference Conditions on Russian Reflexivization. *Language* 56: 777-796.

Ueno, M. (in preparation). ERP Inquiries into the Processing of Japanese Wh-Questions. Doctoral dissertation, University of California, San Diego.

Ueno, M. and R. Kluender. (in press). Event-Related Brain Indices of Japanese Scrambling. *Brain and Language.*

Yamashita, H. (in press). Scrambled Sentences in Japanese: Linguistic Properties and Motivations for Production.

9

Generative Grammar and Beyond

S.-Y. KURODA

Part 1: Generative Grammar and a Unification of Sciences

1 Galilean/Cartesian Linguistics

In *Cartesian Linguistics*, Chomsky summarizes the significance of the rationalist grammarians in the 17th and 18th centuries as follows:

> ...the universal grammarians of the seventeenth and eighteenth centuries have made a contribution of lasting value by the very fact that they posed so clearly the problem of changing the orientation of linguistics from "natural history" to "natural philosophy" and by stressing the importance of the search for universal principles and for rational explanation of linguistic fact, if progress is to be made toward this goal. (Chomsky 1966: 59)

For Descartes, (natural) philosophy was an empirical inquiry by means of the testing of hypotheses through observations and experiments.[1] The discovery of the experimental/empirical method, however, is attributed to Galileo.[2] Descartes and the Cartesian rationalists do deserve credit, however, for applying the scientific (i.e. empirical/experimental) method to the study of language; their legacy is Cartesian linguistics. However, in a broader his-

---

[1] *Discourse on the Method*, Part VI and *Principles of Philosophy*, Part III Principles 43-47; Part IV Principles 204, 205.

[2] According to A. D'Abro, though, "it was [Archimedes] who inaugurated the experimental method," but "the lesson taught by Archimedes was soon forgotten." (D'Abro 1951: 5)

The Nature of Explanation in Linguistic Theory.
John Moore and Maria Polinsky (eds.).

torical perspective it is perhaps more fitting to call it Galilean/Cartesian linguistics.

Chomsky sees generative grammar as a contemporary reemergence of Galilean/Cartesian linguistics. It is, I believe, a widely held feeling that the progress made by generative grammar from the nineteen sixties to eighties brought linguistic theory to the equivalent of a Galilean stage in the history of natural science.

2 Parable 1. A Story of Super-Genius Mega-Ptolemy, the Discoverer of a Mathematical Description of Mega-Ptolemaic Astronomy

Some might maintain that generative grammar has progressed even further. But such an evaluation is not generally agreed upon among theoretical linguists. Newton's decisive contribution in surpassing the Galilean-Cartesian stage is undisputable. In order to assess the present state of linguistic theory properly, I would like to review one aspect of Newton's historical significance.

For this purpose, let me indulge at this point in the fanciful play of a counterfactual history of natural science.

> Copernicus put the Ptolemaic order of the universe in serious doubt, and Kepler gave a further blow to it by discovering that the planets move around the sun along elliptic orbits observing his three laws. With the benefit of hindsight, let me invent a Greek supergenius, Mega-Ptolemy, who succeeded in discovering a mathematical theory of the Ptolemaic order of the universe.
>
> Imagine a coordinate transformation that makes the earth the origin of the coordinates, and apply the transformation to the elliptical orbits of the planets around the sun. In principle, the class of such curves, and more generally, the class of quadratic curves a focus of which is the sun, should be transformed into a certain natural class of curves, perhaps a certain kind of algebraic curve. Since we are simply engaging in a fanciful counterfactual, or even counterconceptual imagination for the sake of argument, let us suppose that we obtain by this mathematical transformation a class of non-elementary but mathematically highly interesting objects. Let us call them Mega-E-curves.
>
> Now, imagine also that a supergenius, Mega-Ptolemy, was born in Alexandria. By a truly miraculous stroke of genius, Mega-Ptolemy found out that the planets (and even comets) orbit around the earth along curves that were characterized as Mega-E curves. At the same time Mega-

Ptolemy demonstrated many remarkable properties of Mega-E curves. He could even have predicted the course of a comet on its way toward the earth along a Mega-E curve. The people of Fanciland would have been mesmerized with this great discovery and struck by the truth of mathematical order governing the universe.

Now let us assume that after our Mega-Ptolemy's fame had been enshrined and a paradigm set by Mega-Ptolemy's theory had dominated astronomy for over fifteen centuries, Copernicus and Kepler came around and challenged the Mega-Ptolemaic order of the universe. The Fancilanders now have two competing theories. From the perspective of scientific methodology, Mega-Ptolemy and Copernicus/Kepler stood on the same footing. They both belonged to the pre-Galilean, observational stage of scientific method. Neither can claim superiority over the other on methodological grounds. Nor by our assumption does either have advantage over the other on empirical grounds.

One might say that the choice is a simple matter of simplicity criteria: Quadratic curves would have to count as formally simpler objects than Mega-E curves. Nonetheless, the Mega-Ptolemaics could still have appealed to the intuitive naturalness of their theory to their advantage: Perceptually the earth does not move, the sun and the planets do. This is also a kind of conceptual simplicity argument. The choice between the two theories can be made only on conceptual grounds.[3]

[3] In this parabolic exploitation, I simplify the history and put aside Galileo's role in the fight for the Copernican theory. For Galileo's use of his discoveries with the telescope as evidence for the Copernican theory, see Swerdlow (1998).

In the Ptolemaic geocentric theory, only the ratio of the radii of the epicircle and the deferent can be determined for each planet empirically. Hence, the epicycle for each planet can be set freely. In contrast, in the Copernican heliocentric theory with circular planetary orbits the epicycle translates into the distance between the sun and the earth and must be kept invariant. Hence, the Ptolemaic theory contains more free parameters than the Copernican theory. The Ptolemaic theorist determined the epicycles on a transcendent principle. See, for example, Sugimoto and Hamada (1975: 11). In reality, the orbits of the planets are not circular, and neither the Copernican nor the Ptolemaic theory accounts for the observed planetary movements perfectly. But disregarding the mismatch between data and prediction in this regard, one could argue formally against the Ptolemaic theory for the reason of excessive indeterminacy. One might contend that our Mega-Ptolemy would also be plagued with free parameters as the Ptolemaic theory was, and on this ground the Mega-Ptolemaic theory can be dismissed. The moral of our parable, however, is that the Newtonian unification can overrun the Mega-Ptolemaic theory even without questioning the relative advantage in terms of the number of free parameters.

3 The Moral of Parable 1

It is a truism to say that Newton's contribution to the advancement of the science was decisive and significant. The moral of the preceding parable is to put in relief one aspect of this significance by exaggerating the weight of the view against which the progress of the modern physics had to be made.

While Kepler inquired into the movement of celestial bodies and attained a descriptive theory through observational methods, Galileo opened a new stage of science, the science of the experimental/empirical method, and attained a descriptive theory of the movement of masses on the earth. Newton then pursued the idea that heavenly bodies are nothing but the same masses as on the earth and must be controlled by the same forces. From this insight, he developed the concept of universal gravitation.

On the one hand, Newton elevated both the Keplerian and the Galilean theories from a descriptive to a decisively explanatory level. On the other hand, in so doing, Newton unified Keplerian astronomy and Galilean mechanics in one science of physics. In reality, these are but two aspects of a single historical incident. But conceptually we can distinguish these two aspects and evaluate their significance separately to some extent. In fact, counterfactually, we could imagine Mega-Newton discovering Newtonian mechanics on the basis of Keplerian astronomy alone, without Galilean mechanics preceding it. If that were the case, Mega-Newton would have lifted Keplerian astronomy to an explanatory level, but there would not have been a unification of sciences.

The progress of scientific method from observational/experimental to speculative/mathematical and a shift in the nature of theories, from taxonomic/descriptive to explanatory, was momentous in the Newtonian revolution. Nonetheless, as we contemplate the future of the science of grammar and reflect on the history of science in this context, I submit that what characterizes the decisive step taken by the Newtonian revolution in the progress of the science of nature is the unification of sciences. Not only did this unification vindicate the Keplerian understanding of astronomy and Galilean mechanics, but it also weeded out all the unjustified hypotheses and ill-conceived speculations in celestial astronomy as well as in terrestrial mechanics that did not fit in this unification; Keplerian astronomy and Galilean mechanics emerged out of the chaos of intellectual activities of the time as integral parts of the unified knowledge of nature. The conclusive effect of the sudden clearing of the perspective by the Newtonian unification of Keplerian astronomy and Galilean mechanics would have been the same, or perhaps greater, even if the Ptolemaic point of view had been reinforced by the Mega-Ptolemaic theory of Parable 1.

4 Generative Grammar and a Unification of Sciences

Let us now return to generative grammar. The enthusiasm and optimism that prevailed in the early nineteen sixties, and again in the early nineteen eighties, seems to have subsided as the end of the second millennium approached. While a dominant current in generative grammar is still unmistakable in professional meetings and a conceptual program has been proposed (cf. Chomsky 1995b), it would seem fair to say, however, that we continue to be deluged with manipulated descriptive technology in the guise of the advancement of a conceptual program.

Three hundred years from now, the present state of the art of grammar might well be viewed as we now do the state of mechanics before Newton. Galilean mechanics surely formed a part of pre-Newtonian mechanics. But Galilean mechanics was immersed in bodies of speculations and hypotheses, including the tradition of Cartesian mechanics, which was then discarded by the Newtonian theory of universal gravitation.

In this context, we must recall that generative grammar, a scientific inquiry into human language, must be an integral part of the scientific inquiry into the human mind/brain, a scholarly endeavor within what Chomsky calls methodological naturalism.

> A naturalistic approach to linguistic and mental aspects of the world seeks to construct intelligible explanatory theories, taking as 'real' what we are led to posit in this quest, and hoping for eventual unification with the 'core' natural sciences: unification, not necessarily reduction. (Chomsky 1995a: 1)

Naturalism in the sense intended in this context is '"methodological naturalism", counterposed to "methodological dualism".' Methodological dualism is 'the doctrine that in the quest for theoretical understanding, language and mind are to be studied in some manner other than the ways we investigate natural objects, as a matter of principle.' (Ibid.: 28) One hopes that the unification of the sciences of mind with the core natural sciences will be achieved, but it must be left as an open question if such a unification is indeed a possibility.[4]

---

[4] A remark on the reference to naturalism may be in order in this context. According to Chomsky, generative grammar is, on the one hand, a modern re-emergence of Cartesian linguistics and, on the other hand, an inquiry into language following methodological naturalism. But language is a hallmark of mind in Cartesian metaphysical dualism. Cartesian linguists of the seventeenth and the eighteenth century would, one might say, protest for being identified as 'naturalists', and one might wonder if Chomsky's conception of history is incoherent. Such

A new form of behaviorism might be able to explain away generative grammar. This is conceivable, but I am not suggesting such a possibility here. If that feat should be realized, that would be a reduction, not a unification. Generative grammar would be dissolved, not incorporated as an integral part of a unified science.

I suggest that our concern should be a unification within the soft sciences, the sciences of cognition and human communication. I am suggesting the possibility of a unification that makes generative grammar an integral part of a unified science, a unification which thereby clears up our current opaque perspectives in generative grammar, just as Newtonian physics did with the pre-Newtonian mechanics by incorporating Galilean mechanics into the unified science.

For such a unification to be possible, or even conceivable, however, there would have to be another science of mind with which generative grammar is to be unified. Is it conceivable that such a science exists? Where could we expect it to emerge? A plausible candidate would be found among a variety of formal or mathematical studies in semantics, pragmatics and information structure that are intensively explored among linguists and philosophers. But I would like to leave that aside for now and turn to another possible direction.

---

concern, however, is unwarranted.

As Chomsky elaborates, methodological naturalism is an attitude according to which theoretical inquiry (call it philosophical, as Cartesians did, or scientific, as we do) does not assume that the objects of inquiry, whether physical, mental or whatever, dictate different canons of methodology. Descartes, and the Cartesian grammarians who succeeded him, took this attitude for granted, while Chomsky had to counterpose it to methodological dogmatism, due to the different intellectual environments in which they worked.

Metaphysical dualism, as long as it is free of dogmatism, is logically orthogonal to methodological naturalism. A particular argument for metaphysical dualism could even be entertained as a hypothesis within methodological naturalism, subject to possible refutation. This is conceptually a coherent position. Metaphysical dualism, however, also served historically as a springboard for subjectivist anti-naturalist foundationalism.

In the middle of the nineteenth century Franz Brentano advocated essentially the same thesis as methodological naturalism in philosophy and psychology. He apparently held the view that the immortality of the soul is a legitimate hypothesis for study in naturalist philosophy.

In contrast, Husserl, who started his philosophical career as a student of Brentano from inside this movement, drifted away to Cartesian epistemological foundationalism and at the close of his life ended up as a staunch advocate of anti-naturalism.

For Brentano, Husserl and Chomsky concerning naturalism, see Kuroda (1997b, 1999b).

5 The Possibility of a Science of Rationality: Communicative (Grice)

Some time ago I presented an axiomatic formal theory that is intended to account for Grice's work on communicative intentions (Grice 1957, Kuroda 1986, 1989). Grice himself thought he was engaged in a theory of meaning, but that is, in my view, a mischaracterization of the core idea of his work. Grice's formula for nonnatural meaning is well-known:

(1) A meant$_{NN}$ something by x' is (roughly) equivalent to 'A intended the utterance of x to be produce some effect in an audience by means of the recognition of this intention'.

The formal system I constructed in those articles is based on three operators {A}, [A], and <A>, corresponding to *believe*, *know* and *intend.* I set up a system of axioms that express basic formal relations among these operators in terms of equality and entailment. I then derived three formulas from these axioms, that is, I proved three theorems of this axiomatic system. I maintained that each of these theorems could be taken as a formal representation of one of the three alternative interpretations of Grice's formula.

I thus claim that the English sentence form in which Grice clothed his idea can be parsed in three different ways, though none of the readings yields a perfectly grammatical parsing in ordinary English. Nonetheless, each of these readings represents a proposition expressing a characteristic property of communicative intentions, at different depths of analysis. All these propositions are proven as theorems in this axiomatic system.

Believe, *know* and *intend* are the three basic mental acts/states of the rational agent. The axioms of our formal system characterize a structure of rationality based on these mental operations. Grice's formula embodies a rare philosophical insight into the rational performance of human mind. The fact that the interpretations of Grice's formula can be proven as theorems of this formal system acquires dual significance when put in complementary perspectives. It vindicates Grice, who discovered these theorems by the penetrating power of philosophical intuition. Or, reversing the viewpoint, it vindicates the system as a viable model of an aspect of rationality that relates to linguistic performance.

I do not have even a vague idea how this theory might be unified with generative grammar within a formal theory. But it seems intriguing to speculate whether grammatical theory maybe unified with a science of rationality. I am referring to this work to give an example of a possible formal inquiry into rationality within the spirit of methodological naturalism. If grammar is a characteristic of human instinct, rational communication is a characteristic of human practical reason. Language and rationality are two pillars of human nature. Would it be a vain hope, surprising though it might seem now, that formal inquiries into innate endowments in linguistic competence and rationality in linguistic performance may be unified in a science of mind?

Part 2: The Perceptual Order of Nature vs. the Phenomenological Disorder of Mind

1 The Demise of Newton Physics and the Historico / Methodological Significance of the Kantian Epistemology in the Sciences of Nature

The foundations of the Newtonian order of the universe began to shatter around the turn of the last century. By the 1920s Newtonian physics had to relinquish the throne of science to the new physics, i.e., relativity theory and quantum mechanics. It is not that Newtonian physics must be discarded as a wrong theory. Rather, Newtonian physics turned out to be the right approximation of the order of the universe under limiting conditions in which the parameters that characterize relativity theory and quantum mechanics can be ignored, as infinitesimal.

Around the turn of the century prior to the last, the philosopher Kant speculated that Euclidean geometry was synthetic *a priori* knowledge. The Kantian order of epistemology can be seen as motivationally tied to the Newtonian order of the universe. A century later, as they saw the Newtonian order crumble, some philosophers began to scoff at Kant's shortsightedness. However, as a matter of fact, it is much to Kant's credit that he realized that our PERCEPTUAL epistemology can be grounded on the synthetic *a priori* principles of Euclidean geometry. In fact, it should strike us as remarkable that our perceptual world is shielded securely from the reality of relativity theory and quantum mechanics. In this context, let me indulge in another flightof fancy.

2 Parable 2. The Struggle of Mega-Galileo, Mega-Kepler and Mega-Newton in Weirdland

In this Weirdland, some crucial physical constants are sufficiently off from their real values, so that relativity and quantum effects could not be shielded from our everyday perceptual world. In this Weirdland the Newtonian and Euclidean picture of the universe cannot emerge in our perceptual natural experience. We could imagine that the intelligent organism nonetheless emerges, so well adapted evolutionarily as to perceptually cope with quantum and relativity environments, perhaps with synthetic *a priori* knowledge of a non-Euclidean geometry. But it is harder to imagine that environmental pressures could equip this organism with a super faculty of reason that is capable of producing a Mega-Einstein and a Mega-Heisenberg/Schroedinger who could discover relativity theory and quantum mechanics *ex nihilo*, that is, without the benefit of Galilean mechanics, Keplerian astronomy and Newtonian physics which the new theories were to replace. Would Mega-Einstein not have to be preceded by Mega-Galileo, Mega-Kepler and Mega-Newton? But what would these Mega-heroes have to achieve? They would have to somehow hit upon and isolate phenomena that appear to escape relativity and quantum effects; they would have to idealize such phenomena as supporting evidence for Galilean mechanics, Keplerian astronomy or Newtonian physics, a theory that would look like an ill-fitting theory and relate to only a fraction of the perceptual reality. The philosophers of science in Weirdland might insist that the sciences of Mega-Galileo, Mega-Kepler and Mega-Newton would not qualify as empirical sciences.

3 The Moral of Parable 2

What is the moral of our second parable? Luckily, the physical design of our real universe lets our faculty of perception see only what appears to us, that is, PHENOMENA in Kant's sense; it spares us from seeing reality itself, or NOUMENA.[5] But that is precisely why the human faculty of theoretical reason succeeded in taking off on its journey towards the scientific understanding of physical reality. Newtonian physics is the physics of PHENOMENA, but it was a necessary step towards the post-Newtonian physics of NOUMENA.

In contrast, we may not be so lucky in the sciences of mind. Put ironically, it may be the case that we intuit our inner life all too well. Our faculty of inner perception lets us observe mental phenomena indiscriminately. We would face phenomenological data that are not *naturally* modularized. As a consequence, in our inquiry into the mind, we might not be able to take the initial step corresponding to the Newtonian stage in the science of nature. The more we try to look for relevant data phenomenologically for testing

[5] In what follows I small-capitalize the words PHENOMENA and NOUMENA when they are intended as terms in Kantian philosophy (or as their parodies).

hypotheses and advancing our scientific knowledge of the mind, the more deluded and trapped we might be by data, metaphorically speaking, data of post-Newtonian kinds.

It may be in order to elaborate on the above point. Generative grammar, as it is practiced currently, is a phenomenological science in the following sense; it is ultimately founded on the intuition (inner perception) of investigating scientists or other speakers on their native languages. The significant part of empirical data on which the theory is constructed and on which it is empirically tested is phenomenological. This is not to say, of course, that the concepts that constitute the theory are phenomenological. If generative grammar posits a rule or principle, it does not entail that the native speaker, or the scientist as a native speaker, can access it by intuition, phenomenologically. In this sense, the theory is formal, but it is empirically grounded on intuition.

Galilean mechanics and Keplerian astronomy were phenomenal sciences in the sense that the empirical data on which they were constructed were obtained directly by perception, aided, to be sure, by instruments that extended the human visual capacity. We are drawing a parallel analogy Galilean mechanics and Keplerian astronomy are also 'phenomenal' and mathematical; generative grammar is phenomenological and formal.[6]

Now, we are speculating if a unification of generative grammar with a science of rationality might take us to a higher stage of the science of mind, and secure firm foundations for generative grammar, just as Newtonian physics did for Galilean mechanics. Assume our analogical parallelism should run its course to the end. Then, the unified science of mind that we are hoping for would be attained as a science of MENTAL PHENOMENA, in the way Newtonian physics was a science of PHYSICAL PHENOMENA. By this, what I mean is: Our faculty of inner perception would luckily be so limited as to let us intuit just about the right kind and the right amount of data with which our theoretical reason could construct a first stage of the science of mind, just as Newtonian physics was a first stage of the science of nature. But the moral of our Parable 2 is that the reality may not favor us in the science of mind as it did in the science of nature. Perhaps our faculty of inner

---

[6] An optimist might suggest that unpredictable advances in information technology, could allow generative grammar in the future to rely more and more on corpus linguistics and diminish native intuition in generative research, thus rendering generative grammar a non-phenomenogical science. But in the context of our metaphorical/analogical argument, the function of linguistic corpora might be compared with that of photographic/cinematographic records of natural events. In the intended sense, the perceptual character of Newtonian mechanics would not change with the extended use of photographic/cinematographic recordings; neither does the phenomenological character of generative grammar with corpus linguistics.

perception is not so structured as to isolate MENTAL PHENOMENA and let us intuit only those; rather, it leaves us groping in the dark forever, lets us descend into the abyss of our mind indefinitely and see detail after detail of mental phenomena (not small-capitalized) indiscriminately. Would it be the case then that a unification of generative grammar with a science of mind must be achieved, if ever possible, only as a science of MENTAL NOUMENA?

4 An Illustration of the Structure of the Argument: Operator Movement and Japanese

To facilitate the understanding of the point I am trying to make, let us consider the issue of operator movement (abstract *wh*-movement) in Japanese. It is well known that Japanese topicalization and relativization, the most plausible constructions where we would expect to encounter movement effects, appear to be able to violate the movement constraints. It is common to assume that these constructions are base generated, apparent gaps being filled *in situ* with an empty category of some sort. But it is not entirely clear when we get readily acceptable forms and when less acceptable or unacceptable forms.[7]

However, there are some constructions that do seem to observe the movement constraints. Those are constructions that involve IMAGINARY argument/adjunct positions. By an IMAGINARY argument/adjunct position, I mean a position where only an empty category of some sort can be selected, that is, a position which a non-empty category cannot occupy but which is posited as a place holder for an empty element. One such construction is the comparative construction, for which we posit an empty degree adjunct. As Kikuchi (1987) demonstrated, Japanese comparatives obey subjacency, as English comparatives do. Another construction in Japanese that exhibits subjacency effects is the construction called the PSEUDO-RELATIVE. Functionally the Japanese pseudo-relative corresponds to the English construction in which a head noun takes a gerund complement, as exemplified by phrases such as *the smell of John's broiling tuna*, *the sound of Mary's knocking at the door.* Unlike this English construction, however, the Japanese pseudo-relative exhibits long-distance filler-gap relations. Observe:

---

[7] For examples of topics and relative clauses that apparently violate island constraints, see Kuno (1973) and McCawley (1976), among others. For an analysis of such examples without involving island violations, see Kuroda (1992: ch. 8,9).

(2) a. John ga maguro o yaite iru nioi
John NOM tuna ACC broil is smell
'The smell of John's broiling tuna'

b. Mary ga John ga maguro o yaite iru to
Mary NOM John NOM tuna ACC broil is QUOT
omotte iru nioi
think is smell
'*The smell of Mary's thinking that John is broiling tuna'

Here, in the second example, the attempted translation into English fails as indicated by the star, but the Japanese counterpart is acceptable. As pointed out by Murasugi (1997), the pseudo-relative appears to display characteristics of *wh*-movement:

(3) a. *Mary ga maguro o yaite iru hito o mite
Mary NOM tuna ACC broil is person ACC look-at
iru nioi
is smell
'*The smell of Mary's looking at a person who is broiling tuna'

b. *Mary ga John ga maguro o yaite iru
Mary NOM John NOM tuna ACC broil is
aida ni kimono o kikae ta nioi
while DAT dress ACC put on smell
'*The smell of Mary's putting on a dress while John is broiling tuna'

c. *Mary ga dare ga maguro o yaite iru
Mary NOM who NOM tuna ACC broil is
ka John ni kiita nioi
INTERR John DAT ask smell
'*The smell of Mary's asking John who is broiling tuna'

We can account for the pseudo-relative by assuming that its embedded clause has an empty event argument selected by the pseudo-relative head, and an operator moves from this argument position to the head noun position, *nioi* smell, in the above examples.

Yet another example of a construction involving the movement of an operator from an imaginary adjunct is the construction Ishii (1990) calls the *half* RELATIVE. The embedded clause, indicated by the brackets in the examples below, directly precedes and modifies the measure term noun *han-*

bun half. As Ishii pointed out, the *half*-relative obeys the constraints of *wh*-movement.

(4) a. John wa [Mary ga yatin ni tukau] hanbun o
John TOP Mary NOM rent DAT use half ACC
gyanburu ni tukau.
gamble DAT use
'John spends for gambling half as much as Mary does for rent.'

b. John wa [Mary ga Bill ga yatin ni
John TOP Mary NOM Bill NOM rent DAT
tukau to omote iru] hanbun gyanburu ni tukau.
use QUOT believe is half gamble DAT use
'John spends for gambling half as much as Mary believes Bill does for rent.'

c. *John wa [Mary ga Bill ga kaseida zizitu o
John TOP Mary NOM Bill NOM earn fact ACC
mitometa] bai o kasegou to omotte iru.
acknowledge two-times ACC earn QUOT think is
'*John is thinking of earning twice as much as Mary acknowledges the fact that Bill earned.'

d. *John wa [Mary ga kaseide kara Yooroppa ni itta]
John TOP Mary NOM earn after Europe DAT go
hanbun mo kaseg-anak-atta.
half even earn.NEG.past
'*John did not earn half as much as Mary went to Europe after she did.'

We can assume that the *half*-relative requires and selects an empty degree adjunct; this empty element moves to the head of the construction.

Now, I maintain that a number of factors together contribute to produce the effect that gives rise to the impression that operator movement involving NON-EMPTY categories does not obey island constraints in Japanese. First of all, following Kuroda (1988), I assume that structural Case marking and abstract movement are manifestations of one and the same underlying effect, Abstract Agreement, the sharing of a feature between a head X and a maximal category in an external (i.e. Spec) or internal complement of X. I further assume that Abstract Agreement is not obligatory in Japanese, in contradistinction to obligatory Agreement languages like English. Instead, a mechanism is provided to obviate Abstract Agreement. Thus, for structural Case marking, there is a device of morphological case, *ga* for the nominative and *o* for the accusative case, that obviate Abstract Agreement by finite

Infl and a transitive verb, respectively. But Case is not our present concern. Abstract movement is also due to Abstract Agreement and for each case of Abstract movement there is normally a way to obviate movement. Let us take a look at the two most plausible phenomena where one would expect to find island effects for movement.

First, consider the *wh*-question. A *wh*-phrase moves to Spec (C) and 'agrees with' the *wh*-feature at Comp. In Japanese, this Agreement can be obviated simply by leaving the *wh*-phrase *in situ*. Besides, although the *wh*-phrase may be put at sentence-initial position, it is hard to tell whether this positioning is the effect of *wh*-movement or scrambling. Thus, the effect of the *wh*-movement, let alone its island effect, is hard to identify.

As far as scrambling is concerned, there appear to be a couple of operations of different kinds: clause-bound scrambling, VP-internal scrambling, and one with long-distance effect; these phenomena may be manifestations of one underlying operation, as Saito (2001) claims, or they may not, as Ueyama (1998) maintains. As Saito (2001:42) states 'Japanese and (Korean) scrambling is potentially theoretically significant because of its unique properties.' Be that as it may, scrambling is not a unified phenomenon easily shown to demonstrate the island effects of a movement.

Secondly, let us consider the so-called topic construction, which is characterized by the sentence-initial *wa*-phrase.[8] There is, I assume, a crucial syntactic difference between the topic construction and the *wh*-question. The *wh*-question does not necessarily require *wh*-phrases to be moved to the Spec(C) position in overt syntax, as seen in multiple *wh*-questions in English; that is why *wh*-phrases may stay at an argument or adjunct position in Japanese. In contrast, for it to be properly interpreted the topic must occupy a specific peripheral position (say, Spec(C)) in overt (as well as covert) syntax.

For this condition to be satisfied, the topic conceivably could be either generated *in situ* or moved from an argument or adjunct position. Japanese topic *wa*-phrases appear to involve movement. Take, for example:

---

[8] For the function and semantics of the so-called topic *wa*-phrases, see Kuroda (1992: ch. 1) and Kuroda (to appear). From the functional/semantic perspective, the term TOPIC can be misleading, but I retain this term for the convenience of syntactic treatment. I employ English topicalization (left dislocation) for glossing Japanese *wa*-topic sentences for the convenience of syntactic discussion only; functional equivalence between the two constructions is not guaranteed.

(5) kono ronbun wa John ga NLLT e okuroo
this paper TOP John NOM NLLT to send
to omotte iru.
QUOT think is
'This paper, John is thinking to send to NLLT.'

It is plausible to assume that topicalization moved *kono ronbun* 'this paper', leaving a trace [*t*] at the direct object position inside the embedded clause:

(6) *kono ronbun* wa John ga [PRO NLLT e [*t*] okuroo to] omotte iru.

We can assume that the Comp of a topic sentence contains the *wa*-feature and the *wa*-phrase is moved to Spec(C) to agree with this feature. However, there is a way to obviate this process of movement and Agreement. Spec(C) is not a theta position, hence presumably a term can be generated there *in situ* without being locally governed, and licensed, by a theta-role discharger, provided that a derivation eventually converges. Recall that Japanese has the unconstrained empty pronoun, *pro*. In the above example, we can have *pro*, instead of [t], and have it bound to *kono ronbun* at Spec(C), deriving without movement the same phonetic form as above:

(7) *kono ronbun* wa John ga [PRO NLLT e *pro* okuroo to] omotte iru.

Thus, the same topic sentence can be generated either by moving a topic phrase from an argument or adjunct position to Spec(C), or by generating a topic phrase at Spec(C) and pro at an argument or adjunct position.

But, then, topicalized sentences with apparent violation of the island constraint are also readily generated. Take, for example, the famous example by Kuno (1973), which appears to show topicalization does not observe the island constraints:

(8) sono sinsi wa, kite iru yoohuku ga yogore iru.
the gentleman TOP wearing is suit NOM dirty is.
'Speaking of that gentleman, the suit he is wearing is dirty.'

This sentence can be assigned the following structure with *pro* bound by *sono sinsi*:

(9) *sono sinsi* wa [*pro* kite iru yoohuku] ga yogore iru.

Then, movement is not involved in the derivation of this sentence. The bare noun phrase *sono sinsi* is licensed *in situ* as a topic, by *wa,* or perhaps more properly, by *wa* in Spec(C) and is allowed to be interpreted, say, by the ABOUTNESS condition or, as I claim, as the subject of a predicational (or categorical) JUDGMENT.[9] The same phrase *sono sinsi* is also understood as the subject of *kite iru,* with the intermediary of *pro*, which it binds.

The above observation might lead one to conclude that there is no movement, let alone Agreement feature, that is responsible for generating any topicalized sentences; it would suffice to generate all topics *in situ.* However, observe the following sentence:

(10) Russell ni wa nihonzin ga oozei atta.
Russell DAT TOP Japanese NOM many meet
'Russell, many Japanese met.'

Here, *Russell* is a topic, but it is accompanied by *ni*, an inherent (or, quirky) case marker chosen by the verb *atta*. The marker *ni* has to be locally licensed by *atta*; *Russell ni* must be moved from the complement position governed by *atta* to Spec(C):

(11) *Russell ni* wa nihonzin ga oozei [*t*] atta.

But if a noun phrase with an inherent (or, quirky) case marker or postpositional phrase, like *Russell ni* above, must move to become a topic, such a topic phrase cannot violate island constraints. This prediction in fact holds, as the observation made by Saito (1985) demonstrates. Take, for example:

(12) **Russell ni* wa John ga [[*e*][*t*] atta] nihonjin] o
Russell DAT TOP John NOM meet Japanese ACC
oozei sitte iru.
many know is
*'Russell, John knows many Japanese who met with.'

Here, [*e*] is an empty category coindexed with *nihonjin* and [*t*] is, as before, a trace left by *Russell ni.* This form is ungrammatical, as predicted; *Russell*

---

[9] See Kuroda (1992, to appear). Matsushita (1928) is an earlier work that presents a similar view (Kuroda 1992:75, n. 6).

ni moved out of the noun phrase [[e t atta] nihonjin], violating an island constraint. In contrast, the following form is grammatical:

(13) *Russelli* wa John ga [[[*e*] *pro* atta] nihonjin] o oozei sitte iru.

Here, *Russell* is generated *in situ* and *pro*, coindexed with *Russell*, is selected by *atta* as its object; the quirky case marker is absorbed in *pro* and invisible. No movement, and *a fortiori*, no island constraint violation, hence a grammatical form.

Thus, as Saito concludes, postpositional phrases (or, quirky case-marked phrases) are topicalized by movement, obeying the island constraints. I do not assume, though Saito (1985) seems to, that topicalization as a movement is restricted to postpositonal phrases (pied-piped topics), since such a restriction is *ad hoc*. I grant derivational ambiguity for non-pied-piped topicalized sentences that can be generated without violating island constraints; the same phonetic form could be generated with a topic *in situ*.

The whole story about the Japanese *wa*-topic involves more complication, however, due to the phenomenon involving the major subject (Kuroda 1992, chps. 6 and 8-10). Consider again Kuno's example cited above and replace the topic marker *wa* with the nominative marker *ga*. We get a double nominative, hence apparently a double-subject sentence:

(14) sono sinsi ga, kite iru yoohuku ga
the gentleman NOM wearing is suit NOM
yogorete iru.
dirty is
'The gentleman is [such that] the suit he is wearing is dirty.'

This form is grammatical and can be used in contexts where non-topicalized sentence forms are expected, for instance, in conditional clauses:

(15) mosi sono sinsi ga, kite iru yoohuku ga
if the gentleman NOM wearing is suit NOM
yogorete ireba
dirty is.COND
'If the gentleman is such that the suit that he wears is dirty,...'

Then, Kuno's original topic sentence can be derived from the double-subject sentence with multiple Spec(C) position without violating any island constraint. The topicalized sentence is derived from the following underlying structure by moving the MAJOR SUBJECT:

(16) a. [sono sinsi ga [[*pro* kite iru yoohuku] ga yogorete iru].
b. sono sinsi wa [[*t*] [[*pro* kite iru yoohuku] ga yogorete iru].

Here, [*t*] is the trace left at the major subject position, that is, the outer Spec(C) position.

The same conclusion may be drawn for Saito's example (130 above, to the extent that the double subject form is deemed acceptable; we can entertain the derivation suggested by the following forms, where *pro* is bound by *Russell* and [*t*] is a trace of *Russell*:

(17) a. [*Russell* ga [John ga [[*e*] *pro* atta nihonjin] o oozei sitte iru.
b. *Russell* wa [[*t*] [John ga [[*e*] *pro* atta nihonjin] o oozei sitte iru.

To recapitulate, at least some apparent violations of island constraints can be resolved by deriving them from the double-subject structure. The problem is shifted from island constraints to the conditions for the double-subject structure. Given the possibility of the major subject construction, only in cases where the corresponding double-subject structure is impossible, do we have uncontestable evidence for the possibility of the *in-situ* topic, a device to obviate movement, and hence to obviate Agreement. The acceptability judgment for multiple-subject sentence forms is often not quite clear, but the acceptability degenerates rapidly as the *pro* bound to the topic *wa*-phrase is more deeply embedded. Compare the following topicalized sentence and the double subject sentence forms:

(18) a. Russell wa itumo Mary ga John ga atta
Russell TOP always Mary NOM JOHN NOM meet
nihonzin o takusan sitte ita to itte iru.
Japanese ACC many know was QUOT say be
b. Russell ga itumo Mary ga John ga atta
Russell NOM always Mary NOM JOHN NOM meet
nihonzin o takusan sitte ita to itte iru.
Japanese ACC many know was QUOT say be
'Russell, Mary always says John knows many Japanese who met (him).'

The double subject form here, I believe, is very difficult to accept, and contrasts sharply with the more readily acceptable corresponding topicalized sentence. One might wish to resort to performance limitation in order to account for the gradual decrease of the acceptability of double subject forms, but the fact would remain unaccounted for that the topicalized counterpart is decisively much more acceptable than the double-subject form. A natural explanation is that the topic phrase can be generated *in situ,* not derived from the major subject by movement.

To conclude, then, there are two ways to generate topic *wa*-phrases, [1] by movement and [2] by *in situ* generation. Among those derived by movement, there are [1a] those which involve movement from an argument or adjunct position of the ordinary type and [1b] those which involve movement from a MAJOR SUBJECT POSITION (i.e., a higher position in the multiple Spec(V) position). Pied-piped topic phrases, however, are necessarily generated by movement and provide evidence for the movement option. In contrast, bare topic *wa*-phrases may, in principle, have three different possible derivations, by movement from an argument or adjunct position, movement from a major subject position or by *in-situ* generation. One might take this derivational ambiguity against the proposed account. I, for one, on the contrary, take it as supporting evidence vindicating the proposed analysis; for this ambiguity is predicted from our fundamental assumption that Abstract Agreement is not forced in Japanese.[10]

Let us now return to the constructions where the affected category is an empty category of an imaginary constituent, such as the comparative, the pseudo-relative and the half-relative construction. We note that none of these factors discussed above can contribute to obliterate the obligatoriness of Agreement as well as the effect of island constraints. For, an empty category that can occupy an imaginary constituent, like a degree adjunct in the comparative construction or an empty event argument in the pseudo- or half-relative construction, just like a quirky case-marked phrase, must be locally chosen by the head that requires it; it cannot be generated at Spec(C) or Spec(V), and bind *pro* that occupies an imaginary constituent position. Even though Agreement is assumed to be optional in principle, for these constructions there is no way available to obviate Agreement, and movement.

As a consequence one can observe movement effects in Japanese constructions clearly and unambiguously if and only if a construction necessarily selects an empty category at an imaginary constituent position and requires it to move. This is precisely why we see movement effects in Japa-

---

[10] Structural ambiguity entailed by a theory, however massive it might be, should not be taken just for its own sake against the theory. One cannot fault New York City for its street planning for the sake of the multiple ways possible for going from 47th Street and Park Avenue to 57th Street and 7th Avenue.

Be that as it may, our immediate concern here is not to determine what the right theory for the topic construction is, but to see that, whatever that might be, and however much it is difficult to determine it, movement is responsible for some cases and see that island constraints are observed with topicalization if we restrict our attention to the right kind of data.

nese transparently with the comparative, the pseudo-relative and the *half*-relative construction, but not with the *wh*-question or topicalization.[11]

The analogy to be drawn is: The relevant part of English grammar (the syntax related to Abstract movement) is to that of Japanese grammar what Newtonian physics is to post-Newtonian physics. Metaphorically speaking, a part of the core syntax of English singles out itself and can be observed as if we have secured a syntax of PHENOMENA which enables us to take off for the construction of grammatical theory, while the functionally corresponding part of Japanese syntax is as if submerged in the chaos of NOUMENA.

However, at a crucial point, this metaphor is inadequate and misleading. It is not the case that the generative theory of movement was achieved thanks to any restriction nature imposed on the power of our inner perception, while it did on the power of our outer perception and allowed our theoretical reason to start the science of the physical world from a science of PHENOMENA and to move on to that of NOUMENA. An analogy always breaks down if stretched beyond its usefulness. We must guard against taking this danger, so another parable may be in order.

5 Parable 3. Micro-Chomsky and Micro-Ross in Skewland Japan

It would be instructive to try to imagine how our faculty of inner perception could counterfactually be so structured that, in the study of language, as in physics, we could take off from the science of PHENOMENA, before we move towards the science of NOUMENA, without benefit of an English-type language.

> In our imagined Skewland, Skew-Japanese speak in just the same way as their doppelgängers do in our familiar world. But their reflective consciousness is so restricted that they cannot reflect upon linguistic forms that obviate Agreement. Thus, Skew-Japanese have the ability to use such

---

[11] As explained above, topicalization exhibits island effects, *if* one limits one's attention only to the pied-piped case. If one is already familiar with the theory of movement, as we are, the significance of this fact might seem obvious, and one can even deduce it from the theory, as we did above. In the absence of the theory, however, the discovery of the fact and the understanding of its significance would be anything but trivial. For the concept about the optionality of Agreement and a comparative syntax of English and Japanese on the basis of this concept, see Kuroda (1992), in particular, Chapter 10. For a similar idea implemented with a different technical orientation, see Fukui (1995). For *imaginary* arguments and adjuncts see Kuroda (1997a); for *half*-relatives and pseudo-relatives see also Kuroda (1999a).

forms and they do use them as facilely as their doppelgängers without being aware of, and in fact without being able to become aware of, using them.

Martian scientists investigating Skew-Japanese linguistic behavior might take note of such forms in use and might try to determine the grammatical characteristics of such forms. The Martian scientists might present data pertaining to their task to Skew-Japanese and ask for grammatical judgments; they might find out to their consternation that Skew-Japanese are totally at a loss as to how to respond; unbeknownst to the Martians, the faculty of inner perception is so limited that Skew-Japanese cannot reflect upon the presented data. But precisely because of this limited faculty of inner perception, Skew-Japanese scientists would have the advantage over their doppelgängers on our planet for initiating a science of grammar; had Micro-Chomsky been born in this Skewland, he, and Micro-Ross following him, could have gotten generative grammar to take off in the same way as Chomsky and Ross did in Boston on our planet, because Micro-Chomsky and Micro-Ross don't see and are therefore not disturbed by, Skew-Japanese sentences involving any extra mechanisms that obviate Agreement and allow them to bypass licensing by Agreement.

6 The Moral of Parable 3

In reality, English exists, and luckily Chomsky was born in the United States. Generative syntax was able to take off from Boston and we are in a position to survey Japanese syntax from the impressive height it has attained. But note that it is not the structure of our faculty of perception, as in the case of physics, but a serendipitous state of affairs with English that favored the discovery of the syntax of PHENOMENA in English and enabled us to isolate corresponding PHENOMENA in Japanese. A serendipitous state of affairs, because English happens to be an obligatory Agreement language and forces REAL (i.e., non-empty) arguments/adjuncts to move for Agreement.

One could draw a moral from our parable that generative grammarians need to survey widely typologically divergent languages. But such a moral just expresses a truism; the methodological point of the parable would be lost. What we need to realize is that the student of grammar must be lucky in ways the physicist does not have to be. Linguistic reality reveals itself in different guises in different languages thanks to the variability of language.[12] Besides, this luck is indeed dependent on fortuitous contingent facts manifested in existing languages like English that let aspects of the reality, NOUMENA, seep through to our inner perception.

But we are concerned with rationality as well as grammar as an object of the scientific inquiry into the mind. Unlike grammar, rationality is supposedly invariable; it can be latent but to the extent that it is actual, it is invariant under environmental variability. To put it ironically, we do not posit universal rationality in the way we have to posit universal grammar, precisely because rationality is universal. The scientific inquiry into rationality could not then count on serendipity in the way the science of grammar could. Neither, perhaps, would it have the good luck of the physicist, due to the unconstrained phenomenological faculty of inner perception.

Generative grammarians would have to face the same fate if English-type languages ceased to exist. Let us imagine such a situation, in order to appreciate the predicament that the science of rationality might have to face.

7 Parable 4. Mega-Chomsky and Mega-Ross Starting a Cognitive Revolution in Loneland Japan

Assume that Chomsky was not born in the United States and did not start generative grammar. Imagine, furthermore, that English and languages resembling English in the relevant respects had since long ceased to exist. Assume that Mega-Chomsky was born in Loneland Japan and launched a revolution in linguistics, and Mega-Ross was to follow and discover the grammatical phenomenon of movement.

What would Mega-Ross have to do under such circumstances? He would have to discover that some constructions in Japanese involve imaginary argument/adjunct positions, that is a position where only empty categories can be selected. He would discover then that those constructions display a remarkable phenomenon, known to us as abstract *wh*-movement. Only after this remarkable insight of Mega-Ross could mega-generativists start constructing a syntactic theory resembling anything near what we know today.

---

12 At least for the moment. I say "lucky for the moment" for the obvious reason that the variability of languages is rapidly diminishing.

8 The Moral of Parable 4

Even without the luck physicists had and without the luck generative grammarians have in the real world, generative grammar could perhaps have been developed by Mega-geniuses like Mega-Chomsky and Mega-Ross in Loneland Japan. They would have to have unusually penetrating insights, to be sure, and unflinching intellectual courage and commitment as well. For they would have to largely bypass most common sentences constructed with non-empty arguments and/or adjuncts and pay attention only to constructions that involve IMAGINARY constituents, which select only empty categories. Mega-Chomsky and Mega-Ross would be hard-pressed by philosophers of science to justify maintaining that they are engaged in an empirical science of real languages, rather than indulging in the idle pastime of recording curiosities.

Those who might wish to engage in the scientific study of rationality would face the difficulty that Mega-Chomsky and Mega-Ross would have had to overcome in Loneland Japan. These pioneers might (have to) circumscribe data without apparent empirical justification (without perceptually/ phenomenogically drawn plausible natural boundaries) and construct a theory to account for the chosen data by virtue of their theoretical perspicacity. They would have to come up with what might correspond to a science of PHENOMENA in the natural sciences. That would prepare a stage for a science of NOUMENA for those who follow their steps to continue their work. But the pioneers would have to achieve this feat without the same benefit that the faculty of perception afforded to natural scientists by shielding them from NOUMENA. The limited structure of perception provided natural scientists with a safe passage towards the science of PHENOMENA by following the canons of the empirical method. Indiscriminate phenomenological intuition might not afford the same benefit to those who inquire into the mind.

Part 3: Summary and Conclusion

I first suggested the possibility of a science of rationality and expressed hope for a unification of the sciences of grammar and of rationality, a hope for a clear determination of the legacy of contemporary generative grammar as part of secure knowledge of the mind in a unified science. I next argued that we humans might intuit ourselves too well, which might impede the orderly progress of empirical inquiry by the faculty of theoretical reason to get to know our inner life. In the sciences of mind, we might not be so lucky as in the science of nature. The physicist could take off from the science of PHENOMENA and proceed to that of NOUMENA, thanks to the limited faculty of perception that shielded us from the reality of the physical world. Generative grammar seems to have managed to get around this hurdle, thanks to the variability of language. But rationality is presumably determined uniquely, and is invariant among humans. The science of rationality would not be able to benefit from the fortuitous collaboration of physical nature and human nature, as natural science did, nor could it take advantage of environmental variability.

Soon after Kant, classical physics outgrew the science of PHENOMENA with the development of thermodynamics and electromagnetism. The data base of physics was enlarged beyond the confines of (visual) perception and its straightforward instrumental extensions. Nonetheless, thermodynamics and electromagnetism are unified with classical Newtonian mechanics, mediated by the concept of energy. It is not obvious for the moment whether, or how, the science of mind, or more particularly, the science of language, can outgrow a phenomenological science, and be unified with generative grammar. Nor is it likely that a science of rationality that is to be unified with generative grammar can emerge as a science transcending phenomenological foundations.

A science of rationality is for now destined to be built within phenomenological confines, as generative grammar is. It would then require some daring and ingenious methodological strategies. Here lies a challenge if we wish to undertake an inquiry into rationality and to try for a unification of the inquiries into grammar and rationality and yet remain faithful to the spirit of methodological naturalism.

References

Chomsky, N. 1966. *Cartesian Linguistics.* New York: Harper and Row.

Chomsky, N. 1995a. Language and Nature. *Mind* 104: 1-61.

Chomsky, N. 1995b. *The Minimalist Program.* Cambridge, MA: MIT Press.

D'Abro, A. 1951. *The Rise of the New Physics.* vol. 1. New York: Dover.

Fukui, N. 1995. *Theory of Projection in Syntax.* Stanford: CSLI Publications.

Grice, H. P. 1957. Meaning. *Philosophical Review* 66: 377-388.

Ishii, Y. 1990 Half-Relatives and Syntactic Operator Movement in Japanese. *MIT Working Papers in Linguistics* 12: 80-95.

Kikuchi, A. 1987. Comparative Deletion in Japanese. Unpublished manuscript, University of Connecticut.

Kuno, S. 1973. *The Structure of Japanese.* Cambridge, MA: MIT Press.

Kuroda, S.- Y. 1986. A Formal Theory of Speech Acts. *Linguistics and Philosophy* 9: 495-524.

Kuroda, S.- Y. 1988. Whether We Agree or not: A Comparative Syntax of English and Japanese, *Linguisticae Investigationes* 12: 1-47.

Kuroda, S.- Y. 1989. An Explanatory Theory of Communicative Intentions. *Linguistics and Philosophy* 12: 655-681.

Kuroda, S.- Y. 1992. *Japanese Syntax and Semantics: Collected Papers*. Dordrecht: Kluwer.

Kuroda, S.- Y. 1997a. Nihongo shubu-naizai kankeisetsu. Handout. Taiwanese American Citizens League.

Kuroda, S.- Y. 1997b. A Second Look at Marty, Husserl and Chomsky: The Significance of the Revolution in Linguistics. *Tohoku Daigaku Bungakubu Kenkyu Nenpo* 47, 1-37. Sendai, Japan: Faculty of Arts and Letters, Tohoku University.

Kuroda, S.- Y. 1999a. Shubu-naizai kankei-setsu. *Kotoba no Kaku to Shuen*, eds. S.- Y. Kuroda and M. Nakamura, 27-103. Tokyo: Kurosio.

Kuroda, S.- Y. 1999b. Bunpo-riron to tetsugakuteki shizenshugi. Appendix to N. Chomsky, *Gengo to Shiko* (*Language and thought*), translated by Masayuki Oshi. Tokyo: Shohakusha.

Kuroda, S.- Y. to appear. Focusing on the Matter of Topic: A Study of *wa* and *ga* in Japanese.

McCawley, J. D. 1976. Relativization. *Syntax and Semantics Volume 5: Japanese Generative Grammar,* ed. M. Shibatani, 295-303. New York: Academic Press.

Matsushita, D. 1928 *Kaisen Hyojun Nihongo Bunpo.* Tokyo: Chubunkan.

Murasugi, K. 1997 Hanbun o shuyobu ni motsu hukugo meishiku: sono kozo to bunpo-tokuseu. *Kinjogakuin Daigaku Ronshu (Eibungaku Hen)* 38: 279-298.

Saito, M. 1985. Some Asymmetries in Japanese and Their Theoretical Implications. Doctoral dissertation, MIT.

Saito, M. 2001. A Derivational Approach to the Interpretation of Scrambling. Unpublished manuscript, Nanzan University, Nagoya.

Sugimoto, D. and H. Takashi. 1975. Uchu chikyu kagaku. Tokyo: Tokyo Daigaku Shuppankai.

Swerdlow, N. M. 1998. Galileo's Discoveries with the Telescope and Their Evidence for the Copernican Theory. *Galileo*, ed. Peter Machamer, 244-270. Cambridge: Cambridge University Press.

Ueyama, A. 1998. Two Types of Dependency. Doctoral dissertation, University of Southern California.

10

Explanation in Cognitive Linguistics and Cognitive Grammar

RONALD W. LANGACKER

1 Introduction

I will address the topic of this volume from the standpoint of COGNITIVE LINGUISTICS (Langacker 1999c) and, in particular, the theory of COGNITIVE GRAMMAR (Langacker 1987a, 1990, 1991, 1999b). The latter, it might be noted, is one of the older theories currently being pursued. Its formulation was initiated a quarter century ago (when many of its central ideas were far more radical than they seem today), and its basic organization (first outlined in print in Langacker 1982) has remained intact for over two decades. Cognitive grammar has, moreover, been successfully applied to a wide range of languages and linguistic phenomena (e.g. Achard 1998; Casad 1982; Cook 1988; Dabrowska 1997; Doiz-Bienzobas 1995; Israel 1998; Kumashiro 2000; Langacker 1999a; Lindner 1982; Maldonado 1999; Manney 2000; Nomura 2000; Rubba 1993; Smith 1987; Taylor 1996; Tuggy 1988; van Hoek 1995, 1997; Vandeloise 1991).

A question that is commonly asked about both cognitive linguistics and cognitive grammar pertains to the label 'cognitive'. Why, it is asked, do they merit that label, when other theoretical approaches are also concerned with the nature and status of language as a mental entity? The tone of righteous indignation that sometimes accompanies this question is, I think, misplaced. (After all, nobody interpreted the term RELATIONAL GRAMMAR as implying that no other framework was concerned with grammatical relations. Nor was the term PRINCIPLES AND PARAMETERS taken as indicating that no other theory could formulate principles.) The question, though,

The Nature of Explanation in Linguistic Theory.
John Moore and Maria Polinsky (eds.).

is legitimate. The simplest and most widely accepted answer is that, insofar as possible, language is seen in these approaches as drawing on other, more basic systems and abilities (e.g. perception, attention, categorization) from which it cannot be dissociated. To the extent that this is validated empirically, leading in a principled way to well-supported linguistic analyses, it affords an inherent explanation for many properties of language structure. These properties are characteristic of linguistic organization because they are features of cognition, and language is an integral facet of cognition.

Obviously, in the space available I cannot begin to offer even a minimally adequate description of cognitive grammar, or outline the case for its empirical validation. What I propose to do instead is focus on just two basic descriptive constructs adopted in the framework, as illustrations of a primary working strategy I employ with some consistency (Langacker 1993). By its very nature, this methodology incorporates the kind of explanation just indicated.

2 Cognitive Grammar

The central and most distinctive claim of the framework is that grammar is *symbolic* in nature. A SYMBOLIC STRUCTURE is defined as the pairing between a form (i.e. a phonological structure) and a meaning (a conceptualization, in the broadest sense). It is claimed that lexicon, morphology, and syntax make up a continuum consisting solely of *assemblies* of such structures (i.e. symbolic structures linked by relationships of correspondence and categorization). Consequently, all elements validly posited in grammatical description have some kind of meaning (often quite schematic).

Here I can only state these claims as relevant background, without providing the detailed explanation and justification they require. I would however call attention to the intrinsic desirability of the vision they represent. If it proves workable—and I believe this has already been demonstrated—this view of language ought to be eagerly embraced by linguistic theorists because its organization directly reflects the SEMIOLOGICAL FUNCTION of language, that of allowing conceptual structures to be symbolized by sound structures. To fulfill this function, language must at least comprise semantic structures, phonological structures, and symbolic links between the two. Cognitive grammar claims that *only* these elements are necessary. It thus achieves a striking *conceptual unification* as well the *reduction* of linguistic structures to the minimal basic elements (sound, meaning, symbolization).

The reduction of grammar to assemblies of symbolic structures ought to be especially welcome. Symbolic structures reside in correspondences between the two basic content domains of language, conceptualization and sounds. There is no independently existing content domain of grammar. It seems to me quite natural, then, that grammar should itself be symbolic, residing in the reinforced commonality observable in sets of complex expressions at a certain level of abstraction. Grammatical 'rules' (or constructions) are simply schematized patterns immanent in the successive combination of symbolic structures into complex assemblies. I should add that grammar does exist—the conventional patterns of a language have to be specifically learned by children and explicitly described by linguists. The reduction of grammar to configurations of symbolic structures does not imply its non-existence, any more than the non-existence of water is implied by its characterization as a configuration of hydrogen and oxygen atoms.

Cognitive grammar is also highly *restrictive*. Whatever may be its reputation, it is in fact both down-to-earth and highly constrained in what it postulates. It is a *usage-based* model, in which all linguistic structures are seen as straightforwardly reflecting the primary data of actual language use (Langacker 2000). Its restrictiveness stems from the *content requirement*, which specifies that the only elements ascribable to a linguistic system are: (i) semantic, phonological, and symbolic structures that are (part of) overtly occurring expressions (hence directly apprehended); (ii) abstractions (schematizations) of permitted structures; and (iii) categorizing relationships between permitted structures (e.g. the relationship between a schema and a specific structure that instantiates it). Thus the content requirement limits the linguistic elements one can posit to structures that occur as part of the primary linguistic data, or that derive from such structures via the fundamental cognitive processes of abstraction (schematization) and categorization.

A symbolic account of grammar presupposes an appropriate, independently justified CONCEPTUALIST SEMANTICS. A fundamental notion is that an expression's meaning is not simply the array of conceptual *content* it evokes: equally important is how that content is *construed* for linguistic purposes. Construal can be characterized as our ability to conceive and portray the same situation in alternate ways. Every lexical and grammatical element, and every linguistic expression, embodies—as an inherent aspect of its meaning—a particular way of construing the conceptual content evoked (either its own content or that supplied by the structures it combines with).

By way of brief illustration, one dimension of construal is the level of SPECIFICITY (or conversely, SCHEMATICITY) at which a situation is characterized. The expressions in (1), for instance, might all be used to describe the same entity, depending on the degree of granularity (precision and detail) the speaker deems appropriate.

(1) thing ∅ creature ∅ animal ∅ dog ∅ poodle

Various dimensions of construal pertain to the *perspective* taken on a scene. One such factor is exemplified by the following contrast:

(2) a. This road winds through the mountains.
b. This road is winding through the mountains.

Sentence (2a) presupposes a *global* perspective on the scene, of the sort available from an airplane or when viewing a roadmap. By contrast, (2b) reflects the kind of *local* perspective one has when actually traveling along the road. (For detailed analysis, see Langacker 1987b.)

An essential aspect of construal is the degree of PROMINENCE accorded to the various components of a conceptualization. Numerous sorts of prominence need to be recognized and clearly distinguished from one another. Here I will only consider two, which prove to be especially significant for grammar. These factors–PROFILING and TRAJECTOR/LANDMARK ALIGNMENT will be used to illustrate the working strategy for adopting descriptive constructs in cognitive grammar. This strategy consists of seeking CONVERGING EVIDENCE from three sources: (i) a particular construct is shown necessary for the adequate semantic description of multiple phenomena in various languages; (ii) this construct is related to an independently observable cognitive ability; and (iii) this same construct proves critical for the explicit characterization of varied grammatical phenomena.

3 Profiling

Within the array of conceptual content it evokes (its conceptual *base*), there is invariably some substructure that an expression is construed as designating, or referring to (in a conceptual sense). This substructure is called its PROFILE. For instance, as sketched in Figure 1, the word *hypotenuse* evokes as its base the conception of a right triangle, within which it profiles (designates) the side opposite the right angle. Similarly, *aunt* evokes a network of kinship relationships and profiles a particular relative of the reference individual (ego). Observe that profiling is indicated diagrammatically by means of heavy lines.

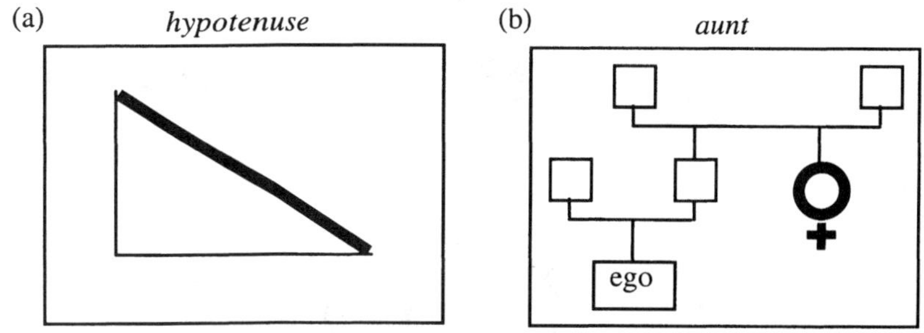

Figure 1

Expressions that evoke the same content may contrast semantically by virtue of their choice of profile within this base. Some examples are given in Figure 2. The terms *husband* and *wife* each presuppose as their base the conception of a particular kind of institutional relationship (abbreviated as a line) between a male (M) and a female (F). The primary difference between them does not reside in this largely shared content, but rather in which element is singled out for profiling (conceptual reference). The same holds for the semantic distinction between the verb *admire* and the derived noun *admirer*. Both evoke as their base the conception of a particular relationship between two things (given as circles), wherein the first bears a positive mental attitude (represented by a dashed arrow) toward the other. The verb profiles this relationship itself in its extension through time. By contrast, the noun designates only the individual who holds the mental attitude. Since their content is essentially the same, the difference in meaning between *admire* and *admirer* has to be ascribed to the alternate profiling they impose on this content.

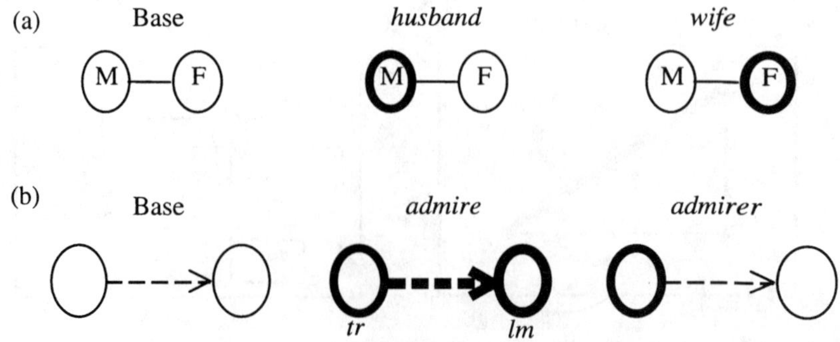

Figure 2

I see no way to adequately describe conceptual meanings without the construct of profiling, or something equivalent to it. This is especially clear in cases where, since the content is for all intents and purposes the same, the semantic contrast can only reside in the choice of profile. This is also the basis for METONYMY, e.g. the use of *church* to designate either a building where religious services are held (I take this to be the primary sense) or else a religious organization:

(3) a. That church needs a new steeple.
b. Despite its radical doctrine, their new church is growing quite rapidly.

Metonymy can be characterized as a shift in profile: an expression that normally profiles one entity is used instead to profile some other entity within the same conceptual base. For *church*, this base comprises the conception of both a building used for religious services and the type or organization that meets in such a building, as shown in Figure 3.

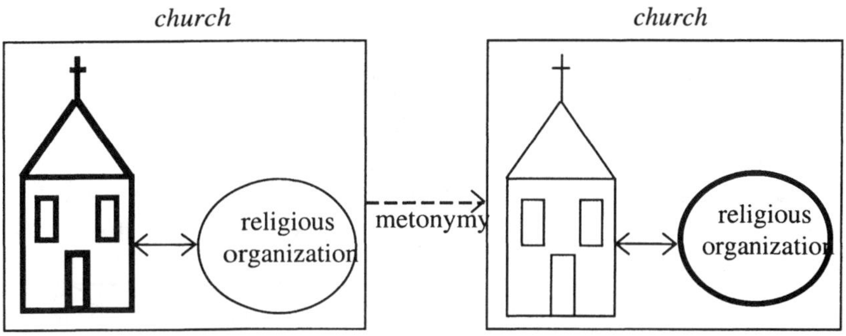

Figure 3

The foregoing discussion argues the need to adopt the construct of profiling just for purposes of formulating revealing semantic descriptions. This consideration is one of three types of converging evidence in the working strategy followed in cognitive grammar, the others being psychologically plausibility and grammatical utility. How does the notion profile fare with these other two?

With respect to psychological plausibility, I try to show that a construct is related to an independently observable cognitive ability. It should be evident that profiling is a FOCUSING OF ATTENTION within a conceived situation. In non-linguistic cognition, it has both perceptual and more abstract mental analogs: looking at one particular person in a group; focusing on a particular lineman making a block (amidst the welter of activity constituting one play in a football game); or—in the case of linguists—thinking of one particular node in a syntactic tree structure. The focusing of attention is such a basic phenomenon that it is hard to imagine it not having a basic linguistic manifestation. There may of course be many kinds and levels of attention, but here the important point is that profiling is reasonably considered one of them.

Thus, just for purposes of semantic description—independently of grammar—one could justify the construct profile and see it as the linguistic application of a broader, more fundamental cognitive phenomenon. Grammar is another source of evidence, the third factor in the working strategy. It turns out that, once expressions are properly described in purely semantic terms, profiling is just what is needed for the characterization of various grammatical notions. Here are some grammatical applications: (i) an expression's GRAMMATICAL CLASS is determined by the nature of its profile; (ii) the imposition of a particular profile constitutes the essential meaning of certain GRAMMATICAL MARKERS; (iii) in a grammatical construction, the HEAD is the component structure whose profile is inherited by the composite structure; and (iv) a SUBORDINATE CLAUSE is one whose profile is overridden at a higher level of grammatical organization. Obviously, space does not allow me to argue in detail for these applications. The following is merely intended to give some indication of what is meant.

The first point is the most controversial (see especially Langacker 1987a, 1987b). From cases like *admire* vs. *admirer* (Figure 2(b)), it is evident that an expression's grammatical class is not determined by its overall conceptual content, but rather by the nature of its profile. Expressions can profile either *things* or *relationships* (both abstractly defined). A noun profiles a thing. A verb profiles a *process*, defined as a relationship whose evolution through time is rendered salient. Classes like adjectives, prepositions, and participles profile different sorts of *non-processual* relations. Thus *admire* is a verb because it designates a process, and *admirer* a noun because it profiles a thing. Though based on the verb *admire*, the present participle *admiring* is non-processual because it profiles an arbitrary internal portion of the verbal process, and construes it holistically (i.e. its temporal evolution is backgrounded).

The elements traditionally considered *grammatical* (as opposed to *lexical*) are quite schematic in terms of their conceptual content. Hence their primary semantic import resides in the construal they impose on the content supplied by lexical items. Often this construal is a matter of profiling. Consider the derivational suffix *-er*. Like most lexical and grammatical elements, *-er* is polysemous (Ryder 1994). In its prototypical sense, *-er* evokes a schematic process as its base, and profiles a thing characterized by its active role in that process. In the *V+er* construction, the base process is identified with the one designated by the verb stem. The composite expression inherits the specific conceptual content of the stem, together with the profile imposed by *-er*. The imposition of its profile constitutes the semantic contribution of the suffix. (This is typical of derivational morphology.)

The example also illustrates the conceptual definition of a HEAD as the element which (at a given level of organization) contributes its profile to the composite expression (cf. Williams 1981; Zwicky 1985; Hudson 1987). Thus *-er*, itself a schematic noun (because it profiles a thing), is the head within the *V+er* construction.

Providing further illustration of these points is the past participial morpheme, as in *broken*. In one of its senses, it profiles the resultant state of a change-of-state process, e.g. *break*, as shown in Figure 4. The circle in Figure (4a) stands for a thing undergoing a change of state, and the horizontal line inside it indicates the extent to which the incipient state is manifested. The bar along the time arrow represents the salience of the relation's temporal evolution: through time, the change runs its course until the new state is fully implemented.

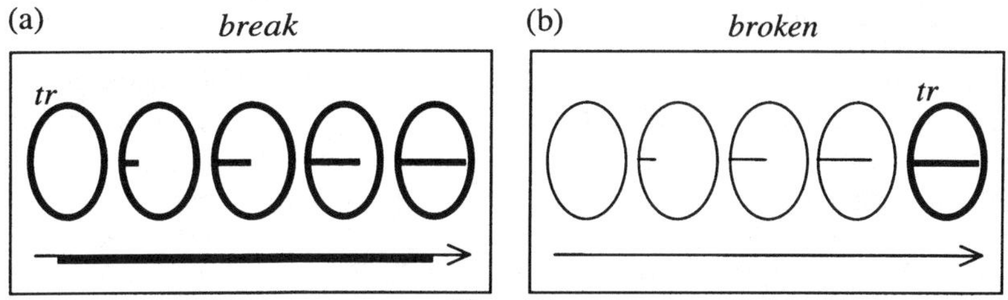

Figure 4

The process profiled by *break* constitutes the conceptual base for *broken*. As shown in Figure 4(b), *broken* profiles only the resultant state, namely the relationship of a thing exhibiting a certain property. The imposition of this profiling constitutes the meaning of the participial morpheme. This morpheme is the head within the construction, for it imposes its profile on the composite expression. In fact, the overall expression (*broken*) is categorized as a kind of adjective, defined as profiling a non-processual relationship whose single focal participant is a thing.

Finally, profiling allows one to characterize the notion SUBORDINATE CLAUSE. This can be defined in various ways, depending on the range of phenomena one wishes to subsume by the term (Langacker 1991: 10.1). For sake of illustration, let us simply assume that the bracketed clauses in (4) are all to be included:

(4) a. I admire anyone [who can pole-vault 16 feet].
b. She tried [to lift the box].
c. [After they finished] they went home.

In a complex sentence, the main clause can be characterized as the one whose processual profile functions as such for the sentence as a whole, and a subordinate clause as one whose profile is overridden at higher levels. The bracketed clauses in (4) are thus subordinate, granted that the complex sentences—taken as wholes—respectively profile the process of admiring, of trying, and of going home. Internally, the subordinate clauses designate the acts of pole-vaulting, lifting, and finishing, but these profiles are overridden at higher levels of grammatical organization.

In sum, converging evidence from three sources—semantics, cognition, and grammar—strongly supports the adoption of profiling as a basic descriptive construct.

4 Trajector and Landmark

Our second illustration of this working strategy, trajector/landmark organization, is another dimension of prominence. Let us start once more with semantic evidence. The need for this additional construct is apparent from the existence of numerous pairs of contrasting expressions which differ semantically despite evoking the same conceptual content and profiling the same relationship. Here are a few such pairs: *before* and *after*; *above* and *below*; *in front of* and *in back of*; *precede* and *follow*; *lead* and *trail*; *like* and *please*. I would also suggest that an active and a passive are comparably distinguished, e.g. *admire* and *be admired by*.

Consider *before* and *after*, in the basic sense exemplified in (5):

(5) a. He washed the car before he waxed it.
  b. He waxed the car after washed it.

Both expressions profile a relationship of temporal precedence between two events. Moreover, as seen in Figure 5, they both profile the same relationship: referentially, a *before* relation is also an *after* relation. Clearly, though, *before* and *after* are not synonymous, despite invoking the same conceptual content and profiling the same relationship. Something else is needed to distinguish them.

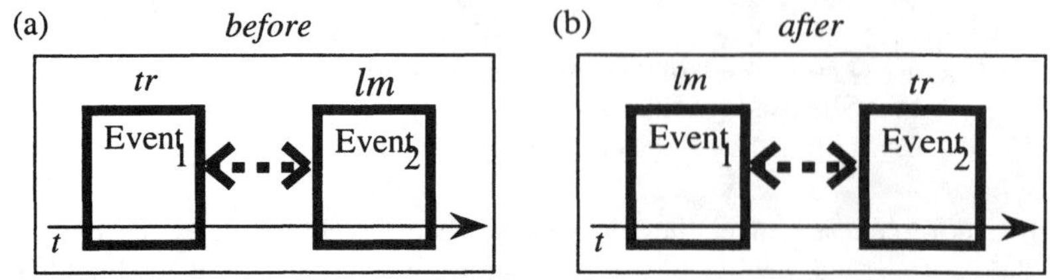

Figure 5

The only plausible option is to ascribe the semantic contrast to the status of the relational participants. In *X before Y*, it seems evident that *X* is the entity being located, with *Y* invoked as a landmark for this purpose. In *Y after X*, the opposite is true. Comparable remarks hold for all such pairs. It is on this basis—purely semantic—that trajector/landmark alignment is initially proposed. It is required for viable semantic descriptions, to properly distinguish pairs of relational expressions which would otherwise be identical.

I claim, then, that when a relationship is profiled, its participants are made prominent to varying degrees. The most prominent participant, called the TRAJECTOR (*tr*), is construed as the entity being located, evaluated, or described. It is the PRIMARY FOCUS (or FIGURE) within the profiled relationship. Often another participant is made prominent as a SECONDARY FOCUS. This is called a LANDMARK (*lm*). Expressions can have the same content, and profile the same relationship, but differ in meaning because they make different choices of trajector and landmark. This is shown in Figure 5. By analogy, trajector/landmark alignment can also be ascribed to relational expressions without a lexical converse (an example is *admire* in Figure (2b)). If there is only one focused participant, by definition it is the trajector (e.g. *break* and *broken* in Figure 4).

Another such pair, *above* and *below*, is sketched in Figure 6. The profiled relationship holds between two things, which occupy different positions along the vertical axis (and comparable locations in the horizontal plane). Once again, the conceptual content evoked may well be the same, nor is there any distinction in their profiles: an *above* relation, differently construed, is also a *below* relation. The semantic contrast is a matter of prominence, of which participant the expression makes its primary focus (trajector). In either case, it invokes the other participant as a landmark to specify the trajector's location.

(a) *above* (b) *below*

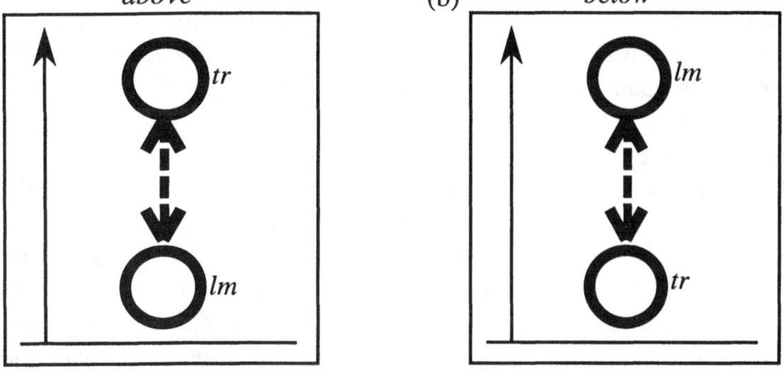

Figure 6

Data like the following supports this characterization:

(6) a. Where is the lamp?
(i) The lamp **(tr)** is above the table **(lm)**.
(ii) *The table **(tr)** is below the lamp **(lm)**.
b. Where is the table?
(i) The table **(tr)** is below the lamp **(lm).**
(ii) *The lamp **(tr)** is above the table **(lm)**.

In (6a), the question makes it evident that the object of concern is the lamp, so the answer is expected to put the lamp in focus as trajector. Answer (i) is thus felicitous, for it observes this alignment, whereas answer (ii) is problematic because it reverses it. Naturally, the situation is reversed in (6b), where the table is asked about.

Adopting the constructs trajector and landmark gives us an explicit way to characterize various instances of what are called RELATIONAL OPPOSITES (or CONVERSES) in semantics. What does it actually mean to say, for instance, that *above* and *below* are relational opposites? That is only a term, and terms are not self-explanatory at the analytical level. Once it is recognized that trajector/landmark organization is a basic feature of relational expressions in general, involving degrees of focal prominence, we have succeeded in characterizing the phenomenon rather than simply labeling it. Moreover, these constructs allow us to recognize certain distinctions that might otherwise go unnoticed. Not all pairs of relational opposites are explicated in terms of alternate choices of trajector. Compare *husband* and *wife* in Figure (2a). Here the contrast resides in the choice of profile.

Let us turn now from semantic to psychological considerations, the second potential source of converging evidence. Are there non-linguistic manifestations of this ability to variably impose focal prominence in conceptualizing a relationship? I suggest that the relative prominence accorded to relational participants is very much akin to the FIGURE/GROUND ORGANIZATION observed in gestalt psychology, with alternate choices of figure being analogous to FIGURE/GROUND REVERSAL.

But can we speak of two degrees of figure status, a 'primary figure' and a 'secondary figure', corresponding to the constructs trajector and landmark? I believe so. We certainly do have the ability—independently of language—to focus selectively on one participant in an interaction. If I watch a boxing match, for example, I can focus primarily on one boxer: to observe his techniques, which hand he favors, his footwork, even the number of blows he absorbs (this is analogous to a passive construal). Moreover, as I do so the other boxer naturally becomes a kind of secondary focus: I am following $boxer_1$ mostly in relation to his interaction with $boxer_2$, being concerned in only in a peripheral way with his corner, the referee, or the audience. Thus, while there may be some question about the precise psychological characterization of trajector/landmark organization and how it relates to other kinds of attention (like profiling), we have good reason to think that the kind of cognitive ability being appealed to does in fact exist.

I therefore posit trajector/landmark alignment for purposes of viable semantic description, and would argue for its psychological validity. What about its grammatical import, the third source of converging evidence? It seems quite obvious to me—and elsewhere I have argued at great length (e.g., 1990, 1991, 1998a, 1998b, 1999c)—that this independently established semantic/conceptual factor is precisely what is needed to characterize the grammatical notions SUBJECT and OBJECT. The SUBJECT, at a given level of grammatical organization, is a nominal element which specifies the trajector of the relationship profiled at that level. An OBJECT is a nominal element which specifies the landmark at a given level.

5 Constructions and Grammatical Relations

To be more precise about this characterization, we need to look at grammatical constructions. A CONSTRUCTION is a symbolic assembly in which a set of COMPONENT symbolic structures and a COMPOSITE symbolic structure are linked by CORRESPONDENCES. Viewed compositionally (but see Langacker 1999d), one obtains the composite structure by superimposing corresponding elements of the component structures and merging their specifications (i.e. by 'unification', if you will). This is done in accordance with conventionally established grammatical patterns. Such patterns are represented by CONSTRUCTIONAL SCHEMAS, i.e. *schematic* symbolic assemblies that serve as templates governing the formation of novel expressions. A particular expression is simultaneously categorized by numerous constructional schemas pertaining to different facets of its structure, its well-formedness being a matter of how well it conforms to them (Langacker 2000). From its outset, therefore, cognitive grammar has exemplified what are now referred to as 'unification' and 'constraint based' approaches.

For illustrative purposes, an obviously oversimplified example is presented in Figure 7. There are two levels of composition, representing two constructions: at the lower level, the component structures *admires* and *Bill* are integrated to form the composite structure *admires Bill*; this in turn functions as one component at the higher level, combining with *Alice* in a higher-order construction to form the composite structure *Alice admires Bill*. A symbolic assembly is therefore capable of exhibiting a kind of CONSTITUENCY, which emerges when the composite structure at one level of organization functions in turn as component structure at a higher level. Constituency, however, is neither fundamental nor essential in this framework (Langacker 1997). Nor are 'trees' like Figure 7 analogous to syntactic phrase trees as traditionally conceived in generative grammar. In particular, each 'node' in Figure 7 is a symbolic structure, with both conceptual and phonological content, whereas generative phrase trees, per se, are thought of as purely 'syntactic' objects with no intrinsic semantic or phonological content. In my view, constituency is merely the manifestation, in the realm of symbolic assemblies, of the very general tendency for simpler behaviors to be successively combined into progressively more complex ones. The constituency observed in grammar is seen as being flexible, variable, and often partial if not indeterminate.

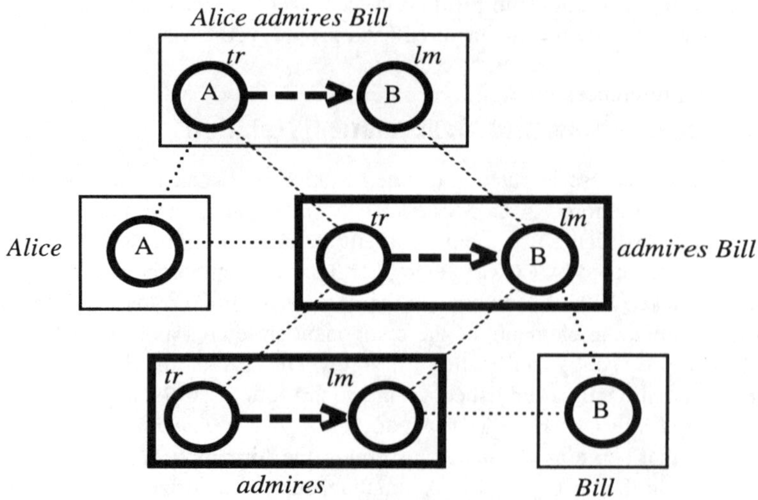

Figure 7

The real grammatical work is done by correspondences, represented in Figure 7 by dotted lines. Correspondences indicate which elements of the component structures are conceptually identified, hence superimposed in forming the composite structure. In *Alice admires Bill*, the schematic landmark of *admires* is put in correspondence with the profile of *Bill* (whose semantic specifications are abbreviated as B). Likewise, the schematic trajector of the *admires Bill* is put in correspondence with the profile of *Alice* (whose semantic specifications are given as A). Within each construction, the box enclosing one component structure is drawn with heavy lines. This identifies the PROFILE DETERMINANT, i.e. the component structure whose profile is the same as the composite structure profile. This is what it means to be the HEAD at a given level of organization.

Grammatical relationships reside in conceptual and phonological correspondences. A SUBJECT can now be defined, more precisely, as nominal structure (i.e. one designating a thing) whose profile corresponds to the trajector of a profiled relationship. Likewise, an OBJECT is a nominal structure whose profile corresponds to the landmark of a profiled relationship. By observing both 'horizontal' and 'vertical' correspondence lines, we see that *Alice* is the subject with respect to *admires*, *admires Bill*, and *Alice admires Bill*. In the same way, *Bill* qualifies as the object at all three levels. It can also be noted that constituency plays no role in these characterizations. Provided that the same composite structure obtains, and the same correspondences, there is no difference in grammatical relations with the alternate constituencies *(Alice (admires Bill))*, *((Alice admires) Bill)*, or even *((Alice) (admires) (Bill))*. I believe in fact that all three occur.

In the references cited, a long series of considerations are offered supporting the characterization of subject and object in terms of focal prominence, and further exploring the precise nature of that prominence. Here I will simply observe that linguistic scholars representing widely divergent theoretical perspectives have found good reason to describe subject (and secondarily object) in terms of notions like 'focus', 'centrality', 'prominence', and 'starting point'. These intuitive descriptions reflect the special proclivity of subjects (and secondarily objects) to be pivotal in grammatical constructions, to function as the antecedents of pronouns, to be interpreted as having wide scope in quantification, and so on. The high level of grammatical activity of subjects (and secondarily objects), often cast in the form of 'prominence' or 'accessibility hierarchies', is on my account *symptomatic* of their conceptual characterization. This in turn is part and parcel of a general view of conceptual meaning in which construal, including various kinds and degrees of prominence, holds as much linguistic importance as conceptual content.

It is important to be clear about the nature of the claim. It is *not* being claimed that the most salient entity in a scene—if that salience can be determined independently—is automatically chosen as the subject. Rather, I maintain that primary and secondary focal prominence constitute the conceptual import of trajector and landmark status, the ascription of this status to certain participants being one facet of the meaning of relational expressions. By using an expression with a particular trajector/landmark alignment, we *impose* this organization on a scene, regardless of whether the entities thus singled out for focal prominence would have it independently of linguistic encoding. In (6), for example, there is no inherent reason why the table would be more salient than the lamp, or conversely. Either can be singled out linguistically for focal prominence, depending on the discourse context and speaker intent.

What about supposedly meaningless subjects, like 'dummy' *it* and *there*? I deny that these are meaningless—it is just that their meanings are schematic and abstract. Briefly sketched, the argument hinges on a conceptual distinction in the construal of nominal elements, which can designate either SETTINGS vs. PARTICIPANTS. Though often covert, this conceptual contrast is strongly supported on independent grounds and has extensive grammatical ramifications. Transitivity, for instance, depends on the subject and object nominals being construed as participants (Langacker 1987c; Rice 1987). For this reason a SETTING-SUBJECT CONSTRUCTION like (7a) is non-transitive, as indicated by its inability to passivize:

(7) a. The next few decades will witness many startling technological developments.
b. *Many startling technological developments will be witnessed by the next few decades.

Elements like *it* and *there* are analyzed as designating settings that are abstract and characterized quite schematically. Despite an apparent object, sentences containing them are non-transitive:

(8) a. It is raining big drops.
b. *Big drops are being rained (by it).

The settings they profile are not specifically spatial or temporal, but more abstract, pertaining to the discourse realm and the presentational function of the sentences they appear in. They designate mental spaces, establishing presentational frames where a situation will subsequently be introduced. In view of this discourse function, it is natural that the abstract setting should be chosen as subject. This dovetails with other evidence suggesting that the focal prominence of a trajector consists in its serving as initial point of access to a profiled relationship.

Be that as it may, it is useful to think of trajector and landmark metaphorically as primary and secondary SPOTLIGHTS of focal prominence, which can be directed at various elements of a scene. The choice of which elements to illuminate is often motivated by reasons of inherent salience, but even in those instances the speaker must still opt to confer focal prominence on an intrinsically salient entity as one facet of construing the situation for linguistic purposes. Given the symbolic resources a language provides, the speaker usually has lexical or grammatical options for putting the primary focus on alternate participants in the same interaction.

Let me note just in passing that some independent experimental work (Tomlin 1995, 1997; Forrest 1996) lends support to this way of looking at subjects. These experiments were designed to focus attention on one participant in a relationship, to see what effect this would have on the grammatical organization of an utterance describing it. The working hypothesis was that, at the time of utterance formulation, the speaker codes the referent currently in focal attention as the syntactic subject of the utterance. A key design feature was a minimal time lag between focusing of attention and prompting for the utterance, an interval too brief for attention to wander in between. Under this condition, the experimental results strongly corroborated the hypothesis.

The proposed characterization of subjects pertains to construal (primary focal prominence) and is thus independent of any specific conceptual content. Its schematicity makes it applicable to the full range of subjects: both active and passive subjects, both settings and participants, etc. This is not to deny, of course, that certain semantic roles are prototypical for subjects (likewise objects). Nor does it imply that anything whatever is permitted. Through its inventory of constructional schemas, each language specifies a conventionally sanctioned array of clause types, thus defining the permissible range of semantic roles for subjects.

6 Further Illustration

Let me finish by briefly examining a variety of related expressions. Their analysis may help clarify how the constructs discussed—profile/base and trajector/landmark—allow us to state explicitly just what the expressions have in common and how they differ. At issue are the boldface portions of the sentences in (9). Diagrammatic representations of their essential conceptual import are respectively given in Figure 8.

(9) a. The fire will **melt** it.
b. It will **be melted** by the fire.
c. It should **melt** easily.
d. It may **melt** in the heat.
e. It is finally **melted.**
f. It is now **liquid**.

As a transitive verb, in (9a) and Figure (8a), *melt* profiles a force-dynamic interaction (Talmy 1988) between two participants. The double arrow indicates that the trajector directs some kind of force or influence at the landmark. As a consequence, the landmark undergoes a change of state (single arrow) resulting in it having the property of being liquid (L). This sense of *melt* is prototypically transitive, since the trajector and landmark are both participants, linked in a causal relationship. It can therefore be passivized, producing *be melted*, sketched in diagram (b). The passive has the same content as the active, and profiles the same process. Their semantic contrast, due to the meaning of the past participial morpheme (Langacker 1982), is a matter of focal prominence: trajector status is conferred on the patient, the agent being defocused (cf. Shibatani 1985). A passive sentence thus has a subject, specified by means of the general subject construction, but does not have an object.

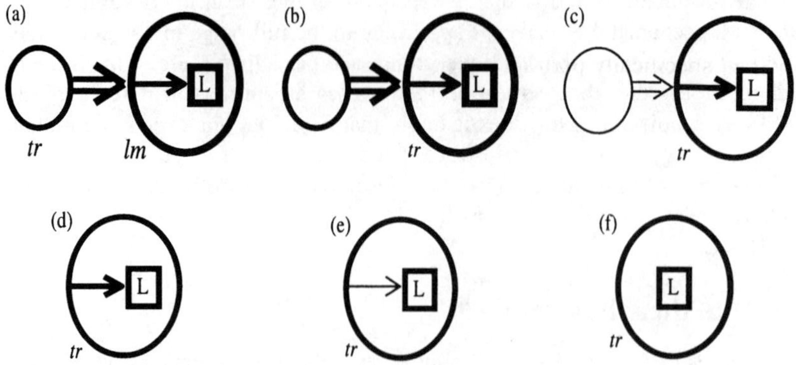

Figure 8

Examples (9c-d) represent different construals of the intransitive version of *melt*. It contrasts with the transitive *melt* by profiling only the patient undergoing its change of state and becoming liquid. Hence there is only one focal participant, namely the patient, which is thus the trajector by default. The exertions of an agent (or some other type of causation) may still be invoked as part of the conceptual base, but they remain unprofiled, their salience and nature being determined by other elements. In (9c), the adverb *easily* makes tacit reference to an agent who experiences the patient's lack of resistance. On the other hand, (9d) suggests the absence of an agent and portrays the heat as a kind of setting. Although we naturally interpret the heat as inducing the melting, the sentence does not specifically present it in a causal role.

Sentence (9e) employs the stative-adjectival participle *melted*, analogous to *broken* (Figure (4b)). As shown in Figure (8e), its conceptual base is the change-of-state process profiled by the intransitive verb. Within this base, it profiles only the resultant state, in which the trajector exhibits the property of being liquid. It is therefore a type of adjective, since—unlike a verb—it does not render salient the evolution through time of the PROFILED relationship. (This static relationship, in which the trajector exhibits the property of liquidity, is however given temporal extension by *be* at a higher level of grammatical organization. As opposed to *melted*, the composite expression *be melted* counts as a verb and functions in (9e) as the clausal head.)

Finally, let us compare the participle *melted* with the adjective *liquid* in (9f). The properties they ascribe to the trajector are essentially the same. Instead their difference in meaning resides in an unprofiled facet of the base: *melted* specifically portrays the liquid state as resulting from the process of melting, whereas *liquid* is neutral in this regard. Something can only be described as *melted* by virtue of having undergone the process coded by *melt*. If something is *liquid*, however, it may always have been in this state, which may also result from the liquifaction of a gas.

In summary, the similarities and differences among these expressions are straightforwardly captured by the descriptive constructs adopted. The transitive *melt* and the passive *be melted* have the same content and profiling, but differ in their choice of trajector. The transitive and intransitive *melt* may have the same content but differ in their choice of profile. Alternate construals of the intransitive *melt* vary in regard to unprofiled facets of their base. However it is construed, the intransitive variant resembles the passive by putting the patient in focus as trajector, but contrasts with the passive in that it only profiles the change of state. The stative-adjectival participle *melted* has the same content as the intransitive *melt*, but profiles only the resultant state, not the process leading to it. Finally, the participle *melted* and the adjective *liquid* profile the same state but differ in that only the former includes the change-of-state process in its base.

7 Conclusion

It has not of course been possible to present a full justification of the many constructs and analyses alluded to. I hope to have indicated, however, that they have been arrived at in a principled manner in the context of a coherent overall descriptive framework. Moreover, a limited set of constructs have proved adequate and revelatory for describing a wide and representative array of structures in diverse languages. Achieving a high degree of descriptive adequacy, assessed in terms of such factors, constitutes one level of explanation in linguistics. Certainly it has been a primary level in cognitive grammar. Everything posited in the framework has been strongly motivated on internal linguistic grounds, as being necessary for an optimal characterization of linguistic structure.

Of course, other levels of explanation can and should be sought. One in particular is consistently aspired to in cognitive grammar: That the description of language structure rely exclusively on mental phenomena which on independent grounds are known to exist or at least to be highly plausible. In the strategy of converging evidence, this corresponds to the requirement that a descriptive construct be related to an independently observable cognitive ability. It is at this level that cognitive linguistics is said to provide an inherent explanation for many properties of language structure—they are characteristic of language because they are features of cognition, of which language is an integral facet.

A further level of explanation resides in the experimental confirmation of predictions derivable from linguistic descriptions. I resist the common attitude (apparently based just on the word 'cognitive') that a cognitive linguistic description cannot be taken seriously unless experimental evidence is provided for it. A burden of this kind would be impractical and unreasonable. No such obligation is imposed on any other linguistic theory, nor should it be imposed on cognitive grammar just because the constructs employed are natural rather than arbitrary. As for any other framework, considerations of descriptive adequacy ought to be sufficient in themselves as a basis for initial assessment.

I nonetheless consider it important that cognitive grammar be evaluated with respect to other, external sources of evidence—not just experimental, but also clinical, acquisitional, and practical (e.g. its application to language pedagogy). While not entirely lacking (see, for instance, Kellogg 1993; Tomasello 1992; Pütz, Niemeier and Dirven 2001), efforts along these lines have thus far been quite limited. I hope and expect that they will be much more numerous in the future, providing the framework with additional sources of empirical justification.

References

Achard, M. 1998. Representation of Cognitive Structures: Syntax and Semantics of French Sentential Complements. *Cognitive Linguistics Research* 11. Berlin and New York: Mouton de Gruyter.

Casad, E. H. 1982. Cora Locationals and Structured Imagery. Doctoral dissertation, University of California, San Diego.

Cook, K. W. 1988. A Cognitive Analysis of Grammatical Relations, Case, and Transitivity in Samoan. Doctoral dissertation, University of California, San Diego.

Dabrowska, E. 1997. *Cognitive Semantics and the Polish Dative*. Berlin and New York: Mouton de Gruyter.

Doiz-Bienzobas, A. 1995. The Preterite and the Imperfect in Spanish: Past Situation vs. Past Viewpoint. Doctoral dissertation, University of California, San Diego.

Forrest, L. B. 1996. Discourse Goals and Attentional Processes in Sentence Production: The Dynamic Construal of Events. *Conceptual Structure, Discourse and Language*, ed. A. E. Goldberg, 149-161. Stanford: CSLI Publications.

Hudson, R. A. 1987. Zwicky on Heads. *Journal of Linguistics* 23: 109-132.

Israel, M. 1998. The Rhetoric of Grammar: Scalar Reasoning and Polarity Sensitivity. Doctoral dissertation, University of California, San Diego.

Kellogg, M. K. 1993. When a 'Cat' is a 'Cow' and 'Hearing' is 'Understanding'; Paraphasia and the Conceptualization of Nouns and Verbs. Papers from the Regional Meeting of the Chicago Linguistic Society 29.2: 201-215.

Kumashiro, T. 2000. The Conceptual Basis of Grammar: A Cognitive Approach to Japanese Clause Structure. Doctoral dissertation, University of California, San Diego.

Langacker, R. W. 1982. Space Grammar, Analysability, and the English Passive. *Language* 58: 22-80.

Langacker, R. W. 1987a. *Foundations of Cognitive Grammar*, vol. 1, *Theoretical Prerequisites*. Stanford: Stanford University Press.

Langacker, R. W. 1987b. Nouns and Verbs. *Language* 63: 53-94.

Langacker, R. W. 1987c. Grammatical Ramifications of the Setting/Participant Distinction. Proceedings of the Annual Meeting of the Berkeley Linguistics Society 13: 383-394.

Langacker, R. W. 1990. *Concept, Image, and Symbol: The Cognitive Basis of Grammar*. Berlin and New York: Mouton de Gruyter.

Langacker, R. W. 1991. *Foundations of Cognitive Grammar*, vol. 2, *Descriptive Application*. Stanford: Stanford University Press.

Langacker, R. W. 1993. Grammatical Traces of some 'Invisible' Semantic Constructs. *Language Sciences* 15: 323-355.

Langacker, R. W. 1995. Raising and Transparency. *Language* 71: 1-62.

Langacker, R. W. 1997. Constituency, Dependency, and Conceptual Grouping. *Cognitive Linguistics* 8: 1-32.

Langacker, R. W. 1998a. Conceptualization, Symbolization, and Grammar. *The New Psychology of Language: Cognitive and Functional Approaches to Language Structure*, ed. M. Tomasello, 1-39. Mahwah, NJ and London: Erlbaum.

Langacker, R. W. 1998b. Topic, Subject, and Possessor. *Linguistic Notes from La Jolla* 19: 1-28.

Langacker, R. W. 1999a. Double-Subject Constructions. *Linguistics in the Morning Calm* 4, ed. S.-Y. Bak, 83-104. Seoul: Hanshin.

Langacker, R. W. 1999b. *Grammar and Conceptualization*. Berlin and New York: Mouton de Gruyter.

Langacker, R. W. 1999c. Assessing the Cognitive Linguistic Enterprise. *Cognitive Linguistics: Foundations, Scope, and Methodology*, eds. T. Janssen and G. Redeker, 13-59. Berlin and New York: Mouton de Gruyter.

Langacker, R. W. 1999d. Correspondences, Compositionality, and Grammar. *Actas del XXI Congreso Internacional de A.E.D.E.A.N. (Asociación Española de Estudios Anglo-Norteamericanos)*, eds. F. T. Iglesia et. al., 55-74. Seville: Secretariado de Publicaciones de la Universidad de Sevilla.

Langacker, R. W. 2000. A Dynamic Usage-Based Model. *Usage Based Models of Language*, eds. M. Barlow and S. Kemmer, 1-63. Stanford: CSLI Publications.

Lindner, S. 1982. What Goes Up Doesn't Necessarily Come Down: The Ins and Outs of Opposites. Papers from the Regional Meeting of the Chicago Linguistic Society 18: 305-323.

Maldonado, R. 1999. *A media voz: Problemas conceptuales del clítico se*. Mexico City: Universidad Nacional Autónoma de México.

Manney, L. J. 2000. *Middle Voice in Modern Greek: Meaning and Function of an Inflectional Category*. Amsterdam and Philadelphia: John Benjamins.

Nomura, M. 2000. The Internally-Headed Relative Clause Construction in Japanese: A Cognitive Grammar Approach. Doctoral dissertation, University of California, San Diego.

Pütz, M., S. Niemeier, and R. Dirven. eds. 2001. *Applied Cognitive Linguistics II: Language Pedagogy*. Berlin and New York: Mouton de Gruyter

Rice, S. 1987. Towards a Cognitive Model of Transitivity. Doctoral dissertation, University of California, San Diego.

Rubba, J. E. 1993. Discontinuous Morphology in Modern Aramaic. Doctoral dissertation, University of California, San Diego.

Ryder, M. E. 1994. Ordered Chaos: The Interpretation of English Noun-Noun Compounds. *University of California Publications in Linguistics* 123. Berkeley: University of California Press.

Shibatani, M. 1985. Passives and Related Constructions: A Prototype Analysis. *Language* 61: 821-848.

Smith, M. B. 1987. The Semantics of Dative and Accusative in German: An Investigation in Cognitive Grammar. Doctoral dissertation, University of California, San Diego.

Talmy, L. 1988. Force Dynamics in Language and Cognition. *Cognitive Science* 12: 49-100.

Taylor, J. R. 1996. *Possessives in English: An Exploration in Cognitive Grammar*. Oxford: Oxford University Press/Clarendon.

Tomasello, M. 1992. *First Verbs: A Case Study of Early Grammatical Development*. Cambridge: Cambridge University Press.

Tomlin, R. S. 1995. Focal Attention, Voice, and Word Order. *Word Order in Discourse*, eds. P. Downing and M. Noonan, 517-554. Amsterdam and Philadelphia: John Benjamins.

Tomlin, R. S. 1997. Mapping Conceptual Representations into Linguistic Representations: The Role of Attention in Grammar. *Language and Conceptualization*, eds. J. Nuyts and E. Pederson, 162-189. Cambridge: Cambridge University Press.

Tuggy, D. 1988. Náhuatl Causative/Applicatives in Cognitive Grammar. *Topics in Cognitive Linguistics*, ed. B. Rudzka-Ostyn, 587-618. Amsterdam and Philadelphia: John Benjamins.

van Hoek, K. 1995. Conceptual Reference Points: A Cognitive Grammar Account of Pronominal Anaphora Constraints. *Language* 71: 310-340.

van Hoek, K. 1997. *Anaphora and Conceptual Structure.* Chicago and London: University of Chicago Press.

Vandeloise, C. 1991. *Spatial Prepositions: A Case Study from French.* Chicago and London: University of Chicago Press.

Williams, E. 1981. On the Notions 'Lexically Related' and 'Head of a Word'. *Linguistic Inquiry* 12: 245-274.

Zwicky, A. M. 1985. Heads. *Journal of Linguistics* 21: 1-29.

11

Meaning, Function, and the Autonomy of Syntax

FREDERICK J. NEWMEYER

1 Introduction

The purpose of this paper is to take on difficult and controversial question of whether syntax is 'autonomous'. To be specific, it will provide a definition of syntactic autonomy, discuss what the autonomy hypothesis implies about the relation between syntax on the one hand and meaning and discourse on the other, and evaluate the kinds of evidence that might be relevant to establishing or refuting the hypothesis. The paper will conclude that the autonomy of syntax is indeed a correct hypothesis and will stress that it is in no way incompatible with the hypothesis that much of syntax might be motivated functionally.

The paper is organized as follows. The remainder of this section characterizes the autonomy hypothesis. Section 2 provides empirical support for the hypothesis, while 3 rebuts published arguments against it. Section 4 argues that the hypothesis is compatible with the idea that syntactic structures might owe their properties to external functional factors and 5 is a brief conclusion.[1]

Let us begin with a working definition of the autonomy of syntax:

[1] Some of the material in this paper originally appeared in Newmeyer (1998) and is reprinted with the permission of MIT Press.

The Nature of Explanation in Linguistic Theory.
John Moore and Maria Polinsky (eds.).

(1) The Autonomy of Syntax

> A central component of the grammar of a language is a formal system characterizing the set of syntactically well-formed sentences in that language. This system makes no reference to the meaning or discourse function of the sentences generated.

In other words, the distribution of syntactic elements is governed by distinct principles of combination that make no reference to the semantic or pragmatic properties of those elements. Hypothesis (1), henceforth 'AUTOSYN', has been characteristic of most approaches to syntax that fall under the heading 'generative', though this hypothesis has been weakened in various ways in various approaches (for discussion, see Newmeyer 1998: 2.3).

2 In Defense of AUTOSYN

Section 2.1 discusses the factors that bear on the correctness of the autonomy hypothesis. The two following sections provide motivation for two key components of the hypothesis: 2.2 for the idea that purely formal generalizations are central to syntactic patterning and 2.3 for the idea that these generalizations interlock systematically.

2.1 What Bears on the Correctness of AUTOSYN?

What sorts of facts bear on the question of whether syntax is autonomous? One extreme position is held by many formalists, who appear to believe that a sufficient demonstration of autonomy is to point to some mismatch between form and meaning or form and function. But if that were all that were necessary, then almost every linguist would be a partisan of autonomous syntax. Most agree that such mismatches are widespread. Hudson, Rosta, Holmes, and Gisborne (1996) catalogue a number of them from English, a few of which are illustrated below: *Likely* occurs in a 'raising' structure, while *probable* does not (2a-b); *allow* occurs with an infinitive marker, while *let* does not (3a-b); *enough*, unlike *sufficiently* and other degree modifiers, does not occur prenominally (4a-b):

(2) a. He is likely to be late.
    b. *He is probable to be late.
(3) a. He allowed the rope to go slack.
    b. *He let the rope to go slack.

(4) a. He isn't sufficiently tall.
 b. *He isn't enough tall. / He isn't tall enough.

Clearly, then, arguing for AUTOSYN must involve more than showing that mismatches exist.

Some functionalists (e. g., Payne 1998) have taken the opposite extreme position, namely, that AUTOSYN can be refuted simply by showing that form is in a systematic relationship with meaning and function. But all generative theories posit such a systematic relationship. There would be no autonomous syntacticians at all if, in order to qualify as one, one had to reject rules linking form and meaning.

What is involved, then, in establishing the correctness of AUTOSYN? In my view, it is necessary to establish the correctness of the following two hypotheses:

(5) a. There exists an extensive set of purely formal generalizations orthogonal to generalizations governing meaning or discourse.
 b. These generalizations 'interlock' in a system.

In other words, a full defense of AUTOSYN involves not merely pointing to extensive formal generalizations, but showing that these generalizations interact in a manner graphically illustrated in (6) (where 'FG' stands for 'formal generalization'):

(6)

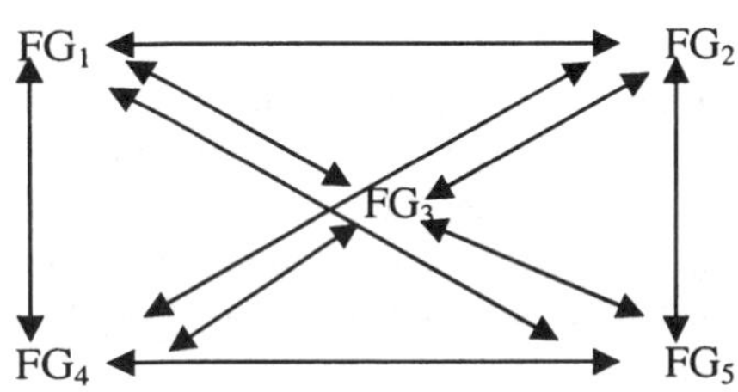

2.2 Purely Formal Generalizations

In the realm of morphology, nobody questions the idea that there exist purely formal generalizations that cannot be linked in one-to-one fashion to meaning or function. Consider, for example, processes such as Tagalog reduplication and German umlaut. Each has a multitude of semantic effects:

(7) a. Tagalog reduplication: gerunds, plural comparative adjectives, occupational nouns, aspect, causative adjectives, moderative verbs, intensive verbs, ...

b. German umlaut: some plurals, some abstract nouns, diminutives, some derived feminine nouns, agentive and instrumental nouns, some derived adjectives, ...

Few linguists would question the idea that the grammars of Tagalog and German contain 'autonomous' statements characterizing the purely formal processes of reduplication and umlaut respectively.

However, when it comes to syntax there is a curious resistance among many linguists to stating processes in purely formal terms, that is, independently of their particular semantic or discourse effects. Nevertheless, there is considerable evidence that it is correct to do so. Consider, for example, structures with displaced and fronted *wh*-phrases:

Wh-constructions in English:

(8) *Questions:*
Who did you see?

(9) *Relative Clauses:*
The woman who I saw

(10) *Free Relatives:*
I'll buy what(ever) you are selling.

(11) *Wh (Pseudo) Clefts:*
What John lost was his keys.

We have here a profound mismatch between syntactic form and the semantic and discourse properties associated with that form. In each construction type, the displaced *wh*-phrase occupies the same structural position, namely, the left margin of the phrase immediately dominating the rest of the sentence (in Principles-and-Parameters terminology, the 'Specifier of CP'):

(12)

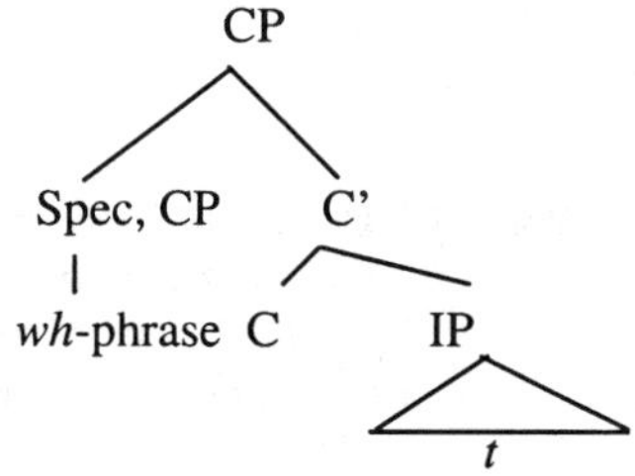

Despite their structural parallelism, the *wh*-phrases in the four constructions differ from each other in both semantic and discourse function. As far as their semantics is concerned, one frequently reads that it is the (semantic) function of a fronted *wh*-phrase to set up an operator-variable configuration or to act as a scope marker. But only in the least complex cases, is such the case. Consider simple *wh*-questions, for example. In (13) *what* does indeed behave as a semantic operator and as a scope marker:

(13) What did Mary eat? = for what *x*, Mary ate *x*

But the full range of *wh*-constructions gives no support to the idea that the semantic role of the attracting feature *in general* is to set up operator-variable relations. So in (14), for example, with an appositive relative clause, there is no operator-variable configuration corresponding to trace and antecedent:

(14) Ralph Nader, who several million Americans voted for, lost the election.

By way of confirmation, as pointed out by Lasnik and Stowell (1991), there is no weak crossover effect with appositive relatives:

(15) a. Gerald$_i$, who$_i$ his$_i$ mother loves t$_i$, is a nice guy.
b. This book$_i$, which$_i$ its$_i$ author wrote t$_i$ last week, is a hit.

Nor does the fronted *wh* element reliably act as a scope marker. Consider partial *Wh*-Movement in German and Romani (McDaniel 1989):

(16) Was$_i$ glaubt [$_{IP}$ Hans [$_{CP}$mit wem]$_i$ [$_{IP}$ Jakob jetzt t$_i$
what think Hans with who Jacob now
spricht]]]?
speak
'With whom does Hans believe Jacob is now talking?'

(17) So$_i$ [[$_{IP}$ o Demìri mislinol [$_{CP}$ [kas]$_i$ [$_{IP}$ I Arìfa dikhl'a t$_i$]]
what that Demir think who the Arif saw
'Whom does Demir think Arifa saw?'

The same point can be made in cases of multiple *wh* phrases, where one is left in situ:

(18) Who remembers where we bought which book? (Baker 1970)

There are two interpretations, in neither of which the *wh*-phrase in SPEC of CP acts as a scope marker:

(19) Two interpretations of (18) (Chomsky 1973: 283):
  a. For which *x*, *x* remembers for which *z*, for which *y*, we bought *y* at *z*
  b. For which *x*, for which *y*, *x* remembers for which *z* we bought *y* at *z*

Indeed, Denham (2000) argues persuasively that *Wh*-Movement and scope marking are completely dissociated in UG.

Furthermore, fronted *wh*-phrases in different constructions play very different roles in terms of information structure. In simple *wh*-questions, the sentence-initial *wh*-phrase serves to focus the request for a piece of new information, where the entire clause is presupposed except for a single element (Givón 1990). Fronting in relative clauses, however, has nothing to do with focusing. Haiman (1985) suggests that the iconic principle, 'Ideas that are closely connected tend to be placed together', is responsible for the adjacency of the relative pronoun to the head noun. In free relatives, the fronted *wh*-phrase actually fulfills the semantic functions of the missing head noun. Semantically, the fronted *wh*-phrase in pseudo-clefts is different still. As Prince (1978) argues, the clause in which the *wh*-phrase is fronted represents information that the speaker can assume that the hearer is thinking about. But the function of the *wh*-phrase itself is not to elicit new information (as is the case with such phrases in questions), but rather to prepare the hearer for the focused (new) information in sentence-final position. In short, we have an easily characterizable structure manifesting a profound mismatch with meaning and function.[2]

Let us turn to another example. Consider the structure in which an adjective occurs with an infinitival complement:

(20) NP – COP – [$_{AP}$ A – *to* – V]

[2] An anonymous referee suggests that the four *wh*-constructions of (8-11) do in fact share some semantic /pragmatic similarities. In each case, the referee suggests, there is some element *X*, denoted by the extracted *wh*-phrase, and which is defined by the rest of the clause *Y* (as 'the *X* of which *Y* is true'). While not incorrect, such a characterization does not distinguish *wh*-constructions from a multitude of other constructions, including those with fronted topic and focus phrases and even garden-variety active declarative sentences, in which a subject is followed by a predicate.

There are six logically possible ways that the NP subject can relate (in terms of understood grammatical relations) to the A and the V. All six occur:

		Rel^n to A	Rel^n to V
(21) a.	Mary is eager to please	subject	subject
b.	Mary is easy to please	none	object
c.	Mary is liable to dance	none	subject
d.	Guns are cheap to buy	subject	object
e.	It is useless to try	none	none
f.	It is (too) dark to see	subject	none

One concludes from this and many similar examples that the multiple uses to which any syntactic expression can be put argue for the independent characterization of formal patterning.

It is easy to find examples of the converse situation as well, that is, where a particular semantic or discourse-based construct maps onto a multitude of syntactic structures. Consider first the telic/atelic distinction, as discussed in Jackendoff (1997). The formal embodiment of this distinction can be signaled by the choice of verb (22a), the choice of preposition (22b), the choice of adverbial (22c), and the choice of determiner in the subject (22d), the object (22e), or the prepositional object (22f):

(22) a.	John destroyed the cart (in/*for an hour)	(telic)
	John pushed the cart (for/*in an hour)	(atelic)
b.	John ran to the station (in/*for an hour)	(telic)
	John ran toward the station (for/*in an hour)	(atelic)
c.	The light flashed once (in/*for an hour)	(telic)
	The light flashed constantly (for/*in an hour)	(atelic)
d.	Four people died (in/*for two days)	(telic)
	People died (for/*in two days)	(atelic)
e.	John ate lots of peanuts (in/*for an hour)	(telic)
	John ate peanuts (for/*in an hour)	(atelic)
f.	John crashed into three walls (in/*for an hour)	(telic)
	John crashed into walls (for/*in an hour)	(atelic)

Since all of these formal devices can be used to express other semantic distinctions having nothing to do with aspect, we are justified in factoring out generalizations about meaning from those about form.

2.3 Interlocking Formal Generalizations

This section will present supporting evidence for (5b), namely the idea that purely formal generalizations interlock in a *system*. Let us return to *wh*-constructions. As we have seen, they exhibit a one-many relation between form and meaning. However, this fact in and of itself is not a knock-down argument in support of AUTOSYN. An advocate of this principle would posit a simple set of formal principles and link their output to a variety of semantic functions. An opponent could presumably posit the same relationship in reverse. But what does support AUTOSYN is that the formal principles involved in *wh*-fronting interact with *other* formal principles involved in other types of constructions. That is, not only do *wh*-constructions have an internal formal consistency, but they behave consistently within the broader structural system of English syntax. For example, in all four cases, the *wh* phrase can be indefinitely far from gap:

(23) a. Who$_i$ did you ask Mary to tell John to see ___$_i$?
b. The woman who$_i$ I asked Mary to tell John to see ___$_i$
c. I'll buy what(ever)$_i$ you ask Mary to tell John to sell ___$_i$.
d. What$_i$ John is afraid to tell Mary that he lost ___$_i$ is his keys.

And as (24) shows, each *wh*-construction is subject to principle of Subjacency, informally stated as in (25):

(24) a. *Who$_i$ did you believe the claim that John saw ___$_i$?
b. *The woman who$_i$ I believed the claim that John saw ___$_i$
c. *I'll buy what(ever)$_i$ Mary believes the claim that John is willing to sell ___$_i$.
d. *What$_i$ John believes the claim that Mary lost ___$_i$ is his keys.

(25) Subjacency
Prohibit any relationship between a displaced element and its gap if 'the wrong kind' of element intervenes between the two.

But Subjacency, as it turns out, constrains movement operations that involve no (overt) *wh*-element at all. For example, Subjacency accounts for the ungrammaticality of (26):

(26) *Mary is taller than I believe the claim that Susan is.

In other words, the formal principles fronting *wh*–phrases interlock with the formal principle of Subjacency. One might try to subvert this argument by claiming that Subjacency is a purely *functional* principle, rather than an interlocking grammatical one. In fact, there is no doubt that the ultimate roots of Subjacency are a functional response to the pressure for efficient parsing (see Berwick and Weinberg (1984), Newmeyer (1991), Kirby (1998)). But over time, this parsing principle has become grammaticalized. Hence, there are any number of cases in which sentences that violate it are ungrammatical, even in the absence of parsing difficulty. Sentence (27a), a Subjacency violation, is ungrammatical, even though it is transparently easy to process. Minimally different (27b) does not violate Subjacency and is fully grammatical:

(27) a. *What did you eat beans and?
b. What did you eat beans with?

In other words, the *wh*-constructions of (8-11) are integrated into the structural system of English, of which Subjacency forms an integral part.

We find analogous instances of interlocking formal principles with the adjective - complement structure illustrated in (20). For example, all manifestations of this structure allow subject-aux inversion, regardless of their meaning:

(28) a. Is Mary is eager to please?
b. Is Mary is easy to please?
c. Is Mary is liable to please?
d. Are guns are cheap to buy?
e. Is it is useless to try?
f. Is it (too) dark to see?

They even all allow VP preposing:

(29) a. Eager to please though Mary is ...
b. Easy to please though Mary is ...
c. Liable to dance though Mary is ...
d. Cheap to buy though guns are ...
e. Useless to try though it is ...
f. (Too) dark to see though it is ...

Again, such interlocking formal generalizations point to the correctness of AUTOSYN.

3 Attempts to Refute AUTOSYN

Let us turn now to some recent published attempts to refute AUTOSYN. I will argue that such attempts fail because too little attention is paid to the full set of relevant data.

We will begin with two arguments presented in Lakoff and Johnson (1999) (L&J). L&J point out that deictic locatives and rhetorical questions like (30a-b) respectively have traditionally been assumed to occur only in main clauses. They show, however, that they occur in subordinate clauses introduced by *because* (31a-b), though not in those introduced by *if* (32a-b):

(30) a. Here comes the bus! (Deictic Locative)
b. Who on earth can stop Jordan? (Rhetorical Questions)

(31) a. I'm leaving because here comes my bus.
b. The Bulls are going to win because who on earth can stop Jordan?

(32) a. *I'm leaving if here comes my bus.
b. *The Bulls are going to win if who on earth can stop Jordan?

L&J's generalization is that those supposedly 'main-clause' constructions that can occur in subordinate clauses are the ones that convey statement speech acts. Since *because*-clauses express a reason and the statement speech act *is* the reason, deictic locatives and rhetorical questions can occur in such clauses. L&J's conclusion is that a pragmatic generalization unites (30a-b) with (31a-b) and so therefore syntax cannot be autonomous.

L&J's analysis, however, is too limited and construction-specific. The relevant generalization is not one pertaining to grammatical structure, but rather about what constitutes a coherent/cohesive discourse. Notice that (33a) is as good as (31a) (and for the same reason), while (33b) is as bad as (32a) (and for the same reason):

(33) a. I'm leaving. Do you know why? Here comes my bus.
b. #I'm leaving if the following condition is met. Here comes my bus.

In other words, we're not dealing with a *grammatical* generalization at all. English grammar does not distinguish between *because* and *if* clauses with respect to the issues that concern us here. A (presumably universal) condition on cohesive discourse is at work here that accounts for why (31a-b) sound fine, while (32a-b) seem bizarre.

L&J's second example involves the Coordinate Structure Constraint (CSC), formulated in Ross (1967): 4.2 as in (34):

(34) Coordinate Structure Constraint: In a coordinate structure, no conjunct may be moved, nor may any element contained in a conjunct be moved out of that conjunct.

Ross illustrated the second clause of the CSC with examples like (35a-b):

(35) a. *What did John eat hamburgers and Bill drink ___?
b. *What did John eat ___ and Bill drank milk?

But there are many counterexamples to the second clause of the CSC:

(36) a. What did John go to the store and buy ___? (Ross 1967)
b. How much can you drink ___ and still stay sober? (Goldsmith 1985)
c. What did he go to the store, buy ___, load ___ in his car, drive home, and unload ___? (Lakoff 1986)

L&J put forward a construction-specific solution to account for the well-formedness of (36a-c). All-or-nothing movement can be violated if there exists a 'natural sequences of events' or (in the two conjunct cases) where the first conjunct enables or causes the second. Since the CSC appears to have a discourse-based condition, L&J conclude that it violates AUTOSYN.

In these cases, however, there are straightforward syntactic explanations for the examples presented by Lakoff. Sentence (35a) is ungrammatical because it violates the principle of Relativized Minimality (Rizzi 1991). The *wh*-phase object of *drink* has a closer possible landing site than SPEC, CP of the leftmost clause, namely the SPEC,CP of its own clause. Note that if it had moved to the closer position, the sentence would have been grammatical:

(37) Did John eat hamburgers and what did Bill drink?

The ungrammaticality of sentence (35b), on the other hand, has nothing to do with movement at all. The following sentence is just as bad:

(38) *Did John eat hamburgers and Bill drank milk?

Questions like *Bill drank milk?* are ungrammatical in English, save as expressions of astonishment. And one would hardly conjoin a simple information question with an expression of astonishment.

On the other hand, the grammatical sentences (36a-c) violate no syntactic constraints, other than the second clause of the CSC. Clearly, the puzzle of their grammaticality is solved, if there *is no* second clause to the CSC.[3]

Quite often attempts to refute AUTOSYN fail because too little attention is paid to the interaction of syntax with principles of meaning or discourse that are needed anyway. For example, there is no need to complicate the statement of grammatical generalizations by appealing to notions like 'degree of prototypicality', 'radial categories', or 'metaphors' (as in Lakoff 1987), since, invariably, independently-motivated principles from different domains interact to yield the desired results. Take existential-*there*, for example. As argued in Newmeyer (1998), all that is required of the grammar is to specify that it is an NP and is either meaningless (the traditional generative characterization), or denotes conceptual space (Lakoff 1987) or an abstract setting (Langacker 1991). But what about the deviance of (39a-b), taken from Ross (1973)? Don't they show that it is necessary to appeal to lack of prototypicality of existential-*there* as an NP?

(39) a. *There surprised me by being heat in the furnace.
b. *There, there are three armadillos in the road.

Not at all. Sentence (39a) is bad because meaningless elements (or conceptual spaces or abstract settings) cannot intrude into one's consciousness and (39b) is bad because they cannot serve as discourse topics. In other words, there is no reason that the grammar itself needs to tag *there* as 'nonprototypical'.

Turning to deictic uses of *there*, Lakoff (1987) argues that they have to be characterized as a complex 'radial construction', linked by 'metaphors'. Why? Because there are specialized subcases of deictic-*there* that seem quite restricted in their distribution. He cites (40-41) by way of example. According to Lakoff, the 'perceptual deictic construction' needs to characterized in such a way as to exclude (41b):

(40) a. There's Harry.
b. Harry is there.
(41) a. There's the beep.
b. *The beep is there.

---

[3] None of L&J's examples bear on the first ('A-over-A') clause of the CSC, which can be subsumed under Subjacency (see §2.3).

In Lakoff's analysis, the construction-specific metaphor (42) licenses (41a), but not (41b), since (41b) is not part of the construction:

(42) NONVISUAL PERCEPTUAL SPACE IS PHYSICAL SPACE

But (41b) is odd for a non-construction-specific reason: transitory beeps in general make poor discourse topics. In fact, the sentence is fine, given a setting making *the beep* a clear topic:

(43) a. Have you figured out where inside the wall that annoying beep is coming from?
b. As far as I can tell, the beep is *there*.

Hence, there is no need for a specific perceptual deictic construction sensitive to a 'metaphor'.

A number of publications by Ronald Langacker (Langacker 1987a, b; 1991; this volume) have attempted to subvert AUTOSYN by arguing for an intimate link between formal and cognitive categories. For example, Langacker (this volume) provides notional definitions of the categories 'Noun' and 'Verb' as follows:

> ... an expression's grammatical class is not determined by its overall conceptual content, but rather by the nature of its profile. Expressions can profile either *things* or *relationships* (both abstractly defined). A noun profiles a thing. A verb profiles a *process*, defined as a relationship whose evolution through time is rendered salient. (Langacker, this volume, 244)

It is not at all clear how these notional definitions can be made to work. What insures that inherently relational words like *parent* (44a) or temporal processes like *explosion* (44b) will surface as nouns and non-temporal, non-process words like *die* (44c) will surface as verbs?:

(44) a. Al is the parent of Don.
b. The explosion went on for hours.
c. Alice died (*in/*for hours).

Langacker goes on to define 'Subject' as follows:

> Grammatical relationships reside in conceptual and phonological correspondences. A SUBJECT can now be defined, more precisely, as nominal structure (i.e. one designating a thing) whose profile corresponds to the trajector of a profiled relationship. Likewise, an OBJECT is a nominal structure whose profile corresponds to the landmark of a profiled relationship. (Langacker, this volume, 252-253)

But unless I misunderstand what Langacker means by 'trajector of a profiled relationship', this construct seems like neither a necessary nor a sufficient condition for subjecthood. It is hard to imagine how the bold-faced NPs in (45) could be 'trajectors':

(45) a. **There** are 12 people in the room (expletive-*there*)
b. **It** is likely that Tom will be late (dummy *it*)
c. **The jig** is up (idiom chunk subject)
d. Mary regrets that **somebody** left a hostile message on her machine (embedded indefinite subject)

4 Autonomy and Functional Explanation

There is a widespread belief (see, for example, Givón 1984) that once a system is characterized as autonomous, any functional explanation of that system (or its properties) is impossible. Such is not the case, as a look at other formal systems will make clear. Consider for example, a formal system par excellence — the game of chess. Chess is an 'autonomous system' in the sense that it comprises a finite number of discrete statements and rules and, given the layout of the board and the pieces and their permissible moves, it is a mechanical task to generate the set of well-formed chess matches. But nevertheless, usage-based considerations went into design of system — presumably the goal was to make it a satisfying pastime. Furthermore, usage-based considerations can change the system. A decree from the International Chess Authority, for example, could result in a change in how the procedure of 'castling' is carried out, thereby leading to a change in the set of possible matches. Extending the analogy still further, the autonomy of chess does not prevent the particular move made by a particular player at a particular time from being subject to the conscious will of that player any more than AUTOSYN prevents any act of speaking from being a product of the conscious will of that speaker. In other words, chess is both autonomous and motivated functionally.

To take a more biological analogy, consider any bodily organ, say, the liver. The liver is an autonomous structural system, in the sense that it can be characterized in terms of its component tissues and their formal properties. Nevertheless it has been shaped by its function and use; presumably the liver evolved in response to selective pressure for a more efficient role in digestion. Moreover, the liver can be affected by external factors. For example, a lifetime of heavy drinking can alter its structure.

It is not the purpose of this paper to present a detailed model of how autonomous grammar can be shaped functionally. However, a few brief remarks are in order. As is argued persuasively in the rich functionalist literature, parsing ease, pressure for an iconic relationship between form and meaning, and so on are forces that shape grammars. These forces influence adult speakers, in their use of language, to produce variant forms consistent with them. Children, in the process of acquisition, hear these variant forms and grammaticalize them. In that way, over time, certain functional influences leave their mark on grammars. The input and the output to this process is an autonomous grammar; variation takes place in the arena of language use, either in the use of one of a number of variant possibilities already allowed by the grammar or in the extragrammatical use of a structure not provided for by the grammar.

Pressure for an iconic pairing of form and meaning is an important functional factor that has shaped grammars. Therefore, models such as Cognitive Grammar (Langacker 1987a), Functional Grammar (Hengeveld 1989), and Role-and-Reference Grammar (Van Valin 1993) are correct to attach importance to such a pairing. But in general, such approaches tend to see much tighter iconic form-meaning match up than actually exists. Very often, of course, syntactic units *do* correspond directly to cognitive ones. Hence, the head noun - relative clause sequence in (46) is both formally and conceptually a unit:

(46) [A man [who was wearing a silly-looking red hat]] came to visit today.

But beside (46), we *also* have grammatical (47), where the iconic form-meaning relation is distorted, presumably by parsing pressure:

(47) [A man] came to visit today [who was wearing a silly-looking red hat].

Unfortunately, no simple formula exists to predict when one pressure will dominate another. In (46-47), iconicity and parsing respectively make their pressure manifest in grammatical sentences. But in certain cases, only iconicity 'wins out'. Adjective phrases cannot be extraposed from the nouns that they modify, no matter how heavy they are:

(48) a. An extremely peculiar-looking man dropped by today.
b. *A man dropped by today extremely peculiar-looking.

On the other hand, in certain cases parsing pressure alone appears to be the winner. When comparatives are used attributively, the adjective is separated from its complement by the head noun, despite the fact that together they serve to modify semantically that head noun (49a-b). Their structural unity can be obtained only in a manner that is consistent with parsing pressure (49c):

(49) a. That's a more boring book than any I have ever read.
b. *That's a more boring than I have ever read book.
c. That's a book more boring than any I have ever read.

Cases of competing functional motivations such as these strike at the heart of the attempt of Cognitive Grammar and related approaches to establish the close form-meaning correspondence that is so central to their view of language. Indeed, I would speculate that AUTOSYN is correct *because of* competing motivations. That is, AUTOSYN is a clever 'design solution' to the chaos inherent in the possibility that formal structure might be pushed this way and that willy-nilly by different functional motivations. It allows for a structural system that is beholden exclusively to no one motivation and thereby acts as a stabilizing factor facilitating language acquisition and use (for more discussion of this point, see Newmeyer 1998: Ch. 3).

5 Conclusion

This paper has argued that syntax is autonomous, that is, that grammar embodies a formal structural system whose principles of combination make no reference to meaning or discourse function. The autonomy of syntax is fully compatible with the external functional shaping of grammatical structure.

References

Baker, C. L. 1970. Notes on the Description of English Questions: The Role of an Abstract Question Morpheme. *Foundations of Language* 6: 197-219.

Berwick, R. C. and A. Weinberg. 1984. *The Grammatical Basis of Linguistic Performance*. Cambridge, MA: MIT Press.

Chomsky, N. 1973. Conditions on Transformations. *A Festschrift for Morris Halle*, eds. S. Anderson and P. Kiparsky, 232-286. New York: Holt Rinehart & Winston.

Denham, K. 2000. Optional *Wh*-Movement in Babine-Witsuwit'en. *Natural Language and Linguistic Theory* 18: 199-251.

Givón, Talmy. 1984. *Syntax: A Functional-Typological Introduction,* vol.1. Amsterdam: John Benjamins.

Givón, T. 1990. *Syntax: A Functional-Typological Introduction,* vol.2. Amsterdam: John Benjamins.

Goldsmith, J. 1985. A Principled Exception to the Coordinate Structure Constraint. *Chicago Linguistic Society* 21: 133-142.

Haiman, John. ed. 1985. *Iconicity in Syntax.* Typological Studies in Language, vol. 6. Amsterdam: John Benjamins.

Hengeveld, K. 1989. Layers and Operators in Functional Grammar. *Journal of Linguistics* 25: 127-158.

Hudson, R. A. et. al. 1996. Synonyms and Syntax. *Journal of Linguistics* 32: 439-446.

Jackendoff, R. 1997. *The Architecture of the Language Faculty.* Cambridge, MA: MIT Press.

Kirby, S. 1998. *Function, Selection and Innateness: The Emergence of Language Universals.* Oxford: Oxford University Press.

Lakoff, G. 1986. Frame Semantic Control of the Coordinate Structure Constraint. Papers from the Parasession on Pragmatics and Grammatical Theory, eds. A. M. Farley, P. T. Farley and K.-E. McCullough, 152-167. Chicago: Chicago Linguistic Society.

Lakoff, G. 1987. *Women, Fire, and Dangerous Things: What Categories Reveal About the Mind.* Chicago: University of Chicago Press.

Lakoff, G. and M. Johnson. 1999. *Philosophy in the Flesh: The Embodied Mind and Its Challenge to Western Thought.* New York: Basic Books.

Langacker, R. W. 1987a. Foundations of Cognitive Grammar, vol. 1. *Theoretical Prerequisites.* Stanford: Stanford University Press.

Langacker, R. W. 1987b. Nouns and Verbs. *Language* 63: 53-94.

Langacker, R. W. 1991. *Foundations of Cognitive Grammar,* vol. 2. *Descriptive Application.* Stanford: Stanford University Press.

Lasnik, H. and T. A. Stowell. 1991. Weakest Crossover. *Linguistic Inquiry* 22: 687-720.

McDaniel, D. 1989. Partial and Multiple *Wh*-Movement. *Natural Language and Linguistic Theory* 7: 565-604.

Newmeyer, F.J. 1991. Functional Explanation in Linguistics and the Origins of Language. *Language and Communication* 11: 3-28.

Newmeyer, F.J. 1998. *Language Form and Language Function.* Cambridge, MA: MIT Press.

Payne, D.L. 1998. What Counts as Explanation? A Functionalist Approach to Word Order. *Functionalism and Formalism in Linguistics*, eds. M. Darnell et. al., 135-164. Amsterdam: John Benjamins.

Prince, E. F. 1978. A Comparison of *Wh*-Clefts and *It*-Clefts in Discourse. *Language* 54: 883-906.

Rizzi, L. 1991. *Relativized Minimality*. Cambridge, MA: MIT Press.

Ross, J. R. 1967. *Constraints on Variables in Syntax*. Doctoral dissertation, MIT

Ross, J. R. 1973. A Fake NP Squish. *New Ways of Analyzing Variation in English*, eds. C.-J. N. Bailey and R. Shuy, 96-140. Washington: Georgetown University Press.

Van Valin, R. D. ed. 1993. *Advances in Role and Reference Grammar*. Amsterdam: John Benjamins.

12

Minimalism and Explanation

ROBERT D. VAN VALIN, JR.

1 Introduction

Chomsky's Minimalist Program (Chomsky 1995, 1998) portrays itself as an attempt to simplify generative syntactic theory while enhancing its explanatory potential. This paper explores some of the questions of language design raised in the Minimalist Program, especially in Chomsky (1998), from the point of view of syntactic theories which do not accord syntax a privileged status and which seek to view grammar in terms of the complex interplay of syntax, semantics and pragmatics. In other words, the perspective is non-syntactocentric, to use Jackendoff's (1997) term.

Chomsky (1998) explores the issue of the design of the language faculty and argues for a conception in which there are only two levels of representation, PF and LF, which are the interfaces with non-linguistic cognition. The derivational process which results in LF is aptly named 'narrow syntax', and it excludes many of the phenomena which have been central to syntactic theory, both principles and parameters theories and others, over the last few decades, e.g. binding. Chomsky (1995) maintains that C_{HL}, the computational procedure for human language that derives LF (and PF), is invariant across languages, and since narrow syntax is equated with C_{HL} as a mapping between the lexicon and LF (Chomsky 1998: 13), narrow syntax must also be invariant across languages. This may account for the exclusion of binding from narrow syntax: it clearly shows cross-linguistic variation and therefore cannot be part of the invariable C_{HL}.

The Nature of Explanation in Linguistic Theory.
John Moore and Maria Polinsky (eds.).

Within this framework, he addresses the existence of two alleged major 'imperfections' in language design, the existence of uninterpretable features and displacement. He argues that the two go together: displacement exists because of the necessity of movement to permit checking and hence erasure of uninterpretable features, in order to satisfy legibility conditions at the LF interface. Since narrow syntax is invariant across languages, it may reasonably be concluded that displacement and the existence of uninterpretable features are universal features of human language. If the core of human language, narrow syntax, is uniform across languages, why, one wonders, should cross-linguistic syntactic variation exist at all?

The discussion will proceed as follows. First, Chomsky's claims about the necessary cooccurence of two alleged imperfections, displacement and uninterpretable features, will be examined. Second, two central syntactic phenomena, binding and displacement, will be analyzed with respect to what is universal about them and what potentially motivates the cross-linguistic variation they exhibit. Finally, the conclusion raises the issue of possible motivations for cross-linguistic variation in syntax.

2 Issues of Language Design

The existence of uninterpretable features and displacement in human language constitute, for Chomsky, part of narrow syntax, and as such must be universal features of human language. However, it is not obvious that every language has uninterpretable features or displacement phenomena. A language which appears to lack both is Lakhota, a Siouan language. Lakhota has no voice oppositions of any kind, and question words appear *in situ*; this is exemplified in (1).

(1) Lakhota

a. witʃháʃa ki tuwá na-Ø-Ø-xų́ he?
   man the who hear-3sgA-3sgU Q
   'Who does the man hear?'

b. tuwá witʃháʃa ki na-Ø-Ø-xų́ he?
   who man the hear-3sgA-3sgU Q
   'Who hears the man?', *'Who does the man hear?'

Lakhota is a head-marking SOV language, and the affixes on the verb signal actor and undergoer. (The verb *naxʔu* 'hear' takes its affixes as infixes.) A question word like *tuwá* 'who' is interpreted in terms of its position in the clause; in (1a) it can only be interpreted as the object (undergoer), while in

(1b) it can only be interpreted as the subject (actor). Relative clauses do not involve *Wh*-Movement, as they are internally headed. Finally, there is no raising of any kind in the language. Chomsky (1998) characterizes displacement as a situation in which 'the surface phonetic relations are dissociated from the semantic ones' (35), and no such dissociation exists in Lakhota. The only instances of a discrepancy between the occurrence of an overt argument and its interpretation are control structures, which do not involve movement and therefore do not fall into the category of displacement phenomena.

This has important consequences for the relationship between syntactic functions and semantic roles and hence for the linking between syntax and semantics in the language: the syntactic functions in a clause are completely predictable from the semantic role properties of the verb, and vice versa. If a verb, e.g. *naxʔu* 'hear', takes actor and undergoer arguments, then the actor will always function as the subject and the undergoer as the direct object; there is no other possibility. The single argument of an intransitive verb will be subject, regardless of whether it is actor or undergoer. Given the morphosyntactic form of a clause, its semantic roles are completely predictable and directly derivable. There are no grammatical processes akin to passive or dative shift to affect the relationship between syntactic functions and semantic roles. This aspect of the linking between syntax and semantics in such a language is straightforward and uncomplicated. Furthermore, the interpretation of *wh*-expressions presents no difficulties, since they occur in the canonical position for their interpretation. Hence such a one-to-one correspondence between syntactic functions and semantic roles should make for maximum legibility at the interface with cognitive systems.

The second alleged imperfection is the existence of uninterpretable features in a language. Chomsky (1995, 1998) analyzes the person and number features of verb agreement (ϕ-features) in English as uninterpretable. Does this analysis hold for a language like Lakhota? English agreement morphology on verbs has no ramifications for the semantic interpretation of the sentence; is the same true in Lakhota? Consider the following examples.

(2) a. miye witʃháʃa ki na-wítʃa-wa-xʔų.
1sg man the hear-3plU-1sgA
'I hear the men.'
a′. miye witʃháʃa ki na-Ø-wa-xʔų.
1sg man the hear-3sgU-1sgA
'I hear the man.'

b. na-witʃhá-wa-xʔų.
hear-3plU-1sgA
'I hear them.'

b′. na-Ø-wá-xʔų.
hear-3sgU-1sgA
'I hear him/her.'

In (2a) the affixes on the verb look like agreement morphology, duplicating the inherent and interpretable features of the NPs, but in (2b) the situation is very different; here the affixes are crucial to the semantic interpretation of the sentence, because they are the sole overt expression of the arguments of the verb. Hence it would appear that they are in fact interpretable. In GB, the structure of (2b) would be as in (3) (from Williamson 1984).

(3) $[_{IP}$ *pro*$_i$ $[_{VP}$ *pro*$_j$ na-witʃhá$_j$-wa$_j$-xʔų]]

In such an analysis, *-witʃhá-* '3plUndergoer' and *-wa-* '1sgActor' are simply agreement and presumably carry uninterpretable features, just as in (2a), with the interpretable features being carried by the null pronominals. But such an analysis would seem to be excluded from the Minimalist Program by the Inclusiveness Condition: 'no new features are introduced by C_{HL}'(Chomsky 1998: 27). Chomsky asserts that it excludes any superfluous elements or structure and elaborates its implications as follows:

> It requires that there be no phrasal categories or bar levels, hence no X-bar theory or other theory of phrase structure...It also rules out the introduction of traces, indices, lambda operators, and other new elements in the course of operation of C_{HL}. (28)

The minimal analysis of (2b) requires a lexical array (numeration) consisting of *naxʔų́* 'hear' – *witʃha*– '3plU' and –*wa*– '1sgA', and the derivation of (2a) would simply be combining them. Adding tree branches to carry null pronominals, as well as the introduction of the null pronominals themselves, would seem, at the very least, to run counter to the spirit of this condition. Furthermore, it seems counterintuitive to claim that overt morphemes like –*witʃha*– and –*wa*– are the morphological manifestations of uninterpretable ϕ-features, while the interpretable ϕ-features are carried by phonologically null elements. After all, the basis of the hearer's interpretation is the phonological form of the sentence.

The other major candidate for an uninterpretable feature is the EPP feature of T, and it is not obvious that it is applicable to this language. If the EPP feature is construed as requiring a structural subject (i.e. an external argument), then it is not satisfied by (2b, b′). The structure in (3) would satisfy this feature, but it is problematic, as we have seen. There are no expletives in Lakhota, and weather expressions consist of a single verb which cannot have 'agreement' morphology and which cannot have any NPs accompanying it, as illustrated in (4).

(4) (*hé/iyé) magádʒu-kte
(that/it) rain-FUT
'It will rain.'

Hence it appears that T lacks the uninterpretable EPP feature in this language.

Lakhota thus appears to be a language without the imperfections of displacement and uninterpretable features, and because of this a language of this type would seem to be, in Chomsky's terms, the optimal solution to the interface legibility conditions.

It is important to recognize that it is of course possible to simply stipulate that person-number features on NPs are always interpretable and the ones on verbs are always uninterpretable and to stipulate that there is always displacement in a language, even if it involves only covert displacement or the displacement of phonologically null elements. This would, however, seem to run counter to the spirit of the Minimalist Program, and in the latter case, displacement of a phonologically null element would not in fact meet Chomsky's definition of displacement, given earlier (1998: 35). The claims in this section are based on the existence (or lack thereof) of *overt* displacement in a language and whether the agreement features on the verb do or do not contribute to the semantic interpretation of the sentence.[1]

One could reasonably argue that the lack of displacement and uninterpretable features is just what the analysis in Chomsky (1998) would predict:

[1] It is important to distinguish 'displacement' from 'movement'. As Chomsky's definitions makes clear, he is referring to a dissociation between overt phonetic elements and their semantic interpretation; hence movement of empty categories or movement after spellout would not count as displacement phenomena. H. Lasnik, in his remarks after this paper was presented, suggested that the existence of verbs like 'die', etc. in the language shows that there must be movement in the language. But such alleged 'movement' would in fact not meet Chomsky's definition of displacement, since there would be no discrepancy in the overt form of the sentence between the position of the NP (or the cross-reference morpheme on the verb) and the position of its semantic interpretation. Displacement is a theory-independent phenomenon which all theories must account for, regardless of whether they posit movement rules or not. Movement, on the other hand, is a theory-internal concept which is distinct from that of displacement.

since the motivation for displacement is the existence of uninterpretable features, if a language lacked uninterpretable features, then it should lack displacement. Lakhota seems to confirm this rather nicely. This immediately raises the question, are there any languages in which there is a dissociation between displacement and the existence of uninterpretable features? It appears that there are. Mam, a Mayan language (England 1983), is a thoroughly head-marking language like Lakhota, and the agreement morphology on the Mam verb leads to sentences exactly like those in (2b, b´), as illustrated in (5).

(5) Mam

a. Ma Ø-tzaj ky-tzyu-7n kab' xiinaq Luuch.
REC 3sg ABS-DIR 3plERG-grab-DIR two man Pedro
'Two men grabbed Pedro.'

b. Ma Ø-tzaj ky-tzyu-7n.
REC 3sgABS-DIR plERG-grab- DIR
'They grabbed him.'

Unlike Lakhota, however, Mam has an extensive variety of displacement constructions, including *Wh*-Movement (in *wh*-questions and topicalization), passivization and antipassivization. The other possibility, a language with uninterpretable features but no displacement, is exemplified by Mparntwe Arrernte (Wilkins 1989), a language of central Australia. This language has optional number agreement with the subject, as well as case features on nominals, which Chomsky argues are also uninterpretable; these are illustrated in (6).

(6) Mparntwe Arrernte

a. Artwe therre-le nwerne-nhe twe-(rlenerre-)ke.
man two-ERG 1pl- ACC hit-(DUAL-) PAST
'The two men hit us all.'

b. Nwerne-Ø re-nhe awe-(rrirre-)ke.
1pl-NOM 3sg-ACC hear-(PL-)PAST
'We all heard it.'

c. Artwe therre-Ø lhe-(rre-)me.
man two-NOM go-(DUAL-)PRES
'The two men are walking away.'

Thus we may conclude that there are uninterpretable features (ϕ-features) in Mparntwe Arrernte syntax. However, unlike English and like Lakhota, Mparntwe Arrernte lacks raising, voice oppositions, and *Wh*-Movement in questions. The only candidate for possible displacement would be externally-headed relative clauses; the language also has internally-headed and headless relative clauses as well. The situation in English, Lakhota, Mam and Mparntwe Arrernte is summarized in Table 1.

Language	Displacement	Uninterpretable Features
English	Yes	Yes
Lakhota	No	No
Mam	Yes	No(?)
Mparntwe Arrernte	No(?)	Yes

Table 1: Interaction of Displacement with the Existence of Uninterpretable Features

The '(?)' indicates that more analysis is needed to fully establish the claim, but nevertheless two conclusions can be drawn from Table 1. First, displacement and uninterpretable features are not necessary facets of language design, and therefore they are not a necessary part of what Chomsky calls the optimal solution to the legibility conditions at the interfaces. Second, both Mam and Mparntwe Arrernte strongly suggest that the two phenomena are not necessarily correlated with each other, as Chomsky claims. Furthermore, since displacement is not a universal feature of human languages, it cannot be part of narrow syntax. It thus would fall outside of I-language, along with other phenomena such as binding, into the extra-linguistic cognitive systems.

Despite the existence of languages like Lakhota and Mparntwe Arrernte, displacement phenomena, as Chomsky notes, are very common cross-linguistically, and it seems highly counterintuitive to exclude these phenomena, as well as binding phenomena, which are likewise pervasive, from the scope of syntactic theory. It would be highly desirable to account for them as principled deviations from the truly universal aspects of syntax, and in the next section we will undertake this task.

3 Binding and Displacement: The Universal and the Language-Specific

Chomsky characterizes the universal core of syntax in terms of his notion of 'narrow syntax', which refers to the syntactic derivational machinery he posits. Van Valin and LaPolla (1997) offers an alternative conception of the universal structural core of human language, formulated in terms of Role and Reference Grammar [RRG] (Van Valin 1993, 2002). They argue that what is truly universal in universal grammar is *semantically driven*, and the grammatical phenomena which show substantial cross-linguistic variation are not purely semantically driven but involve non-semantic motivating factors. From an RRG perspective, the universal part of what Chomsky terms C_{HL} contains only semantically-driven syntactic phenomena. If the core case of binding is taken to be an antecedent binding a reflexive anaphor, then reflexive binding, like displacement, is not a universal feature of human language, but they nevertheless have universally valid properties in the sense of properties found in all languages that manifest them. We will look at reflexivization first.

There are three main types of reflexive constructions: lexical reflexives, clitic reflexives, and coreference reflexives. The first two types are lexical in nature and do not involve binding, according to the RRG analysis of them in Van Valin and LaPolla (1997). Lexical reflexives are exemplified by the following sentences from Lakhota and Dyirbal (Dixon 1972).

(7) Dyirbal

a. bala yugu-Ø baŋgul yaɽa-ŋgu buyba-n
NM.ABS stick-ABS NM.ERG man-ERG hide-TNS
'The man is hiding the stick.'

a´. bayi yaɽa-Ø buyba-yiri-ɲu
NM.ABS man-ABS hide-REFL-TNS
'The man is hiding himself.'

Lakhota

b. na-ní-Ø-xʔų.
hear-2sgU-3sgA
'She heard you.'

b´. na-n-ítʃ'i-xʔų.
hear-2- REFL
'You heard yourself.'

There is no independent reflexive anaphor in either language; in both cases, a reflexive verb form is derived, and the interpretation is limited to expressing identity between two arguments of the verb, normally the actor and the undergoer. Clitic reflexive constructions such as those in Romance and Slavic languages are also lexical in nature, following the line of analysis initiated in Grimshaw (1982), in that the reflexive clitic signals the suppression of the highest ranking semantic argument in the argument structure of the verb.

True binding is found only with coreference reflexives, the kind found in e.g. English, Norwegian, Japanese and Mandarin. Slavic and Romance languages have coreference reflexives in addition to the clitic reflexives, but languages like Lakhota and Dyirbal do not. Hence reflexive binding is not found in all languages, as noted earlier. Since coreference reflexives involve two independent elements, the antecedent and the anaphor, there are two fundamental issues to be resolved with respect to them: (1) what is the hierarchical relationship between them?, and (2) what is the syntactic domain in which they both must occur? The answer to the second question must be syntactic in nature, but the answer to the first need not be. Jackendoff (1972, 1992) proposed semantic answers to the first question, and his approach has been adopted in RRG, *mutatis mutandem.* One of the universal semantic constraints on reflexivization argued for in Van Valin and LaPolla (1997) can be paraphrased as in (8).

(8) Role Hierarchy Condition on reflexivization:
The reflexive pronoun must not be higher on the following hierarchy than its antecedent: Actor > Undergoer > Other

This says simply that actor arguments always bind undergoer arguments and never the other way around. In most cases, this makes the same predictions as syntactic binding conditions like Condition A of the GB binding theory. There is an interesting set of data from Toba Batak, an Austronesian language of Indonesia (Shugamoto 1984), with reference to which the two types of account make different predictions. The basic Toba Batak facts are presented in (9).

(9) a. Mang-ida si Ria si Torus. 'Torus sees Ria.'
ACT-see PNM PNM
b. Di-ida si Torus si Ria. 'Torus sees Ria.'
UND-see
c. Mang-ida si Torus si Ria 'Ria sees Torus.'
ACT–see
d. Di-ida si Ria si Torus. 'Ria sees Torus.'
UND-see

Toba Batak is VOS with an interesting voice system. In (9a) the verb carries the prefix *mang-*, and the NPs following the verb are interpreted as undergoer-actor; hence in this example *Ria* is the undergoer, and *Torus* is the actor. When the verb carries the prefix *di-* as in (9b), the order of arguments is actor-undergoer; hence in this example *Torus* is the actor and *Ria* the undergoer, yielding the same meaning as in (9a). The two possibilities with *Ria* as the actor and *Torus* as the undergoer are given in (9c,d). The relevant examples involving reflexivization are given in (10), and phrase structure trees for these examples are given in Figure 1.

(10) a. Mang-ida diri-na si Torus.
ACT-see self-3sgPOSS
'Torus sees himself.'
Torus c-commands *dirina* - Actor binds undergoer

b. *Di-ida diri-na si Torus.
UND-see self-3sgPOSS
'Himself sees Torus.'
Torus c-commands *dirina* - *Undergoer binds actor

c. *Mang-ida si Torus diri-na.
ACT-see self-3sgPOSS
'Himself sees Torus.'
**Dirina* c-commands *Torus* - *Undergoer binds actor

d. Di-ida si Torus diri-na.
UND-see self-3sgPOSS
'Torus sees himself.'
**Dirina* c-commands *Torus* - Actor binds undergoer

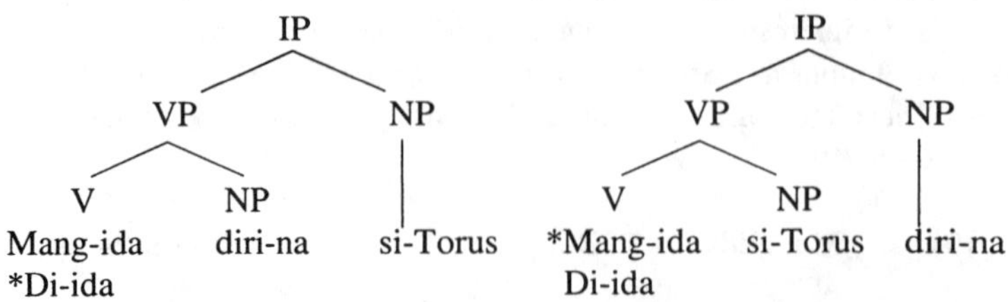

Figure 1: Phrase Structure of Toba Batak Sentences in (10)

Both approaches would predict that (10a) would be grammatical and that (10c) would be ungrammatical, since the first example satisfies both (8) and Condition A and the second one violates both of them. The two approaches diverge with respect to (10b, d) however. Condition A predicts that (10b) should be grammatical, since *Torus* c-commands the reflexive *dirina*, and that (10d) should be ungrammatical, since the reflexive *dirina* c-commands *Torus*, the antecedent.[2] The RRG analysis, on the other hand, predicts just the opposite: (10b) should be ungrammatical, because the undergoer binds the actor, and (10d) should be grammatical, since the actor binds the undergoer. The RRG predictions, not those of Condition A, are correct, and this

---

[2] See Clark (1985) for arguments that the immediate postverbal NP is in the internal argument position in Toba Batak sentences.

supports the semantic approach to reflexive binding.[3] In terms of the issue of universality, the principle in (8) would be the core principle governing reflexive binding, with the main variation cross-linguistically being whether only subjects (actors) may serve as antecedents or whether non-subjects (undergoer, other) may as well. It would predict that in every case the higher ranking argument would be the antecedent.

But the condition in (8) says nothing about where the antecedent and anaphor have to be in relation to each other: in the same core, the same clause, or the same sentence? This is not a semantic question, and there is no universally valid answer. Indeed, there are several answers, as Dalrymple (1993) shows. They range from being co-arguments within the core to being in different clauses. The restriction to co-arguments within the core is essentially semantic, and highly restricted coreference reflexives like these are very close semantically to lexical and clitic reflexives. When the domain of reflexivization extends across core and even clause boundaries, however, the constraints are no longer semantically motivated. Rather, discourse-pragmatics becomes a potential motivating factor. Coreference involves reference, and reference is ultimately a discourse notion. Hence once reflexivization involves coreference between two referring expressions, the door is open to a potential discourse function for the reflexive, and this is just what is found in languages with long-distance reflexives such as Mandarin, Korean and Japanese (see e.g. Zubin, et al. 1990). Such a discourse function for reflexivization is quite impossible for lexical and clitic reflexives. Thus, it would appear that at least part of the motivation for the cross-linguistic variation in the domain of coreference reflexives is the varying discourse function of reflexives in different languages.

The prime example of displacement phenomena, *Wh*-Movement in questions, clearly involves discourse-pragmatics, since *wh*-words are narrow foci (Lambrecht 1994). There appear to be four main patterns cross-linguistically with respect to *wh*-questions: (1) the *wh*-word remains *in situ*, as in (1) from Lakhota; (2) the *wh*-word is displaced to the unmarked focus position in the clause, as in e.g. Turkish; (3) the *wh*-word is displaced to a special clause-initial position, as in English, and (4) the *wh*-word is displaced to a special clause-final position, as in a number of south Asian lan-

3 There are a number of other phenomena which have been argued to provide evidence against a semantic approach to reflexivization such as this one. See Van Valin and LaPolla (1997) and Van Valin (2002) for discussion of these phenomena and arguments that they are not in fact problematic for this approach.

guages. The situation in Turkish is illustrated in (11), from Underhill (1976).

(11) Turkish

a.	(Siz)	Gazete-yi	Halil-e	ver-di-niz.
	2pl	newspaper-ACC	Halil-DAT	give-PAST-2pl
	'You (pl) gave the newspaper to Halil.'			
b.	(Siz)	Halil-e	ne	ver-di-niz?
	2pl	Halil- DAT	what	give- PAST -2pl
	'What did you (pl) give to Halil?'			
b´.	*(Siz)	ne	Halil-e	ver-di-niz?
	2pl	what	Halil- DAT	give- PAST -2pl

The sentence in (11b) is a *wh*-question with a ditransitive verb, and the *wh*-word *ne* 'what' must occur in the immediate preverbal position; it cannot occur initially or medially, as (11b´) shows. The immediate preverbal position is the unmarked focus position in the Turkish clause (Erguvanli 1984), and this is the normal situation in OV languages (Kim 1988). The clause-initial position in which *wh*-words appear in *wh*-questions in English and other languages is associated with contrastive topics and foci, as in sentences like *That book I wouldn't buy.* Perhaps the most surprising pattern is the rightward displacement found in a languages like Dhivehi (Cain and Gair 2000), an Indo-Aryan language of the Maldives. In this language, which is SOV, the *wh*-word may occur either *in situ* or in a special post-verbal position. This is shown in (12).

(12) Dhivehi

a.	alī	kīkē	bunī	ta?	
	Ali	what	say.PST.FOC	Q	
	'What did Ali say?'				
b.	alī	bunī	kīke	ta?	
	Ali	say. PST.FOC	what	Q	
	'What did Ali say?'				
c.	māle		ulunīma	aharen	bonī
	Male		be.PST.PROG	when 1sg	drink.PRES.FOC
	ais kurīmu.				
	ice cream				
	'When in Male, it is ice cream that I eat.'				

In the question in (12a) the *wh*-word is in the normal object position, which is also the unmarked focus position. However, in (12b) the *wh*-word appears postverbally in what is otherwise a special focus construction with a special form of the verb; an example of this focus construction is given in (12c). Hence in Dhivehi, Turkish and English, displacement of *wh*-words involves positions which are independently associated with pragmatic functions, in this case focus. Here again, as with reflexivization, the breaking of the one-to-one correspondence between syntax and semantics involves discourse-pragmatics.

When languages like Lakhota are analyzed from a standard generative perspective, the question that is inevitably raised is, why don't *wh*-words move (overtly) in this language? The presumption, clearly stated in Chomsky (1998), is that displacement is a universal feature of human language, and therefore the default is for *wh*-words to be displaced. This is, however, the wrong question to ask. A reasonable starting hypothesis regarding the correspondence between the syntactic positions in which arguments appear and their semantic (thematic role) interpretation is that it should be consistent and uniform. From this it follows that the preferred way of expressing *wh*-questions should be with *wh-in situ*, since the *wh*-word would occur in the position appropriate to its semantic interpretation, and therefore this, not displacement, should be the universal default and, one might reasonably expect, the most frequent type. It does seem to be the case that a clear majority of human languages are not like English in this respect; in Matthew Dryer's typological database, only 33% of the languages have obligatory initial *wh* in questions (Dryer, p.c.). Hence the correct question from this perspective is, why do *wh*-words move in languages like English, Turkish and Dhevehi? Given that *wh*-words are focal and that the positions in which they occur are associated with (contrastive) focus, it is clear that a significant part of the answer will involve discourse-pragmatics, as noted above.

Another very important type of displacement phenomena is voice constructions. This is a huge topic, but the following points are relevant to this discussion. Much of the early work in RRG (Foley and Van Valin 1977, 1984, 1985; Van Valin 1980, 1981, 1987) and a considerable amount of typological work during the 1970's and early 1980's (e.g. Li 1976, Givón 1984) was devoted to showing that in at least some languages subject is a kind of grammaticalized topic. In essence, this means that in some languages the choice of which argument of a multivalent verb will serve as subject can be influenced, sometimes very strongly, by discourse-pragmatic factors. From this it has been argued that one of the motivations for the use of voice constructions has been the desire of the speaker to keep the primary topical participant in subject position in a sequence of clauses about that participant.[4] Hence in at least some instances the displacement found in

[4] See e.g. Foley and Van Valin (1984), Van Valin (1987, 1993), Van Valin and LaPolla (1997) for examples from a variety of languages, both accusative and ergative. See Branigan

voice constructions is motivated by discourse-pragmatics. This contrasts strikingly with the situation in Lakhota-type languages, in which the choice of subject with a multivalent verb is completely predictable from its argument structure. Here again the breaking of a potential correspondence between semantics (thematic roles) and syntax (grammatical functions) involves discourse-pragmatics.

4 Conclusion: Language Design and Cross-Linguistic Variation

This paper began with Chomsky's speculations about language design and has presented evidence that the correlation between the existence of uninterpretable features and displacement phenomena proposed in Chomsky (1998) does not hold. This result raises questions about the content of narrow syntax, since it excludes non-universal phenomena, one of which is clearly displacement. It has further argued that the truly universal part of universal grammar is semantically driven and has proposed that deviations from this semantic core are motivated at least in part by discourse-pragmatics. The question that immediately arises is, why should this be the case? Why should the universal core of universal grammar be semantically driven?

Regardless of whether one holds that 'human language is a system for free expression of thought, essentially independent of stimulus control, need-satisfaction or instrumental purpose' (Chomsky 1980: 239) or that its primary function is communication, a crucial function of language is representing states of affairs in the world, and this is accomplished by means of reference and predication. Chomsky's super-engineer, faced with the task of designing a language which is optimal in terms of referring and predicating, on the one hand, and interfacing with other cognitive systems, on the other, would, I would argue, come up with languages of the Lakhota type: displacement-free, lacking uninterpretable features, hence with a one-to-one correspondence relationship between syntactic functions and semantic roles, ensuring maximal legibility at the cognitive interface, as he puts it.[5] If this is so, then we would expect the universal core of C_{HL} be semantically driven, in order to preserve the desired syntax-semantic correspondence. However, this assumes a rather 'solipsistic' view of language: the cognitive interface is the speaker's own. Suppose the super-engineer's task were to

and Prat-Sala (2000) and Heydel and Murray (2000) for cross-linguistic psycholinguistic evidence of a discourse motivation for passives in certain contexts.

[5] See Van Valin and LaPolla (1997), section 6.5, for arguments that the Lakhota-type is in fact the most common language type cross-linguistically.

create a linguistic system that is optimal in terms of referring and predicating by the speaker, on the one hand, and interfacing with the cognitive systems of the hearer, on the other. In this case the issue arises, as it does not in the first scenario, of structuring the utterance in order to facilitate the assimilation of the information by the hearer. Now a conflict may arise between the optimal correspondence between syntax and semantics, on the one hand, and the optimal coding of information for assimilation, on the other. In such a situation, various options must be explored, in order to reconcile the competing concerns. This is what gives rise to the kind of cross-linguistic variation discussed in this paper, in which the optimal syntax-semantics correspondence is undone by the introduction of discourse-pragmatic factors into grammar, and it is a natural consequence of the non-solipsistic view of language.

5 Notes

Abbreviations: A 'actor', ABS 'absolutive', ACC 'accusative', ACT 'actor-as-subject voice', DAT 'dative', DIR 'directional', ERG 'ergative', FOC 'focus', FUT 'future', NM 'noun marker', NOM 'nominative', pl/PL 'plural', PNM 'proper noun marker', POSS 'possessive', PROG 'progressive', PST 'past', Q 'question particle', REC 'recent past', REFL 'reflexive', sg 'singular', TNS 'tense', U 'undergoer', UND 'undergoer-as-subject voice'.

References

Branigan, H. and M. Prat-Sala. 2000. *A Cross-Linguistic Perspective on Discourse Context and Syntactic Processing in Language Production*, eds. M. De Vincenzi and V. Lombardo, 205-226. Dordrecht: Kluwer.

Cain, B. and J. Gair. 2000. Dhivehi (Maldivian). *Languages of the World*, Materials 63. Munich: Lincom Europa.

Chomsky, N. 1980. *Rules and Representations.* New York: Columbia University Press.

Chomsky, N. 1995. *The Minimalist Program.* Cambridge, MA: MIT Press.

Chomsky, N. 1998. Minimalist Inquiries: The Framework. *MIT Occasional Papers in Linguistics* 15. Cambridge, MA: Department of Linguistics, MIT.

Clark, R. 1985. The Syntactic Nature of Logical Form: Evidence from Toba Batak. *Linguistic Inquiry* 16: 663-69.

Dalrymple, M. 1993. *The Syntax of Anaphoric Binding*. Stanford: CSLI Publications.

De Vincenzi, M. and V. Lombardo, eds. 2000. *Cross-Linguistic Perspectives on Language Processing*. Dordrecht: Kluwer.

Dixon, R.M.W. 1972. *The Dyirbal Language of North Queensland.* Cambridge: Cambridge University Press.

England, N. 1983. *A Grammar of Mam.* Austin: Texas Press.

Erguvanli, E. 1984. The Function of Word Order in Turkish Grammar. *University of California Publications in Linguistics* 106. Berkeley & Los Angeles: University of California Press.

Foley, W. A. and R. D. Van Valin, Jr. 1977. On the Viability of the Notion of 'Subject' in Universal Grammar. *Berkeley Linguistics Conference* 3: 293-320.

Foley, W. A. and R. D. Van Valin, Jr. 1984. *Functional Syntax and Universal Grammar.* Cambridge: Cambridge University Press.

Foley, W. A. and R. D. Van Valin, Jr. 1985. Information Packaging in the Clause. *Language Typology and Syntactic Description,* vol. 1, ed. T. Shopenĕ, 282-364. Cambridge: Cambridge University Press.

Givón, T. 1984. *Syntax: A Functional-Typological Introduction*, vol. 1. Amsterdam & Philadelphia: John Benjamins.

Grimshaw, J. 1982. On the Lexical Representation of Romance Reflexives. *The Mental Representation of Grammatical Relations*, ed. J. Bresnan, 87-148. Cambridge, MA: MIT Press.

Heydel, M. and W. Murray. 2000. Conceptual Effects in Sentence Priming: A Cross-Linguistic Perspective. *Volume on Cross-Linguistic Sentence Processing Research, Architectures and Mechanisms for Language Processing 96*, eds. M. De Vincenzi and V. Lombardo, 227-254. Dordrecht: Kluwer.

Jackendoff, R. S. 1972. *Semantic Interpretation in Generative Grammar.* Cambridge, MA: MIT Press.

Jackendoff, R. S. 1992. Madame Tussaud Meets the Binding Theory. *Natural Language and Linguistic Theory* 10: 1-31.

Jackendoff, R. S. 1997. *The Architecture of the Language Faculty.* Cambridge, MA: MIT Press.

Kim, A. H. O. 1988. Preverbal Focusing and Type XXIII Languages. *Studies in Syntactic Typology*, eds. M. Hammond, E. Moravcsik, and J. Wirth, 147-72. Amsterdam & Philadelphia: John Benjamins.

Lambrecht, K. 1994. *Information Structure and Sentence Form.* Cambridge: Cambridge University Press.

Li, C. N., ed. 1976. *Subject and Topic.* New York: Academic Press. Shugamoto, N. 1984. Reflexives in Toba Batak. *Studies in the Structure of Toba Batak, University of California Los Angeles Occasional Papers in Linguistics 5,* ed. P. Schachter, 150-71. University of California Los Angeles, Department of Linguistics.

Underhill, R. 1976. *Turkish Grammar.* Cambridge, MA: MIT Press.

Van Valin, R. D., Jr. 1980. On the Distribution of Passive and Antipassive Constructions in Universal Grammar. *Lingua* 50: 303-27.

Van Valin, R. D., Jr. 1981. Grammatical Relations in Ergative Languages. *Studies in Language* 5: 361-94.

Van Valin, R. D., Jr. 1987. Aspects of the Interaction of Syntax and Pragmatics: Discourse Coreference Mechanisms and the Typology of Grammatical Systems. *The Pragmatic Perspective: Selected Papers from the 1985 International Pragmatics Conference*, eds. J. Verschueren and M. Bertuccelli-Papi, 513-31. Amsterdam & Philadelphia: John Benjamins.

Van Valin, R. D., Jr. 1993. A Synopsis of Role and Reference Grammar. *Advances in Role and Reference Grammar*, ed. R. Van Valin, 1-164. Amsterdam: John Benjamins.

Van Valin, R. D., Jr. 2002. *A Short Introduction to Role and Reference Grammar.* Cambridge: Cambridge University Press.

Van Valin, R. D., Jr. and W. A. Foley. 1980. Role and Reference Grammar. *Current Theories of Syntax*, Syntax & Semantics, vol. 13, eds. E. Moravcsik and J. Wirth, 329-52. New York: Academic Press.

Van Valin, R. D., Jr. and R. LaPolla. 1997. *Syntax: Structure, Meaning & Function.* Cambridge: Cambridge University Press.

Wilkins, D. P. 1989. Mparntwe Arrernte (Aranda): Studies in the Structure and Semantics of Grammar. Doctoral dissertation, Australian National University.

Williamson, J. 1984. Studies in Lakhota Grammar. Doctoral dissertation, University of California, San Diego.

Zubin, D., S. A. Chun, and N. Li. 1990. Misbehaving Reflexives in Korean and Mandarin. *Berkeley Linguistics Conference* 16: 338-54.

Index